AC/DC Maximum Rock & Roll

For the first time, Murray Engleheart along with Arnaud Durieux tells
the full story of Australia's greatest and loudest rock and roll export.
One of the most respected music journalists in Australia, Murray has
written for magazines all over the world in the past quarter of a century
and interviewed the members of AC/DC on many occasions. Arnaud is
a former rock journalist who has followed AC/DC's career for 25 years,
amassing what is without question the largest archive of AC/DC
material anywhere in the world.

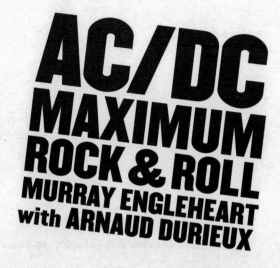

AC/DC
MAXIMUM
ROCK & ROLL
MURRAY ENGLEHEART
with ARNAUD DURIEUX

Aurum e
entertainment

First published in Great Britain
2009 by Aurum Press Ltd
7 Greenland Street
London NW1 0ND
www.aurumpress.co.uk

This edition first published in 2012 by Aurum Press.

First published in Australia by Harper Collins
Publishers Australia Pty Limited in 2006.

ISBN 978 1 84513 576 8

3 5 7 9 10 8 6 4 2
2012 2014 2016 2015 2013

Text design by Natalie Winter
Typeset in 10.5/15pt Sabon by Kirby Jones
Printed and bound by CPI Group (UK) Ltd, Croydon, CR0 4YY

In memory of Peter Wells
— Murray

To Ascar and Sydney
— Arnaud

CONTENTS

1996
Cliff Williams, Phil Rudd, Brian Johnson, Malcolm Young
and Angus Young — VH1 'Uncut', London.

INTRODUCTION

*t*he story goes something like this. Jerry Lee Lewis knew there was a problem. For reasons he couldn't for the life of him understand, whoever was sitting in the royal boxes of the theatre was attracting more attention than he was.

'The Killer' took this disrespect for as long as he could, then stalked from the stage, showering the audience with a murderous glare. No-one was more disappointed than the celebrity couple high above it all — John Lennon and Yoko Ono. They made their way to Lewis' dressing room, the former Beatle intent on re-establishing the pecking order of respect. He assumed a worshipful position on his knees before his hero and declared, 'Jerry Lee Lewis! The true king of rock and roll!'

Over the past 30 years, Malcolm Young, and manic schoolboy guitarist brother, Angus, have been unswervingly focused on paying that same respect to Jerry Lee and the likes of Chuck Berry, Little Richard and Fats Domino, all channelled through a monstrously loud sound system.

With that sound, and sales of well over 150 million albums, AC/DC have helped celebrate the sexual encounters, drunken adventures, fights, weddings, births, funerals, new cars and new tattoos of millions of people from Brussels to Brisbane, Montreal to Manchester and all points between.

And that makes AC/DC not just a rock band but a global cultural institution.

From day one, it was all about the near-psychic musical bond between Malcolm and Angus, their tenacity, self-belief and Swiss-precision sense of timing and swing.

While their imprint is their endless catalogue of crushing guitar riffs, which they honed firstly with Bon Scott and then polished with Brian Johnson, it's the space — the breather holes if you like — between those chords that's become their signature.

As Steve Marriott from The Small Faces and Humble Pie once told guitarist Chris Turner, later of Rose Tattoo, 'It's the gaps what rocks.'

And so it is with AC/DC who, interestingly, originally wanted to call themselves The Younger Brothers — after the Old West outlaws who at one point ran with Jesse James — only to find that the name had already been registered by Turner.

So what's their secret elixir? What has allowed them to raise rock and roll to a deceptively simple and utterly pure art form that additives, preservatives and the musical fashions of any given moment simply bounce off?

Why have they managed to continue while others have fallen by the wayside and been able to watch with contempt as the bodies of their many detractors float past?

What's really difficult to equate is The Brothers Young simply don't look or act the part. As a result, it's almost like finding that the puny guy on the bus every morning, with the ill-fitting clothes and the massive glasses with the three-inch-thick lenses, is actually a champion boxer who women absolutely adore.

Children have been named in their honour, none more comprehensively than the kid who is officially registered as Angus Malcolm George (elder brother, former member of The Easybeats and the band's mentor), with Bon tagged on to complete a cramp-inducing birth certificate entry.

Then there's the Danish stripper who only works to AC/DC music, the Melbourne fan who kicked alcoholism by walking around for a week listening through earphones to the *Powerage* album on full blast, or the Los Angeles radio station that once had a segment called the AC/DC hump hour in homage to the couple who kept calling in to announce which of the band's songs they had just had sex to.

Even the grave of The Doors' Jim Morrison reportedly has the names of each member of the classic Bon Scott-led band etched into it.

This book plots the journey from the crucial influence of The Easybeats through to Bon's legendary days and his death in February 1980, through to the recruitment of Brian Johnson, the landmark *Back In Black* album and the enormous success and reverence that the band continues to enjoy to this day.

Originally, this project was undertaken in an attempt to give the first in-depth view of AC/DC. But in the process of putting it together, we discovered a far greater need for this book than we had imagined.

While AC/DC don't do an enormous amount of interviews, when they do, journalists almost invariably pose the same questions that have been asked and answered countless times since the band's beginnings.

Yes, it is true that AC/DC don't volunteer much, but they have shown themselves to be more than happy (between the endless jokes, of course) to open up if the right question is posed. The fact is that interviewers have so rarely chosen to make that leap.

The result has been that while there are notable exceptions, such as Australia's Christie Eliezer, it's quite possible to scour hundreds of AC/DC interviews and come out the other end only a bare fact or two better off.

In a sense, this lack of depth in the band's media history made our work a little more difficult, but at the same time strongly validated and highlighted the need for what it was we were trying to do.

As for AC/DC themselves, suffice to say that the world is a delicately balanced place and removing something as staple as them from the equation might have perilous consequences socially, environmentally and on any other level you care to name.

Try just for a moment considering life without them.

Murray Engleheart
Arnaud Durieux

circa 1962-63

Angus with the 'King of Carnaby Street', designer
John Stephen, in his shop Lord John in London.

chapter 1

WITH A
GLASGOW KISS

*t*he crushing mid-1960s summer heat in North Queensland, Australia's last wild frontier and Deep North to America's Deep South, was punishing enough. But the attitude of the locals presented a danger to The Easybeats and their touring partners, The Purple Hearts, that was far greater than heatstroke. No-one liked strangers in these parts, certainly not strangers that looked as they did. Something had to give and in Cairns it did, while Hearts guitarist Barry Lyde, aka Lobby Loyde, waited for a hamburger. An old local who objected to the length of Loyde's hair leapt up and put a knife to his throat. Thankfully, The Easybeats' George Young and Harry Vanda were on hand.

Lobby Loyde: 'George headbutted the prick. He's about two foot tall but, mate, don't get in his road, he's a killer! He just went, "Boof!" and Harry said, "Don't get up!", which he didn't do. Harry could throw a good blow too, I might tell you.'

George's headbutt first, ask questions later approach was an instinctive reaction from his days growing up on the streets of Cranhill, Glasgow.

Cranhill came into being in the '50s when the government decided to forcibly move a mix of people from the tenements of central Glasgow to an area in the east. The housing scheme was based on similar highly successful projects in southern Germany, however on the outskirts of Glasgow it failed spectacularly. The venture became a ticking social time bomb compounded by being out of sight and so out of mind when it came to facilities. By the '60s, razor gangs had emerged on the streets.

It was in this environment that William Young (born 1910) and his wife, Margaret (born 1915), were raising eight children — Steven (1933), Margaret (1936), John (1938), Alex (1939), William (1941), George (1946), Malcolm (1953) and Angus (1955).

Steel production and shipbuilding were the city's key industries, but work was hard to come by, a situation that weighed heavily on William, a spray painter who had been a ground mechanic in the air force during World War II.

Music was an ever-present distraction. Margaret, the revered and only sister among the seven brothers, acted as an evangelist of sorts for all manner of blues, jazz — such as the glorious freewheeling of Louis Armstrong — R&B and the earliest driving rock and roll recordings of Fats Domino, Little Richard and Chuck Berry.

It wasn't long before various members of the family began to play a range of instruments, from guitar, piano and sax to accordion and clarinet. John and Alex picked up the guitar first, while Stevie squeezed the life out of the piano accordion.

In the early '60s, Alex took that grounding into the wider world and secured work in Germany playing saxophone and bass with Tony Sheridan, whose former backing band was a then unknown Beatles.

The decision of Alex to break free with music dramatically increased the daydreams of George, who had shown great promise on the football field. The Youngs were, of course, football fans and supported Glasgow Rangers who, in the '50s, coincidentally boasted a fullback by the name of George Young. In 1961, Rangers became the first Scottish side to reach a European final only to be well beaten, 4-1.

As the '60s progressed, though, the club continued to rack up the trophies on home soil, including winning the Scottish championship and FA Cup in 1964.

By then the Youngs were on the other side of the world, after relocating to Sydney in 1963 on the strength of the Australian Government's £10 immigration package. Maybe in Sydney, Angus, who was eight, could avoid being hit by a car a second time, as he had been in the streets of Cranhill. He made his mark as soon as he arrived, decorating the airport with whatever was in his stomach.

Despite Australia's sun-drenched reputation, it poured rain constantly for six weeks when the family first arrived. To make matters worse, they had to share their basic living quarters in barrack accommodation at the Villawood Migrant Hostel in the city's western suburbs with local snakes and lizards desperate to find somewhere, anywhere that was dry. Everyone was horribly homesick and one night both William and Margaret were reduced to tears. From that moment on, the already strong bonds between the family tightened even further and they were determined to make a success of their move.

William had an additional headache. Apart from the increased employment prospects, he had hoped that the relocation would also act as a circuit breaker on the growing musical career aspirations of some of the family. It was a major if understandable miscalculation. Rock and roll was well established in Australia by the time the Youngs arrived. The switch had been flicked in 1955 with the screening of teen rebellion movie *Blackboard Jungle*, and its musical soundtrack in the form of Bill Haley and The Comets' Rock Around The Clock transformed normally sedate cinemas into virtual dancehalls. Then came the main players in person.

In January 1957 it was Haley and in October Eddie Cochran, Gene Vincent and Little Richard, while the arrival in Australia of the music of Elvis Presley and a January 1958 tour by Jerry Lee Lewis and Buddy Holly and the Crickets slammed shut all the remaining fire exits.

Not content with a typically manic performance, Little Richard also made history. During the flight to Australia, the deeply spiritual singer felt that the plane was being kept in the air by angels. Then when Russia's Sputnik satellite appeared in the night sky over the Sydney Stadium, he believed the sight was a directive from God. In response, he promptly announced his retirement from rock and roll and his entry into a life of religious service. The huge ring he threw into Sydney Harbour the following day in order to demonstrate the level of his faith is still somewhere in the murk.

All this, coupled with the Australian contingent of rockers led by the wildly popular Johnny O'Keefe, amounted to William Young's worst nightmare. None of this was lost on George, who was almost 18 and had just started playing rock and roll on guitar and demonstrating a fine ear. Then The Beatles arrived in June 1964 and everything changed again.

For George, the family's accommodation held more promise and possibility than it suggested to most. The fact he was old enough to venture out on his own was a huge advantage, and he wasted no time in making whatever musical associations he could with others in the district. There was a community hall and eating area in the hostel so mixing was easy, but it was in the laundry where the music began. George soon teamed up with two young Dutchmen — Dingeman Vandersluys (a bass player, known as Dick Diamonde) and hostel resident Johannes Vandenberg (Harry Vanda, guitar) — and Englishman Stevie Wright (vocals), who was in his mid-teens and lived in the Villawood area.

The initial meeting of George and Wright was more confrontational than cordial after Wright mistook George for the brother of someone he had recently fought. George denied all knowledge of the situation, although he could have easily handled himself had the more slightly built Wright foolishly chosen to go on with it.

The band's earliest performances were low-key affairs at the hostel as part of events which were humorously christened 'Wogs and Rockers' gigs, a reference to the participants' various countries of origin. All the outfit required was a regular drummer, a spot that was finally filled by another Englishman, Gordon 'Snowy' Fleet, who was up to eight years older than some members of the band.

When the Young family were on their feet, they moved to Burwood which was much closer to the city, a better area on a major railway line with more attractive employment and schooling prospects. In time, Wright, who had developed a strong bond with George, moved in with the family.

Stevie Wright: 'Getting lost in amongst the clan of the Youngs — I loved it and they shared their love. That was the atmosphere that those earlier Easybeat songs were written [in].'

The move brought about a spreading of the band's territorial wings and, with the assistance of de facto manager, Allan Kissick, they did a number of auditions in the city. From there — although too loud and with hair too long for some, particularly as far as visiting sailors were concerned — they soon exploded with a simple exciting understanding of what The Beatles and The Kinks were doing.

Within a few months, Mike Vaughan approached with an offer of management which they accepted without knowing just how smart a move it really was. Vaughan knew aspiring producer Ted Albert from J. Albert and Son, the son of Alexis Albert, the respected and warmly admired friend of the cream of Sydney and international society who would be knighted in 1972. The family owned Commonwealth Broadcasting — part of which was Sydney radio station 2UW — Albert's head office building in King Street in the heart of the Sydney business district, and ran by far the most successful music publishing business in Australia. Accordingly, there were few, if any, more important ears in Australia than those of Ted Albert. Within days of a private showcase at the 2UW Theatre, Albert had The Easybeats in the studio under his direction.

Albert Productions released the first single, Stevie Wright and George Young's For My Woman, in March 1965 to little response. However, a second single in May, Wright and Young's She's So Fine, gleefully grabbed the number one slot by the collar and didn't let go.

Melbourne radio, though, had been relatively slow to fall for the band's charms, so an introductory function for the city's radio stations was organised. Trouble began when some local labourers began to taunt the band over their appearance, little realising that they were playing with fire.

Stevie Wright: 'Some of the drinkers were calling us "poofter!" and whatever, and then somebody punched me in the back. I went over to the boys and said, "I just got hit!" George was really pissed off with the carry on. We went over to approach them and make peace and they started in on us, so George kicked one of them between the legs and dropped one.'

Music wasn't the only trait that the Easys had in common with the famously volatile Kinks and The Who. But despite the incident Melbourne opened its arms to the band. In fact, like the rest of the country, it quickly succumbed to 'Easyfever'.

The experience of having She's So Fine in the number one position on the national charts, which ignited Australia's frenzied answer to Beatlemania, would ultimately help shape George Young's hard-nosed views on the music industry.

'That's where all the bullshit started,' George told Glenn A. Baker in Australian *Rolling Stone* in July 1976. 'We weren't really playing any more, we were just trying to satisfy demand . . . We went out and did our half hour, nobody could hear us.'

A performance at Brisbane's Festival Hall in December 1965 before 5000 rabid fans lasted for little more than half that time before police moved in and shut it down. Outside, the band's taxi was surrounded by overexcited admirers who set about demolishing what lay between them and their horrified heroes. At the other end of the scale at a club in Bankstown in Sydney's southwest, some of the local boys grabbed the band, held them down and attempted to cut their hair.

George's youngest brother, Angus, came face to face with the band's female fans when he arrived home from school one afternoon to find that several hundred had placed the house under siege after a magazine had printed their address. The police arrived and sealed off all access to the house. Not to be outmanoeuvred, Angus ran around the block, jumped a neighbour's fence and made it home. What he didn't know was that he had been followed and within seconds a screaming horde smashed down a door and trampled the tiny teenager. Having the police clear the house was surreal and the memory and excitement of it all was indelible.

The police were exactly what was needed when the Easys toured North Queensland with The Purple Hearts, but chances are they would have been as bewildered and threatened by the presence of the visitors as the locals.

Lobby Loyde: 'At the end of one gig it was everybody [all the band members] out the back waiting for the doors to open with mic stands and nulla nullas [aboriginal clubs] and stuff because half the town was there to fight us, and to get to the truck to get out it was like an all-in brawl at the back door. Just thinking back to it, mate, it's scary. But it was a brawl to get out of most of the joints.'

The powerhouse singles kept coming, with Vanda and Young's Wedding Ring in August 1965 and then the *Easy* album in September.

By early 1966, with the *It's 2 Easy* album released in Australia in March, plans were laid to replicate Easyfever in the US. A deal with United Artists was arranged, with a slot on the hugely influential 'Ed Sullivan Show' lightly pencilled in. Casual remarks by Beatles producer George Martin were wildly interpreted by the media as a virtual agreement to defect to the Easys camp. Everything seemed set. Even the Rolling Stones, who made their second visit to Australia in February, were caught up in the mania and Keith Richards expressed an admiration for the band. Eventually, however, a trip to London was considered to be a stronger option than America.

Not long after they arrived in London in July 1966, a trip to the Marquee Club left The Easybeats awestruck as The Move savagely set about destroying the place, along with the hearing of anyone in the general area. Faced with that level of competition, the entire exhausting journey from the other side of the planet suddenly seemed a massive exercise in futility. Nonetheless, they began work with Ted Albert at Abbey Road Studios only to have United Artists recruit producer Shel Talmy, who had worked with The Who and The Kinks.

The subsequent sessions, which included pianist and soon-to-be Rolling Stones associate Nicky Hopkins, weren't immediately thrilling. A band trip to the movies one afternoon changed all that. A pre-feature short about French doo-wop outfit The Swingle Singers gave George and Harry the idea for the riff and backing vocals for what would be Friday On My Mind.

Meanwhile, back in Australia, Stevie Wright and George Young's Sorry was released in October. With it came the public unveiling of something that most insiders already knew. That is, George was one hell of a rhythm guitarist.

Lobby Loyde: 'No matter what anyone says about the birth of that rhythmic guitar playing, it was George. It was a style, it was like no-one else in the world. George had it in spades. It was how that rhythm fixated itself around the centre of the beat. George has always known it. His rhythm was right in your face. It wasn't sissy rhythm playing. George was always the fucking engine room, mate. He drove like a semi-trailer.'

The more subtle Friday On My Mind was released in October 1966 in the UK, in November 1966 in Australia — just as the *Volume 3* album came out — and May 1967 in the US, and became a huge hit internationally.

For Harry Vanda, the song was an act of simple genius, from a guitarist's standpoint alone.

Harry Vanda: 'I think the only really clever thing we've ever done was the bloody riff out of Friday On My Mind. It sounds like one guitar but it's two. A lot of people say, how do you manage to go down and go up? One plays one part of the riff and keeps it going and the other one goes down against it, you see. But it sounds like the one guitar. So people come up and say, how did you do that? Trade secret.'

Friday On My Mind had its first live outing at what was also the band's English debut at Beatles manager Brian Epstein's Saville Theatre on 13 November 1966, in circumstances that were anything but relaxed.

'We looked out at the audience and saw the Rolling Stones and

The Beatles in the first row,' Vanda told *Beat* magazine's Christie Eliezer, 'and we were shitting blue shit!'

While Friday On My Mind was Vanda and Young's gem, writing a suitable follow-up became an almost impossible task. A European tour with the Rolling Stones in March 1967 provided the pressure release, even if the bands were met at the airport in Vienna by 13,000 fans and a 500-strong contingent of riot police.

Back in Australia in May, just as the *Good Friday* album was released in Europe and the *Friday On My Mind* album in America, it was obvious that Easyfever hadn't diminished in the slightest. At the end of the tour and just prior to the band's first crack at America, drummer Snowy Fleet took his leave and on their return to London, Tony Cahill, formerly of The Purple Hearts, was called in.

Cahill's debut performance was a baptism of fire in Scotland, where it was quickly confirmed once again that the band were easy in name only. Courtesy of long guitar leads, George and Harry took a hands-on approach to crowd problems and ventured out to personally resolve any disputes.

By contrast, the American tour in August 1967 was far more sedate, although the band's celebrity status was on high beam. At seminal punk watering hole, Max's Kansas City in New York, the single Falling Off The Edge Of The World had the honour of a place on the jukebox and was regularly spun by a besotted Lou Reed, while patron Andy Warhol also made himself known to the band.

Meanwhile, the search for something even in the same ballpark as Friday On My Mind continued. For George, that search was frustrating enough. For the band to be dipping into all manner of other styles in the process, including big ballads, was infuriating.

'It was a classic mistake from our point of view,' George told Glenn A. Baker in *Rolling Stone*. 'We were a rock and roll band and what was a rock band doing with this cornball schmaltzy shit?'

The going was beginning to get tough and cracks emerged. The Easybeats' situation, not to mention the drug culture that was increasingly prevalent in the music industry, didn't go unnoticed by the Young family back in Sydney. As far as William was concerned, it was time George found himself a more stable employment situation with a regular weekly pay packet. It also hardened his resolve that his youngest sons, Malcolm and Angus, would do something else with their lives other than music.

After the release of the *Vigil* album in Australia and Europe and the *Falling Off The Edge Of The World* album in the US in June 1968, The Easybeats did hit their stride again with the rousing Good Times, which was released in Australia in July and September in the US and UK. It was here that their friendship with The Small Faces came into its own, with Steve Marriott's distinctive rasp making its presence felt in backup vocals. A story circulated that when Paul McCartney first heard Good Times he pulled his car over at the nearest phone booth to call the BBC and request they play it again.

By this time, George's brother Alex was in London working as a songwriter for The Beatles' Apple publishing division and had been snapped up to be part of an Apple band to step into the pop shoes that The Beatles had vacated. John Lennon had come up with the idea of naming the project Grapefruit — in which Alex was known as George Alexander — in a nod to a book by Yoko Ono, and the Beatle connection didn't end there. The presence of Lennon, McCartney and Ringo Starr, along with Rolling Stone Brian Jones, elevated a function to officially unveil the band to a level most acts only ever dream of. Lennon's fingerprints are also thought to be on the band's third single, C'mon Marianne, and along with McCartney's on the production of their debut album, *Around Grapefruit*.

George's luck wasn't quite as good. His disenchantment with the music industry was almost doubling in weight each week, and listening to ska music at London clubs like the Bag O' Nails was a rare pleasurable diversion. The band still had a magic, as 1969's thumping single St Louis proved, but it was to be the last hurrah from an outfit now barely functional as a unit. An after-the-fact report that Brian Epstein had at one point expressed an interest in managing the band, a situation that would more than likely have dramatically altered their fate, by now seemed like a cruel joke.

After the worldwide release in August of the *Friends* alb
which was essentially a collection of demos from Vanda and Young
that was owed to Polydor Records, a quickly arranged September
tour of Australia saw the band in stripped-down, foot-to-the-floor,
jeans and T-shirt mode. The general response was strong but it was
a far cry from the mania of just over two years prior. Nonetheless,
the Easys put in some blistering performances which, by the time
they hit Sydney in the second half of October, included old friends
and openers, The Valentines, with their two singers, Vince
Lovegrove and Bon Scott. Ironically, Scott was doing the stage
moves of Wright, his hero, as well as Wright himself had ever done.

When the tour wound up, The Easybeats called time and George
and Harry were left holding the financial bag to the tune of an
estimated $85,000. There were such black comedy acts as one single
being released on two separate labels in Canada and recordings
being exclusively signed to numerous others. Even, as was
discovered later, the Gold record for sales of Friday On My Mind
that had hung proudly on the wall in the Young family's living room
turned out to be a single of Sorry.

George and Harry headed back to London in 1970 where, for the
next few years, they immersed themselves in the private world of
recording they found so fascinating and forged a formidable joint
identity in a variety of guises. This included Tramp and Moondance
(1970), Paintbox (1970–71), Grapefruit's last single with Alex
Young in 1971, and Haffy's Whisky Sour, also in 1971, singles that
were released with various degrees of success in Britain and Europe.

The pair wound up their UK stay in mid-1972 with a far from
serious project with former Pretty Things bassist, Alan 'Wally'
Waller (Wally Allen), titled the Marcus Hook Roll Band. The 'band'
was the brainchild of Waller, who was in charge of liquid
refreshments during the sessions at Abbey Road Studios. But after
recording two singles — Natural Man in August 1972 and Louisiana
Lady in February 1973 — the party wound down.

When George arrived back in Australia in January 1973 and
Harry late in the year, they were amazed to receive word that the

project had attracted some serious interest in America, where Natural Man had been released. After all they'd been through with The Easybeats they didn't know whether to laugh or cry, but decided to finish what they had started in London. With Waller again in charge of the liquid catering, the studio team in Sydney was expanded to include George's brother Malcolm on guitar, although Angus was also on hand.

Harry Vanda: 'Malcolm got involved because it was just me playing guitar and George hacking away on a bass. So we said we need a drummer and another guitar player. I did some singing and so did George.'

They spent a month in EMI's Sydney studios with engineer Richard Lush, an Englishman who had arrived in Australia just a few months before with enormously impressive credentials that included being second engineer on The Beatles' *Sgt Pepper* album. Lush was stunned by the skills of Malcolm and Angus.

Richard Lush: 'I was amazed at the talent in people that were so young because they were like little kids. I thought, wow! This is amazing! Especially Angus.'

The result was the 1973 album *Tales Of Old Grand-Daddy*, which was initially only released in Australia, but typically it came with yet another kick in the teeth. To George's disgust, the original cover art showed an old man in a rocking chair, when a bottle of Old Grand-Dad bourbon was the true source of the name and a more-than-likely nod to the nightly fuel for the recording sessions. Just to further rub salt in old wounds, despite the fact that it was interest from America that pushed the project to be completed in the first place, the results didn't see daylight in the US for another six years. It was the Easybeats' cycle of shit all over again. George was adamant that his brothers would never be taken on a similar ride but also had great sage-like hope for the future.

'One day,' he told one magazine, 'an act is going to come along that has the same relevance to our present day society as Dylan had in the '60s. That act will blow everyone's minds.'

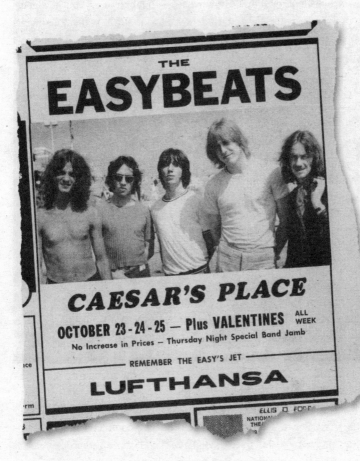

1971
Malcolm in the Velvet Underground.

chapter 2

THE RHYTHMATIST

$\mathcal{M}$alcolm Young was born on 6 January 1953, the same year Elvis Presley walked out of the sweltering heat and through the doors of the Memphis Recording Service to make his historic first recordings. It made sense that in time Malcolm was playing along to Elvis records and then The Beatles when they struck.

Malcolm's first guitar was one of two cheap acoustics his mother bought for Angus and himself that doubled as an entertainment buffer between the fiery duo. The surf instrumentals of the day were his early targets. Malcolm's small hands and reach forced him to play with open strings.

Music at first was an interest rather than a driving and all-consuming passion. Like George, Malcolm was a talented soccer player and had very definite designs on a career in the sport. But at 13 or 14, the growth spurts of everyone in his age group — except him — put paid to that. Malcolm remained locked in a tiny frame, due, it's been said, to the lead in the pipes while the family was still in Glasgow. Almost overnight, every male around him was much taller, more robust and, most important of all, much faster on their feet. Worse still, Malcolm's mates looked so much older than he did and therefore were more easily, if still not legally, able to taste pub culture — something Malcolm's severely under-aged-looking figure couldn't possibly pull off to the satisfaction of even the most easy-going publican.

It was at that point that Malcolm's serious interest in music kicked in and at much the same time as the faith of big brother George was on a downward spiral with The Easybeats.

The 15 year old's refocused enthusiasm roughly coincided with several pivotal moments. In 1968 Malcolm's schooldays at Ashfield Boys High School ended, which was like being released from a five day a week prison, although he had been something of a lady-killer possibly due to his good looks as much as his musical abilities. Having a big brother who had slightly long hair, a sure sign in those days of a hooligan, not to mention being a prominent member of one of the biggest rock and roll bands in the world, made Malcolm a marked man and placed him squarely behind the eight ball as far as his teachers were concerned.

It was also in 1968 that Harry Vanda presented Malcolm with his treasured Gretsch Jet Firebird guitar that had served him so well that year. The international success of The Easybeats and the excitement they generated was a powerful motivator for Malcolm, and now he actually had one of the tools that Harry had used to get the job done.

George had been stoking Malcolm's growing interest while he was overseas and made sure that his brother received what he felt were the best and most noteworthy albums and magazines from wherever he was at the time. The only problem was that these treasured packages were invariably sent by sea freight, an agonisingly slow process when the ultimate destination was an impossibly distant Australia.

The journey sometimes took up to several months and more often than not, despite tough packaging, resulted in the covers of many of the albums — which of course were as mystifying and sacred as their actual contents — ending up bent and their corners folded.

But even with the delay in transit, Malcolm was still many months ahead of most radio playlists and Saturday morning music television shows, which, over cups of tea, the entire family would watch and critique the acts that appeared.

When he was at home in Sydney, George would play bass in jams in the family home and yell out time and chord changes as best he could over the racket. He even performed crude surgery on the guitars and forcibly removed some of the 'un-rock and roll' strings. To George, some guitar strings were as useful as going into a street fight armed with a toothpick. You had to be properly equipped to play rock and roll.

Malcolm coupled this rough-house tutoring in both style and attitude with repeated studious listens to Eric Clapton's blazing work with John Mayall's Bluesbreakers, the Peter Green and Jeremy 'Deltahead' Spencer-led Fleetwood Mac, Paul Butterfield and Mike Bloomfield.

The great blues men who inspired them, such as Muddy Waters, as well as early rock and roll figures like Little Richard, Jerry Lee Lewis and, of course, Chuck Berry, were also a major part of his musical diet.

Malcolm: 'As a kid it started with Chuck Berry. You can't forget Chuck Berry. I mean, just about everything he did back then was great.'

But it was the English acts who had styled blues and R&B into roughly three-minute pop radio fodder who shook him to his core.

Malcolm: 'The first time I heard My Generation by The Who, that was something. The Beatles and the Stones were the big thing and then all of a sudden this thing sounded heavier. That changed my whole thing. Later on I guess Jumpin' Jack Flash, and I'll give you two more, Honky Tonk Woman — and these are all just tracks out on their own — and then Get Back by The Beatles. That's just pure rock and roll as it evolved, I reckon.'

Ironically, Malcolm's first exposure to The Who's My Generation was as part of an Easybeats performance. At first he thought the anthem was another Vanda and Young masterstroke until he was told it was a song that the band themselves had heard on Radio Luxembourg.

William Young's work ethic dictated that Malcolm get himself a job rather than just practise guitar in his bedroom, and keep an eye out for good-looking women and equally good-looking cars. Accordingly, he entered the workforce and took on a number of positions, from a sewing machine repairman to an apprentice fitter and turner and storeman.

But unlike his colleagues, Malcolm didn't hear the usual workplace noise during the day. Instead, the repeated clunkings and clickings of the various pieces of machinery around him blurred into a tribal rhythm after a while which, with a little imagination, helped him formulate song ideas and structures.

This was helped by the fact that Malcolm, like George, was blessed with a fine ear. He also had a clear talent for the guitar and an ability to pick up almost any tune in a matter of minutes, a talent made easier thanks to a record player that allowed him to adjust the speed of his albums, so he could play along without having to fiddle with the tuning of his guitar.

When it came time to make a racket in a band of his own with bassist/singer Mick Sheffzick and drummer Brian Curby, the initial exercise was short-lived.

A more serious attempt came in 1968 with Beelzebub Blues which sometimes went under the name of Red House and even the Rubberband, all with singer Ed Golab, drummer Gerry Tierney, George Miller on guitar, bassist Sheffzick and Malcolm on lead guitar. Occasionally, Larry Van Kriedt, an accomplished jazz-influenced guitarist who had only just arrived in Australia from America, would sit in.

Malcolm was the tiny guitar virtuoso and impressively and quite effortlessly tore his way through songs by Bloodwyn Pig, Savoy Brown, Black Sabbath, The Animals, Eric Clapton in his

Bluesbreakers period, as well as virtually all of Cream's first album and *Are You Experienced?* by Jimi Hendrix. It was all blues based and slightly left field, nothing from the radio playlists of the day. As radio friendly as they got was The Beatles' Come Together.

Ed Golab: 'He was THE guitarist, I mean we used to do a lot of Cream covers, Hendrix covers, he had [them] just down pat.'

Songs were often sketched out in Malcolm's bedroom and then given some volume at a scout hall at Rhodes in Sydney's inner-north, which they'd break into and occasionally sleep in.

In quieter moments, Golab and Malcolm, who began to pen his own songs, toyed with Latin rock and listened to Stevie Wonder. But there was nothing lightweight about the amplifier Malcolm used, which was made by an electronics wiz friend of the band, Bevan Boranjee.

Ed Golab: 'He made up Malcolm this huge box, a big black speaker box, it was the size of, say, two doors put together side by side. Imagine something that size, and we used to roll this sucker into the hall and these people would go, "Whoa, this is gonna be something else." Little did they know there's only four speakers in the bloody thing. Malcolm used to stand in front of it; it used to bloody dwarf him! Made him look even smaller.'

And Malcolm was already small enough and still looked very young for his age.

Ed Golab: 'When we were sort of 18–19, he was looking like he was 12–13, just because of his height. And it was something that I guess he always had a hard time with, 'cause all his girlfriends were sort of really young girls who thought that he was a very young boy. And that was always a problem for him.'

As was getting the band into a church for a gig. But given their name, Beelzebub Blues, it was always going to be difficult.

On this memorable occasion, the driver of the band's van mistook the walkway into the classic old-style stone church for the driveway, and it was only when the vehicle became jammed between two pillars that it became obvious they'd taken the wrong path, so to speak. It was decided that there was only one way to go and that was forward, so the engine was gunned and the entire archway came crashing down, covering the van in rubble.

Other gigs presented far more dangerous situations and the band's other guitarist, George, a towering, intimidating-looking Russian, was a good man to have on their side. He just seemed like the sort of person best not fucked with.

Ed Golab: 'Getting in and out of these places, some of them we would actually walk in there with microphone stands in our right hands, as protection. It was some tough places we played.'

The release of Led Zeppelin's 1969 debut album caused a minor sensation. Malcolm was among the admirers, but he was very specific in his appreciation.

For him, the band's appeal began and ended with the album's opener, Good Times, Bad Times, that like the defining efforts of the Stones and The Who registered strongly with Malcolm as a lesson in how a song should be structured and complemented with great guitar work. Thinking about how music was played, as much as the actual process of playing it, began to become a serious concern as Malcolm toyed with jazz chords and worked out songs on a keyboard.

By 1971, Beelzebub Blues had run its course but Malcolm was always eager to take part in whatever jams there were to be had, on songs such as Joe Cocker's cracking version of The Letter and some standard 12-bar blues, with friends such as Larry Van Kriedt on guitar, Ray Day on piano, Gerry Tierney on drums and Mick Sheffzick on bass.

But in the middle of 1971, opportunity knocked when the Velvet Underground, not to be confused with the legendary New York outfit led by Lou Reed, relocated to Sydney from Newcastle, an industrial city 170 kilometres north of the capital.

The early Velvets had a keyboards-driven Doors-like sound, a wild, destructive stage act like The Move and The Who, and a literally fire-breathing singer in Steve Phillipson.

They'd recorded a single of Jefferson Airplane's Somebody To Love backed with She Comes In Colours by Love and took out the local Battle of the Bands competition in Newcastle, but it was now time to broaden their horizons.

After they settled in Sydney, the reshuffled band brought in singer Brian Johnson — no relation to the man who would later figure prominently in Malcolm's career — and were after a second guitarist. Malcolm's glowing reputation preceded him.

On the recommendation of former Easybeat Stevie Wright, drummer Herm Kovac and guitarist Les Hall went to see Malcolm at the Young home in Burwood where they were amazed to find the family spoke to each other in a thick, almost impenetrable Scottish brogue.

It wasn't the only shock. Malcolm was smitten with T. Rex and the guitar playing of Marc Bolan.

Herm Kovac: 'I used to say to him, "That's shit, Malcolm! All those singles all sound the same!" There were no blues guys or anything like that on his wall — there was a big poster of Marc Bolan.'

After a mandatory cup of tea, it was suggested that when Malcolm was free he come to the band's house in Mona Vale to go through the motions of an audition. To the amazement of Kovac and Hall, Malcolm wasn't about to wait: he grabbed his Gretsch guitar and told his mother he was going out.

They stayed up all night at Mona Vale with Malcolm talking about his blues heroes and Kovac playing him some of his own favourite albums. Malcolm slept in the lounge room and, thinking that their guest — given his size and appearance — was only about 12, Kovac half expected the police to knock at the door sent by the boy's worried mother.

They jammed all the next day and it was blindingly obvious that the Velvet Underground had their new guitarist.

By now the Velvets also had a new singer, so the line-up was — Malcolm (guitar), Kovac (drums), Les Hall (guitar), Andy Imlah (vocals) and Mick Sheffzick (bass). They made their debut in July 1971 at the Parramatta Rivoli in western Sydney.

They soon took on a bad-boy image, much like the Stones, and slogans such as 'Keep your daughters away from the Velvet Underground' were bandied about.

Like most bands of the time, the Velvets were eclectic to say the very least. Almost anything was fair game, from Deep Purple's Black Night and the Shocking Blue's Venus to George Harrison's My Sweet Lord and the Stones' Can't You Hear Me Knocking, as well as songs by Badfinger and Slade. Most of these featured Malcolm on lead guitar.

A particular favourite of Malcolm's was Gary Wright's first album, *Extraction*, which he thrashed at top volume every chance he got and channelled several songs into the band's sets.

At the other end of the scale, he would set up with Kovac in the drummer's room and noodle away on jazz for anything up to eight hours at a stretch, much to the horror of some other members of the band.

Hot Cottage guitarist Kim Humphreys remembers meeting Malcolm for the first time at a Velvets rehearsal.

'I can remember him telling me, I've got this young brother. He was singing his praises even back then and I don't know how old Angus would have been — probably 15 or 16.'

The Velvets would work Saturday and Sunday nights and then, after the Sunday gig, drive Malcolm back to Burwood so he could go to work on Monday morning servicing sewing machines in a bra factory.

When they went to Newcastle, Malcolm, who seemed to be outside the Sydney city limits for the first time, was stunned that there was bushland and farms between Sydney and Newcastle and wanted to stop the car to get out and look around.

Malcolm's hard-nosed character presented itself when they came across Australian singer and songwriter Richard Clapton, who was in the very early stages of his career.

Herm Kovac: 'I remember Malcolm saying to me, "Look at this fucking tosser Richard Clapton! Fuck me dead! He ain't gonna get anywhere trying to copy Eric Clapton's name!" He said with a name like Clapton there's only room for one!'

Malcolm didn't take shit from anyone. Fiercely loyal, he had little time for fools or those he felt were attempting to gain any advantage at his expense.

Those with designs on managing the band who he sensed weren't genuine were quickly and bluntly assessed. 'Nah, fucking don't like him,' he'd snarl. 'It's not fucking rock and roll, he's just into bullshit.'

At the same time, Malcolm was anything but a humour-free zone. Once, when the Velvets were playing in Tamworth in northern New South Wales, he and Kovac were sharing a hotel room. They had scored some female company for the evening and when things got heated Malcolm swung wickedly into action.

Herm Kovac: 'I said, Mal, have you got any frenchies [condoms]? He said no. He said, What sort of socks have you got on — nylon or wool? I said nylon. He said, You're in luck — nylon kills spunk. So anyway, it's dark and I'm going, Fucking hell! Jesus Christ! How the fuck does it stay on? He flicked the light on and I'm hovering over this chick trying to put this black sock on. Malcolm, who's in bed with this girl, is just pissing himself laughing and the girl in front of me is just terror stricken. But I ruined it for everyone so Malcolm didn't even get his oats that night, because whenever he was trying to he just burst out laughing.'

Then there was the time Malcolm and Imlah suddenly developed a strange interest in going fishing near Palm Beach north of Sydney. It would be up to Kovac to arrange it all, from the bait and fishing tackle to the boat itself. But the drummer couldn't figure out why the other two wouldn't fish when they were out there. Even though the exercise had been their idea, all they did was giggle.

In time, Kovac began to notice a link between that laughter and lousy onstage performances.

Herm Kovac: 'It took me about a year to realise that they were hiring the fishing boat out so they could go and smoke dope. That was truly it. I said, "Fucking hell, Malcolm, you're a fucking hippy!" Then, when I knew they were giggling, I said, "That [gig] was shithouse! You played like shit!" He said, "I played great!" So then

I started taping gigs, so whenever they were stoned I'd point it out to them.'

Malcolm had never been keen on the name Velvet Underground. So when the band's sound slowly took on a heavier, tougher tone and their set list began to feature a number of songs by Free, including Ride On Pony, they changed their name — in an act of homage — to Pony in September 1972.

Their first gig under that name was at Manly on Sydney's northern beaches where Malcolm made an equipment and sound connection that would stay with him for the rest of his career.

Herm Kovac: 'Les said, "Why don't you try the Marshall and see what that sounds like?" Malcolm plugged that Gretsch into the Marshall and that's when his love affair with Marshall amps and Gretsch happened. Les didn't get the Marshall back that night! Malcolm just stuck to it and that week he went out and bought himself one, and he's been using that red Gretsch and a Marshall ever since.'

At Malcolm's urging, the band began to place greater emphasis on their own material and recorded a single called Keep Me Company that was never released.

In time they started to back Ted Mulry, an alliance which set the stage for the hugely successful Ted Mulry Gang, or simply TMG. But that teaming leant too much towards pop for Malcolm's liking.

The diminutive guitarist quit soon after.

Herm Kovac: 'The reason he left is because we were getting too poppy and we were also starting to back Ted a lot and he wanted to do something heavier. He wanted to do Deep Purple stuff and everything like that.'

Towards the end of Pony's life, singer Dave Evans took over from Imlah, but within weeks it was all over.

In February 1973, Malcolm witnessed the real thing; one of the Rolling Stones' two Sydney shows at Randwick Racecourse. The band made their entrance in white horse-drawn carriages that looked like something out of a production of *Cinderella*. The fireworks that lit up the sky on the first night were abandoned for the second as the explosions had badly spooked the nearby racehorses in their stables. But for all the pomp and lavish showmanship, the Stones were at their brooding best.

Better still, they talked the talk as well as walked the walk. During their press conference, a wonderfully sullen Keith Richards clashed with a journalist who felt the need to tell him that he looked like a train wreck.

Richards sneered that she didn't look so great herself.

His defiance was perfect. Now, that was a band.

1973
Angus in Kantuckee, Sydney.

chapter 3

THE
SEVENTH SON

*a*ngus Young wasn't the most warm and welcoming sight when Herm Kovac first knocked on the door of the Youngs' home in Burwood.

Herm Kovac: 'This little skinhead, the evilest, meanest-looking guy you've ever seen — shaved head — went, "Yeah! What do ya want?" When he said that I actually stood behind Les [Hall], because I thought this guy's going to beat the crap out of me. I said, "I've come to see Malcolm." "Alright, come in."

'This little skinhead's hovering around. He had the bovver boots, the whole thing. "Hey! Come in 'ere!" Come into his bedroom, puts his SG [Gibson SG guitar] on and then he does the routine. He's on the dressing table, he's kicking his legs up, he's jumping on the bed, he's just all over the place, and he said, "What do ya reckon?" Me being the smart alec said, "Do you know any chords?" Bloody 'ell!'

Kovac had good reason to be shit scared by Angus' appearance.

In the early '70s the Sharpies or Sharps, a more snappily dressed version of the English skinhead movement, were the scourge not only of the dance circuit — particularly in Sydney and Melbourne — but also the railway system. In Hornsby in Sydney's northern suburbs anything up to 400 individuals would congregate, while other main areas were at Burwood, Strathfield, Campsie and Town Hall in the city.

Even if Angus only looked the part, his quick temper and — despite his size — tenacity of a pitbull made him good company when there was trouble on a Saturday night.

Born on 31 March 1955, he was the mythologically famed seventh son, a position considered to have unique powers in blues mythology, and entered the world the same year a sweat-soaked Little Richard first recorded the rampaging Tutti Frutti.

Initially, Angus played a customised banjo, and then, courtesy of his mother, came his first actual guitar as he began to play some of what he heard around the house.

Angus: 'When I was a kid the stuff that I heard, especially coming out of a couple of the brothers putting on records, was like Chuck Berry or Little Richard, and I would say Chuck Berry was the one that I always picked bits of guitar off.

'I think the earliest stuff I ever did — it was probably the first thing I ever played — was just a little 12-bar blues thing. One of my older brothers, Alex, he showed me a couple of little licks and that was probably the only lesson I ever really got!'

Following some heated haggling, Angus inherited an old Hofner guitar from Malcolm after his brother graduated to the Gretsch that Harry Vanda gave him. Coupled with a 60-watt amp, he was able to make it roar.

Like Malcolm, Angus was self taught, treating daily after-school guitar practice as a sacred act and it paid off. And like his brother, he began playing surf instrumentals, and by the age of 11 he was handling Jimi Hendrix songs while his friends were still trying to come to grips with the Top 40.

Although his first-ever public performance was at 13 at a coffee shop, Angus made his debut proper at a local church when he stood in at short notice with some friends only to play so loudly he cleared the room.

His first record purchase was a single of Club A Go-Go by The Animals, followed by I'm A Man by the Yardbirds. He was attracted by their earthiness and fascinated by the science fiction-like guitar sound in I'm A Man. He loved Australian bands like The Missing Links and The Loved Ones for the same gritty bluesy reasons.

And seeing the larger-than-life majesty of Louis Armstrong in all his soulful glory at the Sydney Stadium with his sister left him wide-eyed for days.

The gravitational pull of Little Richard's You Keep A Knockin', however, was nothing short of dangerous and very nearly threatened his wellbeing. Angus played the song, or rather one particular part of it, incessantly until his mother could stand it no longer and firmly advised her youngest son that it would be in his best interests to find something else to do.

Being so close to the madness of Easyfever was hugely influential, as was being heir apparent to the contents of the packages George sent Malcolm while he was overseas. But Angus had to find out more and often took matters into his own hands.

'I would save my pocket money, come into town, and if I wanted a Buddy Guy record I'd have to get it imported because the local stores weren't carrying it.'

The blues was like stepping into another world where people sang like ghosts and demons, and Angus had a hunger for further information about it all. At his father's urging, he took himself to the local library where he soon became a regular fixture, even during school hours.

There the librarian was more than happy to source material from overseas while Angus waded through their back issues of *Downbeat* magazine with articles on his blues heroes like Muddy Waters.

It was a very different type of learning environment to life at Ashfield Boys High. With Malcolm as an older brother, Angus, who was known as The Banker for his ability to save whatever money he received, was poorly regarded long before he walked in the front gates. When the headmaster demanded Angus have a haircut he incurred the wrath of the boy's mother — no-one made decisions about the family but the family itself.

Unlike George and Malcolm, Angus had no interest in football or other sports. Music and guitars were his great passions along with drawing and painting in art classes, a subject well suited to his small hands, which gave him freedom in between his regular bouts of truancy.

Angus: 'I liked art, the art classes, because in art you can get away with a lot!'

Besides, where else could he make a six-foot-long fly out of papier-mâché as he did for one memorable school project?

Angus: 'I remember going to the library which was kind of strange. I used to like going in there too because you could hang out there because the librarian, the teacher, was one of these guys who was meticulous about the reference [the book request form]. So he would never let you have a book!

'It was like you had to fill out a four-page enquiry to get a book. You just used to ask for a book and by the time he'd worked out all the paperwork, that was half your day gone.'

Taking music as a subject wasn't an option.

Angus: 'They wouldn't let me! I remember once they passed around a violin to let us look at it and it never came back! That was the music lesson!'

On another occasion, a frustrated music teacher snatched a triangle out of his hands, saying that he had no sense of rhythm.

In 1969, Angus met 15-year-old Larry Van Kriedt, an accomplished guitarist himself, who had moved to Sydney from San Francisco. Van Kriedt soon found that Angus was rarely alone.

Larry Van Kriedt: 'He had kind of a gang of friends around him, you know, and they were kind of like the tough guys. Angus was the ring leader! He was the smallest one. They were in their school uniforms, and smoking cigarettes.

'Sometimes people might pick on me a bit — I was very quiet. And Angus, even though he was half my size, he used to go, "You leave him alone! I'll tell you, if you touch him I'll see you in the ground!" But Angus never actually did any fighting much or anything like that, it was just like a lot of kinda hard arse or something. I mean, he was a pretty assertive sort of guy.

'He got into trouble quite a lot and he attracted a "gang" culture around him in a schoolboy sense. But I always felt he was very honourable and loyal.'

Angus was very keen to get a Gibson guitar. When a friend of Van Kriedt's mentioned that Van Kriedt had one, Angus looked him up and down contemptuously.

Larry Van Kriedt: 'He said, "Bullshit!" He asked me again, "Have you got a Gibson?" and I said, "Yeah, I've got one." And then he's like, "I can't believe it!" and then he looks at me again and goes, "Can I see it?" Then I thought I was gonna have all these kids in my room and I was a bit worried and I said, "Well, you can come in, but I can't have all these people in there, you know," so he said, "Alright". He kept them all under control. And he and one other friend went in.'

Impressed that Van Kriedt not only owned the guitar of his dreams but also had a Gibson guitar catalogue, Angus and Van Kriedt began to hang out together listening to records and exchanging guitar techniques.

As it had done for Malcolm, Eric Clapton's work with John Mayall's Bluesbreakers made a big impression on Angus, as did Led Zeppelin's debut album. Angus' ultimate idol at this point, however, was Jeff Beck, from the moment he heard Hi Ho Silver Lining. He bought Herm Kovac's copy of the single for two dollars and played it to death in his bedroom.

Despite these endless hours in his room, he was quite capable of handling himself when he stepped outside the house. If a fight broke out at one of the parties where he played, he would swing his guitar like a six-string mace without hesitation. He was no angel and was once locked up overnight after being caught stealing milk bottles, according to *Juke* on 24 February 1979.

By 1970, 15-year-old Angus could take school no longer and came home one last time after being given an ultimatum over his poor attendance.

Career or vocational guidance — as it was known at the time — at school took a fair bit to be desired. Angus wanted to be a songwriter only to be told with a roll of the eyes that those jobs didn't exist any more. He went on to work several jobs including nightmarish night shifts in a butcher shop and, like Malcolm, Angus took on a trade and began a printing apprenticeship.

Contrary to a fitting piece of AC/DC folklore, he was never specifically employed by Sydney porn mag *Ribald*.

Angus: 'I think *Ribald* used to move their publishing [from place to place] because they were always getting busted, and the place where I was printing, I think it [the magazine] came in one week. It just came in for that week, then they'd move on somewhere else! I'd just say I had a hand in putting some type together for them.'

With that weekly pay packet, Angus decided to take the step up and get a new guitar from Chord Music in Burwood. While a Gibson SG was what Angus had dreamt of owning, when it came to the crunch he was said also to be really taken with a Gibson Les Paul.

The problem was that one of the members of teen pop screamers Sherbet bought the one Angus had his eye on. So, determined not to be caught out twice, he snapped up the remaining Gibson SG.

Besides, the SG model was the guitar of choice of his heroes such as Mountain's Leslie West, The Who's Pete Townshend, and the poor bloody donkey on the cover of the Stones' live album, *Get Yer Ya-Ya's Out!*

Angus was a fixture at the gigs by Malcolm's band the Velvet Underground as often as his mother would allow, although strict conditions were imposed on his attendance.

Herm Kovac: 'Angus was allowed to come on the condition that when we played he sat down to the front somewhere where we could keep an eye on him, and the minute we finished playing he'd have to come up to where we were. We'd have to drop Angus home and Angus used to make us all Ovaltine. That's how I got hooked on Ovaltine.'

One of Angus' earliest bands was with Les Golab, the little brother of Ed Golab, who was playing in Beelzebub Blues with Malcolm.

Ed Golab: 'They were the little brother band, you know. And my brother played, he was the lead singer with him for a couple of gigs, I think. We dismissed any of that — they were just kids.'

It was Herm Kovac who tipped Angus off around 1972 about what would be his first serious band, Kantuckee. They were believed to be named after the number one fried chicken outlet in the country at the time. Kovac was teaching drummer Trevor James in a line-up that included John Stevens (bass) and eventually Bob McGlynn on vocals.

When McGlynn joined the band, his initial impressions of Angus were colourful.

Bob McGlynn: 'He had green teeth, never brushed his teeth. He was a funny guy. Quirky — not funny, laughing ha ha! He used to complain a lot about, "Oh, I shouldn't have to go through all this, my brothers didn't have to," although they did. He just didn't think we were sort of treated right. But we didn't have a [known] name or anything like that.

'But, nice guy, he always had a bit of a laugh. Didn't have a lot of confidence in himself, though, but once we started to play his confidence really kicked up. But he still didn't jump around, he still stood there. As a person he seemed more confident, but still on stage he didn't have that sort of showmanship thing. I did all the moving.

'I think they [Kantuckee] were going to be called The Clan or something, which was a very Scottish thing. [Angus] was very protective of his family, friends, things like that.'

For associate Steve Morcom, Kantuckee represented an amazing merger of opposing subcultures.

Steve Morcom: 'Angus was part of the Town Hall Sharps, the Burwood connection, and Trevor was part of The Long Hairs, supposedly two violently opposed gangs which really hardly ever did anything and they ended up playing in a band together. I thought that was a classic.'

Angus played through a small amp, although Malcolm would occasionally lend him his Marshall amp stack which, of course, was taller than Angus and he could only just reach the knobs. His reach was far better within the band where he came to largely dictate their material, which he sourced from a local import record store in Burwood.

He would grab about 10 albums a week — most if not all of which were almost unheard of in Australia at the time — learn everything on them and then somehow take them back and get more. The sole criterion, at least for the band, was that the songs had good strong guitar riffs in them. For that reason, songs by Mountain, Cactus, Argent, Deep Purple, Ursa Major (it's said that Angus once jammed with guitarist Dick Wagner, later of Alice Cooper and Lou Reed fame, in Melbourne), Hendrix, the Stones, and from Jeff Beck's *Truth* and *Beck-Ola* era, all made appearances in their sets.

Rehearsals were on Sundays, or more regularly as the need arose, in a scout hall next to busy Concord Road in Rhodes adjacent to a major bridge, the same place Malcolm rehearsed in. When they really wanted to tighten up they would shift into the hall's small kitchen where the sound wouldn't be lost.

If the scout hall was unavailable there was always the community hall at Hornsby Heights or, at a pinch, Angus' immaculately tidy bedroom where the bed was always made and all his records neatly filed away in order.

At the Young home, there was never anything more potent than buckets of tea, while biscuits and countless cigarettes were always on hand.

Angus would dismiss the regular compliments about the impressive sketches he had done that were sometimes in view and refocus on what they were trying to play. Music was what mattered.

When it was time to take a break, they would play pool on a table so big that the only way to attempt a shot without hitting the walls was to hold the stick at a 90-degree angle. After rehearsals, Angus would lock himself away in his room and practise for another four hours or so.

Their first professional gig was at Batemans Bay on the South Coast several hours' drive from Sydney with none other than the Velvet Underground. In time the band graduated to the occasional spot at Chequers in the heart of Sydney, where they developed a small following after passing a Tuesday afternoon audition for MC Mr Casey.

As the gigs and the travel time increased, transportation for the equipment became a key issue. They thought big.

Bob McGlynn: 'John Stevens and Angus, I think, together bought a big International ex-ambulance. It was a big white thing. They used to travel around in it and it had two amps in the back. It was like a semi-trailer carrying three boxes!'

Their first recording was done by former Hot Cottage guitarist Kim Humphreys during a rehearsal at Rhodes. Humphreys went along as a favour to McGlynn but, as a class guitarist himself, also wanted to see first-hand if Angus was everything his friend had boasted he was.

Kim Humphreys: 'Mate, I just felt like bloody walking out the door! I thought he was that good. I can remember the band did one gig somewhere and someone asked me to get up and play because they saw me standing in the audience. I said, "You're fucking kidding!" Anyway, Angus quite cheerfully loaned me his guitar and I got up and played a few things with them. He was just brilliant back in those days — just very strong. I knew the guy could walk all over me! I knew people in the audience probably couldn't tell the difference, but I could.'

Bob McGlynn: 'His speed was incredible. Kim gave him some advice and said slow that down and don't worry too much about your speed, you can play more tastefully. But he still had it, obviously. I mean, some of the stuff we played was not easy and he could play it even through this 50-watt terrible amp.'

Humphreys also couldn't fathom how Angus got the sound he did with his Fi Sonic amp.

Kim Humphreys: 'I used to have one and I said, "Shit! How does this guy get a sound like that? Mine never sounds like that!" He just made it sound unbelievable, little bastard.

'He was probably more flashy then than he is now, because of the sort of things he was listening to. He really liked Jeff Beck and he also liked Paul Kossoff from Free. [Mountain's] Leslie West was one of his favourite guitar players.

'I've still got a really early *Guitar Player* magazine that Angus loaned me that's got Leslie West on the cover — I never gave it back to him. That's where I think he got that really distinctive vibrato from, Leslie West. The other band he really liked — and I think I've still got his album of this — was Cactus [self-titled album].'

Angus' sense of purpose and dedication didn't leave much time for social niceties and led to some initial misconceptions.

Kim Humphreys: 'I think the guy just believed in what he was doing so much that anybody else just didn't matter. He knew what was going on, he knew what he was doing and he just didn't have the time to chit-chat and talk about the weather.'

Eventually, it was decided to get a second guitarist which would allow Angus, who other bands were constantly trying to poach, more room. Mark Sneddon walked into a baptism of fire with 50 songs to learn in under a week.

Mark Sneddon: 'Angus gave me an absolute pile of albums with each song marked on each album and said, "Go home and learn them." And I'd never heard some of these bands in my life. I went home and I just remember sitting there [practising] for hours and hours every day for the first four days. By the time I got to the gig, I was that tired it was a wonder I could remember anything.'

With Sneddon up to speed, the now five-piece band with twin guitar firepower were really able to stretch out, particularly at Chequers, which required them to play up to four hours a night.

Thankfully for Angus, he was yet to start doing his St Vitus' dance on stage, otherwise he would have been hospitalised with exhaustion by the end of the night.

Mark Sneddon: 'Angus used to move his own way. He used to stand there and just pose and move a bit, like shake his leg. But he didn't do a lot of jumping around.'

In addition to originals like The Kantuckee Stomp, at one point the band had up to 10 songs by Mountain in their set, including Long Red, Blood Of The Sun and Mississippi Queen, as well as material by Leafhound, Bulldog and Cactus, who were a particularly strong influence. Cactus' 1972 effort, *'Ot 'N' Sweaty*, was a cornerstone in the Kantuckee set, with almost the entire album part of their pool of material.

The dynamic began to shift when Sneddon showed he could sing as well as play guitar. McGlynn saw the writing was on the wall and decided to leave.

At this point, Dave Evans, who had done time as singer in latter-day Velvet Underground outfit Pony after Malcolm left, was offered a role in the band. Like McGlynn, Evans was immediately struck by the colour and condition of Angus' teeth.

Dave Evans: 'That put me off. I went, "Fuck! He's got to clean his teeth!" And he had this big fat tall bass player with him. He looked really strange. The guy's about six foot and Angus is five foot tall, it was like the weirdest sight. He introduced himself as Angus Young, brother of George Young from The Easybeats, and also the brother of Malcolm Young. I obviously heard of Malcolm because of the Velvet Underground thing. They were playing lots of sort of heavy guitar-based music rather than songs with lyrics that much. I listened to it and I really wasn't into it and I didn't join them.'

The downsized band continued with Sneddon on vocals and guitar under the new name of Tantrum.

The band's work schedule slowly began to expand to include places like Blacktown RSL in western Sydney and the Coogee Oceanic in the city's eastern suburbs. The Manly Vale Hotel on Sydney's northern beaches was a favourite gig until Stevens got into a scuffle with a few patrons and at the end of the night the beaten locals wanted to tear the band apart.

On another occasion they were mistakenly booked as a good old boy country and western band. After six songs and having blown several eardrums they were firmly told that their services would not be required any longer.

Then there was the time they had barely plugged in before they were asked to move on.

Mark Sneddon: 'We loaded down two flights of stairs, set up and we were doing the soundcheck, and a bloke comes up and goes, "Hey mate, you're not 18." Angus goes, "Yes I am." It was his birthday and he pulled out his birth certificate — Scottish birth certificate with a thistle on it — and he showed it to the guy and said, "Look, I'm 18, it's my birthday," and they wouldn't believe us. So we had to pack all the gear and get out again.'

Angus took full advantage of being of age when Sneddon threw a party one night and not a soul showed up but the band.

Mark Sneddon: 'He turned up absolutely sloshed with a bottle of Bond 7. He liked his Bond 7, at the time. But he wasn't a big drinker, he was a big cigarette smoker. Pretty sort of self-contained. He had one idea in mind and that was pretty well it.'

Malcolm would occasionally come to the band's rehearsals at Rhodes and jam, not only to keep his hand in and support his brother but because he genuinely liked what they were doing.

Malcolm: 'Actually, they weren't a bad band. I was surprised when I saw him the first time. It was loud and he was making a big noise on that stage.'

It was only a matter of time before George also checked out what his little brother was up to. During 1973, George and Harry Vanda arrived with a large reel-to-reel tape recorder and got the group down on tape for a second time. On playback the band just couldn't believe it was actually them.

Mark Sneddon: 'I remember listening back to it one time and going, "Holy shit! Is that us? Fuck! It sounds huge!"'

They subsequently went into EMI Studios with George and Harry and recorded the pair's Evie and, possibly, Guitar Band.

Tantrum continued for about another six to nine months and then the rot began to set in.

Mark Sneddon: 'Angus had a few altercations with Trevor, the drummer. Angus couldn't handle him and they came to blows a few times. Finally, Angus just went, "That's it! Let's get another drummer and kick him out!"'

But getting a replacement was tough and, for Angus at least, other opportunities presented themselves.

Mark Sneddon: 'Malcolm had half a band together, I forget what they sound like now. Somewhere along the way the suggestion came up: why don't you go and play with Malcolm? At first Angus wasn't real happy about it [but] the idea caught on.'

Angus' initial reaction to the prospect of playing with his brother was sheer horror.

Mark Sneddon: '"Oh no, we can't do that, we'll kill each other." But three weeks later they were doing it. I don't know if someone had a talk to him or whether Angus just saw the light.'

Kim Humphreys, on the other hand, recalls that teaming with Malcolm was always on Angus' agenda.

'He said, "Oh look, not too far down the track I'm going to be getting a band together with my brother." He said that was his ultimate aim.'

Mark Sneddon: 'They had the AC/DC idea long before that and the school uniform idea too. I think it was mentioned some time that here's a name, AC/DC — that'd be a good name to use, wouldn't it? I don't think any of us took it really seriously at the time.'

1974
Malcolm, Peter Clack, Rob Bailey,
Dave Evans, Angus, Chequers, Sydney.

chapter 4

IN THE
BEGINNING

*O*ne of George Young's regrets was that The Easybeats went off message and turned their backs on the simple magic that could be conjured up with three chords, all in an attempt to be more impressive musically. He wasn't about to let Malcolm fall into the same trap with his band.

When George arrived back in Australia, he told Malcolm tales of the great English rock and rollers of the day like the Stones and The Faces.

But Malcolm had been doing some homework of his own. He hadn't just been listening to the greats, he'd been studying them, and made a discovery. Both the Stones and The Beatles had had their experiments, such as the Stones' *Their Satanic Majesties Request* and scholarly concept albums like The Beatles' *Sgt Pepper* and *Magical Mystery Tour*.

But they had both gravitated back to their original rock and roll roots, the Stones supremely with *Exile On Main Street* and The Beatles to a lesser degree on *Let It Be* and songs like Get Back.

The lesson was clear.

'You're gonna come back there anyway,' Malcolm told David Horowitz in *Juke* on 23 February 1991, 'so why leave in the first place? Why not simply work better and harder at what you've got?'

While Status Quo, Slade and Foghat were popular, Malcolm had something more grassroots in mind. With the enormous impact of Muddy Waters' Australian tour in May 1973 still bouncing off many a musician's household wall, Malcolm wanted to reclaim the lost art of real rock and roll, of the raw energy, emotion and drive of Little Richard, Chuck Berry, Jerry Lee Lewis, The Beatles' rock and roll songs like Get Back, and, of course, the Stones stripped bare of hippy bullshit and druggy excesses.

What he had in mind when he left Pony simply hadn't panned out as he'd hoped and this stuff was almost his birthright.

Malcolm: 'I was initially looking for a keyboard and try a bit of rock and roll with piano and be versatile. And it just didn't work out, probably because I didn't feel confident enough as a solo player. Even though I didn't want to do a lot of solos but just to pick up the odd licks. It wasn't working out, couldn't find a good thing and it [working with Angus] just came about. I just didn't even think about Angus [previously].'

He initially teamed with the Velvets and Pony bassist Mick Sheffzick and former Masters Apprentices drummer Colin Burgess. It was close but no cigar.

Then in November, after Larry Van Kriedt — with whom Malcolm already had several years of history — replaced Sheffzick, it was decided to get a singer to handle the words that Malcolm had already penned.

After a string of less than successful candidates, Dave Evans had his second brush with the Young clan via an advertisement in *The Sydney Morning Herald*. The former Velvet Underground/Pony vocalist had long been intrigued by the cryptic references of his bandmates to a previous member known as 'the little fella', and now he finally got to meet him.

Evans hadn't exactly been popular among his bandmates in Pony, so some were surprised that Malcolm considered taking him on as a singer.

An audition was arranged at an old office in Newtown in the city's inner-west, which was owned by well-known and respected Sydney scene identity Allan Kissick, who was far more powerful than his unassuming look indicated.

He had been de facto manager, agent and general guiding hand for many bands, and a decade earlier had linked Stevie Wright with The Easybeats and handled the subsequent band's early affairs. It was he who had introduced Colin Burgess to Malcolm's equation.

Evans was stunned when he walked in and saw Burgess, given that the Masters Apprentices were one of Australia's top bands in the late '60s and early '70s and had been to London.

Dave Evans: 'Colin was like a fucking star to me, because when I was a kid in school the Masters Apprentices were big.'

They ran through some standard 12-bar rock and roll and some Free material and everyone was pleased. Even though the band didn't have a name, Evans was amazed that even at this point Malcolm knew exactly where they were headed.

Dave Evans: 'He used to say, "I don't give a fuck about this country! I don't give a fuck about Australia! We're gonna make it fucking big, man! The world!" His vision was always to be huge around the world.'

After a few more rehearsals, Malcolm thought of Angus entering the fold. Apart from sharing a strong work ethic, the pair had seen a number of major overseas acts together and had formed very similar and strong views on what had worked, what hadn't, and why, all of which made Angus the perfect ally.

Their first concert experience had been seeing the Yardbirds at the Sydney Stadium in January 1967. Despite the fact that the band were in the final phase of their career and the short-lived dynamic guitar axis of Jimmy Page and Jeff Beck had parted ways only a few months prior, the Englishmen still had plenty of power and blues-drenched magic. Even from the cheap seats something clicked in Angus' brain as he sat and watched. This was the stuff.

Angus: 'I suppose it didn't kick in until I was around about 10 years old [when] I remember seeing the Yardbirds, me and Malcolm. It was just a great atmosphere. I always thought they were a good band. They came on, they played, they were really short and sweet. I thought, this is very flash. I think at the time they had that fast and furious thing but it was quality.'

Almost a year to the day later, The Who and The Small Faces scorched Australian soil with a violent stage act and monstrous volume. The Small Faces' Steve Marriott spewed venom at the crowd at the Sydney Stadium and The Who trashed everything that they couldn't blow up. The entire show was an exercise in attitude and Malcolm and Angus Young took it all in with eyes and jaws wide open.

In April and May 1971, another lesson in English rock touched down at Sydney's Randwick Racecourse in the form of Deep Purple, Free and Manfred Mann, who by that point were as keyboard-heavy as Purple themselves. Again, Malcolm and Angus were in the crowd; however, the teachings and inspiration didn't come from the heavyweight headliners, who Angus thought weren't doing anything he himself couldn't do at least as well, but from the searing blues rock of Free. The day was a seminal moment, with Free guitarist Paul Kossoff and drummer Simon Kirke, and Manfred Mann's drummer Chris Slade and bassist Colin Pattenden, in a testament to Malcolm's steel trap of a memory, all destined to brush against the Young brothers in some form or other in the years to come.

Then in March 1972, the Led Zeppelin juggernaut rumbled into Sydney Showgrounds with a marathon performance, although Angus much preferred what he'd seen guitarist Jimmy Page do several years earlier in the Yardbirds.

Angus: 'When I saw Led Zeppelin it had seemed to tone down a lot [from the Yardbirds] and I always liked the Yardbirds' thing, their approach, better. When I saw Led Zeppelin maybe I was disappointed because I expected more of the same.

'I think the singer grated on me a little. He'd sing like he was picking his nose and he was more concentrated on swivelling his hips than singing. I'm not knocking Zeppelin. I just expected more because the Yardbirds had a great singer in Keith Relf. He didn't dazzle you with his hips. He concentrated on what he was there for — to make a bit of rock and roll.'

That was exactly what Malcolm had in mind.

Malcolm: 'I came in one day and I said [to Angus], "How's things, anyway? How's the band?" "Ah, it's not really happening. I'll just hang out with John who's still here — the bass player." So I said, "Well come down and have a jam and check this guy out for us. I've found this singer, I'm not sure of him. At the same time, I don't mind, we can have a blow because it's a bit empty just with me and the bass player and the drums."'

Malcolm raised the idea with the band and some members had reservations as to whether Angus could cut it next to the blindingly obvious skills and versatility of Malcolm.

Colin Burgess: 'Malcolm was playing lead and rhythm guitar at the same time. I thought it was incredible then — the band sounded fantastic. When Angus came along, I thought, well, is he gonna be good enough?'

Being up to the mark musically wasn't the issue. The proximity of a hospital and how fast an ambulance could get the two brothers there seemed likely to be a far greater concern.

Angus and Malcolm had long had a fiery if fiercely brotherly relationship. Angus would work on his guitar heroics in his room and Malcolm on song structures in his, an area of the house which was a virtual no-go zone for the younger brother. Over time, their interests spilt together and a strong mutual admiration grew, as did a hair-trigger defence mechanism for one another. The fireworks, however, were never far from the surface.

William Young was amazed that both his youngest boys had even considered joining forces and gave the exercise a week before it and they exploded. But on the most basic level, them getting together was simply a matter of the mutual needs of both, while the potential of the pairing would not have been lost on George, who some have said was the architect of the whole thing.

If Angus had any reservations himself, Malcolm's broad vision for the band dulled the pain of any potential cuts and grazes. No-one was playing rock and roll properly any more, Malcolm, who was fired up after seeing his hero Marc Bolan and T. Rex at Sydney's Hordern Pavilion, told him. It was time to take a stand.

Angus asked where to sign.

Larry Van Kriedt: 'Malcolm was a bit of a visionary. He's always like that, he always sees a whole band. He didn't just think of the guitar. I remember hearing him say that he would like to be like the guy that plays guitar who's organised — you know, sort of writes parts and does things like that — and Angus would be the showman and would be the lead guitarist.'

Angus was quiet and nervous at the first rehearsal, slightly overawed with the calibre of the other members, like Van Kriedt, and Burgess, of course, was still a bona fide star.

He need not have worried.

Malcolm: 'He came down and all the guys in the band went, "Oh fuck, this is great!" It just instantly happened. I was surprised. I'm sure Angus was too.'

Dave Evans recalls being quite happy for Angus to become involved and welcomed him aboard. But Malcolm remembers that first rehearsal very differently to the singer.

'This singer had to go! [laughs] It was a case of instant hate. The singer didn't like Angus because Angus is smaller than me and thinner at the time. He didn't want Angus in the band, which we thought was unbelievable.'

Nonetheless, the line-up locked in and one of the earliest — if not *the* first — gigs by the still nameless band was in December in the middle slot of a three-band bill, always the prime position, at The Last Picture Show in Sydney's south.

Working without a name couldn't last, so it was decided that some ideas be drawn from a hat at rehearsal.

While Margaret, the sister of Malcolm and Angus, has long been credited with the name AC/DC after she saw the term on the back of either her vacuum cleaner or sewing machine, another source credits the genius of George Young, while George's wife was initially cited as the originator of the tag.

'George's wife, Sandra, thought it was a good name for a group,' Malcolm told Michele O'Driscoll in *Go-Set* on 15 June 1974.

Albert's Rocka Souvenir Songbook confirmed this in August 1976, saying, 'George's wife devised the name AC/DC', a statement backed up by Angus when he spoke to Bob Hart the following month in *Spunky*. '[The name came] off the back of my sister-in-law's sewing machine.'

The name had strong gay connotations at the time and, as a result, some of the band's initial bookings were in gay bars, a situation which ran totally against the testosterone-oozing nature of what the outfit was all about.

The band, though, almost revelled in the ambiguity of it all and Malcolm and Angus relished the prospect of putting some idiot who really did think they were gay back in their place.

Where the pair were coming from musically was far more straightforward. The Yardbirds, The Who, The Kinks, The Small Faces, the Stones and even The Spencer Davis Group were favourites. They were both also fascinated by the rhythmic interplay of Billy Gibbons and Dusty Hill — the guitarist, much admired by Jimi Hendrix, and bassist respectively of ZZ Top — along with classic belters like Fats Domino and Ike and Tina Turner.

The first time Angus visited the offices of *Juke* magazine, he was more interested in going through their files on Jerry Lee Lewis than doing an interview. He drew from watching the technique of flamenco guitarists, while the fingerpicking of Southern country swamp guitarist Jerry Reed held great sway with them both.

Malcolm: 'We'd always had a sort of Stones or a Beatles ... everyone at that point in time had that sort of influence. Then your Led Zeppelins and your heavier [stuff], Hendrix came along. We grew up through all of that and Jeff Beck — guys like that.

'We were always into the blues, especially Muddy Waters and a lot of the Willie Dixon Chess stuff. Little Richard, Chuck Berry for the rock and roll side, Jerry Lee Lewis, and we just used to party on this music, basically. So it was all rough and tumble and just fucking grin and go for it. That's all it was to us. We had really good influences around, you know, in music.'

For Malcolm it was almost a dumbing-down exercise, although the attraction was simple; he and Angus loved the way rock and roll was played, the subtle techniques involved that only made it seem basic.

Steve Morcom recalls a conversation with Angus about Yes and their guitarist Steve Howe.

'Angus said, "Look, Malcolm can play all that stuff but we're just going to stick to this bottom line thing." But he meant it in a really positive way and I knew Malcolm was well up on that [more complex material] and could pull stuff off like that. Malcolm was a really accomplished player when AC/DC started.'

What is historically seen as the official launch of that formula came courtesy of Allan Kissick on New Year's Eve 1973 at Chequers. The band had played there previously, sometimes simply to fill in at short notice. But this time it was serious and they were headlining what was to be a week-long booking at the club.

In the southern end of the central Sydney business district, Chequers was not just any gig and, in the '60s, had been the city's number one nightclub. Set deep down from street level via a white mottled marble staircase, it had all the glitz and class of the artists who'd performed there, from Frank Sinatra to Shirley Bassey. The immaculate, often purple-suited host was Mr Casey.

Although by the early '70s the club was more a music industry drinking hole than the palace it had once been, it retained a certain status as the place to be seen at and heard in, although AC/DC were all just dressed in their street clothes for the occasion.

Angus: 'I suppose we were a bit nervous. But we figured we were on good territory 'cause, well, it's New Year's Eve and as the night wears on the bulk of the place is going to be drunk, so we thought, well, that's one guard we've got. Casey was always good with

Malcolm and myself. The good part about it [was that] we were one of the few bands he ever paid a bit more. Everyone was impressed by that fact, I think!'

Playing Chequers involved three or four sets a night which meant up to five hours on stage. That required some fast thinking and plenty of jamming, Van Kriedt occasionally moving to sax and Malcolm to bass. They had originals such as The Old Bay Road and Midnight Rock and there was even some joke telling to fill out the time.

Angus: 'I think we did a couple of the Stones, a lot of Chuck Berry and Little Richard — I remember we were doing School Days, we did Nadine, and the other one, No Particular Place To Go. I think we did [The Beatles' I Want You (She's So Heavy)]. Then I think some of the other ones we busked through. Malcolm would say, "This is our jazz moment now — Ang will do you a guitar solo. Keep you amused for half an hour."'

The dates at Chequers were followed with other gigs on the Sydney circuit and transport was courtesy of Malcolm's VW Kombi van. Every night the star attraction was the musical fireworks between the two tiny guitar players.

Dave Evans: 'The two boys would be doing guitar solo duels on stage. And two little guys fucking blowing people away, you know. Malcolm would just go for it, then Angus, then Malcolm would go for it again, and they'd be both playing at the same time. It was pretty exciting stuff.'

There were the unusual gigs, like the time the band were asked to play at the Greek wedding of the cousin of a friend of Dave Evans in Sydney. Everything was steaming along until the not entirely unexpected request for a version of Zorba The Greek. After some initial horrified looks from the stage, Malcolm came to the rescue.

Dave Evans: 'He's got a brilliant ear. He'd never played it before in his fucking life, you know. And he said, "Yep, no worries! Just follow me, guys." So AC/DC did Zorba The Greek and killed it at the Greek wedding, man.'

George Young quietly took in all that was going on with pride. For him, AC/DC represented a reawakening, a renewed hope, and helped him regain the enthusiasm that had been beaten out of him in the latter days of The Easybeats.

Every few weeks George would attend the band's rehearsals and offer suggestions. Malcolm and Angus eagerly gulped down his wisdom, as did other open-mouthed members of the band.

Larry Van Kriedt: 'I remember I was impressed because he [George] had some words and he had a bit of a song, and he said, "What do you think of this?" And Dave said, "I don't like the words." So he said, "How come?" "Well they're a bit negative," or something like that.

'So George, instead of going, "I don't think they're negative," he just goes "Oh," and wrote some more — he wrote some positive ones just like that.'

Chris Gilbey began work at Albert Productions, the recording home of The Easybeats, in February 1973 as Artists and Repertoire (A&R) Manager. After a few months, Ted Albert requested that he also take over promotions duties. By the end of the year Gilbey was vice president and he too saw George playing a primary role in assisting the band.

Chris Gilbey: 'I think in the early period of time George was a far greater controlling influence on AC/DC than any of the members of the band, because George was big brother and he'd been there with The Easybeats, he knew the ropes, he'd gone to England, he'd had hit records. I think he imparted a very strong ethic as to what the music business was about, what music was about and staying close to the roots. I think that was one of the things that George really communicated.'

In January 1974, George and Harry Vanda took the band into EMI Studios in Sydney with engineer Richard Lush, with George subsequently re-recording Van Kriedt's bass tracks. A number of songs were recorded, including Can I Sit Next To You, Girl and Rockin' In The Parlour, along with Sunset Strip (later known as Show Business), Soul Stripper, and an early version of Rock 'N' Roll Singer which was firmly earmarked for the band's debut album.

For Harry Vanda, the sessions highlighted a clear divide between what Malcolm and Angus were doing and Evans' position within that plan.

Harry Vanda: 'I think the guys were still looking for their identity then and all that. I think Dave always leant a bit more towards the glittery part of rock, which is fair enough if that's what you want to do. But I think that was pretty alien to the guys, it's not their thing. And I think by what was coming off those demos at the time, you could tell it was going to be a rock band regardless.'

A week after the session, Colin Burgess collapsed on stage at Chequers.

Colin Burgess: 'Someone must've spiked my drink or something, because it knocked me right out, and I actually fell off my drums. I know it sounds bizarre. I'd never done that before.'

He was dismissed on the spot and, with one of the heels of his boots broken, he hobbled off into the night. Malcolm immediately rang George who sat in on drums for the rest of the show.

But Burgess' departure set a purge in motion and Van Kriedt was also shown the door. Other changes had been in the wind while Van Kriedt was still on the payroll.

Larry Van Kriedt: 'There was a mention of everyone having a character, and Angus was a schoolboy. I was gonna be like an American cop — sounds a bit like the Village People, but they didn't exist then! Malcolm was gonna be like a pilot or something and have blue hair or something. And I remember Angus, at first, was pissed off because he didn't want to be like a cabaret performer! Malcolm brought him into line though.'

All the while George and Harry had been working on another recording, having struck up a warm working relationship with Ted Albert and Albert Productions late in 1973. That project was the debut album for former Easybeat Stevie Wright, who had been involved in the Australian cast of *Jesus Christ Superstar*.

Hard Road featured not just the production skills of George and Harry but the guitar front line of Malcolm and Harry. The centrepiece of the album was Evie, an 11-minute Vanda-and-Young-penned epic, which was divided into Parts 1, 2 and 3 and took up much of the first side.

Drummer Russell Coleman was involved in some sessions for the album and was amazed by the musical instincts and talents of George, who was also a stunning vocal mimic.

Russell Coleman: 'He used to go and listen to heavy duty steel presses — you know, like stamps, things like that, but 20 tons. He'd go and have a listen to that and say, "That's how I want the snare drum to be!" I came in with Stevie Wright one time and had all my shiny cymbals, and he said, "Get rid of that rubbish, mate!" He brought out the ugliest cymbals I've ever seen in my life and went, "That's rock and roll!" And he had a stack of guitars, beautiful Gibsons and Epiphones and Fenders, all neck to neck, just stacked up in the corner.'

Malcolm had been surprised and disappointed when he saw the complex cut-and-paste process involved in recording with the Marcus Hook Roll Band — George and Harry's studio project that spawned the *Tales Of Old Grand-Daddy* album — and the methods used in the *Hard Road* sessions only served to confirm his quiet horror.

In response, he took drastic action when he got home. All his records — with virtually the sole exception of the Stones' *Get Yer Ya-Ya's Out!* and his blues albums, which he knew had character through their mistakes — were thrown out.

Meanwhile, in February, Allan Kissick enlisted Malcolm to fill in on guitar with Sydney band Jasper, whose frontman — John or Johnny Cave — was a very early contender to be AC/DC's singer. Cave later changed his stage name to William Shakespeare, adopted a blindingly glittering fashion sense and had two major pop chart successes for Albert's in 1974 with Vanda and Young's Can't Stop Myself From Loving You and My Little Angel.

Impressed by what he heard and felt thumping away behind him in Jasper, Malcolm asked if bass player Neil Smith and drummer Noel Taylor would be interested in joining AC/DC. The pair were quite a bargain as they not only came with a van like Malcolm's, but also a PA system.

In late February, the revamped band secured themselves a month-long residency at the Hampton Court Hotel after greatly impressing the publican while rehearsing there. Like Chequers, the Hampton was a gruelling schedule of three 45-minute sets that, with half-hour breaks, saw them clocking up roughly five hours' work a night.

AC/DC didn't have one but two showstoppers to keep the crowd's attention. One was a fiery version of Jumpin' Jack Flash which clocked in at around the 12-minute mark, with Malcolm and Angus duelling off one another like madmen. The other was an extended version of Baby, Please Don't Go, which featured Malcolm on vocals.

Both Angus and Malcolm still had day jobs which involved early starts, so between sets, Angus would take himself off and find as quiet a corner as he could and grab some sleep.

Neil Smith quickly got the sense that he'd signed up to something pretty special, and not simply because of the combined talents of Malcolm and Angus and the fact they were George's kid brothers.

Smith was amazed that Malcolm and Angus never socialised in the rock and roll industry and basically wanted to keep as far from it as they could. After gigs Angus would just go home and practise, and the pair had granite-hard, black and white views in relation to the music and musicians of the day.

'I remember going down to Chequers one night, and Malcolm's having a Scotch and I'm having a beer, and he goes, "What d'ya think of this band?" And I said, "I think they're sort of alright." He said, "Are they good?" I said, "Well, not really ..." "They're shit then, aren't they?" That's how they used to think. It was all black or white, there was no middle. They just knew, mate, they knew how to do it.

'Angus once said to me, "It's a shame Hendrix died 'cause we could've blown him off stage!" You're having a couple of beers in the pub and then he tells you, "You know we're gonna be one of the greatest bands in the world." I mean, a 20-year-old guy who says that [and] you're going, "Hang on a minute, what? What are you saying, mate? Would you like a beer?"'

It was during February and March that Geordie, a tough glam band from Britain with singer Brian Johnson, toured Australia. Chris Gilbey at Albert's helped organise the tour as Albert's were representing the publishing interests of a UK company called Red Bus Music who had signed Geordie. Angus saw them at Hornsby Police Boys Club and Malcolm at Chequers.

Ever eager to document his brothers' progress, George again made arrangements to capture AC/DC on tape at his home in Epping, where he had a studio set up. Unfortunately, Smith's bass amp blew up and the sessions didn't really fire. The sole result was just another take of Can I Sit Next To You, Girl.

While they had been gigging regularly, April brought a new chapter at an open air gig at Victoria Park on the outskirts of the central business district of Sydney. AC/DC were determined to make an impact. A lasting impression at such a big show would be invaluable publicity.

It was at this gig that the costumes which had been under discussion were finally unveiled.

Dave Evans: 'We decided to dress pretty bizarre to get some attention. [For] Angus, his sister came up with the idea of him wearing a schoolboy uniform with short pants and a satchel on his back. The bass player, he decided to wear jodhpurs and a crash helmet and dark glasses, sort of like a highway copper. The drummer wore a kind of clown outfit with a top hat — sort of harlequin — and Malcolm had a white jump suit and blue boots like an airman. I had red boots and fucking tight pants and a red-and-white striped jacket that was very colourful.

'People went, "Whoa! What's this?" especially the schoolboy uniform. The whole look of the band was just completely from outer space. It was just something different. We did the gig and it went over great, of course.'

Of all the outfits, Angus' role as a schoolboy was the most memorable and believable. The look was a direct connection to his schooldays when he would burst in the front door in the afternoons and make straight for his guitar, a change of clothes lost in his enthusiasm.

His big sister, Margaret, saw the possibilities of a stage costume which would time freeze Angus as a 16 year old. He was shy and so less than enthusiastic about the school uniform at first, and again it took Malcolm and George to talk him around.

For all its eye-catching impact, the schoolboy outfit was not the only character that Angus had in circulation over the coming months. In Zorro mode, for example, Angus would play the guitar with a bowing action with his plastic sword in a quiet nod to Jimmy Page's experimentation with a violin bow when he and Malcolm saw the Yardbirds in the late '60s.

Dave Evans: 'He used to also have fights on stage with me, like he'd sword fight me. I had the mic stand, you know, and he'd sort of sword fight me and then I'd put him on my shoulders. He used to play up on my shoulders.'

The Victoria Park show was a turning point in the band's career, but for Neil Smith and Noel Taylor it was the end of the line and they were fired soon after, having been on the payroll for just six weeks. With them went their respective stage characters and the edge fell from the entire concept.

Neil Smith: 'These guys kept telling us, "We're gonna be the biggest band in the world!" We'd go, "Yeah, yeah, yeah," and have another beer. We didn't take it as serious, obviously, as they did. I can just imagine how frustrating it must have been for Malcolm.'

Smith and Taylor were out, and the band held auditions at their rehearsal space in Newtown. Bassist Rob Bailey, who had played with Flake at the Victoria Park concert, and drummer Peter Clack were recruited.

Dennis James: 'At the time they were both playing in my band, which I think was called Train. They got a call from [AC/DC's first manager] Ray Arnold telling them of the audition. I went along with them. Those two, plus my singer Wayne Green, were asked to join. Wayne unfortunately (for him) declined. I of course had no offer ... being a lead player myself!'

Stevie Wright's Evie was released in May 1974 and would go on to be the biggest Australian single of the year. It was also the world's first opportunity to hear Malcolm on record. On 9 June, while the momentum of Evie was building strongly, Wright, now a huge solo star on the back of the *Hard Road* album which was released in March, performed at the Sydney Opera House. An estimated crowd of 10,000 arrived for the free show, although there was only space to accommodate a few thousand at best.

In an Easybeats reunion of sorts, Wright was backed by George Young on bass and Harry Vanda on guitar — their first public appearance together since The Easybeats folded — with Malcolm on rhythm guitar and Dave Evans, John Paul Young and Blackfeather's Neil Johns on backing vocals. Both Malcolm and Dave Evans did double duties as AC/DC opened the event.

Go-Set's review in the 22 June 1974 issue said the opening act 'were a force to be reckoned with' and that 'AC/DC look great and sound great'.

It was priceless coverage particularly as the band were officially signed to Albert Productions that same month.

Around this time a piece of AC/DC's future identity presented itself when they arrived at a gig in Sydney's southern suburbs to find a poster for the show with a lightning bolt separating AC and DC, an idea Albert's Chris Gilbey had come up with to emphasise the sense of energy in the band's name. It was perfect and it stuck.

On 22 July, AC/DC's first single, Can I Sit Next To You, Girl backed with Rockin' In The Parlour, both taken from the January EMI sessions, was released in Australia. Due to the creative imprint of George and Harry, copies made their way overseas where they were snapped up by enthusiastic fans.

The first overseas review was in the spring '75 issue of Greg Shaw's *Who Put The Bomp* magazine by Shaw himself, a long-time Easybeats fan and admirer of the talents of Vanda and Young, who, without any information to the contrary, made some interesting observations.

'AC/DC is most likely Vanda & Young with some studio guys; if it is a real group, their similarity to the early Easybeats is startling ... a modern evolution of that classic sound ... a stunning record.'

A film clip of the band doing the song was shot in an empty movie theatre called The Last Picture Show in Cronulla where they played regularly. Bernie Cannon, producer of ABC Television's 'GTK' (Get To Know) program which screened for 10 minutes from 6.30 p.m. Monday to Thursday, directed the video that Sunday morning with one startling innovation; he decided to shoot it in colour before there was colour transmission.

Despite its general low-key format and timeslot, 'GTK' was a national outlet and a vital tool in exposing the band in regional areas they had yet to reach in person. This situation was partially remedied with a small-scale Australian tour to capitalise on the chart success of Can I Sit Next To You in areas such as South Australia and Western Australia, the song having even hit the Top 5 listings in some places.

In Sydney, the band's energy and enthusiasm were winning over even the most intimidating of audiences. Wizard, from the 60-member-strong Annandale/Leichhardt Sharpies, recalls a night at Hornsby Police Boys Club: 'One of the guys jumped up on stage, knocked Angus' hat off and gave him a Sharpie hat, which was just a golf hat, and he'd have his hat. We gave it back to him — it was just for a few songs.'

In August, Can I Sit Next To You debuted on 'GTK' the same month Lou Reed, the king of rock and roll decadence, toured Australia for the first time. Who better to open for Reed than a young band, with a schoolboy guitarist, with what many assumed to be a name with bisexual connotations? The tour was national and as such was a prime promotional opportunity for AC/DC.

At a Melbourne show during the tour, when it was discovered that AC/DC's use of the sound system was to be drastically cut, Malcolm exploded and jumped on the phone to George.

Dave Evans: 'George flew down to Melbourne immediately. He fucking went up to the guys [Lou Reed's sound technicians] and said, "You give these boys the fucking lot!" and he stood by the fucking

PA, by the mixer. He made sure that we fucking had the full rig. Nobody fucks with George Young, man!'

It was in Perth during the Reed dates that a major shift of responsibilities took place within the band. Malcolm announced that Angus would play lead guitar and he would play rhythm, rather than mixing the roles between them, as had been the case.

Dave Evans: 'He said, "We need a focus in the band." He's a very canny guy, you know, very business minded. I remember saying to Malcolm, "Man, I fucking love your guitar playing!" I said, "It's gonna be a fucking waste if you're not playing [lead] guitar. You're great. You're better than fucking Angus!" He said, "Don't matter."'

Angus had always wanted to be the show-stopping, jaw-dropping soloist and besides, if he needed to check on technical points, Malcolm, the master of such things, was somewhere just over his shoulder. It was the perfect arrangement.

The clear separation of the guitar roles of Malcolm and Angus tied in with other changes. The rise of Melbourne's heavily costumed and theatrical Skyhooks had put the final nail in the coffin of AC/DC's own stage characters. They weren't about to get into a fashion race with anyone, particularly the outrageously dressed 'Hooks. All that stayed was Angus' schoolboy get-up.

In turn, rather than just standing still and concentrating on his playing, Angus was becoming more active under the lights — powered and empowered by little more than gallons of milk, handfuls of chocolate bars and countless cigarettes.

In a television interview in the early '90s, fellow Scot Billy Connolly spoke of his early days wearing strange costumes and how he felt he could do whatever he liked, because in those outfits he didn't represent anything. Angus came to see the school uniform the same way and it began to free him.

With the urging of George and Malcolm, he slowly found that he was able to tear around like a madman, tap into the emotional depth he admired so much in instruments such as saxophones, and do his heroes like Jeff Beck and Mountain's Leslie West proud at the same time.

With the spotlight being directed more towards Angus, the simmering tensions between Dave Evans and the Youngs, which seemed to be based on a clash of personalities more than anything else, increased.

One night, Evans, with help from a bottle of Drambuie, played right into the hands of Malcolm and a frustrated Angus who kicked the shit out of the below-par singer. The aggression Angus unleashed helped firm up his growing stage character and put everyone on notice. There was more friction over money — there was precious little of it despite all their hard work — and management. Evans and Dennis Laughlin, the band's second manager, got physical in Adelaide and the pair had to be pulled apart.

Despite all these sparks, or maybe because of them, the Young brothers had no doubt AC/DC were destined for big things. Geordie Leach, then of Melbourne's Buster Brown, recalls running into Malcolm and Angus outside an Adelaide gig.

Geordie Leach: 'We went in to get the keys to the Hospital Hotel and we were walking back and Angus and Malcolm were sitting on the steps of this joint, playing electric guitars, just acoustically, just playing with each other. Someone said, "You guys are cooking!" And they said, "Yeah, we're going to be huge."'

In Adelaide, they found the man to help them get that job done.

1969

Bon Scott with The Valentines, Melbourne.

chapter 5

COULDN'T MAKE A LIVING AS A MANIAC

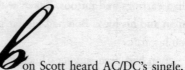on Scott heard AC/DC's single, Can I Sit Next To You, on the radio in Adelaide. It was the sort of stuff that he always loved to yell along to. Then the announcer said the name of the band and the enjoyment of the previous few minutes was replaced by sneering contempt; they were gay.

By 1974 and at the age of 28, Ronald Belford Scott had already carved out a sizable legend for himself in the Australian music industry.

Born on 9 July 1946 in Forfar, near Kirriemuir, Scotland, Bon was six when his family emigrated to Australia. They settled in Melbourne for a few years before relocating to Perth in 1956. At school his accent made him a target and he was given an ultimatum; either speak like everyone else or there'd be trouble. Bon wasn't about to be threatened.

'I didn't take any notice,' he told *Record Mirror*'s Daniela Soave on 18 August 1979. 'No-one railroads over me.'

There were other complications. In his class at school, there was another boy by the name of Ron, so to draw a line between them, he opted to be called Bonnie in homage to his homeland.

It was a move that fitted in perfectly with his decision to join the Fremantle Scots Pipe Band with his father and from 1958 to 1963 Bon was beginner side drum champion. Much to the delight of his parents, he was also part of the pipe band that played during the opening ceremony of the Empire Games in Perth in November 1962.

But by the time he reached his mid teens the notion of being called Bonnie was anything but ideal for a boy — like most his age — out to prove himself.

He worked various jobs after he left school, including as a postman, but no single experience in his life to that point had the impact of working alongside a hard nut on a crayfishing boat who had earrings and tattoos. Taken with the no bullshit attitude of the man and his look, Bon had his ear pierced and had an etching done on his arm.

Bon had been singing Chuck Berry and Elvis since the late '50s, much to the horror of his mother who felt that rock and roll didn't qualify as proper music. But it wasn't until he was 18 in 1964 that he made his first proper public appearance at Port Beach Stomp in Perth with his first band, The Spektors, named after Phil Spector, the man who created music's wall of sound studio effect.

Rehearsals took place in a small church hall but were hampered by the fact that Bon was doing time in reform school for being less than angelic.

Wyn Milson: 'We could only do gigs on Saturdays and Sundays because he was in the slam for the rest of the week. He'd been a little bit of a wild boy — he got into a bit of trouble. I think the reason they had him in the reform school was because he and a few friends had stolen a car and driven it off the Fremantle traffic bridge into the harbour when he was under age. I remember that when they let him out on weekends they used to just about cut his hair back to nothing with the clippers.'

When his time was served, Bon was freed up and the band began to make some progress, developing a following all over Perth and in some regional areas.

Bon divided his stage time between drumming and his preferred option, occasionally singing. The singer also played drums but Bon reckoned he was far better. Dennis James recalls seeing The Spektors at his high school dance in November 1964.

Dennis James: 'Bon was the drummer, but I can *still* see him jump up front and sing [The Kinks'] You Really Got Me. Even then, the kids saw something unique there.'

When The Spektors melted away in 1966, Bon and Wyn Milson joined forces with singer Vince Lovegrove from Perth's other top band, The Wynstons. At the suggestion of Alan Robinson at Radio 6KA in Perth, they named themselves The Valentines and began to tackle the soul music of Wilson Pickett and Sam and Dave.

Their progress in the scene was rapid and they opened for P.J. Proby in Perth in October and then, in March 1967, signed to Clarion Records. Their first single followed in May — Everyday I Have To Cry/I Can't Dance With You, Arthur Alexander and Small Faces covers respectively. Bon did backup vocals on the A-side and lead vocals on the B.

In June came The Valentines' big moment; opening for The Easybeats, fresh from their overseas triumph, at the Capital Theatre. Bon, being a huge fan, would have been more than happy to buy a ticket to see the show, but instead struck up a friendship with George Young.

The relationship also provided fuel for The Valentines' march forward and in turn showed Bon's musical versatility.

Wyn Milson: 'George said he had this song for us. We went out and recorded it with just George playing guitar and singing in a hotel room in Scarborough. We recorded it on a pretty crappy tape recorder, and then went back and cut it onto an acetate at the radio station, and then we learnt the song from there.

'The thing about She Said is that it had this little piece of recorder on it and Bon played the recorder. He was actually good at a lot of instruments — he was a passable guitar player, he could just about pick something up and learn to play.'

Soon, Everyday I Have To Cry was the biggest-selling single in Western Australia and the band were working six nights a week. But after The Valentines won the Western Australian Hoadley's Battle of the Bands competition the following month they crossed the country to perform at the national finals in Melbourne, where the excitement in the city got them thinking about expanding their horizons.

In August, the Vanda-and-Young-penned She Said was released and reached the Top 10 in Western Australia. It was something of a farewell to their home state.

In October 1967, The Valentines relocated to Melbourne where the pace of the music scene was nothing short of frantic, and on Saturday mornings, large department stores often had three or four bands performing on their rooftops.

With the band's new surroundings came a shift in how they presented themselves. Bon, who had been splitting his time between singing and drumming, had been desperate to take up a position in front of the band on a full-time basis, and now he got his wish alongside Vince Lovegrove.

The soul music they were playing also had to go in order to compete in Melbourne, so they began to tackle the Rolling Stones, Them and The Who. Right up Bon's alley.

In time, while the band were doing up to four different shows on a Saturday night, sometimes all within a few minutes' drive of each other, they were living in the one house making barely enough to survive. At one point they were forced into going to the supermarket and filling their mouths with food and then leaving, hoping that no-one asked them anything requiring a verbal response on the way out.

In February 1968, The Valentines' first original material, Why Me?/I Can Hear The Raindrops, was released. While home-state support kicked in and it reached the Top 30 in Perth, it flopped in Melbourne and nationally.

By the middle of the year the decision was made to move temporarily to Sydney where they recorded a version of Soft

Machine's Love Makes Sweet Music and Peculiar Hole In The Sky, which was written for them by Vanda and Young. By August, it reached the Top 20 in Adelaide and Perth but national impact was still elusive.

In November came another image shift to that of an unashamed pop band that played largely covers, in line with the popular 'bubblegum' movement of the day. With that came brightly coloured stage outfits with sheer sleeves and that presented a problem for Bon.

While he wasn't changing on the inside for anyone, he had to cover his tattoos — a great social taboo at the time — with pancake makeup, even though when he got sweaty the material on his sleeves became see-through anyway. But he had to try.

However, anyone who felt Bon was a soft target because of the way he dressed on stage was in for one hell of a shock.

Wyn Milson: 'He was tough and he knew it, and I've been in plenty of situations where people would sort of threaten me or hassle me and he stepped in and wanted to punch them out. He wasn't one of those guys who goes looking for trouble, but if it happened he wasn't about to back down from it.

'He was always out there looking for the edge. Whatever anyone used to do, he always used to do it a bit too much. Whether it'd be drinking, or speeding, or anything. If you were his friend, you were his friend forever, no matter what. And that's the kind of person he was — you could trust him with your life. If you were ever in trouble, in a dodgy situation or an emergency, this was the guy to have with you.

'I was with him one night and I think some police pulled us over in Melbourne and he ended up swearing at one of them and spent the night in the joint. We had to go and get him out in the morning. And that was because occasionally he wouldn't be able to shut up when it would've been smart to.'

Noel Jefferson, an associate of The Valentines, also saw Bon as an excellent left-hand man. 'Bon impressed me as being a very tough man, tough but gentle. I never ever saw him get beaten in a street fight. He was very quick with his left hand. Very powerful.

'He'd always fight people bigger than himself. I should imagine there was the occasional time when it got a bit hard for him, but every time I saw him he never had a mark on him.'

In March 1969 came the single of Ebeneezer/My Old Man's A Groovy Old Man, which was originally to be released on Valentine's Day. My Old Man, which had again been penned especially for them by Vanda and Young, became a national hit and suddenly, for the first time, money was no longer a problem and neither was recognition.

Record crowds began to flock to see them at Melbourne's dances and The Valentines were offered previously unheard-of fees for gigs in Sydney. Stages were stormed by fans minutes into performances, and when they couldn't be controlled the show was halted.

What the screaming hordes didn't know was that there were really two Valentines; one that did the early shows for a young audience and the other that was much louder and more heavy handed with no flash suits or commercial pop sounds, which played late at night in clubs.

It was in this more aggressive setting that Bon came into his own sometimes with the set of timbales he'd bought.

Wyn Milson: 'Real early Led Zeppelin, stuff off the first Santana album — Bon was singing those. We needed that kind of voice for it. I wanted to, and Bon definitely, we wanted to go that particular way. There was no satisfaction for us in jumping about in coloured suits singing baby lyrics.'

It was in Melbourne that Bon ran into his old mate Billy Thorpe, who he had first encountered in the mid '60s in Perth. Thorpe had just arrived in town and developed a new and very loud version of his band, The Aztecs. Bon was one of the first people to come and be belted in the chest by them.

Billy Thorpe: 'He [Bon] was a fucking madman, mate, a madman. All little blokes have got that little bloke syndrome. I suffer from it. We've all got that, "What did you fucking say to me??!!! What are you fucking looking at!"

'Bon was no different and there was a certain amount of heinous chemicals floating around in those days that made us move a lot faster than we did under normal conditions, and topped off with whisky it made for a fairly aggressive environment. And Bon was very much a part of that. He was like the rest of us. We're talking 24, 25 years old. I think Bon was a bit younger than me. He was a good bloke, staunch.

'It was funny watching the makings of Bon the rock singer from Bon the cabaret singer, because they were two extreme personalities. One was making a living in a tuxedo with a bow tie, and the other Bon — at the same time — was, after those gigs, backstage smoking dope and drinking booze with The Aztecs and jumping up on stage and having a wail every now and again, whenever he could get a look in.

'I remember him saying to me, "You know I'm going to make it, I'm going to fucking make it," one night out of the blue. He was very frustrated because he was stuck in The Valentines thing and wanted to be a maniac and couldn't make a living as a maniac.'

And a romantic to boot. Bon once caught a train from Melbourne to Sydney just to take a girl to the movies, and then returned to Melbourne the next day, a round trip of 2000 kilometres.

All the while the madness around The Valentines stormed on, aided by coloured smoke bombs and Bon and Vince leaping around like mountain goats on the band's amps. A clearly pleased Lovegrove told *Go-Set* that the secret to their success was their singer combination.

'I'm more popular than Bon,' Lovegrove said in the magazine in the 14 June 1969 issue, 'but he's a far better singer than I'll ever be. In fact, I think he's the most under-rated singer in Australia.'

The pop edge in The Valentines became even more obvious in July with the release of Nick Nack Paddy Whack (with Bon's lyrics for the first time on the B-side, Getting Better), and they were voted number nine in the best Australian band category of *Go-Set*'s annual readers' poll.

In September, the band's public image of clean-cut young men took a severe battering when a carload of police raided a surf lifesaving club near Melbourne that the band had chosen to use as a writing and rehearsal base. They were arrested for possession of marijuana after a member of another well-known group reportedly gave them up to save their own neck.

The charges, and the band's subsequent move to turn the situation into a positive of sorts by openly supporting marijuana legalisation, did nothing to diminish their popularity.

To Bon's delight, after an appearance on The Easybeats' TV Special they again supported the Easys, this time at Sydney's Caesar's Place, where The Valentines received at least as much adoration as the returned international act. One night, Stevie Wright caught the band in their darker alter ego at a club and couldn't believe the pitch of Bon's voice as he roared through Led Zeppelin's Whole Lotta Love.

Despite the afterglow of the Easybeats gig, things were about to go downhill. Hopes of My Old Man's A Groovy Old Man being released in the UK disappeared, and when they only achieved third place in the Hoadley Battle of the Sounds competition, it seemed ominous. It was.

The band were just starting to enjoy flexing their creative muscles and stepping into a sound of their own, when a crippling radio dispute over copyright payments saw Australian content shoved from playlists. The band's February single, Juliette, for which Bon wrote all the words and the melodies, was effectively killed off in the airwaves storm.

The problems didn't end there. The band had to attend court in Geelong to face the charges of possession and smoking marijuana. Each member pleaded guilty and received a $150 good behaviour bond, and then the ABC's 'GTK' television program decided to hand down a penalty of their own and ban The Valentines.

On a brighter note, and much to everyone's relief, the bubblegum image was finally put into storage, in favour of more conventional jeans and T-shirts.

In April, the band relocated to Sydney, but the writing was now unmistakably on the wall. Bon, in a typical show of loyalty, was reluctant to move on, but he wanted more and felt the world and what he wanted to do in it was starting to pass him by.

Wyn Milson: 'I think he felt restricted both artistically and personally in The Valentines. I think he really wanted to be the one and only major frontman, didn't want to share that limelight with somebody, like he had to in The Valentines.'

In early July 1970, the band did its last show at Bertie's in Melbourne just as they were voted number six best Australian group in *Go-Set*'s annual readers' poll. They officially broke up on 1 August.

By then, Bon had joined Fraternity, who featured Bruce Howe (bass), Mick Jurd (guitar), John Bisset (keyboards) and Tony Buettel (drums), who was later replaced by John Freeman. They were precisely what he was after at the time. It was a whole new and far more serious direction and he loved it.

Initially, not everyone in the Sydney band was sure Bon would work.

John Bisset: 'One day, out of the blue, Bruce announced that Bon wanted to come on board as our singer. I was a bit sceptical up to the first gig, because I wasn't a big fan of The Valentines. But everybody reassured me that Bon was serious. The Valentines were a pop band and we saw ourselves as a hard rock band. So there was a certain amount of snobbery there.'

Any doubts were blown away with Bon's first gig. They hadn't even rehearsed together but typically he took it all in his stride, as he had long been listening to the same music as his new bandmates. Besides, he had such a strong voice. His role in the band was confirmed: Bon moved into their house in the eastern suburbs of Sydney.

Fraternity had already recorded a single, Why Did It Have To Be Me?, and were in the process of recording other songs.

When on the road it wasn't unusual for the band to play three shows in three places a night in Melbourne, and have to set up and then strip down the gear each time. It was hard, unromantic work. But there were rewards of sorts for former stars like Bon.

John Bisset: 'There was actually a whole bunch of groupies in Melbourne, that we came to call the "Baby Brigade", and they all had babies to rock stars, or would-be rock stars. They were unashamedly getting pregnant to musos. Once, I think it was at the Battle of the Sounds in Melbourne, he [Bon] introduced me to this beautiful chick, who was about eight months pregnant, and she was pregnant to him. And I was shocked, and I went, "Oh, you're gonna get married?" and they both just cracked up laughing. They hadn't even thought about it — she just wanted to have his kid.'

Bon couldn't believe it when Fraternity landed a support slot for a rampaging Jerry Lee Lewis at White City in Sydney. Unfortunately, it wasn't Fraternity's finest hour. For many in the crowd, Bon being covered in war paint was as exciting as Fraternity got.

The sound system made Bon's vocals inaudible and forced the band to revamp their set into an almost entirely instrumental performance. But the exercise wasn't a total loss. Bon was a huge fan of Jerry Lee and he and 'The Killer' got on famously.

Following Jerry Lee back to the US seemed a possibility when a single for Adelaide's Sweet Peach label reportedly attracted the attention of MCA Records in America, who were then, so the story went, eager for a full album from the band. The album was completed in Sydney in December and was done in less than 14 hours, with no after-the-fact polishing.

Bon was never one to pass up a gig, particularly with friends, and had taken part in the sessions for Blackfeather's *At The Mountains Of Madness* album around the same time. He played a haunting recorder on Seasons Of Change and timbales and tambourine on The Rat (Suite), and in so doing unwittingly set the stage for a looming bitter irony.

First, Fraternity would make a major change, and in the middle of the scorching summer of January 1971, they relocated to South Australia to live communally on a seven-acre farm 27 kilometres from Adelaide in the hills at Aldgate.

While The Band's 1968 rural rock and roll masterpiece *Music From Big Pink* was a huge influence, Bon's 'Super Screw' T-shirt was an advertisement for his availability for something more down and dirty. Like their American heroes, Fraternity saw themselves as more than a band; more like *the band*, as in, the only one that matters.

The move to Adelaide was driven by a proposition from local businessman Hamish Henry, a dynamo with family wealth, a shrewd business sense and an ambitious plan to take over the music world from South Australia. A collection of artists, photographers, booking agents, roadies, drivers and general rock and roll helpers were constantly in and out of his office, and Henry bought a 26-seater bus to transport his charges.

When he first arrived, Bon was working for Henry, trying to make a few extra dollars by cleaning up his backyard, mowing lawns and doing general odd jobs. It was mundane but there was an excitement in the air.

Former Valentine Vince Lovegrove had also made the move to Adelaide and had become a one-man promotional unit as a journalist, band agent, promoter, TV show producer and host.

The first demonstration of Henry's clout came with the Myponga Festival, which featured the newly arrived Fraternity and emerging English heavyweights Black Sabbath, who didn't have the best time of it.

Ozzy Osbourne: 'We flew in, wrecked the hotel, drove four cars into the ocean.'

On the homeward journey, the plane stopped off at Perth to refuel.

Ozzy Osbourne: 'I sat on a fucking wall for 15 minutes and I got sunburnt like a son of a bitch. Then I had to sit for 36 fucking hours in one of the old 727s in economy, fucking frying. I've never forgotten that.'

Fraternity then opened for the Deep Purple, Free and Manfred Mann juggernaut when it hit Adelaide in April 1971.

Their schedule was gruelling but no-one complained. Rehearsals often ran to six hours a day with gigs at night and then a party until they could party no more. It was hard work but was taken deadly seriously because it was serious music.

Sometimes it was taken too seriously, as band associate Peter Head recalls.

Peter Head: 'It was always a harrowing experience. The guys would argue over the finest details — the voicing of a chord, the sound of a reverb, a word in a lyric — then they would start to raise their voices, and then be shouting at each other, and sometimes even came to blows over how to do things.'

Life in the Adelaide Hills was more idyllic.

An integral part of the scene was artist Vytas Serelis. On the occasional Sunday off, a number of the group would end up at Serelis' 17-acre place in Carey Gully, where his paintings, sculptures and inventions were everywhere, along with old cars and buses.

Peter Head: 'Vince, Bon, Vytas and I were very close at this time, and would often sit around by the campfire, playing guitar, singing, writing new songs, jamming with Vytas on sitar, getting stoned on marijuana, magic mushrooms, acid, booze, whatever, and generally having a wonderful time. Wives, kids, girlfriends, fellow musicians and artists would all join us for sometimes days on end.'

It was the calm before a storm of disappointment. John Ayers joined the band in March, and in May their second single, Seasons Of Change — their first with Bon — was issued on the Sweet Peach label. The same song Bon had recorded with Blackfeather, it had been committed to tape by Fraternity between February and March in Adelaide. It went on to top the South Australian charts.

But Blackfeather's *At The Mountains Of Madness* album had been released in April and, cruelly, their version of Seasons Of Change was a huge hit right across the country. This was despite the fact that Infinity/Festival Records had reportedly, and somewhat bizarrely, promised not to release Blackfeather in competition with Fraternity. Bon had a furious and very physical argument on national television about the issue, which put his low-level tolerance for bullshit on display.

John Swan, who later drummed in Fraternity, was in a band called Hard Time Killing Floor at the time and often played the same gigs as Fraternity.

'They were big everywhere, but in Adelaide they were fucking huge because they had that sound. They sounded like The Band and nobody really appreciated The Band in those days. Personally, I think Fraternity shit all over them — no disrespect to The Band.

'And it was nothing to do with being friends with them then, because you were more in awe of, as opposed to being friends, because you couldn't believe that people that you knew — or would know you — would be that fucking talented.'

The cancellation of a planned trip to America around the same time was marginally countered by Fraternity being voted one of the best bands in Australia by *Go-Set* magazine. Winning the Hoadley national Battle of the Sounds competition in July and picking up a trip to Los Angeles, $2000 in cash and $300 recording time at studios in Melbourne also helped. While the band never went to the US, they used the studio time to record their second album.

The arrival of Sam See on guitar and piano saw an expansion in their musical dynamic to bring in a more country feel. That shift was only accentuated by the fact that when Fraternity's long-awaited debut album, *Livestock*, was finally released late in 1971 — a year after it had been recorded — the band that made it had clearly moved on.

While nothing, it seemed, was falling into place, the release in March 1972 of a single, Welfare Boogie, was at least further proof that despite his high-brow musical surroundings, Bon's earthy lyrical poetry was quietly on simmer. But any thoughts that Welfare Boogie was going to turn Fraternity into Status Quo were swept away by the band's performance of Peter Sculthorpe's musical, *Love 200*, with the Melbourne Symphony Orchestra and Jeannie Lewis.

Lobby Loyde: 'He might have been in fairly sort of avant-garde bands in Adelaide, but you always knew from three blocks away that Bon was singing, because he was out there at the very edge of the bloody range all the time. He wasn't tarting around with the fancy phrasing. He was just going for it.'

By that point their real focus was on the UK. So several months into 1972, the band relocated to London, but not before Bon's marriage to his girlfriend, Irene, an attractive blonde.

The band's second album, *Flaming Galah*, which was Australian slang for idiot, was issued in their absence in April.

Unfortunately, England wasn't nearly as glamorous as it appeared to be from the other side of the planet or in the overseas reports in magazines like *Go-Set*. They rehearsed a great deal, but gigs were scarce if they existed at all. The band and their partners, 17 people in all, lived in an unheated three-storey house in Finchley, a suburb that later in Bon's career would treat him even more harshly.

For the first few months all they could do was watch their debts spiral and relationships shatter. To try to help make ends meet, Bon worked behind the bar in a local pub.

Late in 1972 a German tour presented itself, with club dates in Berlin, Frankfurt and Wiesbaden. Things were looking up.

John Bisset: 'They just wanted us to rock, and the band responded accordingly. Bon spoke to them in German, and they absolutely loved him.'

On the way back to the UK, the band jammed with Brian Auger's Oblivion Express in a town in France, while on another occasion, former Vanilla Fudge and then Cactus bassist Tim Bogert was eager to take the stage with the Australians.

But playing with the odd minor celebrity and occasionally opening for more established names (like Status Quo, although they steamrolled over the support act) wasn't paying the bills, and in March 1973, Bisset left the band. Sam See had already moved on.

John Bisset: 'We weren't really serious about anything other than just trying to have a good time. In England, our good times started to get a little bit grim. And some of the charm went off it, and we had no money to get pissed. But really, the music and writing songs was all totally secondary.'

In desperation, the decision was made to rename the band Fang in a bid to somehow blend in with bands like Slade and Geordie. But with their beards and several well-advanced receding hairlines, Fang neither looked like their English counterparts nor sounded like them, despite a shared passion for volume and a good time.

Fang supported Geordie at Torquay Town Hall on 23 April and Plymouth the following day. Bon was taken with the raspy voice, warm personality and earthy nature of Geordie's singer, Brian Johnson, who would often hoist the band's guitarist onto his shoulders during their performances.

Fang followed the shows with Geordie by opening for mind-and-eardrum-melting German space rock outfit Amon Duul II in May, and then in early June they supported the Pink Fairies at the Village Roundhouse in London.

A return to Australia was inevitable, but limping back after their last UK performance in August wasn't the dignified return they'd been hoping for.

John Bisset: 'We paid the price for it ultimately in that we totally lacked direction. The whole Fraternity era, from the beginning right to the very end, we were always just getting by from one week to the next. It was always tough — we never had any money.'

Lobby Loyde: 'Fraternity were a great band, man. I thought they were one of the sensational bands in this country. It was a hard time in those days for that kind of rock and roll.'

At the time, master guitarist Loyde was leading the Coloured Balls, a fearsome Melbourne outfit that delivered a searing rock and roll at ear-oxidising volume with a look that was somewhere between *Clockwork Orange* droogs and skinheads. They were, without a doubt, Bon's kind of band.

Lobby Loyde: 'Bon Scott was up there on the stage with the boys jamming at every opportunity he could, because he loved it — he wanted to be where the fire was. Mate, if Bon could have joined any other band in that early period, it probably would have been somebody like the Coloured Balls. He would have loved to have sung with the Coloured Balls. He used to say to me, "You're a cunt of a singer, mate! You need me!" And it's true, I was a cunt of a singer, but we couldn't find any cunt that wanted to do it like that, so I did it. Not because I wanted to, but because I fucking virtually had to. Bon was the only [other] cunt who could have done it.'

Billy Thorpe: 'Bon used to come and sit backstage. He idolised two bands: The Aztecs and Lobby and the Coloured Balls. He wanted to be the lead singer in either one of those bands! He used to say to me, "I'd fucking kill to be in a band like this!"'

By 1974, Bon was back in Adelaide where he teamed up with his friend Peter Head. They decided to put together a new band, only this time just playing simple country music. Personnel were never set in cement, and the decree never to have the same line-up at more than one gig — by what was now christened the Mount Lofty Rangers — would see over 200 different musicians move through their ranks. It was a long way from Fraternity.

Bon's later replacement in his former band was a young Jimmy Barnes, subsequently of Cold Chisel fame, and his first gig, according to legend, was so loud that it shattered several windows in the pub Fraternity were playing.

During the day, Bon had a backbreaking job filling trucks with fertiliser. At least it was good thinking and songwriting time.

Peter Head: 'He'd come to my place and say that, while working, he had actually been writing songs in his head all day. And because his musical knowledge was scant, he wanted me to help him write the songs, arrange them, and then perform them with the Mount Lofty Rangers.

'He came up with two beauties! Clarissa, a soulful country ballad about a previous girlfriend, and the very funny I've Been Up In The Hills Too Long. During this time, to thank me for helping him with his songs, Bon offered to sing on any demos of my songs in return. That's how I one day paid the princely sum of $40 to hire the new 8-track Slater Studios and record two of mine with Bon singing — Round And Round and Carey Gully.'

For Bon, the Rangers were both a comfort zone and a musical outlet, even if the music didn't always suit the lyrical ideas he'd scrawl down in his exercise book. That was until a late-night argument at rehearsals at the Lion Hotel.

A furious Bon, drunk and upset after an earlier fight with Irene, roared away on his motorbike and came into much too close contact with a car. He lost numerous teeth, slashed his neck, broke his collarbone and was in a coma for three days, during which time his heart monitor flat-lined several times. He also had to have his jaw wired.

The bike was damaged beyond repair and Bon looked much the same way. His wonderful smile was broken, his highly expressive face beaten, and his strut was now a hobble. Worse, his self-esteem fell through the floor.

On the back of the Fraternity misfire, it was a doubly cruel blow. Friends were horrified and heartbroken for him.

Rehabilitation was slow, but in time he was scraping barnacles off boats in dry dock in Port Adelaide Harbour. For extra cash he helped Lovegrove paint his agency office and slapped up posters for him.

Putting up posters for other bands, while painfully day-dreaming of what might have been after all of Fraternity's promise, was tough to say the least. One of the posters Bon put up around town was quite possibly for a band that Lovegrove and his wife were touring through Adelaide. Their name? AC/DC.

1974
Malcolm, Peter Clack, Bon and
Rob Bailey, Hordern Pavilion, Sydney.

chapter 6

IT WAS LIKE A HURRICANE

*t*he first time Malcolm and Angus met Bon, he was pissed off that he'd put on his wife's underwear by mistake. It was a fitting introduction to the hurricane of a human being that Vince Lovegrove appointed as AC/DC's guide, minder and general driver from hell while they were in Adelaide.

The first day Bon got behind the wheel was almost everyone's last. His remark — as they were careering down the road in his 1950s FJ Holden sedan — that he'd just gotten out of hospital after a serious motorbike smash didn't fill anyone with a great sense of calm. Thankfully, somehow everyone always got to their destination in one piece.

But Bon took his role very seriously, particularly as he liked his charges. He virtually attached himself to the band from dawn until dusk, providing huge joints at obscenely early hours of the morning and dropping endless hints about his drumming skills. Whether he knew it or not, Bon was positioning himself perfectly, but not for a drumming role.

George Young had already mentioned to Lovegrove that the band were in serious need of a new singer to replace Dave Evans, whose personality had long clashed heavily with Malcolm and Angus. Stevie Wright had been approached but declined, feeling that the last thing Malcolm and Angus needed was help from him. Lovegrove suggested Bon, and George, who remembered him warmly from the days The Easybeats crossed paths with The Valentines, liked the idea.

With AC/DC booked to appear at the Pooraka Hotel, Lovegrove made arrangements to ensure Bon was also there.

Bon couldn't believe what he was seeing when AC/DC hit the stage. The sight of Angus in continual overdrive made him laugh almost nonstop. He also saw his future flash before him and, one way or another, was determined to grab the opportunity any way he could.

A group of hecklers at the front of the stage baited Angus with everything they had all night. What they didn't know was that his size and their numbers weren't an issue as far as the guitarist was concerned.

He finally exploded and showered the group in venom, then stood at the front of the stage and waited to see if they dared to respond. Bon was stunned that by far the smallest guy in the place was clearly the most fearless.

After the show, everyone met up in the dressing room. Bon, who was now quite drunk, issued a smiling challenge to Malcolm and Angus. They were too young to have a proper grasp on how to really rock and roll, the singer joked, and he was prepared to give them a crash course. The pair laughed and dared Bon, who they knew was much older than they were, to give it his best shot.

The basement of Fraternity's Bruce Howe in suburban Adelaide was the venue for the light-hearted showdown right after the Pooraka gig. Several curious members of Fraternity came along to see their former bandmate kick up some dust with the Youngs.

Malcolm and Angus remembered Bon in The Valentines and later in Fraternity, so they knew he could belt out a song. For his part, Bon had figured out that the Young brothers were the band's central power and knew that George Young was not far from the viewfinder. He also knew he was being presented with a golden opportunity and wanted to put in the performance of his life.

But Bon's love of the drums died hard. While he hungered to front AC/DC as a singer, he also had another line-up of the band sketched out in his head: George on bass, Angus and Malcolm on guitars and him on drums.

Angus: 'He took us down to a little studio thing and he was on the drums playing. We said, "Well, we've already got a drummer, Bon, what we need is a good singer!" And he kept saying, "But I'm a drummer! I started as a rock and roll drummer!" We said, "Yeah, we know that." He was a good drummer.'

With Bon finally behind the microphone and Fraternity's John Freeman on drums, the jam went all night and just as the sun was rising he was offered a place in the band by AC/DC's manager, and his old friend, Dennis Laughlin.

Bon was delighted, but despite his previous teasing challenge was mindful of his age and the youthfulness of the rest of the band. He knew he wasn't 21 and wasn't sure he'd be able to keep pace with Malcolm and, particularly, Angus.

While Bon thought the offer over, the band had commitments on the other side of the country in Perth, including a six-week residency at Beethoven's Disco supporting transvestite Carlotta in what was most likely a booking carry-over from the Lou Reed tour. AC/DC took Evans, now very much a dead man walking, with them to Perth.

The 2700-kilometre trip was done by road across the Nullarbor Plain, a virtual desert that stretches across much of Australia's interior. Said to be one of the longest and straightest sections of roadway in the world, it was at the time unsurfaced and cut through some of the harshest landscape on the planet. To make matters worse, some of the band were forced to travel in the back of the truck.

Dave Evans: 'All the gear was stacked in the back, PA and the fucking lot, and we had to get in there and try to find a little position somewhere, just sort of sit. And then the roller went down and it was pitch black — you couldn't see a fucking thing. We had torches and things and, if you wanted a drink or something, you had to put a lighter on. We had to have bandannas, and handkerchiefs around our nose and mouth, because of all the red dust of the desert.'

Then came a flat tyre; then it started to rain. Thankfully, someone stopped and helped them change the flat.

When they finally arrived in Perth, Evans' voice gave out at one gig and Dennis Laughlin had to handle the vocals. With their commitments completed, one way or another, the band made the gruelling drive east in September and stopped off in Adelaide once more for a weekend of shows.

Bon was waiting, and when he was again offered the spot in the band, was more than ready to sign on.

Following a welcoming jam at the Pooraka, Bon took the stage with his new employers at an Adelaide venue called Countdown. In the audience was Phil Eastick, later to become an AC/DC crew member.

'He just got up and did a couple of songs. I don't think Dave Evans had actually figured out what was happening at that stage, but the minute he [Bon] got up with them you could just see there was something magic happening.'

Peter Head: 'AC/DC was the perfect answer for Bon. He had his ever-present notebook of hand-scrawled lyrics, and they had the rock and roll machine just ready for him.'

For Bon, AC/DC were a wonderfully welcome, over-the-counter, anti-aging elixir. For the first time in his career, he could be himself and think below his belt line with songs like She's Got Balls. The members of Fraternity would have just rolled their eyes at the thought of being in any way associated with such primal screaming.

It was an almost parallel situation to that of his hero Alex Harvey, the Scottish leader of the Sensational Alex Harvey Band. Harvey, like Bon, was no spring chicken and had been through several musical false starts before the SAHB kicked into gear in 1972 and he was finally able to act out what he'd wanted to be for so long.

Wyn Milson: 'That was the real Bon Scott. That was the side of Bon Scott that was trying to get out through The Valentines but couldn't.'

Sadly, his recruitment into AC/DC marked the last breaths in his marriage to Irene, although bravado covered his sadness.

'I dug the band more than I dug the chick, so I joined the band and left her,' he told Anthony O'Grady in *RAM* on 19 April 1975.

That heartache aside, it was a win-win situation. Bon wasn't just signing on with a shit-hot band that was everything he had ever wanted, but a shit-hot band with a great lineage.

He felt that AC/DC were picking up where his heroes, The Easybeats, had left off, and with George Young — who Bon admired enormously — as mentor, there seemed absolutely no reason why the second time wouldn't be the charm. He bought a sizable supply of methedrine and packed up his things for his move to Sydney, where he'd meet up with the band and prepare to begin phase four of his career.

The problem was AC/DC now technically had two singers, but with all the excitement of Bon being in the frame, push was coming to one hell of a shove for Evans. By this point he had almost nothing to do with the band and was only in their company on stage: he knew something was going on, and not necessarily even behind his back.

In Melbourne en route to Sydney, Evans' fate was finally dealt with after a gig at the Esplanade Hotel in St Kilda in late September. The singer went back to Sydney and formed Rabbit, a tough but fully glam band that merged Gary Glitter tribal drumbeats with bad-boy rock and roll and a fire-breathing bass player. They released two albums: *Rabbit* (1975), and the more successful *Too Much Rock n' Roll* (1976).

Once AC/DC made it back to Sydney in early October, Bon made his official debut at Rockdale Masonic Hall, a venue about an hour south of the city. He crammed in as much colourful, brutally expressive language as he could as he conjured up lyrics on the fly and leered and grinned his way through the show in a pair of red satin bib and brace overalls. Most people were too stunned to be offended: no-one had ever heard anything quite like She's Got Balls, which was the first song they put together.

The great mystery was how Bon was able to do anything that night.

Angus: 'I remember all this bourbon and, fucking, there was dope! I said to Malcolm, "Fucking hell, if this guy can walk, Mal, it's gonna be something!" I mean, there was these bottles of bourbon going down. At that time Mal used to drink this Stone's Green Ginger Wine and he'd go, "Ah, who cares!"

'When we walked on, my fucking feet lifted off the ground. I mean, I knew he [Bon] was doing it to impress me, but it was like a hurricane — his voice — and he just let out this almighty fucking yell. That place went ... They just stopped. You had to look. As I said, my fucking feet lifted off the fucking ground and then it was into it.'

The greatest shock was for the fans of the suddenly departed Dave Evans who had shown up to see their hero. Bon broke the sad news to them.

Malcolm: 'On comes Bon even before the band. He strides on, grabs the mic and he announces, "Anyone that's come to see Dave Evans sing with AC/DC ain't gonna see it tonight because the band have fired him because he got married." Of course, we went, "Fucking hell! What's this guy done!"

'When he got on, he just took command. He was very good on stage to work with. You wouldn't believe how professional the guy was, even though you wouldn't see that from the front — it just looked like Bon's having a good time. But he really knew what was going on up there.'

Bon, a great fan of comedian Lenny Bruce and his razor-sharp observations, brought much more to the table than just enormous character — which would have served him well as an actor — and a great voice. While he didn't change the band's appearance overnight — Bon himself was often still in white or red satin overalls, with the rest of AC/DC in boots and generally touched by the glam scene — the group bonded together for the first time, and his experience brought out a new level of stagecraft that Angus and, particularly, Malcolm had been working towards. Bon gave their 'fuck 'em' attitude that extra push.

The comic talents of Angus also became more pronounced with the arrival of the equally witty Bon, as each bounced off the other like a classic comedy team. Angus laughingly claimed that when he first met Bon he had to give him some culture and help him speak in a more socially acceptable manner by saying, 'Excuse me, cunt' or 'Get fucked, if you don't mind'.

As the band soon found, Bon was an absolute magnet for women too, with tales of total strangers soliciting him to pleasure their wives.

Then there was Bon the educator, who would pick up old albums and singles in second-hand record stores and pass them on to Angus, with enthusiastic and detailed rants about the songs and the artists who'd recorded them. Jerry Lee Lewis' High School Confidential and Great Balls Of Fire — Bon loved the wordplay — were among the treasures he presented to the tiny guitarist, who probably didn't have the heart to tell him he already knew those songs intimately.

And Bon could speak about his hero Jerry Lee from first-hand experience, having toured Australia with him in Fraternity.

Angus: 'He [Jerry Lee Lewis] liked Bon as a drinking partner. Bon told me his manager was always hiding the booze. Jerry Lee Lewis said, "Don't forget my boots!" to the guy that was with him, looking after him. He kept saying to this guy, "Don't forget those boots!" And Bon kept going, "Why is he in such a panic about the boots?" Then when they got in the dressing room, he said to Bon, "In here!" and he got the boots and he pulled out two bottles of bourbon!'

With Bon's future with the band cemented after the Rockdale show, dates followed in Adelaide and Melbourne, including the Gay Nights at Michael Browning's subterranean Hard Rock Café. The Gay Nights gave Bon an early opportunity to really stretch out before an audience and see how far he could go.

Some patrons would hold up vibrators and present their breasts, courtesy of T-shirts with strategically cut holes. Bon lapped up the attention — both the good and the bad — not to mention the provocation, and gave as good as he got. He used to bring his own props, like vibrators and even a whip, anything to get a reaction.

Browning, former manager of the hugely successful Billy Thorpe & The Aztecs, was a major figure on the Melbourne scene. He was gobsmacked by the new AC/DC.

On previous trips to Melbourne, the Dave Evans version of the band had stopped him in his tracks, largely due, quite naturally, to the antics of Angus. But with Bon at the helm, AC/DC became a two-ring rock and roll circus that was nothing short of jaw dropping, although with Browning's knowledge of the singer's past, it took some getting used to.

Michael Browning: 'I'd previously known Bon when he was in The Valentines, so my perception of him was that of a teenage idol kind of guy. So it was difficult for me at first to really sort of place him in AC/DC. But obviously he was probably miscast in The Valentines, because he was certainly cast correctly in AC/DC — no doubt about that. That definitely suited Bon's character down to a tee. It worked.'

Browning formulated a management proposal to put to the band and quickly figured out who to pitch the idea to.

Michael Browning: 'Malcolm was the thinker, the internal organiser; no two ways about it, he's the boss. It was just Malcolm's grasp of what was going on around him on a business level. As a manager you soon find out who there is in the band that you can have a rapport with, and I sussed things pretty early in the day and I found out it was Malcolm. He, from the band's perspective, ran the show. If I had something that I wanted to sell them, I'd talk to Malcolm first, and from there we'd go and sell it to the rest of the band.'

The offer of management passed initial muster with Malcolm and then George was called in.

Michael Browning: 'George was very, very aware of the pitfalls of the music industry and didn't want the group to fall into those same pitfalls that he'd experienced. I was continually conscious of that.'

Everything went up several gears when Browning officially moved into the frame in November. He was a sharp strategist and an astute manager.

One of his first initiatives was his biggest; move the band to Melbourne on a permanent basis and put AC/DC before the same tough, enthusiastic audiences that followed The Aztecs and Coloured Balls. Melbourne was a rock city. It was a big step for Malcolm and Angus: for them, family, and the grounding of big sister, Margaret, was everything.

John Swan has fond memories of both the Young home in Burwood and Margaret.

John Swan: 'I used to get the train out to Burwood and they'd just have this big pot of soup on all the time. It was a typical Scottish thing and there'd be musos from all over the place, really great musicians sitting around playing cards, having a drink, and Margaret would be there and she'd make sure that everybody had a bowl of soup so it keeps the drink steady, slow us down a bit. If we had a bowl in front of us, we didn't have a glass! She was like the ultimate mother or sister, that's more like it.

'Of course, you didn't give her any shit either. It was taken for granted you didn't speak to her the way you spoke to other women, because you might get fucking necked because you knew what they were capable of!'

The move meant that AC/DC's opening slots for Black Sabbath's shows at the Hordern Pavilion in early November — Bon's second brush with the English heavyweights in almost as many years — were something of an unofficial farewell to Sydney.

But before the relocation, the band's first album, *High Voltage*, was scheduled to be recorded at Albert Studios in Sydney that month. George Young and Harry Vanda handled the production of the record, which was recorded after gigs — starting work after midnight and wrapping up sometimes at six or seven in the morning.

The personnel on their debut effort were something of a collective. George played bass as did AC/DC's Rob Bailey, while Tony Currenti from The 69ers did most of the drumming. The band's drummer at the time, Peter Clack, along with John Proud, who played on the Marcus Hook Roll Band album, also handled one track each — She's Got Balls, which to the band's amazement was Bon's ode to his former wife, Irene, and Little Lover respectively. It's believed that George also contributed to the drumming on the album.

Herm Kovac almost played on it as well.

Herm Kovac: 'I was just about to go on tour [with the Ted Mulry Gang] when Malcolm rang me and said, "Look, we're having trouble with some of the slow songs on the new album and we need that [Free drummer] Simon Kirke feel. Could you come in and do it?" But I had to go on the road.'

While Malcolm and Angus had begun to develop separate roles on stage, there was still some experimentation in the studio. On Soul Stripper the pair traded off some licks, and on You Ain't Got A Hold On Me Malcolm did some soloing.

Harry Vanda: 'We tried one or two things in the studio, a bit of a role-sharing thing. It could have worked, it would sound alright, but it didn't sound as good as what they finished up doing. It would just confuse the identity of the thing.'

In just 10 days, *High Voltage* was ready to go.

Chris Gilbey: 'I suggested calling the album *High Voltage*, reinforcing the [lightning bolt] logo and the [name] AC/DC and the electrical nature of it. I remember they thought it was a great idea.'

By then, Angus could be heard on the radio ripping it up on Guitar Band, the first single from Stevie Wright's yet-to-be-released second album, *Black Eyed Bruiser*.

Momentum was quietly but strategically building. On 29 November, AC/DC made their first appearance on ABC Television's new Sunday evening music program 'Countdown', with their version of Big Joe Williams' Baby, Please Don't Go.

The song was still months from release as a single, but given that the nationally screened 'Countdown' was very much Melbourne based, the exposure just prior to the band setting up in the city was priceless. A repeat performance on the program three weeks later maintained the excitement levels.

Browning's grand plan was playing out perfectly. He knew from first-hand experience that Melbourne would be AC/DC's town.

Michael Browning: 'If it hadn't been for Melbourne, AC/DC wouldn't have existed. There wasn't enough of a support system anywhere else in the country.'

1975
Bon, Malcolm, Phil Rudd and Angus, Sydney.

chapter 7

SO YOU THINK THAT'S LOUD?

*t*he ear-splitting volume and no-bullshit attitude of Billy Thorpe & The Aztecs and Lobby Loyde and the Coloured Balls, along with the hard-nosed sensibilities of their audiences, paved the way for AC/DC's assault on Melbourne. And nothing had defined the mood of the southern capital better than the first Sunbury Festival in January 1972. A three-day event on the outskirts of the city that became more famous for rivers of beer than peace or love, it had marked the coronation of The Aztecs in front of a 30,000-strong crowd.

In a pivotal moment for Australian rock, The Aztecs' resulting double album, *Live At Sunbury*, went shoulder-to-shoulder in the charts with the Stones' *Exile On Main Street* and Led Zeppelin's mystical fourth effort, without the slightest cultural cringe.

The central issue was the intensity of the music. 'Aztec energy', Michael Browning called it, a term for a sound and a decibel level that was metallic before anyone really knew what heavy metal was.

Operating parallel to The Aztecs in Melbourne between 1972 and 1974 were the Coloured Balls, led by Lobby Loyde. The Balls had a fearsome sound and image to match, but the attention they attracted came for all the wrong reasons.

The Sharpies were enthusiastic about The Aztecs but saw Loyde — whose look mirrored their own — as a messiah and flocked en masse to the Balls' gigs, where all hell broke loose. Under the weight of a cycle of poor media publicity which fed the ever-increasing violence at their shows, by the time the Balls recorded their third album, *Heavy Metal Kid*, in 1974, the decision had already been made to split.

Thanks to heavy attention from the police, by the time AC/DC set up base in Melbourne the roaming hordes of Sharps had largely, though not entirely, died down; but a toughness of spirit and attitude in the city's audiences remained. Melbourne's character was what AC/DC were all about: Michael Browning was dead right.

Their reputation for high-energy performances preceded them thanks to a major New Year's Eve show at Melbourne's Festival Hall, and more notoriously, an incident at Prahran's Station Hotel, when Angus took exception to someone clearly unmoved by the band's performance.

Malcolm: 'Angus jumped out into the crowd and he ran up to this guy, grabbed his beer and poured it on his head. This guy had really fuzzy hair and it formed a puddle on top first and then slowly fucking rolled over his face. I thought, this guy's going to kill Angus! He didn't. He just sat there and took it. He felt so embarrassed. I thought at that time Angus had overdone it, but the place loved it. This guy that had the beer poured over his head became a bit of a cult hero!'

Browning's next move was to sign the band to a deal with agent Bill Joseph, who handled a number of major venues in Melbourne. A six-month contract with Joseph's Premier Artists agency provided each member with a wage of $60 a week, and covered the cost of their sound system and repairs to their tour bus, a huge beast of a thing formerly owned by Ansett Airlines.

While Browning made the necessary longer-term arrangements, the band were initially set up in the Octagon Hotel in Prahran, and the rowdiness and an open-door policy for girls and members of other bands began immediately.

In time, Browning found the band a house in St Kilda, a rambling, almost Victorian, free-standing place in Lansdowne Road. For Malcolm and Angus, it was their first time living away from home and what a way to start being out in the world on their own.

Local waitresses and those working night shift soon figured out that the Lansdowne Road address was a cheaper and more exciting alternative to the local pubs and clubs and so turned up with party supplies in the wee hours of the morning. There was always someone pleased to greet them.

The band often got more than they'd hoped for, so a doctor was virtually on call 24 hours a day to cure that odd nasty itch or rash.

St Kilda was a red-light area and it was no surprise that there was a brothel close by. Nor was it a surprise that Bon managed to charm one of the ladies into a date.

Then there was always whoever else was playing in town at the time, as well as a smattering of local gangsters, and even, at the other end of the scale, members of a local Hare Krishna sect.

The police were regular visitors until they worked out that partying was the occupants' sole crime and became more interested in whether they could play some of the instruments that were strewn about the place than brandishing search warrants.

While Lansdowne Road was party central, the band's live shows were take-no-prisoners type exercises that weren't for the faint-hearted.

Writer Jen Jewel Brown recalls an early gig.

'Angus always had to get up like a mountain goat on whatever was high around, he had to climb on it and leads snaking everywhere. The band were just awesomely powerful and tight and rocking and just thrilling to watch. I can't ever remember them doing a bad gig or being inconsistent. They were like a little army. They were there to entertain and they were going to shove it down people's throats.'

The local music heavyweights were just as impressed.

Billy Thorpe: 'I remember a show in Melbourne at a big cricket ground and we were all on the back of a truck in the middle of the oval. These were the great old big production days of a truck with the PA stuck on it and a few fucking rails and bouncers full of speed with their arms folded, glaring at the crowd. I remember standing on the side of the stage and just watching these guys, going, "This thing is going to go all the way." You could just tell. You recognise when the next wave's coming. [Johnny] O'Keefe [legendary Australian rocker] said to me, "I saw you coming." I saw AC/DC coming.'

But on one occasion at the Hard Rock, Bon's partying got the better of him and he had to sit the show out while Malcolm and Angus did the singing.

Bassist Rob Bailey and drummer Peter Clack didn't get to see much of the 24-hour madness at Lansdowne Road. They were fired in early January 1975. Bailey's departure had been on the cards, not due to him being too tall as has been stated, but because he brought his then wife on the road. Her constant presence didn't go down well.

Clack's replacement, Russell Coleman, was no stranger to the band's circle, having done live work with Stevie Wright and sessions for Wright's *Hard Road* album. When AC/DC and Wright were playing together in Perth, Angus had casually approached Coleman.

Russell Coleman: 'He said, "One day we'll play together," and he used to always say that Stevie Wright would be the singer.'

By the time Coleman was recruited, Bon, rather than Stevie, was fronting AC/DC. Coleman knew Bon from The Valentines, and his partying ways, much to the drummer's discomfort, had not changed in the years since.

'He used to love young girls. I can remember being a bit nervous in the band because their fathers would come around, with baseball bats and things like that. Many times. They [teenage girls] would just throw themselves at him — he couldn't help himself. He was just on a constant party.'

After Bailey's exit, George Young filled in on bass and the last thing he was concerned with was fun. His memories of being forced to ask for cigarettes from whoever was driving The Easybeats around — while Friday On My Mind was a huge hit — were still vivid and painful.

Accordingly, in an act of tough love, George was psychologically preparing his brothers and the band in general for the hardships that lay ahead when they, as he planned, eventually went overseas and had to work their way up from scratch in seedy bars and hotels. For Coleman, that hardship included getting far less pay than he was used to with Stevie Wright and travelling from one end of the country to the other in a matter of days in what he called 'the torture bus'.

Russell Coleman: '[George] just wanted to toughen them up to be strong enough to handle the States and England.'

The band's match fitness wasn't all that George had figured out.

Russell Coleman: 'George used to say to me all the time that he wanted to have the same as The Easybeats, which is an older drummer [as was the case with Snowy Fleet], and he'd put a puppet in the front to make it all work. George's tough way of putting it!

'George always believed. He said, "They're gonna do everything The Easybeats didn't do."'

While Coleman was impressed by George, he was stunned by the dedication of Angus, who was far more concerned with being the best guitar player in the world than partying.

Russell Coleman: 'He would sleep with his guitar in that weird house. They would all go out and have a drink and chase girls and he'd just stay home and practise all day. I gave him all my Chuck Berry and Little Richard and all these live records and he loved them. He'd just put them on all day and play with them, skip around in the house.

'He was probably the most focused person I've known, in that: "I'm going to do it." Didn't very often see him without his guitar in his hands in those days.'

Bon was fearless, he discovered, and would take any risk, whether he knew it or not. One night at a party with some other well-known rock and roll identities, Bon took that ethic to near fatal lengths when — to the horror of Coleman — he unknowingly downed a whole double-O cap of morphine.

Russell Coleman: 'Some groupie girl came and said, "Bon's dead, you gotta come down to the house!" And I went down, and he was blue, lying face down on the ground. I could see these two fuck-ups trying to wake him, nothing happening, showered, nothing happening. So I took him to the hospital.

'Bon just didn't know [about drugs]. He didn't get involved with drugs at all. He was a drinker, he liked his Scotch. I think it [the drug incident] was a bit of a shock.

'There was never any drug use in that band at that time or anything, they just used to drink more. Angus would just eat his flakes, chocolate flakes all day . . .'

Coleman decided it was time to move on. He had had enough. Some time later, when he was working at the ABC's television studios setting up for 'Countdown', he bumped into Angus, who was still convinced AC/DC were destined to take on the world.

Russell Coleman: 'Angus said, "What are you doing?" I said I was playing in a '50s rock and roll band at the time. He said, "You were in the best rock and roll band in the world!"'

Phil Rudd, who was born Philip Hugh Norman Witschke Rudzevcuts in Surrey Hills, Melbourne on 19 May 1954, was next on the band's drumming stool. Rudd caught the drumming bug in high school and drove his mother crazy for a kit, pleas she shrugged off as simply being that week's passing interest.

After he left school at 15 and had enough money, he bought a cheap drum kit himself but could only stand one formal lesson. The last thing he felt he needed was a textbook to tell him how to beat the shit out of some drums.

Free and Bad Company's Simon Kirke and Mountain's Corky Laing were early heroes, as was Ringo Starr. Phil used to play along to Beatles records while sitting as close as he could to the speakers, so he was still able to hear the music and keep time over the racket he was making.

But it was hearing The Small Faces' Tin Soldier for the first time that was his pivotal moment. The way drummer Kenny Jones brought the band crashing back into the song after the brief organ passage gave him the tingles.

Local band Mad Mole was the first outlet for Rudd's skills, along with Krayne, a short-lived weekend-only trio with a Zeppelin, Uriah Heep, Deep Purple and jazz flavour, with Geordie Leach — a school friend of Rudd's — on bass. Charlemagne was next in 1972, although in their year-long existence they only ever tackled the songs of Humble Pie, The Small Faces and Free in small bars and at parties. None of these bands interfered with an electrical apprenticeship Rudd had begun.

Smack, in June 1973, was a far more serious exercise. After a few weeks, Gary 'Angry' Anderson was invited to a rehearsal and joined on the spot as singer. In time, the band were renamed Buster Brown after industry concerns about the implications of the name Smack, which didn't represent the recreational activities of any of the band members.

At Buster Brown gigs, everything from the Stones' Jumpin' Jack Flash, The Faces' Stay With Me and Elton John's Saturday Night's Alright (For Fighting) to Stevie Wonder's Superstition, Jeff Beck and Eric Clapton were served up, all driven by Anderson's great raspy Rod Stewart of a voice.

Geordie Leach, who'd joined the band in December, knew Rudd had a unique rhythmic magic.

Geordie Leach: 'Phil was destined to be a rock and roll star, no matter how you looked at it, and everybody knew it. He had a great sense of time and that's why everybody wanted him in the band: he held the whole thing together, always. He turned me into the solid bass player I am today.

'Digger [Dallas "Digger" Royal, drummer with Rose Tattoo] turned me into a more flamboyant player, but Phil was the one who said, "You fucking listen to me and we'll lock this in so nobody can fucking get in between us." He knew that then, and he would have been 19.'

Just a month after Leach's arrival, the band played at the Sunbury '74 festival. Thirty thousand people in broad daylight was a long way from being unable to see a few hundred in the dark in a club, and they were terrified. But they put in the performance of their lives and were called back for an unprecedented two encores.

The band's work schedule increased in the wake of Sunbury and Rudd was forced to quit his apprenticeship after almost five years, as he had trouble balancing a day job and Buster's commitments.

Buster Brown's tough street-punk image had attracted the attention of the Sharps: they definitely weren't a pop band at a time when the biggest thing in the country, Skyhooks, unashamedly were. They were a rock and roll band and Phil drove a car that fitted the mould perfectly.

Geordie Leach: 'He's always been a car-head. The first car that he bought that we used to drive in Buster Brown was a yellow HK Monaro, four speed, and that was the ant's pants in those days. His dad ran a car yard.'

In March, the band signed with Mushroom Records and in July the single, Buster Brown, was released, followed by appearances on 'GTK' in September and October. In late 1974, the band recorded their first album, *Something To Say*, which — like the single — was produced by Lobby Loyde, in a fevered 12-hour session.

Finances were tight to the point of almost being non-existent, a situation Rudd objected to and so was labelled a troublemaker. He was subsequently sacked in November. The album was released in January 1975 but sounded tentative and was a poor reflection of their raw live appeal. Buster soldiered on for another year, before disbanding.

Washing cars at his father's car yard took up much of the next few months. Then Trevor Young from the Coloured Balls, who had drummed in Buster Brown while Rudd, in turn, was briefly in the Balls, called in. Young mentioned that AC/DC were looking for a drummer and suggested Rudd pay them a visit. Rudd asked Geordie Leach to come along and try out for the band's still-open bass spot, but he declined.

The rehearsal room at Lansdowne Road was the hallway of the house, and that, with everyone in their underwear, was where the drummer was put through his paces. They jammed on material that had been recorded for the soon-to-be-released *High Voltage* album as well as rock and roll classics — basically anything that would demonstrate whether Rudd had the crucial ability to swing.

It was quickly clear that he did and he was hired on the spot, with the promise of solid regular work. He was delighted.

'You don't come across guys like Malcolm and Angus very often,' he told Matt Peiken in *Modern Drummer* in August 1996, adding that 'Bon wanted to be the drummer, but he was too good a singer.'

As an old drummer himself, Bon knew a good striker when he saw one and loved Rudd's no fills or frills manner. He was also slightly jealous. If only he had been that good.

While Rudd's services had been secured — a move that, with his background in Buster Brown, probably brought a few more Sharps to AC/DC's gigs — nailing down a bass player was still tough, although Geordie Leach was approached. In the interim, the role fell to either Malcolm or George, depending on the situation and George's availability.

Just three weeks after Rudd signed on, it was this configuration of the band — Bon, Angus, Malcolm, George and Phil — that drove to the outskirts of Melbourne for the fourth Sunbury Festival on 25 January 1975. There, George almost solved the band's bass-player problems by approaching Lobby Loyde.

Lobby Loyde: 'At Sunbury, he [George] said, "Mate! I know you love playing guitar, but this is a fucking great little band and you'd be a killer bass player because you've got the rhythm." And I really thought about it because actually, for a little while, when we'd ploughed through all the drummers that we near killed in the Coloured Balls, we had Phil playing drums with us and he was a mighty drummer. I loved him. I thought he syncopated like a dunny door. He was a rocker.'

Sunbury '75 was quite different to the previous years of the three-day festival. The 1974 event had featured a then little-known Queen — who were unsurprisingly given hell by the beer-filled masses — and new flashy Melbourne act, Skyhooks.

In 1975, the decision to have Deep Purple rather than The Aztecs as the headliners raised almost as many eyebrows as Skyhooks did with their flamboyant and provocative new singer, Graeme 'Shirley' Strachan. The difference was that Skyhooks were gloriously outrageous while Purple simply outraged when it was found that the British band were reportedly being paid up to $150,000, which didn't leave much for the pockets or the self-esteem of local acts, who were so obviously viewed as second class.

When Billy Thorpe discovered that the David Coverdale-fronted Deep Purple, who were at the time touted as the loudest band in the world, were to headline with the 14,000 watts of additional PA system they had shipped into the country, he wasn't about to give up his own 'Mr Loudness' crown without a hell of a fucking fight.

Billy Thorpe: 'We hired every piece of equipment in Melbourne, all the PAs, and put them on stage as guitar amps. It was the loudest fucker! So, you cunts think you're loud, do you? Right! It was excruciatingly loud.'

Thorpe had also begun to recognise in AC/DC some elements of what The Aztecs themselves had bludgeoned into place. Mainly, the 'Aztec ending', which could last almost as long as the song itself.

Billy Thorpe: 'Every band cottoned on to it, AC/DC being one of them. A lot of that shit and the flourishes they do came directly from The Aztecs, which came originally from Lobby and I playing together. I'd finish, he'd play a little bit, so I'd play a little bit more. We had something to do with the bombast and the volume of it and the sheer power of it, because Michael Browning saw the value that that had in the right hands.

'All the bands that put volume down were the guys that were scared shitless of it. There were only a few bands that could do it [volume]. Lobby and the Balls ended up being able to do it, The Aztecs could do it and AC/DC could do it. They were a direct result of working with us, that's where that came from; that tight riffing, loud-format sound was very much the sound of The Aztecs at that point in time. They then developed. I'm not taking credit for the sound of AC/DC. Their sound came from being influenced by us and having one of the best rock riff writers ever put on the planet as a brother, which was George.'

A decibel contest between Deep Purple and Thorpe wasn't the only battle at Sunbury in 1975. A slot for AC/DC came up suddenly because it was rumoured that for some reason Deep Purple wouldn't be playing. But when they got to the site, not only did they have to walk through the crowd in their stage gear, but found that Purple were playing after all and AC/DC were to follow them.

To make matters even worse, Purple were determined to pull out all stops for their performance, then haul all their gear away again immediately afterwards. That meant that no other act could go on for several hours.

Michael Browning: 'I had the band [AC/DC] at the side of the stage when Deep Purple finished and all of a sudden all the riggers arrived and they started pulling down all the lights. Deep Purple's production manager decided that they were going to take everything that came with them down and the other bands had to wait until something like four o'clock in the morning before they could go on.

'I just said, basically, bullshit! And I gave my instruction to my road crew to set up and the instruction to the band was to start playing. What happened then was I had AC/DC, my road crew, George Young and myself in a major brawl with all of their crew and manager, a full-on brawl in the middle of the stage.'

Michael Browning was a big man and George Young a firebrand in such situations who wasn't going to be intimidated by anyone. They made their point.

AC/DC packed up and drove back to Melbourne without playing a note. An offer to perform the following day was less than politely declined.

The day after the festival, they played at Sorrento RSL Club, quite a comedown from what could have been Sunbury's mass audience. But it was all about character-building and George didn't want it any other way.

1975

Not just a pretty face: Malcolm during the making of the High Voltage film clip,
Supreme Sound Studios, Sydney.

chapter 8

HIGH VOLTAGE

*a*C/DC's debut album, *High Voltage*, was released on 17 February 1975 on the Albert label distributed through EMI, and was the first hard evidence that AC/DC were NTBFW (not to be fucked with).

The back cover was restrained enough, even slightly mysterious. There was just a series of photos of Malcolm, Angus and Bon and a contact address for their then fan club in Sans Souci in Sydney's south, not far from where Bon made his official Sydney debut with the band.

The artwork on the front was an entirely different thing. Again the brainchild of Albert's Chris Gilbey, it showed a cartoon dog pissing on an electrical substation and a pair of what were presumably crushed beer cans.

Chris Gilbey: 'I look at it now and think, how naff is that? But at the time it seemed quite, not revolutionary, but it was kind of confrontational. I had people saying to me, "You can't have a dog pissing on the front cover of an album! That's disgusting! You can't do things like that!"'

Commercial artist Paul Power was working at EMI in Sydney and put himself forward to handle the cover art with the assistance of fellow EMI artist, the late Paul Winter.

Paul Power: 'I recall a few people in higher positions who were giving me shit about my lack of taste in rendering such offensive album cover art. I nearly told the three nameless EMI honchos to get fucked. I was under a lot of pressure. I thought I'd nailed what the band was about. I was about to get fired, I could feel it, when who should turn up? Bon Scott! I guess he heard the fiasco in the hallway. He put his arm around me and said, "Isn't this great? You've really caught what the band is all about! I love it!"

'The three execs were gobsmacked! You could have heard a pin drop! Bon said to them, "I'm taking Paulie out for a beer. You don't mind, do you? I mean, artwork this fucking good should be rewarded, right?" The three execs mumbled, "Right." We waited until we were outside EMI and laughed our arses off. He saved my job and the *High Voltage* album cover.'

If the cover of *High Voltage* set AC/DC well apart from the clean-cut pack of the day, what was inside the album sleeve in tracks like She's Got Balls — the song about Bon's ex-wife — represented an even more brutal act of division.

'She's certainly got balls,' Bon told Sydney radio station 2SM in February, 'she got mine for a long time.'

Stick Around was another insight into Bon's love life at the time, his inability to hold onto a woman for more than one night and his failure to understand why.

'I got a good song out of it,' he told 2SM. 'They still leave. Now I sing it every night in bed.'

Show Business was a preview of what was to come from Bon about life on the road, while Little Lover, a song Malcolm had been toying with since he was about 14, was originally called Front Row Fantasies but was changed to protect the innocent. And the not so innocent. After all, Bon wrote the lyrics about Angus, 'the most prominent littlest lover that I know'.

Like Baby, Please Don't Go, Love Song — as it's called on the album — dated back to Dave Evans' time with the band and was originally known as Fell In Love. Bon had rewritten the lyrics. George Young and Harry Vanda lit up when they first heard it, believing it could do what the 11-minute epic Evie had done for Stevie Wright.

'We're not entirely debauched,' Phil Rudd told 2SM about Love Song in a rare interview grab. 'We've got our soft spots, y'know.' 'Speak for yourself!' Bon fired back.

Interestingly, the single was called Love Song (Oh Jene) thanks to a spelling mistake. It was to have been Love Song (Oh Jean).

High Voltage was launched at the Hard Rock Café in Melbourne on 19 February. Admission was one dollar, or free with 'an AC/DC eyeshade', a sun visor-type fashion accessory inexplicably popular at the time.

By that stage, Bon had shaved his hair short, as a large portion of the band's audience in Melbourne were Sharps. He thought that if he couldn't beat them — well, not all of them at once, anyway — the next best thing was to adopt at least part of their look.

Not that he or anyone else in the band was scared. In fact, a fight one night at the Council Club Hotel between the band's road crew and the notorious Heidelberg Sharps ended in a clear victory to the AC/DC camp.

As far as friend John Swan was concerned, this tenacity, particularly of Malcolm and Angus, was very much in keeping with the old line that it's not the size of the dog that counts, but the size of the fight in the dog.

'The boys — Malcolm and Angus and Bon — would come off the stage because some idiot had fucking thrown a bottle or was abusing Bon, and we were at the side of the stage and they've gone straight off the stage into it. They're not the tallest guys in the world, they're not the best-built guys in the world, but I tell you what, don't fucking upset them. You wouldn't think there would be very much fight in them but ...'

Shortly after the album release, bass player Paul Matters joined the band, following the recommendation of George Young, who had seen him perform with Newcastle outfit Armageddon.

Given that AC/DC's record company Albert's were based in Sydney and the city was yet to fall to the band's assaultive charms, a reception was held there for the release of *High Voltage*, followed by a string of proud homecoming nights at Chequers.

But when the album's first single, Love Song (Oh Jene) backed with Baby, Please Don't Go, was released on 3 March it was still Melbourne and Adelaide radio that registered the bulk of the attention — but for Baby, Please Don't Go rather than the more hearts-and-flowers, prog-rock-styled Love Song.

It peaked at number 10 on the national charts the following month, and it was on the back of this success that the band made their first television appearance outside of 'Countdown', playing Baby, Please Don't Go on a telethon appeal in Melbourne.

In early March, Matters was sacked after just a few weeks and George again filled in on bass. By that time a trip to the UK was in the planning stages and the band went back into Albert Studios to record a new single.

They had loved the title of their album for its imagery and its energy and felt that it represented everything AC/DC stood for, so they decided to take it one step further and write a song called High Voltage, after George, typically, hit on the idea of a tune that contained the actual chords A, C, D, C.

Chris Gilbey: 'I remember after we'd started marketing the album and it was doing very well, George and Harry came in and played me this rough mix they had of a song called High Voltage. I said, "For Christ's sake, guys! We've got the album out called *High Voltage*, now you're bringing me a bloody song called High Voltage! It's too late to pull the album, add another track, there'll be a lot of disappointment blah blah blah." So I was thinking, well, what the hell are we going to do?'

Despite Gilbey's concerns, High Voltage would be released as a single. George played bass on the recording but, as good as he was, it wasn't a long-term solution, so auditions were held at Lansdowne Road.

The missing piece they were looking for arrived on 16 March. His name was Mark Evans. Having grown up in the no-nonsense

Melbourne suburb of Prahran, 18-year-old Evans' background was perfect.

Steve McGrath, a roadie with AC/DC, tipped him off that the band were looking for a guitar player. Evans knew of the group, having seen them on 'Countdown', and went down to meet them.

It was a Saturday and Evans was given a tape of the *High Voltage* album to listen to so he could prepare himself for his audition the following day, which, he discovered, was for a bass player not guitarist.

It didn't really matter. He had begun playing guitar when he was 14, before switching to bass at the age of 17. Even though he had little more than 18 months' bass-playing experience under his belt, it was a role he was comfortable with.

After his audition, Evans went to the Station Hotel and had a fight with a bouncer, which resulted in him being barred from the hotel. The following Tuesday night, when he went back to see AC/DC play, security not surprisingly enforced the ban from two nights earlier and wouldn't let him in. Bon, who Evans had never met before, went in to bat for him. What Evans didn't know when Malcolm told him AC/DC were playing at the Station that night was that he had already been chosen as the new bass player in what was his first serious band.

The timing of the gregarious Evans' arrival couldn't have been better for his own career or for grounding the band with a solid line-up. And with Evans on board, Malcolm, who, like George, had played bass from time to time over the past few months, could move permanently back to guitar. AC/DC were then able to present a unified front for their legendary 23 March appearance on 'Countdown' performing Baby, Please Don't Go.

The band ran through the song at rehearsals, then Bon disappeared right up until the taping of the show. At the last minute he emerged dressed as the planet's most disturbing schoolgirl. Hilariously funny as he looked — the perfect 69 opposite to Angus in his schoolboy suit — there was something strangely threatening and dangerous in Bon's manner and actions.

Sunday evening family television would never be the same again, and all to get a rise out of 'Countdown' host, Ian 'Molly' Meldrum.

Angus: 'Bon came up with the idea. He thought, well, I'm going to shock! So he went out and got that schoolgirl thing. Bon thought, well, if we come along and be who we are, he [Meldrum] will just walk away [thinking], "Oh yeah, ho hum!" But when Bon showed up like that, he just went nuts!'

Billy Thorpe recognised a lot of what he used to do in some of Bon's antics.

Billy Thorpe: 'We used to have beer drinking competitions and wet T-shirt contests with jugs of beer and people pouring beers over their heads. It was all about alcohol. I used to get away with murder and Bon watched what worked, like we all did — like I stole it from [Johnny] O'Keefe. So I saw a lot of myself in Bon. Once again, I'm not saying that Bon Scott came out of Billy Thorpe, but I definitely was an influence on him, as were other people.'

Follow-up performances on 'Countdown' — which between November 1974 and December 1976 would see them appear on the show no fewer than 38 times, either in person or on video clip — were less outrageous but no less theatrical. It was all about making maximum television impact, so 'Countdown' appearances were quite deliberately made into events.

While his schoolboy outfit was the most favoured for live work, for one appearance on the show Angus was transformed into Super Angus, for another a pilot in a home-made plane. Most memorable — apart from Bon's schoolgirl get-up — was Angus dressed in an impossibly hot gorilla suit in a cage, being dragged along by Bon dressed as Tarzan.

'Countdown' producer and director Paul Drane recalls:

'Before the show started we got Angus into the gorilla suit and in this cage, which we elevated up above the audience into the lighting grid before the audience came in. He's suspended up there inside this gorilla suit — which would not have been all that comfortable, I shouldn't imagine — with his guitar, and being really, really quiet. The other guys are somewhere on the studio set.

'So the audience came in and they didn't even know Angus was there. And we dropped him down into the crowd after the intros — so he'd probably been up there for nearly half an hour — and they just went absolutely berserk. It was just incredible.'

At that time, theatrics weren't confined to the band's 'Countdown' appearances. Michael Browning virtually had an in-house carpenter at the Hard Rock Café, who was able to knock together almost any idea that sprang into their minds.

One week it was a huge spider web made of rope and Angus would do a Spiderman routine, or Bon would come out as a spider in a suit with multiple arms and legs. On another occasion, there was a telephone booth on stage in which 'Clark' Ang was meant to transform himself into Super Ang. Bon put a stop to that and locked Angus in, or perhaps the door simply stuck and Angus couldn't get out.

All these ideas fitted comfortably with the very era Angus' schoolboy suit came from.

'Just being in high school [was the inspiration for these theatrics] and, believe it or not, watching Bugs Bunny, Road Runner and Wile E. Coyote,' he told Ben Wener in *Orange County Register* on 13 April 2001. 'They're blowing the hell out of each other, you know?'

The power of their live shows, coupled with the spectacle of what they presented on 'Countdown', was having the desired effect. On 20 April, the band played a show at the Myer Music Bowl in Melbourne billed as the Australian Concert for Bangladesh, organised by Freedom From Hunger, with Daddy Cool at the top of the 11-band bill and AC/DC in sixth place after Hush.

Bon arrived again dressed as a schoolgirl, seemingly unconcerned that his makeup would run in the rain that tumbled down that day. Though the attendance was affected by the poor weather, most waited until after AC/DC played before leaving.

In Sydney, they appeared at the Hordern Pavilion for Channel Nine's new program, 'Polaroid In Concert', which gave the band their first national TV exposure as a blistering live act, as opposed to 'Countdown' where they performed to a backing track with live vocals. This was the real deal.

Their balls-out attitude, a general low tolerance for bullshit and a seeming delight in outraging the establishment led to an interesting observation in *RAM* magazine on 19 April. Probably for the first time they were labelled a punk band in an article headed up: 'AC/DC: Australia has punk rock bands too, y'know.' Australian *Rolling Stone* also got involved in the name calling, referring to AC/DC as 'Melbourne's biggest punk band'.

But despite the fact that, at the time, they were playing 'Heavy Metal Nites' at the Hard Rock Café, in a very broad sense the punk tag fitted. AC/DC were street punks, just as Elvis, the early Stones, Pretty Things, The Who, The Small Faces and The Kinks had been, and had no problem calling a fucking spade a fucking spade.

What was strange was the timing of the *RAM* and *Rolling Stone* declarations. The Sex Pistols wouldn't play their first show for another seven months and The Clash didn't appear publicly until August 1976.

Angus' hellish stage demeanour certainly did little to quell thoughts that AC/DC really were out to pillage and destroy the lives of decent folks. At the end of the week, his school suits were a public health risk, thanks to a combination of sweating a large portion of his body weight into the clothes, cigarette smoke and generous smears of snot. He was continually amazed that the girls at the front of their shows were quite happy, even honoured, to be showered in his saliva, sweat and mucus.

And there was certainly nothing polite and refined about AC/DC's blistering live set at the time, which was drawn largely from the *High Voltage* album with various covers by Chuck Berry, the Stones and even Elvis Presley hip-shakers like Heartbreak Hotel.

While Angus' schoolboy character was becoming more established, Bon still opted to dress up or sometimes down for special occasions, as was the case at a show at Melbourne's Festival Hall with Split Enz and hugely popular headliners, Skyhooks.

Bon wasn't about to be overshadowed, so he dressed as Tarzan in an almost painfully small loincloth and swung on a rope between the PA stacks. It worked perfectly at rehearsals but Bon's physics sums didn't add up at showtime.

Angus: 'These days you've got harnesses and everything, but he [Bon] just got a rope flung up there and swung across the PA system. He cleared it. Then when we were doing the gig, he swung, but it was a bit like that cat in *Bugs Bunny* — Sylvester — swinging into all these dogs. He forgot that all the kids were going to stand on their chairs and he went straight into the crowd. There was a lot of young girls and he crawled back on stage with just his jock strap on. They tore all his clothes off!'

Phil Eastick (crew member): 'That Melbourne show was one of the first times I'd seen them do the on-the-shoulders routine [Angus on Bon's shoulders] through the audience. You've got to remember in those days there was no wireless, this is actually still running a cord for Angus' guitar that came almost to the back end of Festival Hall. And Bon took him out there in this loincloth and took him back.'

A series of daytime concerts for Schoolkids Week in May at the Hard Rock Café were just as chaotic. Bon missed one show and Angus and Malcolm filled in on vocals.

AC/DC were by now a bona fide phenomenon in Melbourne and appeared on 'Countdown' an amazing four times in June. Eager to freeze-frame the mania, arrangements were made to film at least part of the band's headline performance at Festival Hall on 16 June with Stevie Wright and John Paul Young.

A video for the next single, High Voltage — and for Show Business — was later assembled from that footage, with extra 'live' scenes for High Voltage done at Sydney's Supreme Sound Studios in early July. The video for High Voltage was directed by American Larry Larstead and was shot with five cameras, which was virtually unheard-of in those days.

Albert's Chris Gilbey chose Larstead because of his outstanding Coca-Cola commercials, and was impressed by his techniques on the AC/DC shoot. After filming the band live, close-ups were done of Bon. The director constantly sprayed the singer's face with a water atomiser to create the illusion of sweat running down his cheeks, while he also got Bon to sing out loud, rather than the more common lip-synching, in order to show his tensed-up throat muscles. 'He wanted to make sure he captured every aspect of the live image of Bon,' said Gilbey, 'so that the video was as real as possible.'

In the middle of the year the band moved out of Lansdowne Road, a model aeroplane left behind by Phil Rudd a curious reminder of their presence. They took up residence at the Freeway Gardens Motel, a centre of activity for any band in town at the time, where the debauchery continued.

It was there that a huge red-headed Tasmanian woman named Rosie — who along with a friend were collectively known as the Jumbo Twins — stepped into AC/DC's legend and Bon's growing list of bedded conquests. Rosie instantly recognised the singer, who was very much the rock star on the rise. By Bon's calculations, Rosie was over six feet (183 centimetres) tall and almost 20 stone (127 kilograms).

'She was too big to say no to,' he told Bill Scott at WABX in July 1979, 'so I had to do it ... my God, I wish I hadn't ... that was some mountain. You can imagine the problems I had.'

It was classic Bon: life was a circus and he had to go on all the rides before it moved on to the next town. According to legend, the next day, while Bon was trying to make out he was still asleep, he heard Rosie do the maths with her friend. 'That's 28 this week!'

The next time the band sighted Rosie was in February the following year when they were in Georgetown, Tasmania. By then, somehow and much to Bon's disappointment, she was many, many sizes smaller than the great woman she'd once been.

On 23 June, High Voltage backed with Soul Stripper was released as a single in Australia, while *High Voltage*, the album, was certified Gold that same month. The impact of the new single was instant.

Chris Gilbey: 'It immediately got added to all of the major radio station playlists. People loved it. The album *High Voltage* sold about 125,000 copies, I remember, before we put out the next album, and certainly the last 50,000 were sold because of [the single] High Voltage. The amazing thing, of course, was that High Voltage the song was not on the *High Voltage* album.'

With High Voltage, the single, and the thrilling video to go with it, AC/DC really arrived. Yet they maintained an underdog status in the face of the phenomenon that was Skyhooks and Sherbet.

The harmless melodic pop of Sherbet — who would later score an international hit with Howzat — was enormously popular right across the country, with huge record sales and national tours that were mammoth exercises. The band's look and sound made them diametrically opposed to the working-class, blue singlet and occasional tattoo territory that AC/DC were slowly beginning to claim as their own.

Meanwhile, Skyhooks, the brainchild of bassist Greg Macainsh, who was tired of the denim look and blues-based sound of so many acts of the day, took to the stage with increasingly jaw-dropping outfits that made the New York Dolls, The Tubes and Alice Cooper look flat and unimaginative.

Their debut album, 1974's *Living In The Seventies*, was by far the biggest selling Australian album of the era, with unprecedented sales figures.

Unlike both Sherbet and Skyhooks, AC/DC's territory was still largely confined to Melbourne, where the weekly, character-building grind of up to four gigs a day, seven days a week, was a goldmine, but utterly exhausting. A lunchtime show at a school would often be followed by anything up to four other performances before the day ended. Malcolm and Angus lapped it up, knowing it was a fine grounding for what they unshakably believed was coming their way.

For Bon, though he was a seasoned campaigner, there was still a certain romance about it all. But even he occasionally got bored, and on the way home from a gig one night acquired another earring just to kill the time.

'I didn't have anywhere to put it [the earring], see,' he told Anthony O'Grady in *RAM* on 19 April 1975, 'so I got a safety pin and told the roadie to stick it in here. Well, it was something to do to pass the time, anyway.'

Getting to gigs sometimes proved to be complicated. When their bus broke down, which was quite often, Phil Rudd's mate Geordie Leach would get a call.

'Phil would ring me up and say, "Is your mum using the car? Come down and drive us to the gig." I had this Toyota Crown, so the five of them would pile in the car. And there were so many people at the gig that you'd be mobbed getting in. Once I lost the fucking mirror off the car and my mum's fucking spittin' it! Another time the aerial disappeared on the way out of the gig, sometimes hubcaps went ...'

The non-financial rewards for their hard work were extraordinarily good. Over a period of a week, a newspaper attempted to document the number of women who passed through the doors of the band's reasonably fixed address. By their estimates, the figure was around a hundred.

More like 110, corrected Angus, in a mixture of mock horror and hurt pride. In reality, it was probably many more.

Bon's theory of attracting women was based on one principle and it centred around being on stage. The lights, sound and your elevation make you a magnet. That magnetism breeds parties and those parties attract more women. Simple. It was a never-ending, constantly expanding cycle of pleasure.

However, the process did sometimes get a little nerve-racking; like, for instance, the Granny's incident. One night after a gig, a pair of girls approached the band with an offer to wind down at a place mysteriously called Granny's. While a naked Bon was doing all sorts of weird gymnastics, the action began in earnest on the lounge-room floor, until Granny walked in. Her presence quickly cleared the place.

Angus, unlike the rest of the band, rarely went out apart from gigs and preferred to stay home and eat chocolate, read comics, drink tea, milk, play guitar — it never left his side — and lap up any Clint Eastwood movie that was on TV. But he was mystified that some girls would be hugely enthusiastic at the shows but horrified at the thought of spending the night with him.

Bon, on the other hand, was often quite helplessly pulled towards trouble when his hormones kicked in, which was most of the time.

On one occasion, the problem was more to do with the fact that a trail of evidence had been left in the form of a series of photos of Bon and a lady friend in bed.

It was all relatively innocent, until the next morning when Bon's friend — still somewhat party-weary — drew the attention of the police while she was on her way to work. They brought her home, found the photos and threatened to charge the singer with offences in relation to pornography.

Not all the busts Bon was caught up in involved the law. His reaction to a loud knock at the door one day was instant and to the point.

'"Fuck off! I'm having a fuck!"' he later recalled his response to Irvin Sealey in Rock Gossip in 1979.

Wrong answer.

His caller was the father, possibly of the same girl who appeared in the photos with him.

Vince Lovegrove: 'The father of the girl didn't want her going out with Bon. He came around and knocked the door down with a friend of his and dragged Bon out and beat him up and threw him in a rose bush. As a result of that, he lost all his front teeth. When that happened I was horrified, but it was almost like, well, that's Bon, you'd expect that to happen.

'He was a good street fighter and he would be in a rumble but he would prefer to avoid it. Not through not wanting to be in a rumble, but just because he'd prefer to pacify the situation rather than become involved. But if the challenge was put to him he accepted it — he never ran away from a brawl.'

Like Bon, Angus also had to endure some physical punishment, but his was self-inflicted, as by this point his performance on stage resembled someone being beaten up by the invisible man. He was immersed in a frenzied primal ritual where he tirelessly threw his body about like a man possessed. In fact, his movements were so frantic and unusual that wild rumours began to circulate that his antics stemmed from severe behavioural problems.

Angus was certainly utterly fearless. He would leap into crowds and forcibly make floor space for himself by spinning madly in a circular motion on his side, while his guitar cord was tangled into tear-inducing knots for the band's road crew. Stunned members of the audience thought he was going to explode at their feet.

But those wild thrashing movements and time-keeping with alternate legs, a fevered dance he would adopt even in late-night hotel room jams, weren't simply an exaggeration of the way he had always reacted to music with any drive to it. It also came from being utterly focused: he couldn't afford to smile and wave at fans.

The other part of it was entertainment value. Angus had found, after George's urging, that rolling on the floor and doing Chuck Berry's duckwalk, which he adopted from the dance mannerisms of a nephew, was going to have an added impact with any audience.

'I'll shit and piss on people if need be,' he told *Beat Instrumental* in August 1976.

After a while, Angus' nervous energy automatically took over and his frenetic movements became a natural, involuntary action every time he stepped onto a stage and felt the sound from the amps rush through him.

Angus: 'For some unknown reason, whenever I'm playing it's like, being a little guy, where most people bend a note on a guitar, my whole body bends. Then when I hit a chord down at the bottom end of the guitar, I just follow it. Other guys let their fingers do the walking. With me, the body does the walking.'

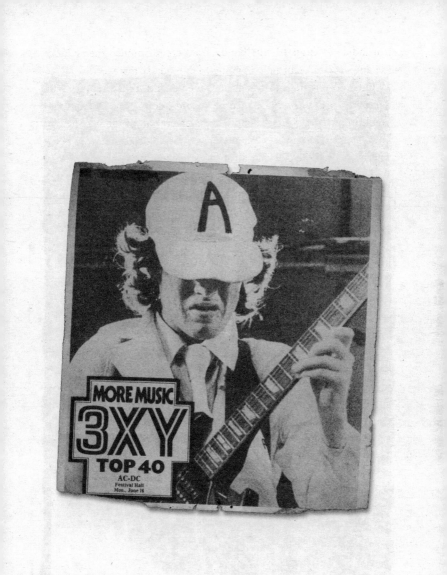

MORE MUSIC
3XY
TOP 40
AC-DC
Festival Hall
Mon., June 16

1975

Bon in Albury, New South Wales.

*a*t first, the voice on the band's introduction tape sounded almost conservative when it heralded AC/DC's arrival on stage. But each time the name was repeated it was faster, more desperate, the pitch higher and more piercing. After a minute or two, the voice sounded like it belonged to a robotic speed-and-caffeine freak. It screamed excitement.

The *TNT* album, which was recorded in July 1975 at Albert Studios in Sydney with George Young and Harry Vanda again handling the production, presented itself the same way.

These weren't the first sessions for the album, with songs like The Jack, which was already a live favourite, recorded back in April.

In the studio, the songs were typically worked up at a piano with George, Malcolm and Angus all often squeezed onto the one stool. Using a piano allowed them to play the guitar and bass sections of a song at the same time. George would always be on patrol, 'bullshit detecting', and fanning the ideas Malcolm came up with into a blue flame.

Harry Vanda: 'A lot of songs we'd try a few takes and most of the time gravitate to the first couple. There was always that sort of immediate, spontaneous thing. They all used to be together in one room anyway — all the amps were lumped in one room with the drums! I suppose it was a recording nightmare, but it worked.'

While in Sydney, the band played a number of gigs, including two nights at the hallowed Bondi Lifesaver. Roger Grierson, later a member of The Thought Criminals, was among those in the Sydney punk scene who found AC/DC's energy at the Lifesaver shows more than slightly attractive.

'The sound just hit you. The sound was so powerful, rocking and economical. I went backstage. Nobody was up for a chat, and they didn't want us drinking their beer, but Phil Rudd let me bum a cigarette. That was the extent of the conversation; they were exhausted. I had never seen anyone put that much sweat into a show.

'I remember telling [founding partner of the Phantom Records store in Sydney and later the label of the same name] Jules Normington that AC/DC were the business, and he said, "Bullshit! You should see this band I manage called [Sydney's Stooges and MC5-inspired] Radio Birdman!" And I laughed and said, "No-one will come near AC/DC! Who are you kidding?" We went along to see Birdman play at the Heffron Hall, and personally I was yet to be convinced. Birdman had lots of good things about them, but they weren't AC/DC.'

The *TNT* album was finished in two weeks and then the band returned to Melbourne. By August, Michael Browning had begun negotiations to get AC/DC out of Australia and before overseas audiences by October. Things certainly couldn't get much bigger or more frantic in their adopted home town.

Late in the month they took part in a week-long series of school holiday lunchtime concerts at the Myer department store in the heart of the city.

On paper, the free gigs seemed like a great marketing idea. But there was anarchy when for show number one — in the girls' clothing section — thousands of fans arrived. Some fainted as the crowd surged towards the band and equipment was toppled when those in the screaming mass with nowhere else to go spilt onto the small stage. After just a few minutes, and only two songs, the show was shut down for the safety of everyone.

The band were forced to make their escape into a change room, but Bon was separated from the rest and had his shoes and most of his clothes, including part of his jeans, torn off by a swarm of girls. Malcolm came out of it all with a cut above his eye but the store was really on the receiving end, with thousands of dollars worth of merchandise stolen as well as general damage.

So much for a four-day engagement.

Stevie Wright's second solo album, the Vanda-and-Young-produced *Black Eyed Bruiser*, was also released in August, nine months after Guitar Band — with a cameo guitar role by Angus — had been issued as a single. The bravado-filled title track had exactly the same tone and vocal delivery as Bon was now doing.

There was little point in going overseas before they'd conquered Sydney as well as Melbourne. Accordingly, Browning arranged a free outdoor show at Sydney's Victoria Park on 7 September to get the ball rolling.

It occurred to Albert's Chris Gilbey that a series of radio ads on Sydney's 2SM would be an ideal way to promote the show. So one Saturday morning he set off to Manly on Sydney's northern beaches with a 2SM tape recorder with the station's logo on the mic, which, he figured, would attract the hip young kids who were bound to know about AC/DC. From that audio he planned to put together a 30-second radio ad.

But getting people on the beach to be interviewed wasn't the problem.

Chris Gilbey: 'Have you heard of AC/DC? "Nah, who are they?" Have you heard of AC/DC? "Nah, what do they do?" Nobody knew who the hell AC/DC was! I was thinking, oh shit! This is going to be dreadful!'

Gilbey went to plan B and decided just to ask people about their favourite bands. With a little creative licence, those answers could be shaped just the way he wanted.

'So we said, "Who's your favourite band?" "Oh, I like Sherbet!" "Why do you like Sherbet?" "I like [singer Daryl Braithwaite] Daryl's legs!" some girl said. So I thought, that's cool, we'll use that for Angus! We'll put in a question saying, "Why do you like Angus?" "I like his legs!"'

With a tape full of quotes, Gilbey headed back into the city and decided to stop off at a friend's home. After a while, Gilbey noticed that his friend's girlfriend had a very deep voice. His mind started racing and he asked if she wanted to be involved in the ad he was developing for AC/DC.

Chris Gilbey: 'I said, "Just do the stoned rave. Or imagine you're a mother of a kid who wants to go out to an AC/DC concert and you don't think that's such a good idea — what would you say?" So we stood her at the front door to get the whole vibe of being there and doing a door knock. She said, "I wouldn't let my daughter go and see a band like them — they're disgusting, blah blah blah." She just went into this rant about this disgusting horrible depraved rock and roll band called AC/DC and it was fantastic!'

The vox pops from the kids on the northern beaches never stood a chance after that. Announcer Mike Drayson, with his big deep voice, added the voice-over tag at the end of it, a single line written by Gilbey: 'AC/DC — they're not a nice band.'

The Victoria Park show was a huge success, so much so that it provided a few heart scares for Angus and Bon.

Angus: 'When the two of us went into the crowd, everyone all stood up at once and moved forward and the two of us went, "Shit! Run!" It was like Custer's last stand.'

Chris Gilbey: 'The record went into the charts the next week and that's how AC/DC were broken in Sydney: by that advertising campaign based on no knowledge of the band anywhere in the marketplace, other than the people in radio and the record industry who knew there was a vibe on AC/DC. Boom. It exploded from there.'

Back in Melbourne not long after, Phil Rudd broke his thumb during a fight at the Matthew Flinders Hotel, a key gig in the suburbs, after he punched out a guy who had thrown a glass at Angus and cut the guitarist's hand open. Rudd later had to have surgery to fix the thumb properly, but even after he injured himself, leaving the stage and not continuing with the show was never an option. Loyalty was everything.

'With one hand, no hand,' he told Phil Lageat in *Rock Hard France* in June 2001, 'I had to be part of the show, to show my support to the band.'

Michael Browning: 'There were a couple of places that were pretty rough and I remember Angus saying to me, "Next time we go back there we want a safety fence or something, a net or something along those lines." But that wasn't so much because of AC/DC, it was just the nature of the venue.'

The next night the band performed behind a wire fence with former drummer Colin Burgess, who sat in for the next few gigs while Rudd was forced to nurse his thumb. The casualties could have been far worse at another gig during this period when someone ran amok with a meat cleaver.

Burgess was pleased to see one of Angus' dreams had, by that point, been realised.

Colin Burgess: 'They had the bus with AC/DC on the front. I remember Angus saying that that's what he wanted early on — a bus with AC/DC on it.'

The drummer was also impressed by one of Bon's pre-gig rituals to warm up his vocal cords.

Colin Burgess: 'Bon was gargling with port every night before the gig. Actually, he wasn't drinking it — he'd spit it out, to make his voice rough enough for the gig. It was quite amazing.'

Bon could also be wonderfully unpredictable.

Colin Burgess: 'I remember one gig we did somewhere and they closed the bar, so Bon said, "Well, no, I'll take over the bar!" and served everyone drinks.'

Angus: 'I remember even Bon ironing his jeans on top of a bar one night. Everyone was a little bit annoyed when he kicked the drinks over, but he got a nice fine crease down those jeans!'

While Burgess was sitting in, the band went to Adelaide where they teamed up with The Keystone Angels, who had just gotten off an Australian tour backing Chuck Berry.

Guitarist John Brewster recalls the thrill of seeing AC/DC for the first time.

John Brewster: 'The music was sensational. A lot of the things you see in an AC/DC show now, they were doing then. Angus was doing this little striptease thing and instead of that hydraulic stage that Angus goes to now at the big shows and spins around on, he'd just jump on a pub table and do the same thing. Of course glasses and bottles and jugs of beer would go west, but unbelievably exciting.

'And Bon used to carry him out into the audience, and in those days Angus didn't have a transmitter guitar so there was this hugely long lead. He'd have these roadies, like the lifesavers with the line that goes out, letting out this lead as Angus went into the audience.'

AC/DC were just as taken with The Keystone Angels. Bon and Malcolm took reports of them back to George and Harry Vanda, which saw the band being signed to Albert's where they would become the hugely popular Angels.

After the final show in Port Augusta, 300 kilometres from Adelaide, Brewster was sitting with Bon in the front section of the band's bus as their gear was packed into the back.

John Brewster: 'He basically just outlined their plans for the future, not bragging, but he knew what he had. He knew he was in a band that was going to take the world by storm — he knew it. Just quite calmly and just being a visionary for the future, he was saying that they were going to go overseas and they were going to stay there until they cracked it.'

By mid-September, sales of the *High Voltage* album had reached 25,000 units, but word that plans for a short promotional visit to London had been scrapped left them with no option but to go back to an endless cycle of touring Australia.

They paused briefly to play High Voltage at the *TV Week* King Of Pop awards in October, even though awards shows and having to deal with hugging and kissing music industry people was at the outer limits of their tolerance.

At the dinner later in the night, Bon, never left wanting when an opportunity to outrage presented itself, pulled out an enormous vibrator in front of a TV executive. That same night, with a few drinks under his belt, the singer acted out the great divide that existed between AC/DC and the rest of the music industry.

In the backstage hospitality area, Bon set about literally tearing his way through piles of *TV Week* magazines with wild-eyed contempt. Not long after, the sight of a turkey on one of the tables got his mind racing. He filled its body cavity with champagne, which he drank in between taking mouthfuls of the bird just to keep his stamina up. Enter Sherbet's Daryl Braithwaite, who accepted Bon's offer to take a few swigs of the bubbly sacrament. The AC/DC frontman stood to one side and watched, roaring with laughter: it had been a big night and he had had to relieve himself somewhere.

AC/DC's first major Australian tour began on 10 November and stretched until January 1976. It didn't just take in the band's major markets in the capital cities such as Sydney and Melbourne, but also the regional centres of the country. That's where the real fun often started.

Hitting towns outside the densely populated coastal areas was often a double-edged sword. On the one hand, those audiences rarely had the opportunity to see in the flesh what they'd watched on television or heard on radio, and as such were usually wildly enthusiastic. On the other, visiting bands, particularly those with a tough stance, were often seen as a threat to the local male order and so were a magnet for trouble.

'Dodge a bottle here, dodge a fist there,' Angus told *Juke* on 30 January 1988. 'The only time they'd stop trying to pick a fight with us was when it was hard and fast. Songs could start off slow but they might have to speed up in the middle!'

At one show in Perth, someone who made it onto the stage thought it'd be fun to put the guitarist in a wrestling hold. Angus retaliated, the locals responded, and the police showed up in force in full riot gear.

Malcolm: 'I remember in Bendigo in Victoria all the youth of the town were ready to beat the shit out of us! It was because somebody had got one of their girlfriends last time they were in town.

'They'd like a bit of a car chase, and Phil is a maniac behind the wheel so if any shit like that went on, Phil was doing his driving and all sorts of tricks. We used to get out in the bush roads and pull around corners, quickly pull over, all lights out, hide! And we'd watch the guys go screaming past, crank up and go back into town, then get their women!'

But if it was necessary to get physical, the diminutive size of the individual band members was never a consideration. In fact, it made retaliation all the more vital.

Malcolm: 'We were all little guys. I mean, let's face it, anyone could knock us over. But the smaller you are, the fucking bigger you think you've got to be. Bon was taller than us guys but he wasn't too solid as a guy either, and he'd drink a lot and he'd always be staggering a wee bit here and there. But we were all brawlers. If we were all jumped on, we all got involved — no-one running away. And that was the thing: we all stuck together, I guess.

'Usually, the toughest guy at the show was backstage introducing himself to Bon — he always got the rough element jumping on him to be his buddies. That was good. But there was moments when you never had guys like that around.'

Bon didn't attract that element because of his etiquette at the dining table (which, as it happened, he also possessed). He was quite capable of walking the walk and talking the talk. Drummer Ray Arnott, a friend of the band who did a number of studio sessions for Albert's with Harry Vanda and George Young, recalls Bon once, wittingly or otherwise, balancing the scales of justice in Melbourne.

Ray Arnott: 'I remember there was this guy who kinghit me once in the Prahran Hotel, and then about a month later Bon headbutted him halfway across Chapel Street!'

On 8 December, the single It's A Long Way To The Top (If You Wanna Rock 'N' Roll), which had been dangled before 'Countdown' viewers twice in the previous month, was released. Its lyrics were an

A-grade example of Bon's street poetry skills pulled straight from his lined exercise book.

Angus: 'That was his greatness. He called it toilet poetry but it definitely was an art form and he took pride in that. He always wrote down stuff as he went along, like Long Way To The Top. George would look through his book. One day George spied the line: "a long way to the top if you wanna rock and roll." It was just sitting there. He hadn't written any lyric for it, just the title.

'You'd say to him, "Bon, you can do better than that," and he would. He'd go away and really work on it, or if he got stuck he'd come and get Mal and say, "Mal, come and bail me out." Mal would help him, give him a few lines or an idea and then he'd flow away or he'd ask me if I had any dirty poetry anywhere! Some inspiration ...'

Bon would only begin to weave his lyrical magic once the band was in the studio and he had a rough idea of a song's sound and, crucially, a sense of its rhythmic stride. Then he'd find a quiet corner, such as a spare office or even the kitchen at Albert's, armed with a pen, some paper and his exercise book of ideas. Lubrication came courtesy of his drink of choice, an economic necessity at the time: bottles of Stone's Green Ginger Wine. George was always on hand to settle and encourage the singer if he was feeling the pressure.

Michael Browning: 'He would pretty much labour over it very intensely. I think it was a very rough time for Bon every time that was to happen, because I think his lyrics were so important: I think every word counted.'

The actual recording of It's A Long Way To The Top was as much a testament to George's extraordinary talents as the band's energy.

'The song was never played in one piece in the studio,' bass player Mark Evans told *Daily Dirt*'s Volker Janssen in 2000. 'It was all cut together from one big jam. That was George Young — the guy is a genius.'

Harry Vanda: 'A Long Way To The Top was just a great blow — we're all going, shit a brick, listen to this! This'd make a good song. So that's how all that started.'

Introducing the drone of the bagpipes was also George's idea, as he was looking for a new angle and a new sound for the central hook of the song that would really slice through the band. Bon, so the story goes, had never previously so much as touched the notoriously difficult instrument, let alone made it sound tuneful.

This came as a surprise to George, who mistakenly thought when Bon said he'd been in a pipe band that he'd played the bagpipes, when in fact he was a drummer. Bon was quickly able to master most instruments he picked up, and coupled with his experience back at school and in Fraternity with the recorder and general knowledge of breathing techniques, he soon added the bagpipes to his list of conquests.

The instrument provided a strange, almost comic relief in the band's otherwise vicious live sets. But while few things are more romantic for a Scotsman — particularly one named Scott — than the pipes, they ended up being a huge millstone around Bon's neck.

Michael Browning: 'They were the bane of his existence, those bagpipes. I think they probably put more pressure on him than any other thing I can think of! They invariably never worked. It's a hard instrument to time to guitars, because you're pumping them and they kind of kick in when the bag's full — very difficult to time to guitars.'

In December, the first major step was taken towards getting AC/DC out into the greater world. After Atlantic in America failed to snap up the band, Atlantic Records' UK head, Phil Carson, signed them to a worldwide deal.

That placed AC/DC in the company of the likes of the Stones, Led Zeppelin, Ray Charles, Aretha Franklin, Buddy Guy and Junior Wells, as well as Angus' beloved Cactus. For an act from Australia, where all the record companies were concerned about was sinking their budgets into the local representation of international artists rather than supporting proven homegrown market performers like AC/DC, it was quite a coup and sweet fuck-you revenge.

Browning had already planned a UK tour for early 1976 and his sister Coral, based in London, was shopping for a record deal for the band and booking club dates. She first met with Carson for discussions in her capacity as manager of keyboard player Rabbit, formerly of Free.

Phil Carson: 'This girl walks into my office, she is drop dead gorgeous. I thought, this chick looks fucking great, you know, I got to get to know her a little better, shall we say. But she's completely professional. And she sits down, we make the deal [about Rabbit], she absolutely knows what she's talking about, and that was the end of that.

'I was about to ask her out for dinner, and she said, "Look, I hope you don't think this is inappropriate, but my little brother manages a group in Australia, and they're very big." In 1975, nobody cared about Australia, and who was big in Australia didn't matter to anybody signing groups at that time. But I wanna go out with the girl, so what am I gonna say — "No"? So I said, "Okay, you wanna leave something and I'll listen to it."'

Coral could do much better than that. She opened her briefcase, which, to Carson's amazement, contained a projector and a screen, and played a film of AC/DC performing. Carson loved what he saw and offered to sign the band and put them on the Back Street Crawler tour of the UK that was scheduled to take place in a few months.

Phil Carson: 'I thought, well, I wanna sign them, and obviously if I wait, she's gonna bring the group to England and someone else will sign them. But I thought I'd better make it a cheap deal because I don't want Jerry Greenberg [President of Atlantic US] going nuts if he doesn't like the band when he comes back from vacation.

'So I made a deal for them in 1975, I think the royalty rate was 12 per cent and the advance was $25,000 an album, for the world outside of Australia. But it was a one-album deal, with an option for two more albums each year, and four options. So for $25,000 I signed AC/DC for 15 albums! That was the initial deal. And I thought, well no-one can shout at me if I make a deal like that! For Christ's sake, I've only got to sell 10,000 records in England and it's okay. And I felt sure that they could do that.'

Carson called Michael Browning at three in the morning and AC/DC had themselves an overseas record deal.

Just before Christmas, the band went back into Albert Studios to cut two new tracks as potential singles, one of which was Jailbreak.

Herm Kovac: 'I remember walking in [to the Octagon Hotel in Prahran] and bloody Malcolm and Angus — everyone except for Phil Rudd — are running around nude! There's girls there and everything and Malcolm said, "Listen to this," and he plays me Jailbreak. He'd just written it. I said, "Mate, it sounds like Gloria!"'

Doc Neeson (The Angels): 'This is a story that George Young told us, that Bon was in the vocal booth [during the recording of Jailbreak], which was a bit out of the actual line of sight of the control room. And he was coming up to the line of "bullet in his back!" and he'd been having a few Green Ginger Wines. They were sort of saying, "Do it again, Bon, a little bit more character!" or whatever. They always tell you to run a few times through a part like that.

'So Bon was going, "With a bullet in his BACK!" and you could hear, guzzle, guzzle, guzzle. "Bullet in his BACK!" Guzzle, guzzle, guzzle. "Bullet in his BACK!" "...Bon?" And you know there's that little stop right then. "Bon? Bon?" And they went around to the booth and he was passed out on the floor. He just put so much into it, he passed out. So they had to finish the song the next day.

'He'd sing and build up a kind of tension — really mean, like he was going to cut somebody's balls off — and then right when you think this is the crunch moment, he'd go, "He he he!" I don't know how you ever imitate that, you couldn't tell someone how to do that. It was just his way of performing.

'You wouldn't know after a while whether he was going to jump down and belt somebody in the audience or let them off. As a result, he had people right under his control. Is it going to be okay or not? He had that danger element going in his performance.'

The TNT album was finally released in late December and heralded the arrival of the classic AC/DC, with Bon's lairy, leery vocals and earthy lyrics, the twin guitars of Malcolm and Angus bonded by brotherly telepathy and a rhythm function you could set a clock to.

Lobby Loyde: 'It's the rhythmic thing that is the unique Australian thing. It's our rhythm sections that make us different to everyone else in the world. If the bloody thing ain't building and ain't going somewhere and it's not rhythmic, well it ain't rock and roll. If it doesn't rock, it's bullshit. Leave it alone, get away from it, it's pox.'

Most of all, *TNT* had an identity and a singular focus that the slightly premature *High Voltage* album lacked. *TNT* was a statement.

Harry Vanda: 'I suppose there might have been one or two tracks on the first album, a few things that they were experimenting with, which probably later on they wouldn't have done any more. So I suppose you could say that *TNT* was the one that really pulled the identity; like, this is AC/DC, there's no doubt about it, that's who it's going to be and that's how it's going to stay. Once you know an identity, then you know what not to do.'

The cover art was something the Sensational Alex Harvey Band might have done, with the inside of the gatefold sleeve containing the mock personal details of all the band members. Birth dates were teasingly obscured for all except, for some reason, Bon.

Juke magazine's Simon Maynard felt that *TNT* was really a make-believe movie soundtrack called *Brats Out Of Hell* and that, overall, the album was a virtual instruction manual for a rock and roll band.

There was the warning of It's A Long Way To The Top (If You Wanna Rock 'N' Roll), the on-the-job training (Rock 'N' Roll Singer), the occupational health pitfalls along the way (The Jack) and the establishment of the singer's persona (Live Wire, TNT and The Rocker), through to the triumphs (High Voltage) and romance (a version of Chuck Berry's School Days).

The album contained a re-recording of Can I Sit Next To You, Girl and a lyrically toned-down version of The Jack, to avoid the wrath of the censors and conservative radio programmers.

Angus: 'When we first made it [The Jack] in the studio they were saying, well, maybe we should do two because it's a hooky song and maybe the radio might pick it up. So Bon said, "Great, now I can really be clever with it." When we would play She's Got The Jack [live], he would always sing the uncensored version and he thought it was a great play with words. Of course, when he was singing that [in the studio] we were on the floor laughing because we know the original lyric.'

The song's origins dated back to a tour of Adelaide and was sparked by a letter Malcolm received after a gig from a girl in Melbourne he'd been having sex with.

Malcolm: 'We were staying in a big house at the time. If I remember, it was Jimmy Barnes and Cold Chisel, all those guys from Adelaide, Swanee [John Swan], bundles of people in there. We were having a singalong with the guitars and I got this note from this chick in Melbourne accusing me of giving her a dose of the clap or the jack, and I never had it. So I thought, hang on a minute, this chick's fucking given it to me then, if anything! So I went down to the clinic and I was cleared.

'But the thing was, when I got the note I gave it to Bon who was sitting next to me and I just started playing a blues and we started together "She's Got The Jack". We sort of threw it away and didn't worry about it, but then a couple of days later we just had a jam with it with the guys, a slow blues, and Bon started singing it again. That song just evolved out of that, really.

'Bon had been to the VD clinic many times in Melbourne and they knew him by first name instead of just a number. Everyone else was called "1102?". But when it came to Bon it was, "Bon?"!'

At one time, the entire band ended up with the disease courtesy of a particular group of ladies. Believing that such acts shouldn't go unrecognised, the next time the women were all in the audience, when the chorus of The Jack kicked in, Bon pointed each of them out as he sang the punchline.

But Bon didn't just give as good as he got, he actually pioneered a brutal, early method of safe sex.

'One time I had the jack,' he told Phil Sutcliffe in *Sounds* on 28 August 1976, 'and this girl wanted fuckin' and she was so ugly

LEFT Stars in stripes: The Easybeats – George Young, Harry Vanda, Dick Diamonde, Snowy Fleet, Stevie Wright, London, 1966

BELOW Riding a rockin' horse; Malcolm and Angus with two cousins, Glasgow, early '60s

BOTTOM The other Velvet Underground: Les Hall, Malcolm Young and Andy Imlah, Australia 1971

Kantuckee: Trevor James and
Angus, Sydney, circa 1972/73

BELOW First known picture of
AC/DC: Dave Evans, Angus,
Malcolm, Neil Smith and Noel
Taylor, Victoria Park, Sydney,
April 1974

RIGHT What's up their sleeves?
The Valentines: (back row)
Ted Ward and John Cooksey,
(middle row) Paddy Beach
and Bon Scott. (front row) Wyn
Milson and Vince Lovegrove,
Melbourne, 1969

BELOW The little drummer boy:
Bon Scott, 1950s

LEFT Any requests? Fraternity:
Bon Scott, Bruce Howe, Mick
Jurd, John Freeman and John
Bisset, Jonathan's Disco,
Sydney, late 1970

BELOW The illustrated man:
Bon with Fraternity, late 1970

Malcolm and Angus face off, Hordern Pavilion, Sydney, December 1974

Crawling from the wreckage: Buster Brown – Geordie Leach, Angry Anderson, Chris Wilson, Phil Rudd, John Moon, Paul Grant, Melbourne 1974

ABOVE The maestros: Harry Vanda and George Young, Sydney, November 1974

LEFT Phil Rudd, Supreme Sound Studio, Melbourne, July 1975

BELOW Prize exhibits: Bon and Angus with George Young on bass, Fairfield Showgrounds, Sydney, March 1975

High voltage: Victoria Park,
Sydney, September 1975

ABOVE Just hanging around: Phil, Malcolm, Angus, Mark Evans and Bon, Melbourne, late 1975

LEFT That killer smile: Bon recording *Dirty Deeds* at Albert Studios, Sydney, March 1976

RIGHT London calling: Mark Evans and Angus, farewell appearance at the Bondi Lifesaver, Sydney, March 1976

ABOVE Letting it all hang out: Angus at the Reading Rock Festival, England, August 1976

LEFT Bon smokes the pipes: It's A Long Way To The Top film clip, Melbourne, February 1976

BELOW Bon, Mark Evans, Angus, Phil and Malcolm, London, August 1976

Brothers in arms: Bon and Angus, the Marquee, London, 1976

ABOVE On the rampage:
Angus at The Old Waldorf,
San Francisco, September
1977

BELOW Early UK gig at The
Nashville Rooms, London,
April 1976

OPPOSITE PAGE, TOP RIGHT
Bon admires Iggy Pop's
body paint, backstage at
the Whiskey, Los Angeles,
August 1977

OPPOSITE PAGE, BOTTOM
Storming the Golden Gate:
Malcolm, Phil, Angus,
Cliff and Bon, The Old
Waldorf, San Francisco,
September 1977

BELOW Calm before the storm:
Angus during the *Powerage*
sessions at Albert Studios,
Sydney, February/March 1978

RIGHT No, this is how it's done:
Bon in Coventry, England,
November 1978

BOTTOM Cliff, Malcolm, Phil,
Angus and Bon, New York,
December 1977

ABOVE *Highway To Hell* goes Gold in the US: AC/DC's attorney John Clark, Perry Cooper, Steve Leber, Ian Jeffery, David Krebs, Bon, Ahmet Ertegun, Angus, Peter Mensch, Malcolm, Atlantic's Sheldon Vogel, Phil, Atlantic's Dave Glew, Cliff, New York, October 1979

LEFT Malcolm, Grenoble, France, December 1979

BELOW Phil, Cleveland Stadium, July 1979

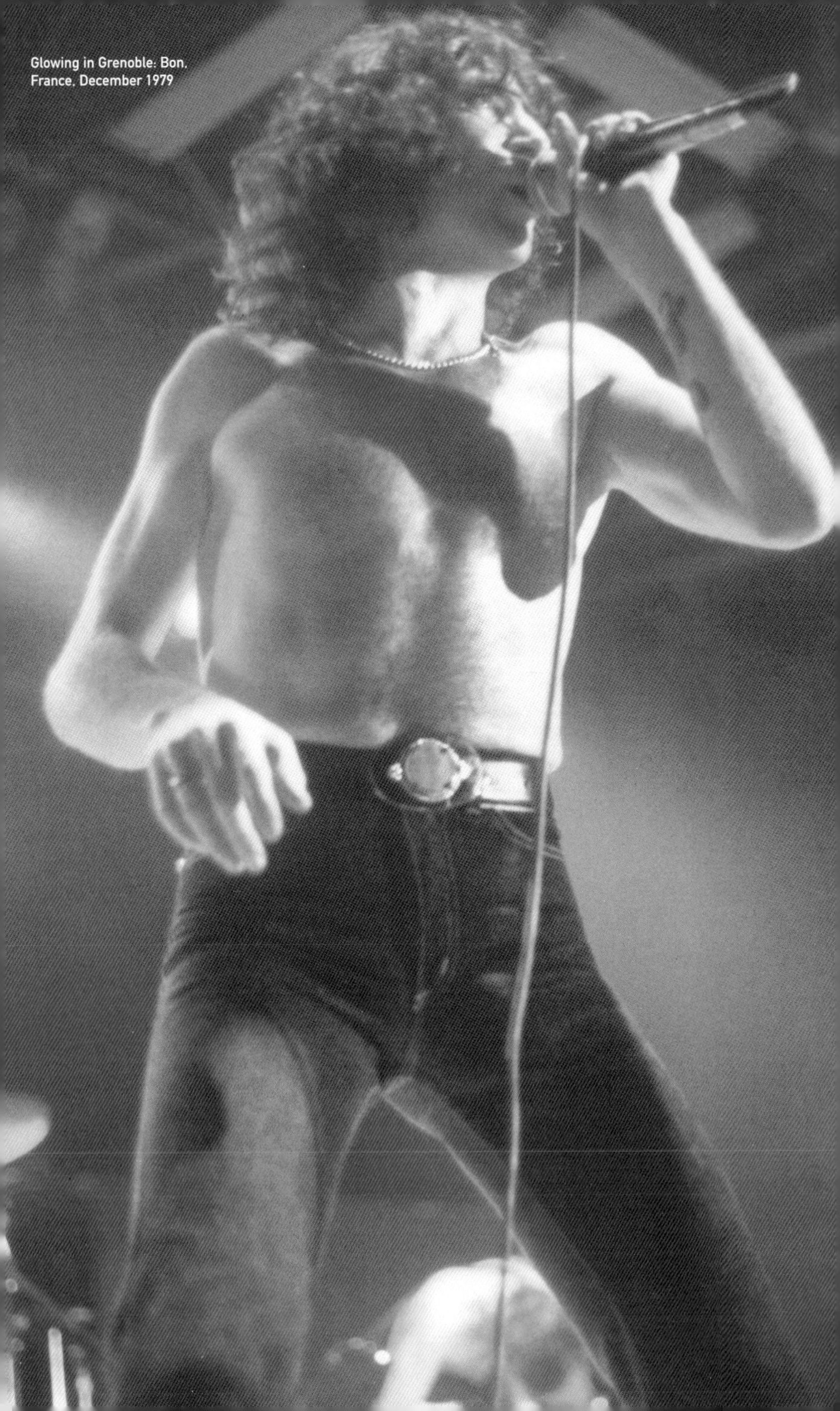

Glowing in Grenoble: Bon.
France. December 1979

I figured, "Shit! Nobody else would have her, so she wouldn't spread it."'

The problem was she then passed the baton to Phil Rudd, who, a few weeks down the track, was contacted by the girl wanting reimbursement for the cost of the medical treatment she had received. Later, when the girl came to see the band, Bon explained during The Jack that it was he who should be paying her bill. It was all about honour.

TNT certainly clearly marked the point where Michael Browning's management technique was really able to kick in.

Michael Browning: 'I came from a school of management where my heroes were people like Andrew Loog Oldham and Gordon Mills, who managed Tom Jones and Chas Chandler and those kind of people. They were very pro-active in terms of the imagery and creating controversial kind of issues. I was very influenced by those guys.

'It was the "If the parents hate them, the kids are going to dig it" concept. Just playing on that sort of bad-boy image.'

One of the main principles in that theory was to build, or at least promote, an us-and-them attitude which was already alive and well in Malcolm and Angus. They had a fierce gang mentality, and other bands, unless they were proven friends, were ignored at gigs in an exercise of intimidation by exclusion. AC/DC simply didn't need anyone else, journalists included.

Writer Jen Jewel Brown recalls going back to the band's hotel one night after a gig for a party and seeing that insular attitude quietly in action.

Jen Jewel Brown: 'You had this feeling like you were in a room with boxers or something. Like there's this whole understanding between them that you can't puncture, that you may not be included in. Part of it felt through being a female and part of it through not being part of the inner circle, the Albert's connection.

'They talked across me. I was quite struck by how insular they were and I think there was a slight macho, not so much chauvinism but an exclusivity ... that's a mateship, that's a male thing.'

TNT's promotional campaign of a mail-out to the media of red underpants with a black and white sign over the crotch that read 'Dynamite?' underlined Browning's bad-boy principle perfectly. Moreover, it worked. *TNT* sold 11,000 in its first week of release.

That in turn brought even more adoring women to the band's flame. Bon was the star and received reams of letters detailing all manner of graphic sexual proposals — one outlining the writer's oral sex intentions on the back of a tampon.

'I thought it was great,' he told Irvin Sealey in *Rock Gossip* in 1979. 'She may have been an old biddie in disguise, but I'm always open for a little excitement.'

Angus: 'Bon once told a story of some girl that came up to him one night when we'd been playing somewhere — she was standing there with two babies under her arms looking at him. He said she didn't say anything, she just said, "Hello, Bon" and talked away, but he said he kept glancing at these two babies. And he was trying to think, do I know ...'

Angus wasn't exactly out of this loop. Girls often wrote to him saying they were holding on to their virginity until they met the guitarist and enclosed contraceptives for the special day. Meanwhile, Angus was doing some saving of his own.

Chris Gilbey: 'I remember Michael telling me at one point that Angus, at the end of every week, used to float the other members of the band with money as they needed because he never spent any money on anything. All he did was drink milkshakes and smoke cigarettes. Whereas Bon was, of course, a drinker. Michael told me that Angus used to have IOUs from Bon for these things.'

But this sex and success didn't dull the fight or fighting spirit of the band. In December, during the nationwide Lock Up Your Daughters Summer Vacation tour, AC/DC opened for Skyhooks at Sydney's Hordern Pavilion.

All hell broke loose during AC/DC's set after Bon, for some reason, was on the receiving end of a band member's boot and found himself not looking down at the audience but actually sprawled among them. Fans at the front couldn't believe their luck and affectionately mauled their idol to the point that when the singer finally emerged, he looked like he'd gone far too many rounds in a heavyweight boxing title fight.

There must have been something in the air because a few weeks later, at Shepparton in northern Victoria, it was on again. Angus had barely tolerated heckling by some locals at the show, but later, with the band's road crew in tow, he was out for revenge and cornered them. It was on. The problem was the fight was raging just a few metres from the local police station. Angus was physically picked up by a cop and spent the night next door in the slammer, according to *RAM* on 23 April 1976.

Angus: 'You get some places where there's a town clown. Nine times out of 10, you ignore them. When they get physical with you, you're not going to sort of stand there and let some guy walk all over you.'

There was something prophetic in Bon giving Angus a T-shirt that read: 'Here's trouble.'

By the end of the year, the *High Voltage* album had reached Triple Gold sales status with 45,000 units. But there were no celebrations on New Year's Eve at a gig in Adelaide: instead there was a riot.

The band, through no fault of their own, had been late going on stage and the power was cut after they'd played just two songs. Bon took control of the situation and was lucky he didn't get arrested for inciting a riot. 'Countdown' host Molly Meldrum handed Bon his bagpipes and the singer was carried on a fan's shoulders out into the crowd, who, in Bon's wake, then trashed the stage and the equipment.

Australia was starting to feel like a very small and restrictive place. AC/DC had to break out.

1976

It only sounds easy to play: Angus, Mark Evans and Malcolm
recording the 'Dirty Deeds' album, Albert Studios, Sydney.

chapter 10

DIRTY DEEDS

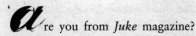

'*a*re you from *Juke* magazine? Are you Al Webb?'

The same menacing question was repeated all night at the Melbourne reception to acknowledge the Gold sales of the *High Voltage* and *TNT* albums. The AC/DC camp were furious about some remarks Webb had made and wanted to take those concerns up with the writer personally.

Frank Peters from *Juke* spent the night trying to steer clear of the Webb lynch mob, some of whom, to Peters' discomfort, seemed to have the impression that he was Webb. Peters was invited back to the band's hotel for a party anyway, and his conversation with George Young resumed where it had left off earlier; he was Al Webb, wasn't he?

After a while, Malcolm came over and grabbed Peters' shirt with a tight fist, and through even tighter clenched teeth, and advised him that he was fucking lucky he wasn't Webb. Not too surprisingly, the cover of *Juke* on 13 March 1976 screamed 'AC/DC attacks *Juke*', with a two-page spread by Peters inside.

Still, the band had made their point: don't cross us.

Frank Zappa would have been proud of their zero-tolerance approach to the media. In the late '60s, he had actively and fearlessly championed music industry oddities such as Alice Cooper and Captain Beefheart by signing them to his Straight label.

When Zappa returned to Australia in January 1976, he crossed paths with AC/DC and loved what he saw; a frenzied rock and roll band of little people, fronted by a virtuoso guitarist in a schoolboy uniform and a singer who was part poet, part pirate and part street fighter.

Malcolm, Angus and Bon loved Zappa's humour and the Young brothers marvelled at the man's musical skills.

'The first man that wanted to take us to America was Frank Zappa,' Angus told Phil Lageat in *HM* in December 1996. 'He saw us in Australia and he loved the way we played.'

The It's A Long Way To The Top single had peaked at number five on the Australian national charts the month before but as the Zappa encounter showed, opportunities for shortcuts did occasionally present themselves.

The Zappa proposal, for whatever reasons, didn't amount to anything, so attention shifted back to the recording of what would be the *Dirty Deeds Done Dirt Cheap* album. Work had begun in January at Albert Studios with George Young and Harry Vanda once again handling production.

Typically, George took a hands-on role in relation to the recording, playing bass on There's Gonna Be Some Rockin'. And not for the first time. While Mark Evans was the band's primary bass player, Malcolm and George had also contributed rhythmic rumble to AC/DC's early albums. As always, George, who could play virtually anything, would often stay back and in the quiet tinker away with what had been put on tape: the studio was his laboratory.

At least one of the songs recorded, Back Seat Confidential, would not make it onto the final album, while the traditional Scottish tune Bonny Banks Of Loch Lomond, which they retitled Fling Thing, would appear only on the Jailbreak single later in the year.

The recording sessions were staggered to allow the band to continue on the Lock Up Your Daughters Summer Vacation tour of the country until 23 January. Then, after returning to the studio in February, again not for the last time, they did dates in Melbourne which included the creation of some Australian rock and roll history.

On 23 February, 'Countdown' filmed the band performing It's A Long Way To The Top on a flatbed truck which was driven up and down Swanston Street in the heart of the Melbourne business district. The idea was a vision that Malcolm had had from the band's early days, although others have claimed the concept as their own — perhaps modelled on the launch of the Rolling Stones' 1975 US tour when they played Brown Sugar on a flatbed truck while driving through Fifth Avenue in New York.

Unsurprisingly, a planned 7 a.m. start didn't happen, but the shoot seemed simple enough — although it took some planning for producer Paul Drane. The budget for 'Countdown' wasn't exactly enormous and Drane had to save up to tackle special events filmed outside the normal TV studio environment.

Paul Drane: 'I think we had two cameras from memory and I was able to have the truck go up and down Swanston Street, although we were only shooting one way, obviously. I think we did it in about two hours, and it took about four passes to get the shots and everything that we needed: the logistics of turning the truck around, bringing the guys back, getting the camera into slightly different positions, organising that sort of stuff. I remember Bon going a bit crazy with the bagpipes, blowing on the bagpipes himself and having a good time.'

Angus: 'A few times a few of us nearly came off the truck — I know that much. It was a case of, you know, Bon would go, "I'll hold the back of your shorts," and Malcolm would lean against Bon.'

Michael Browning: 'If you see the video and look at it closely, you'll see there's not many people taking that much notice of it. But in hindsight, it was a very significant event for the band, although when it happened it was just another day in the life. It wasn't like a big, big thing.'

Total cost? Under $400. While a second version of the video was shot in the City Square, it has never been used. It simply wasn't necessary.

The rapid fire of singles continued on 1 March with the release of TNT backed with Rocker. Rocker began life as a jam around an old rock and roll progression at soundchecks, while TNT — with the opening line in the second verse mimicking an Australian television commercial for fly spray that featured an unhygienic cartoon fly — was written around a progression Malcolm came up with.

Angus: 'We had the title for it — TNT. But when we were doing the lyrics, Bon came in and said, "I'm getting stuck with this chorus." I was in the back there, chanting along, and George said, "What are you doing?" I said, "Just chanting along." He said, "Why don't you hop out and do what you're doing there? Try it." So it started from that.

'Then George said it'd be a great intro too, with that going and then Bon coming in. So it was a case of experimenting. I was never the greatest background singer in the world, so George said, "Hey, this is more your cup of tea."'

Sales of the *TNT* album itself, meanwhile, were going strong and it now held the number two slot on the charts. Those sales were reflected in the way the band was received at Melbourne's Myer Music Bowl, where they appeared before the Little River Band, which was a little like The Who opening for the Eagles.

AC/DC were once again given a wildly enthusiastic welcome, this time by the largest crowd the venue had seen for a while. For some reason, management of the Bowl cut the power before AC/DC could play an encore and the audience responded by turning the stage into a sea of cans. A film crew directed by Chris Lofven was on hand and shot scenes for a movie titled *Oz*, which was retitled as *20th Century Oz* for US release.

With both *High Voltage* and *TNT* certified Triple Gold sales status, the recording sessions for *Dirty Deeds Done Dirt Cheap* seemed less than urgent, but once again continued well into the late night and early morning.

On 13 March, it was as if the Myer Music Bowl show had never happened, with a headline spot in the middle of Warwick Farm racetrack in western Sydney over Sebastian Hardie, Ol' 55 and Finch. It was difficult to tell if the small, scattered crowd of about 200 people was due to the rain or the relatively remote location.

Bon had obviously had a few drinks and it wasn't long before he began to use the stage scaffolding as a personal gym, a fitness program the road crew moved quickly to halt. His bagpipes seemed to have had as big a day of it as their master and typically weren't prepared to function for It's A Long Way To The Top. Fading light late in the early autumn afternoon, and lack of stage lighting, soon made it hard to see who was doing what, anyway.

A free afternoon show on the Sydney Harbour foreshore under the banner of the Bicentenary Rock Stars and Stripes Concert — a curious tribute to the 200th anniversary of American independence — was at the other end of the scale in terms of crowd size. Before thousands of fans, AC/DC, who again played in fading light, were joined by Billy Thorpe, the Ted Mulry Gang and John Paul Young on a stage of floating pontoons.

This didn't present an obstacle for some frantic female fans who attempted to swim out to the bobbing stage, only to be intercepted by water police. Some would probably have been quite happy to paddle all the way to the UK, where AC/DC were headed in the coming weeks.

With the stay in Britain expected to be a lengthy one, a body of work was stockpiled ready for use before the band left. Accordingly, a video for the yet-to-be-released Jailbreak was shot for 'Countdown', once again produced and directed by Paul Drane, in a remote quarry near Sunshine in western Melbourne.

Paul Drane: 'It was fairly early days for our special effects department and because of my budget restrictions I had something like six explosives. We had one take on every one of them; we couldn't afford to stuff it up.'

Jail doors had been made and Bon was supposed to burst through them after an explosion blew them open.

'We didn't really know how much [explosive] we were going to need to make the doors fly open, and I had a couple of guys from props with sticks, trying to push the doors apart, so the hinges are not really there and they're falling over before the take.

'I needed to do some shots with Bon being shot in the back and get the close-ups. It was the first time we'd had access to anything like this, these exploding blood packs. You put this thing in a little pack on his back and it's got a very, very tiny sort of explosion in it so that it pushes the "blood" out through the shirt.

'We had to shoot that when we got back into the city, near the ABC at a tiny little park near the Elsternwick railway station. I think it was around lunchtime the next day, and again here we've got this guy [Bon] running around, we've got somebody [Malcolm] standing there with a toy gun in their hand, and then these little explosions happening. We were getting stuff like this in one take.'

Jailbreak wasn't the only video made during this period. Albert's had a third clip made for It's A Long Way To The Top and a second edition of Jailbreak.

Recording sessions for *Dirty Deeds Done Dirt Cheap* also continued at Albert Studios right up until the last week in March.

Before their departure overseas, a farewell performance by the band took place on 27 March at the Bondi Lifesaver in Sydney. Making the most of such a high-profile moment, Angus exposed his bum on stage for what was thought to be the first time and used the venue's bar, which ran the length of the room, as a catwalk. And he did it in little more than his underpants, much to the amusement and, no doubt, amazement of the audience.

Billy Thorpe joined them for a closing jam, then it was goodbye to Australia for much of the rest of the year and hello to the UK and Europe. It all seemed so sudden: Bon had only been in the band 17 months.

But George Young had a five-year plan to fire Malcolm and Angus at the rest of the world and they were well ahead of schedule.

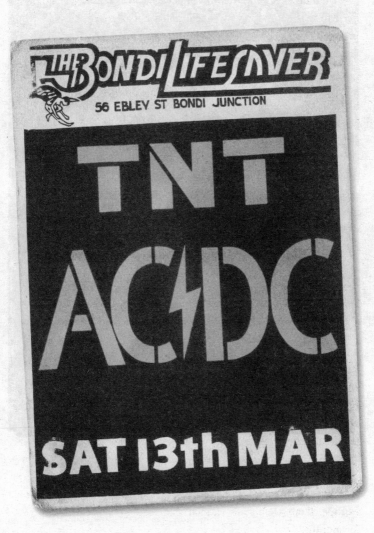

1976
Not too proud to beg: Bon and Angus, the Marquee.

chapter 11

ANARCHY IN THE UK

*a*s a good-luck charm, a leaving gift to himself or simply as an indelible reminder of his spiritual home, Bon increased his tattoo count before AC/DC left for London. His arm became the proud owner of an etching of a lion and a Scottish emblem.

A week after the band unceremoniously flew out on 1 April 1976 for their first British tour, 'Countdown' premiered the video for Jailbreak months before the single was available. The symbolism couldn't have been more powerful; AC/DC really were breaking out of Australia.

Their path in the UK had been cleared in advance with more than just the thrilling footage of High Voltage and the street party of It's A Long Way To The Top, impressive Australian sales figures, countless magazine articles and images of Bon and the ever-manic Angus.

Lobby Loyde made an enthusiastic contribution to their UK campaign.

Lobby Loyde: 'I was writing a lot of shit for them under a bodgie journalist's name. I used to write all that early AC/DC stuff for Browning. All or some of those dodgy names on those early things, that's all me, because I loved the band and all the journalists hated them, and I said, "Man, I can write this fucking shit!" We wrote reams of the shit to take to England, got it typeset and fucking printed the crap, and why not? I loved the band, so at least I was being positive about what they were like live.'

The band's departure from Australia coincided with the UK release of a single on 2 April of It's A Long Way To The Top backed with Can I Sit Next To You, Girl, which became influential radio station Radio Luxembourg's hit pick of the week. It was an encouraging start but no-one was under any illusions about the task ahead.

'We were prepared to start at the bottom again,' Malcolm told Brad Lonard in *Countdown* magazine in February 1988. 'We knew we had something.'

Lobby Loyde: 'People used to say when AC/DC left this country, "Oh mate, taking coals to Newcastle!" I used to always say, "Mate, these guys have got the hypnotic riffs — when these guys fixate on a fucking track, they rock like hell!" And I always knew they'd make it. I said, "Man, I'll bet my balls AC/DC become fucking massive and all the rest of these pricks fail." AC/DC had that international feel.'

The entire band and crew moved into a house in the London suburb of Barnes where Bon had his own room — when he was there to use it — while Malcolm and Angus shared, and Mark Evans and Phil Rudd bunked together.

Rudd soon picked up where he'd left off in Melbourne by taking on hobbies. Back at home, it had been model aeroplanes. Then he began filming everything that moved with an old movie camera he picked up. In Barnes, his attention turned to toy boats. Much to the disbelief of the local kids, he used to carve up the surface of the neighbourhood ponds and then walk away and just abandon the miniature watercraft.

While Michael Browning had been to London with The Aztecs and Bon with Fraternity, for Malcolm, Angus, Mark and Phil, being in the UK was a first. There weren't too many comforts waiting for them: in fact, a mixture of déjà vu and near tragedy had lined up in wait.

First and foremost, AC/DC's touring plans were thrown into chaos. They were originally scheduled to hit the road with The Kids — their UK label mates — who were formerly known as the Heavy Metal Kids, and whose cockney singer, Gary Holton, would later have a brush with the Australian band. Those plans disappeared into the ether.

But they still had the dates that Phil Carson, UK head of Atlantic Records, had promised with Back Street Crawler, the new outfit for former Free guitarist Paul Kossoff, who had so impressed Malcolm and Angus at Randwick Racecourse in Sydney several years earlier. They too were on Atlantic UK and their singer Terry Slesser would also later brush shoulders with AC/DC.

But the dates with Back Street Crawler, or Back Scratcher as AC/DC would come to call them, which were due to kick off on 25 April, were tragically postponed after Kossoff — whose drug difficulties were no secret — died on a flight to New York. Although Kossoff died weeks before AC/DC left Australia, there hadn't been enough time to find a suitable touring partner as replacement.

As a result, AC/DC found themselves in London in not exactly five-star accommodation, with no work but all the expenses of living in a foreign country to deal with.

Carson felt terrible. Back Street Crawler were his act, he'd sent Kossoff to America to do some promotion and now he was dead — as was AC/DC's UK tour.

Bon was in no mood for compassion for the man who brought it all undone for them. 'That cunt Paul Kossoff fucked up our first tour,' he said in a promotional item that appeared in *RAM* on 30 July 1976.

Bon had had troubles of his own. According to a source, not long after the band arrived in the UK he ended up in hospital after what was believed to be an overdose. It was allegedly a virtual repeat of what had happened in Melbourne a year before.

But Bon's English woes didn't end there. One night, he went out on his own to a local pub in Finchley where he'd served behind the bar while with Fraternity years earlier.

Reports of exactly what happened vary. Either someone didn't like the look of him, or perhaps didn't like the way Bon was looking at their girl. There's even talk that Bon tried to break up a brawl. But the result was the same; he copped a pint glass in the head and was knocked out.

For a subsequent photo shoot, he had to don a pair of dark glasses to cover his beaten face, but they only served to make him look strangely sinister. For Bon, it was all part of the rough and tumble.

All this enforced downtime — a proposed gig with heavily percussive Ghanaian outfit Osibisa just didn't seem right — coupled with the fact that they were so far from home and living in such close quarters gave Browning the opportunity to really firm up his views on his charges as individuals.

Michael Browning: 'Angus practised all day, practically just sitting on the side of his bed with his guitar, watching TV — he used to love "Get Smart". He didn't drink, he wasn't somebody who was a connoisseur of fine foods, so eating was just like eating.

'Malcolm loved soccer and going to the soccer; I played a bit of golf with Malcolm. I remember we used to go and eat Indian quite a bit, that sort of thing. He was a little bit more adventurous, I suppose. He liked to drink and go out and have a good time.

'Bon was just into the decadent, sex-crazed ... well, they all liked sex. That was probably one of the biggest pastimes. He was more intellectual, more poetic, more sophisticated in his tastes. His interests were certainly based on the finer things in life — Bon's someone who would have known a good wine.'

Eventually, a local agent, Richard Griffiths, with whom Browning had established a relationship, stepped in and ended the band's stint of unemployment. Griffiths secured AC/DC's first UK gig, a free one-off show at the tiny Red Cow in Hammersmith on 23 April.

Malcolm and Angus had one Marshall amp each and hoped to God nothing went wrong, because there was no backup gear. Legend has it that there were only about 50 people at the gig, which consisted of two 45-minute sets. When the band took a short break — so the story goes — the entire audience raced to the nearest phone booth and called all their friends. For the second set, the place was packed.

Buzz Bidstrup (drummer for The Angels): 'There wasn't a huge crowd, if I remember rightly — maybe 100 or so, 150 — and Bon was doing the thing with Angus on his shoulders and the whole show. A few people were kind of muttering afterwards about how it was a bit over the top. Not "trying too hard", but something like that.'

A few days after the Red Cow show, the band appeared, again for free, at the Nashville Rooms in West Kensington, where just three days earlier, the Sex Pistols had supported Joe Strummer's pre-Clash outfit, The 101'ers. AC/DC were billed on the posters as an 'Antipodean Punk Extravaganza', a tag John Peel, who had been playing the *High Voltage* album long before the band were signed to Atlantic, had used on the BBC's Radio 1.

Sex Pistol Glen Matlock was among those at the show.

Glen Matlock: 'I used to go and see them and I thought that it was alright.'

Lemmy from Motörhead also saw the Nashville show and was more enthused than the Pistols' bass player had been.

Lemmy: 'It was great. Bon did that thing of carrying Angus around the crowd on his shoulders. He was a great singer. He sounded like he was actually having sex while he was singing!'

Bon being Bon, that was not entirely out of the question, and on 30 April his gargle of a vocal sound was available on album for the first time in Europe with the release of *High Voltage*, a compilation of the first two Australian albums — *High Voltage* and *TNT*.

With the sheer intensity of their live shows, the band were quickly pigeonholed as being part of the emerging punk scene by the press. Many of them saw AC/DC as a joke and were fixated on making headlines which punned endlessly on the fact the band came from 'Downunda'.

AC/DC didn't suffer fools of any kind gladly, let alone idiot journalists, who they often lectured fiercely and at length about the poor, rundown state of rock and roll. So this early response only served to fire them up even more.

Malcolm and Angus had worked studiously for much of their lives refining musical abilities that suddenly, with the arrival of punk, were no longer considered necessary. Bon was more philosophical and felt that the whole punk thing was healthy, because it was giving rock and roll a good kick in the arse.

Being tied into the early punk movement might have been an easy marketing and promotional move, but it confused the very audience AC/DC wanted to tap. They were seen by some as being too punk for the rockers and too rock for the punks.

Michael Browning: 'AC/DC were perceived as being a little bit outside of that whole movement and were largely ignored for a while by a lot of people that would have otherwise probably jumped on them straight away. So, if anything, that whole punk movement worked against AC/DC actually.'

Despite the exasperation, they soon began to magnetise audiences with their power and energy and an allegedly 16-year-old Angus — according to the band's publicity, though he was really 21 — during sporadic club dates throughout May.

Their first UK tour kicked off on 11 May and included nine dates opening for the reconfigured Back Street Crawler and AC/DC's first shows at the Marquee on 11 and 12 May. It was there that Angus bared his bum for the first time outside of Australia in an act that, as far as he was concerned, was no different to Little Richard shredding his clothes or Jerry Lee Lewis slamming into his piano keys with the heel of his boots.

The dates with 'Back Scratcher' had been slashed from 30, and to add insult to injury AC/DC were supporting a band that, without Kossoff, were less well-known than they were themselves.

With a night off on 15 May, AC/DC trekked out to the Hammersmith Odeon to see what all the fuss was about with Kiss and their four-ring-circus spectacle of a show. Bon, for one, was hugely impressed.

A week later, they went to see the Rolling Stones during their string of nights at London's Earl's Court.

'They were terrible,' Angus told Bob Hart in *Spunky* on 6 September 1976. 'We would have blown them off the fucking stage.'

Headlining the Marquee for the very first time on 4 June, after recording four songs for the John Peel show on BBC radio the previous day, was a special moment.

The Stones, the Yardbirds, Hendrix and The Who — all heroes of the AC/DC camp — had appeared at the Marquee even if it had switched addresses over the years.

Just a few days after that first tour wrapped up on 8 June, the Lock Up Your Daughters tour, a 19-date club jaunt of the UK sponsored by the weekly *Sounds* magazine at the instigation of Atlantic's Phil Carson, kicked off on 11 June. *Sounds* were early champions of AC/DC. The issue of 12 June carried a leering and sweaty Angus on the cover and posed the question, 'Would you give a job to this school leaver?'

Michael Browning: '[*Sounds*] had a journalist called Phil Sutcliffe and he was very, very instrumental in turning the media vibe around, because *NME* and *Melody Maker* were very cool towards the group and *Sounds* were very, very positive. I mean, it was good for *Sounds* as well.'

The concept of the tour was something of a rock and roll extravaganza. For an admission fee of 50 pence, punters got a DJ and film clips of the big rock and roll names of the day, including the Stones and Kiss, and then an AC/DC performance, with the first few through the doors also scoring a free single. The band were amazed that they were virtually support act to someone playing records.

Ian Jeffery, who had been working with Rick Wakeman from Yes and had been asked by Carson to look after the band on the road while they were in the UK, recalls:

'They had a "best-dressed schoolboy" and "best-dressed school girl" in every place we went to. The punters would designate who was best. "What do you think of her?" And they'd go, "Oh yeah!"

And every guy would get booed, so it would depend on the loudest boo as to who won.'

It was official: AC/DC were a boys' band in the UK. The screaming teenage girls were left in Australia.

The reaction to the tour was mixed depending on where the shows were, but it kicked off in Glasgow, the spiritual home of Angus, Malcolm and Bon, who flashed his new Scottish tattoo to the crowd to wild response.

Fans had a running battle with security at City Hall from the opening song and started to set fire to seats. They also reduced the first half-dozen rows to rubble, while other seats were slashed, after the utterly exhausted band drew the line at doing a fourth encore.

The bagpipes were once again giving Bon headaches of his own.

'I don't know if these bastards will work,' he told a wildly vocal crowd at Edinburgh's Leith Theatre on the second date of the tour. 'It's like trying having sex with an octopus. You never know which one to grab, do you?'

It was during the tour that New York's Ramones made their UK debut at the Roundhouse in London on 4 July, an event that had a seismic effect on the UK punk movement. Dee Dee Ramone had heard about AC/DC through the imported English music papers, which would serve the band well for their American campaign.

Dee Dee Ramone: 'I think they were playing the Marquee and I never got to go. Oh, I wish I could have gone! That's when they had the really good papers, like *Sounds* and *NME* and *Melody Maker*. I used to buy them every week and for a long time they were the only way in America to keep in touch with rock music [in the UK], until they had *Rock Scene*. I got to like AC/DC a lot through creepy press. I think they're wonderful.'

The Lock Up Your Daughters tour concluded at the Lyceum in London on 7 July, with legendary DJ and strong AC/DC supporter John Peel officiating. Atlantic Records had organised a competition for the 'best dressed schoolboy' and 'schoolgirl we'd most like to', with prizes of albums and jeans and, for the winner overall, an

Epiphone 'folk' guitar which sat curiously with the volume of AC/DC.

The schoolboy winner didn't rate a mention, but the lucky female certainly did.

'Beautiful long legs,' Bon told Anthony O'Grady in *RAM* on 27 August 1976, 'long blonde hair, she looked bloody sexy, really sexy, garters, suspenders, stockings, mini-dress.'

While he missed out on sampling these delights, Bon's luck seemed to have changed two days later. On 9 July, the band threw him a birthday party, but while excited and touched by the prospect, he failed to show on the night or for a few days afterwards. No-one batted an eyelid and the party went on regardless. As it happened, he had been having a party all his own.

Bon told *RAM* he had 'fucked' his birthday in. He started at 11.50 p.m. and went until 12.15.

He was revelling in his reputation and was happy to take it up a notch.

'If you think normal behaviour like boozin' and screwing some chick or spitting on the pavement is obscene,' he told *RAM*, 'I'm gonna show you what obscene really is.'

Breathless live reviews began to stack up and there was a growing momentum around the band. The situation was a long way from Bon's idle experiences in the UK with Fraternity several years earlier.

He certainly never made it onto television then, as AC/DC did on 13 July at London's Wimbledon Theatre. They were filmed live for what was to be their first European TV appearance, a Marc Bolan special titled 'Rollin' Bolan' as part of the LWT program 'Superpop', which included a performance from the elf-like star. Malcolm must have been pinching himself.

English audiences were given a brief reprieve from the band's onslaught as they undertook their first dates in mainland Europe with five club shows in Sweden from 16 July. But not before Bon changed one of his onstage habits.

Angus: 'Bon used to never wear shoes on stage — he would always come out bare foot. It was really only when we started gigging around Europe that he started putting on a pair of shoes. I thought, jeez, what's happened here?!'

The day of the first European gig, London's *Sun* ran a full-page feature on the band under the headline 'Power Crazy!' Given a landmark residency at the Marquee had been secured for every Monday from 26 July until 23 August, the article couldn't have been more perfectly timed had it been paid advertising.

Carson had secured the residency after he approached Jack Barry, who ran the legendary club.

Phil Carson: 'The first time [at the Marquee a few weeks earlier], there were about 15 Swedish au-pair girls that somehow had heard of AC/DC — God knows why — and 20 or 30 other people, because people would go there anyway, because it was a rock club. But after the third week you couldn't get a ticket. That's how quickly they caught on. We still didn't sell very many records in the beginning, but they did something to a live audience, which they managed to keep doing all this time. And they built their own audience.'

Before long, a line of fans began to assemble as early as five in the afternoon, all desperate to be among a sea of more than a thousand bodies compressing themselves into the sweltering 700-capacity club to see AC/DC blast away at nine. The situation got to the point where the police had to control the crowd and local TV crews arrived to cover the mayhem. After the show, fans would emerge near naked after stripping down to try to combat the intense heat, which was many times higher than the scorching summer temperatures outside.

The band were forced to do likewise, long before they got back to the Marquee's tiny dressing room. Angus would routinely end up playing in his underwear and even played completely naked on one occasion.

'The place looked like a nudist colony by the time we finished,' Bon told Debbie Sharpe at the Melbourne *Herald* on 4 September 1976.

The Australians smashed the Marquee's attendance record on more than one occasion and, towards the end of their stay, additional nights were put on in an attempt to cope with demand. Little wonder that Jack Barry was quoted as saying AC/DC were 'the most exciting band I've seen play at the Marquee since Led Zeppelin'.

Michael Browning: 'I saw a documentary on the Marquee — which had been around for a while, admittedly — where the owners were talking about bands that had played there and they totally excluded AC/DC, which I found extraordinary. They broke the house record there — what they had there was definitely historic. I've never seen a place as packed and I've never seen so much perspiration pouring down walls. It was literally like there was a hose around the top of the walls.'

Among those who put themselves through the physically taxing experience of seeing AC/DC at the Marquee were, surprisingly, two former members of Creedence Clearwater Revival, who were on a reconnaissance mission.

Michael Browning: 'The guys from Creedence Clearwater — the rhythm section — came down, because Atlantic were talking to me about those guys getting involved in the production with AC/DC.'

The proposed alliance didn't get any further than the preliminary planning stage for unspecified reasons.

Others who crossed paths with AC/DC at the hallowed club threw down a challenge rather than a business proposition. Their rivals for supremacy at the Marquee were Eddie and The Hot Rods, who had recorded a blazing seven-inch single called Live At The Marquee.

Hot Rods singer Barrie Masters recalls the battle for the famed venue.

'With Hendrix and the Stones, it was the prestige really of the name the Marquee. To take the record in there was something else. We was close to the record a couple of times and we never did take it at first, and the guv'nor then, Jack Barry, kept winding us up. When we did finally take it we had a big celebration and a big drink-up afterwards, because we thought, great, our names will be in books and everything! Then literally it was only one week later and AC/DC took the record from us!

'The crush was so much at the front there, especially towards the end of the set, it was just getting silly. It was so hot in there, it was absolutely unbelievable. People were just passing out and the ambulance people couldn't get in to get people out. So, literally, if people passed out or were hurt, people were just picking them up and carrying them over their heads. That's the thing at the AC/DC gig I remember; people being carried out!'

Some of Angus' other antics at the Marquee did little to shut down the media headlines that tied the band to native Australian animals: like his special audience treat of stripping off and hopping around the stage like a naked perspiration- and snot-covered kangaroo, a trick he claimed he learnt from Bon.

With the sweat still stinging their eyes from the Marquee saunas, on 14 August, footage of AC/DC doing Jailbreak — which had been shot the previous month — appeared on Granada TV's 'So It Goes'. The song had been released as a single in the UK on 30 July. Five weeks later, the Sex Pistols appeared for the first time on English television on the same program and unveiled the single Anarchy In The UK.

With the rise of the Pistols and punk generally came the occupational hazard of being spat on. AC/DC, not too surprisingly, didn't tolerate being showered in audience snot and regularly went into the crowd to sort out the offenders.

They didn't come face to face with too many of the major players in the punk scene, although a bout between Bon, the street fighter, and The Stranglers' bassist, J.J. Burnel, who was a black belt in karate with a reputation for not suffering fools gladly himself, would have made for quite a title fight.

For Angus, the Pistols were simply ripping off the way Bon looked when they played at the Nashville.

Angus: 'I remember we were doing this photo shoot and the guy said, "Look, this is the Sex Pistols," and you saw [Johnny] Rotten like a Rod Stewart — blondish. All I know is they were down at this Nashville Rooms when we were playing, and the next time you saw him he had everything fucking Bon had on, every fucking thing!'

But unlike the Pistols, who were busily trying to piss off as many people in the music industry as possible, AC/DC's tireless work ethic was attracting opportunities that had the potential to take them to an entirely new level, such as a slot on the prestigious Reading Festival on 29 August.

However, before an estimated 50,000 people, and on a bill that included Ted Nugent and Eddie and The Hot Rods, for some inexplicable reason Reading was anything but a triumph. The band's performance was typically strong. But for the first time, they were playing to a very broad and very large audience, many of whom probably had no idea who they were. The fact it was raining didn't help.

Bon seemed to sense the mood from the start.

'Hello there!' he yelled. 'With all this rain we're havin', the best thing to do about it is to cause some heat amongst ya to make it evaporate before it fucking hits ya, alright? Let's see what you can do.'

'You're the ones here to prove yourselves!' murmured someone in the crowd.

Michael Browning: 'I think at that stage, we were a little bit influenced by Atlantic Records. They'd previously had Zeppelin do Reading and it was like, "This is the big time. You go there and get your own troupe backstage, sort of role-play being a superstar," and it kind of backfired a little bit.

'The DJ, I think it was John Peel, went, "Yeah?" [We were] Just posturing: "No-one's allowed on the stage, no-one's allowed backstage when they walk through." A lot of things that were just premature.

'I think that kind of set the tone and the vibe of the whole thing a little bit. It wasn't one of their greatest moments. It was just the vibe [not the band].'

Not even Angus dropping his pants to draw attention away from the huge-breasted woman who walked past the front of the stage during their show saved them. With a feeling that months of hard work had potentially gone down the drain in less than an hour, a heated debriefing was held about what the hell had gone wrong and, more importantly, why at such a pivotal, high-profile moment in their English assault.

The reasons were tough to pin-point, as there was certainly nothing lacking in the performance. In any event, it was only a temporary setback. No rethink of methods was required: staying focused was the key.

George Young had come to the UK with Harry Vanda to produce four songs for a planned EP, which was recorded in early September at Vineyard Studios where the pair had worked previously. The EP was eventually scrapped, but the songs Love At First Feel, Carry Me Home, with its disturbing lyric about Bon drinking himself to death, and Dirty Eyes, which would be reworked and retitled Whole Lotta Rosie, would all surface later.

For all the gritty excitement of the recordings, an impending trip to Germany — where AC/DC were billed and reviewed as punk rock — was infinitely more thrilling than being stuck in a studio, and the band were licking their lips in anticipation. Particularly Bon, whose brief was clear.

'We're gonna be like stormtroopers to the audiences and like the Gestapo to the groupies,' he told Anthony O'Grady in RAM on 27 August 1976.

He got half of it right. The strong sales of the High Voltage album gave the impression that the band would be welcomed with open male arms and just as open female legs. But the initial response at one of the handful of German shows was quite different. At first, the audience sat on the floor and it wasn't until the show was coming to a close that they were finally on their feet screaming.

During their stay, and in between checking out local strip shows, the band recorded I'm A Rebel — a song by Alex Young, who was living in Hamburg at the time — at Maschener Studios. George handled the production, but the recording has never been released and the song was later covered by German heavy metal act Accept.

Signing a worldwide contract with John Jackson's Cowbell Agency, who represented such acts as Rod Stewart and Roxy Music, lifted the band into the big league, and from 20 September until late October they embarked on a 19-date European tour.

It included another round of shows in Germany where some promoters insisted on a contractual clause that banned Angus from stripping on stage.

No problem. By that time they were getting around $1000 a night, a 100-fold increase on early European and UK gigs.

The tour involved opening for Rainbow, the new outfit for former Deep Purple guitarist Ritchie Blackmore. While Blackmore was not personally involved when AC/DC slugged it out with Purple's crew at Sunbury in January 1975, he had subsequently started a row all his own when he was quoted as saying that he had seen AC/DC and thought they were 'a new low in rock and roll', with nothing to offer.

The comment is thought to have stemmed from an incident that occurred earlier at the Marquee. According to Angus, who explained the situation at great length to Christie Eliezer in *Juke* on 11 December 1976, Blackmore came to the Marquee with AC/DC convert and English scene veteran Screaming Lord Sutch, who had previously dragged former Jimi Hendrix Experience members Noel Redding and Mitch Mitchell to see the band.

Blackmore wanted to jam with AC/DC during their encore, but as they were feeling the effects of the intense heat in the packed club — Angus had trouble staying upright at the end of the show — they decided not to return to the stage.

The problem was no-one told Blackmore, who was left waiting. A few days later, Blackmore was doing an interview and apparently ended up slagging off AC/DC.

Alex Young, who had known Blackmore for years, had a quiet word with him.

'"The kid brothers are supporting your band,"' Angus quoted Alex to *Juke*'s Christie Eliezer, '"and what's this shit you've been throwing at 'em in the magazine?" ... And then he said, "and I wouldn't worry about what you think of them, I'd be worrying about what they think of you — and they think you're a heap of shit."'

Despite the vitriol on both sides, the situation was soon sorted out and a bond was formed between Alex and Blackmore over numerous drinks.

The band were then free to enjoy the pleasures that cities such as Hamburg had to offer, which of course included sex. While out with Phil Rudd, Angus was confronted by a large hooker who wanted a mere nine Deutschmarks for her services.

'Fur you, little boy, 9DM,' he told 2JJ in November 1976. 'It was an offer too good to refuse! Like, she was twice me size.'

In one club, Bon and Phil Rudd couldn't believe what they were seeing. A guy slouched low in a seat near them was stark naked and jerking off. That was strange enough, then a woman appeared and slowly removed her coat. She wasn't wearing anything underneath. The pair started to have sex on a platform that then somehow floated upwards like some X-rated magic trick.

While a proposed, if premature, live album didn't materialise, AC/DC were on the rise themselves with their biggest UK tour to date; a 15-show run from 27 October, with the single of High Voltage gripped between their teeth.

Ominously, there was trouble almost immediately. The Oxford Polytechnic barred the band from performing, for the puzzling reason that their songs contained 'blatantly vulgar and cheap references to both sexes'.

After Angus took his clothes off in Birmingham and was accused of masturbating on stage, the vice squad in each area were now making AC/DC their poster boys. The wee one was even threatened with arrest in Liverpool and Glasgow if he dropped his pants on stage.

After the carnage of the band's previous visit to Glasgow, this time at the City Hall show there was a strong security presence inside, while the riot squad were stationed in the surrounding grounds.

Angus stripped off anyway, although the band jumped in front of him to block the view. There would have been a riot if he had been arrested. The presence of the riot squad had an unexpected twist as, further into the tour, police would occasionally have a drink backstage after the show and tell the band how much they enjoyed the performance. However, getting on the right side of the authorities didn't stop Bon's bagpipes from being destroyed by fans. He would never play them again.

Angus: 'He [Bon] got these little mics built specially for it, he had them put in all the pipes and he got it happening really well. He was all proud of it but then he put it down at the side of the stage [during the gig] and, of course, all these kids grabbed it and tore it to bits! Then they set fire to the curtains! That was pretty much the end of that.'

AC/DC had only arrived in England in April and had worked from the ground floor up to the point where, on 10 November, they triumphantly took to the stage at London's Hammersmith Odeon. It was their first headline performance at the venue before 2500 howling fans who were treated to a version of Big Balls from *Dirty Deeds* for what was thought to be the first and last time anywhere.

Backstage were members of The Damned, Eddie and The Hot Rods and, possibly, the Sex Pistols.

Steve Jones (Sex Pistols): 'I think I saw them once. Where was it? Fucking Hammersmith Odeon? I was so out of it drunk I don't remember anything.'

According to the media of the day, The Hot Rods were out to settle a score that night which dated back to the great Marquee turf war. It was all a publicity beat-up.

Barrie Masters (Hot Rods): 'We was mates. We came along and everything and we met up with the guys again and had a drink.'

The Odeon show was an unqualified success and a long way from the £10 to £25 gigs early in their UK assault. But it had its stressful moments when Bon, after deciding to take the Tube to the gig, proceeded to get lost on the rail network. He finally arrived at the venue 10 minutes after AC/DC were due on stage.

A few days later, Michael Browning found that he had the moment of Bon's arrival on film. To commemorate the Hammersmith milestone, he had arranged for a photographer to shoot the marquee out the front of the theatre.

Michael Browning: 'We were looking at the proof sheets four or five days later, and lo and behold here's Bon walking along on his way to the gig in front of the marquee. He'd just gotten off the Tube at Hammersmith station. Very casual.'

Before touring commitments in Britain wrapped up on 15 November, AC/DC had one more explosive gift. On 12 November, the *Dirty Deeds* album was released in the UK.

The British version of the album offered a different track listing to the original Australian release, with RIP (Rock In Peace) and Jailbreak left off, and Rocker from *TNT* and Love At First Feel from the Vineyard sessions added.

A completely new cover was also commissioned from Hipgnosis, the design company responsible for Pink Floyd and Led Zeppelin's unique album art.

The review in *Sounds* was headed up: 'Same Old Song and Dance (but so what).' It was a sentiment that a band like Status Quo had long got used to.

Francis Rossi: 'People say, "What? [The same sound] Again?" I go, "Well yeah, I'm sorry, but yeah." One of the questions people ask us is "When are you going to change your music?" And I say, "Well, you wouldn't say that to fucking BB King. He'd chin ya!"'

The 6 November issue of *NME* carried a full-page advertisement which, in keeping with the *Dirty Deeds* album's bad-boy tone, was set out as a trashy tabloid sheet called the *Sunday Purple*. A strategically worded headline, 'AC/DC shock outrage probe', was placed over a shot of the album. A breakout in the top right-hand corner read: 'Depraved schoolboy reveals all', and featured a phone number.

You could almost hear the sound of Atlantic Records drafting advance letters of apology to whoever actually had that number.

Not long after, It's A Long Way To The Top was released in America as a single and the offer of AC/DC's first-ever dates on US soil came through in the form of two gigs in Los Angeles at the Starwood late in November. The increasingly rabid reports in UK music papers such as *Sounds*, *NME* and *Melody Maker* had obviously filtered through.

High Voltage, which, like the English version of the album was the toughest moments from the Australian *High Voltage* and *TNT* recordings, had been released in America on 28 September. A promotional trip had been planned to coincide with its release but had been pushed back to November, which coincided perfectly with the proposed Starwood shows.

'People like Wolfman Jack have been playing our records for two years,' Bon told *Juke*'s Christie Eliezer on 11 December 1976, 'the same way John Peel was doing in England.'

Rolling Stone in America hadn't been among that enthusiastic bunch. Like Ritchie Blackmore, writer Billy Altman scoffed that in terms of hard rock, the album and its creators represented an 'all-time low'.

As it happened, there were visa problems which ultimately brought the entire US exercise to a grinding halt. But what really determined the fate of the trip was the fact that Atlantic in the US simply weren't interested in AC/DC.

Phil Carson: 'In America, nobody gave a shit, nobody cared.'

It was decided to leave the tour until the following year and just return to Australia as planned. Not that coming home was exactly a priority, but with America off the agenda for the moment and good audiences guaranteed in Australia, why not? The money wouldn't go astray. Touring overseas was expensive, and despite wildly enthusiastic audiences in the UK and Europe, their international album sales were not yet anywhere near a level that could sustain them.

Besides, it was coming up to Christmas — always the time to catch up with family and friends — and they needed to think about a new album. America could wait: unlike AC/DC it wasn't going anywhere. But behind the scenes, Atlantic Records were about to play hardball with their investment.

BEWARE!

THE SOUNDS

Lock up your daughters

SUMMER TOUR

'A right summer school-time frolic'

Presents
in conjunction with

ROCKWORLD

AC/DC

with STONES/KISS FILMS and hundreds of GIVAWAYS/PRIZES

AT:

GLASGOW — CITY HALL
Fri June 11th
EDINBURGH — LEITH THEATRE
Sat June 12th
SOUTHPORT — FLORAL HALL
Sun June 13th
SHEFFIELD — TOP RANK SUITE
Mon June 14th
BRADFORD — ST GEORGE'S HALL
Tues June 15th
BEDWORTH — CIVIC HALL
Thurs June 17th
LIVERPOOL — STADIUM
Sat June 19th

DOUGLAS — PALACE LIDO
Sun June 20th
CARDIFF — TOP RANK SUITE
Tues June 22nd
SWANSEA — BRANGWYN HALL
Wed June 23rd
CORBY — FESTIVAL HALL
Thurs June 24th
GUILDFORD — CIVIC HALL
Sat June 26th
BIRMINGHAM — MAYFAIR SUITE
Sun June 27th
SOUTHAMPTON — TOP RANK SUITE
Wed June 30th

GRAVESEND — WOODVILLE HALLS
Thurs July 1st
PLYMOUTH — TOP RANK SUITE
Fri July 2nd
YEOVIL — JOHNSON HALL
Sat July 3rd
BRIGHTON — TOP RANK SUITE
Sun July 4th
LYCEUM — STRAND
Wed July 7th

Starts 7·30pm

Tickets from normal outlets

See SOUNDS music paper for full details and the half-price admission coupon!
(Starts May 29 Issue)

1976
Taking a running leap: Angus, Hordern Pavilion, Sydney.

chapter 12
TROUBLE
AT HOME

'The Little Cunts Have Done It'
was at one point to be the banner for AC/DC's homecoming
Australian tour. And after seven months of enormous, sweat-soaked
strides in the northern hemisphere, they certainly played the bratty
part when they arrived back in the country on 26 November 1976.

Despite a mind-numbing 32-hour flight, they held a media
conference at Sydney Airport when they arrived; and not just in a
corner somewhere. In a first for an Australian band, the conference
took place in the main press room where Frank Sinatra and Bob
Hope previously had held court. The media scrum was so
enthusiastic that even old friends were unable to get anywhere near
the band.

Bon lapped up the attention. He had worked for a long time for
a moment such as this and he dominated the proceedings.

Meanwhile, Angus spent much of the conference innocently
drinking a milkshake as his band mates carpeted the floor with an
ever-widening sea of empty beer cans. Despite his near-shyness off

stage, the guitarist knew when to seize a moment and decided to pull down his pants for the cameras.

The event played right into the hands of a media that had heard about the horrors of punk rock and now had what they thought was the genuine article sneering, swigging and baring its bum right before them.

Well-meaning headlines such as 'Punk Rock Kings Kill The Poms', in the *Sunday Observer* back in August, hadn't helped.

Much of the soundtrack to the coming tour — officially dubbed A Giant Dose Of Rock 'N' Roll — was to be the gritty *Dirty Deeds Done Dirt Cheap* album which had finally been released in Australia on 20 September, preceded by the single Jailbreak on 14 June.

The cartoon cover art of the album couldn't have made a stronger statement about the band's image, or Bon's front-line position within it. His forearm was raised defensively and carried a tattoo of the album's name, while in the background a sullen and much smaller image of Angus, with a cigarette hanging out of his mouth, made a rude gesture. It was Michael Browning's bad-boy image marketing to the max.

The album title came from Angus' days watching a strange early '60s cartoon on television called 'Beany and Cecil'. The pair's arch-enemy was a character called Dishonest John, whose huge business card read: 'Dishonest John — Dirty Deeds Done Dirt Cheap.'

Bon walked Anthony O'Grady through several of the album's songs in *RAM* on 26 August 1976. He explained that Ain't No Fun referred to the simple truth that 'it takes a long time to make enough money to be able to fuck Britt Ekland', the then partner of Rod Stewart.

He also discussed the origins of tracks like Squealer, which was about a virgin ('but after I finish with her ...'), Big Balls ('I have too [got big balls], I just checked'), RIP or Rock In Peace ('fuck off while I'm playing'), Ride On ('about a guy who gets pissed around by chicks ... can't find what he wants') and Problem Child, which centred around Angus.

When Bon teamed up with Angus, the pair gave 2SM a slightly different explanation of some songs. The guitarist said he felt

Problem Child was about Bon, because 'he's been in jail'. Angus added that RIP was Malcolm's idea, in defence of and dedicated to old rockers like Jerry Lee Lewis who found themselves on the wrong side of the law. And Ain't No Fun, like It's A Long Way To The Top, was based initially around a line of Bon's that caught George's attention.

Overall, DDDDC was rougher than TNT and highlighted the difficulties of recording between increasingly demanding touring commitments. Songs like Ain't No Fun, RIP, Jailbreak, and particularly the lonely resignation of Ride On, were almost character studies of Bon and had a sense of impatience, wanting the world to go the fuck away, breaking free and just plain loneliness.

Bon's more mischievous side caused quite a reaction after the 5 October release of the Dirty Deeds Done Dirt Cheap single. The problem was that the number he recited in the lyric led to disturbing phone calls for a widow in Sydney's affluent eastern suburbs, although it was never intended to be a phone number at all.

Chris Gilbey: 'The number was really Bon putting into a song 36-24-36, which were traditionally at that time the optimum measurements for a woman. I said to Bon at the time, "What's the story about the phone number?" And he explained to me, "Chris, it's not a phone number! It's just 36-24-36! What's the problem here?"'

Albert's wasted no time getting the matter sorted out and not only apologised, but had the woman's phone number changed.

The Giant Dose tour was cut back before it even began, with the opening date on 2 December at Perth Entertainment Centre inexplicably cancelled. A show in Adelaide at the Apollo Stadium two days later finally got the ball rolling and it was immediately obvious — and not just from the curious opening instrumental flourish from Love Song — that this was not the same band that left for the UK.

AC/DC had always been tight and well oiled, but now they were something else again. There was no tuning up or stories from Bon, just machine precision that only daily roadwork for long periods can produce.

A film crew under the direction of Russell Mulcahy — who would later direct some of the most lavish music videos of the '80s — travelled with the band and captured all the action for a proposed documentary. Although the subsequent footage, which in rough-cut form was about two hours long, was never released in its entirety, promotional videos for Baby, Please Don't Go and Problem Child were drawn from it and subsequently used in America and Europe. Photographer Colin Stead was also on the tour to take shots for a proposed book.

Meanwhile, the storm over the band's bad-boy crimes, which had been quietly gathering strength, was being unleashed. Already fired up by reports from the UK, as was most of the media, Sydney radio station 2SM, who had been strong supporters of the band, disparagingly referred to AC/DC as a 'punk rock group' and threatened to turn their back on any future promotion of the band if Angus' striptease behaviour continued.

During this period, on a visit to radio station 2JJ with Bon, Angus dropped his pants on air. There were few complaints this time.

Even New South Wales state politicians got into the act in the wake of young female fans tattooing themselves with the name of their favourite AC/DC member. The Minister for Youth and Community Services, Rex Jackson, vowed that tattoo parlours would be policed to ensure that no-one under the legal age of 16 would be able to receive a tattoo without the proper parental authorisation.

On the other side of the planet, far more significant figures were withholding their approval: Atlantic Records in the US had rejected the *Dirty Deeds Done Dirt Cheap* album for American release.

At the time, only the likes of Ted Nugent, ZZ Top and Kiss were offering some resistance to the domination of enormously popular easy-listening acts like Peter Frampton, Fleetwood Mac and the Eagles, who were the favoured sound of American radio.

The tough rock acts only got what little airwave attention they did because they'd built up a fan base through years on the road. AC/DC hadn't had the opportunity to marshal troops through touring in the US and at the time there was no way something as raw and gritty as *Dirty Deeds* was going to make its way onto American radio playlists by itself. It was a brutally simple catch-22.

Although no-one said anything publicly, the American rejection stung. Ruining the hearing and reducing the body weight of several thousand English fans a night was fine, but the main course had always been cracking the US.

To have the second album in that campaign knocked back was a bitter psychological body blow. But far more concerning were the rumblings that continued to emanate from the States: they wanted AC/DC to get a better singer.

Americans were said to have trouble understanding Bon, and if the people working with the band couldn't make out the lyrics, how was his voice going to work on the all-important US radio networks?

The album's American snubbing was ironic given that, around the same time, a reception was held to present the band with Double Gold records for Australian sales of *Dirty Deeds* and two Platinum awards for *TNT*, which by that point had moved in excess of 100,000 copies. This was in addition to the eight Gold record awards they had already received.

What did the Americans know?

The awards reception wasn't all business, of course. Bon displayed a tattoo of a flower and a pair of swallows that was cringingly close to his pubic line, and Angus, in a by-now signature act, dropped his pants.

But, surprisingly, what received the most attention from the media was not these antics, nor the considerable combined weight of all the awards, but that the band bragged — and not entirely unbelievably — of bedding something like 100 girls since their return from the UK.

'AC/DC boast of sex orgies,' screamed the *Sunday Mirror* on 5 December. It was just the publicity they didn't need.

The day the 'orgy' story broke, Melbourne's Myer Music Bowl was in AC/DC's sights while the Bay City Rollers and all their tartan mania were across town at Festival Hall. AC/DC's reworked version of The

Jack subliminally underscored the difference between themselves and the pure, heart-throb pop of fellow Scots, the Rollers. The song featured a near-operatic introduction by Bon about his contraction of a case of gonorrhoea, tastefully set to the tune of Maria from *West Side Story*.

It prompted *RAM*'s Richard Guilliatt to report that the Myer show was 'without doubt the wildest concert I've ever been to. The audience were a bunch of wild teenage girls and male aggromaniacs.'

That feeling was heightened when Bon demanded that the 2000 people who had been listening outside be allowed in, which brought the total crowd to an estimated 5000.

But not everyone in the southern capital — where the band did a surprise gig at the Royal Oak Hotel's Tiger Room in Richmond — was welcoming, even if AC/DC were local boys made good internationally. For Bon, it was a case of history repeating itself.

A runaway teenage girl had made a beeline for AC/DC's hotel. It was only a brief visit, but shortly afterwards, having been contacted by the girl's father, the police arrived. They searched the band's rooms but found nothing. The drama, however, wasn't over.

A little later, the police called and warned that the father was far from satisfied. He'd decided to take matters into his own hands by gathering some friends to come and see Bon.

'This cop said to him,' Angus told Ian Flavin in *National Rock Star* on 5 March 1977, '"If I were you, pal, I'd be singing on my knees!"'

Thankfully, the situation calmed and no prayers were necessary.

Behind the scenes, things were not always quite as rough and tumble, as crew member Phil Eastick recalls.

'Backstage one day, Angus was just sitting about waiting for gear to get sorted or something and he was playing some brilliant acoustic guitar! I remember saying, "Fuck, man! I didn't know you could play like that!" He said, "I can, just no fucker will pay me for it."'

When the tour hit Sydney on 12 December, *RAM*'s Rory Petrie took in the Hordern Pavilion show that kicked off in sweltering summer heat at the strange hour of two in the afternoon.

'Loud seems too tame a description,' he said in the 14 January 1977 issue. 'It's more a living sound that actually penetrates the flesh and bones.'

With only about 2500 fans in the 5000-plus-seat Hordern, the Sydney show was the most glaring example of the changes that had taken place during the band's eight-month absence overseas; combined with the effect of the recent bad publicity.

In addition to the downturn in body count, there was also a shift in AC/DC's audience. Although the band were still fodder for teen mags like *Spunky* — which ran an ad with a picture of a girl who must have been no more than 12 as part of a competition to win the *Dirty Deeds* album — the wildly enthusiastic crowds of teenagers that marked their every appearance during the *TNT* album era had begun to drift away.

In their place, the ranks of the band's male fans had slowly increased from garages and workshops all over the country, maybe in response to the scene of pool hall malevolence on the cover of the *Dirty Deeds* album.

Michael Browning: 'Prior to going to England, they played to screaming girls. England was the exact opposite and then that part was imported back to Australia.'

That suited Malcolm fine. He never wanted AC/DC to be anything more than a street band.

Malcolm Young: 'The band appealed to guys. More and more guys used to come along to the performances. In the end, I remember it was like almost, well, this is a fucking guys' band really, predominantly.'

In the regional areas of the Giant Dose tour, outside of the big cities, the fun really started. There, the media reports had seeped through and welcoming committees had been prepared.

In Canberra and Wollongong, there had been none-too-subtle threats from police that the power would be pulled if Angus didn't remain suitably and fully attired for the show, or if the band's behaviour was otherwise unacceptable. The guitarist got around this in Canberra when Bon covered his bravely bared bum with a 'censored' sign.

At Albury, the concert program was banned from sale and the police seized all copies, because the caption under a shot of Bon was a rerun of his infamous quote about wanting to make enough money to be able to fuck Britt Ekland.

Ms Ekland, incidentally, would attend an AC/DC show at the Los Angeles Forum several years later, no doubt blissfully unaware of her notoriety.

There was a similar situation in Tamworth, where the mayor banned their show outright. The booking for the town hall had earlier been secured and a bond — in the event of any damage — paid. But at a subsequent meeting close to the performance date, the show was banned based on negative media reports.

A series of surprising cartoons supplied by Albert's as part of a press kit, which centred on the outfit's passion for drinking, probably didn't help the cause.

Phil Eastick recalls what he believes to be the root of the problem at Tamworth.

'The story that kind of went around on the tour at the time was that there'd been some young ladies turn up in the afternoon before the band arrived, who made it really clear that they were very, very keen to meet the band. We didn't know, but one of them was apparently the mayor's daughter. So from his perspective, she had gone missing, and that's how it started to take on a life of its own.'

Overall, the band's quite deliberate bad-boy marketing concepts, which had worked so well in the past, had, with the rise of punk rock in the UK and reports of Angus' bum-baring antics, become a public relations Frankenstein.

But the situation went from being a pain to simply surreal. In a rewind move back to the earliest days of rock and roll, when it was believed the music was poisoning the minds of the world's youth, a news crew from a television current affairs program arrived in Tamworth to cover AC/DC's assumed subversions and perversions.

The TV crew came up empty handed, unless poor Coral Browning — Michael Browning's sister and the band's publicist —

being constantly thrown into the pool at the various hotels they were staying in could be considered a threat to the social order.

Sure, hotel pool furniture found its way into the water too, but it was cooler to sit on there than in the searing summer sun. That was the extent of AC/DC's hell-raising.

The positioning in *RAM* of the news item in relation to the Tamworth banning seemed to link AC/DC with what was happening in the UK. Immediately below was a photo of the Sex Pistols' Johnny Rotten and an article about the uproar that the Pistols had created by swearing in their legendary television interview with Bill Grundy.

As it happened, AC/DC had their own 'Grundy' experience on an Australian television talk show. The presenter was chatty and pleasant until they went to air. Then his tone changed and he introduced Malcolm as a member of the 'notorious' AC/DC and, like Grundy, encouraged him to say something outrageous. Malcolm stormed off the set, only to be pursued by the show's director asking if he could storm off once more so they could film it properly.

As far as Malcolm was concerned, AC/DC weren't punks and neither were any of the bands in the UK who had recently been given the tag. He knew who the real troublemakers, the real punks were; his blues heroes, hard men who lived and died the same way and didn't give a fuck about how they dressed.

Malcolm: 'These old blues guys, like Little Walter — he was a harmonica player — just lived what they were. He lived a crazy life. He was a bit like Bon, out drinking all night, things like that, and he used to get beat up a lot. They were the real James Deans. In reality, James Dean was, you know, he wasn't this tough guy, you know what I mean? Mr Cool. He was hiding something. Big!

'The real punks were the black guys: they're the guys who had to fight from the beginning to get accepted, and all the white guys come along and just been influenced by them.'

As far as Angus was concerned, he'd seen the punk thing all before and done much better.

'They're trying to come on like the early Small Faces, remember 'em?' Angus told *Juke*'s Christie Eliezer on 11 December 1976. 'They come on stage swearing 'n' spittin' and telling everyone where to get off. But at least The Small Faces and the Rolling Stones, they were competent musically.'

Locally, AC/DC were about to come blank-expressioned face to blank-expressioned face with one of the leaders of the Australian punk movement, as recently ordained by the British media. Brisbane band The Saints had made a big impact with the single (I'm) Stranded, and were being hailed internationally as Australia's answer to the Ramones, although they evolved in parallel. They were one of two opening bands for the last show for the year on the Giant Dose tour at the Great Miami Hall on Queensland's Gold Coast.

Saints guitarist Ed Kuepper recalls:

'We weren't really used to the whole notion of backstage etiquette, I guess. We were hanging around in the dressing rooms and stuff like that, and I think they expected everybody to clear out. Their road crew got really pissed off with us and our road crew, who weren't a professional road crew — they were just friends carrying our stuff around for free. I think a bit of biffery sort of erupted between The Saints crew and the AC/DC crew.'

Browning was about to get one more headache. Phil Carson, the head of Atlantic in the UK, called.

Michael Browning: 'He [Carson] was having a lot of trouble convincing Jerry Greenberg, the President of Atlantic in America, that they should continue with the group. The advance [on the next album] was only $35,000 but we had to drop it to $25,000. That sounds nothing now, but you've got to remember we're talking about the mid '70s, and it was substantial enough for a company like Atlantic Records to be concerned about. So we had to actually drop the advance down by 10 grand in order for them to continue with the group.'

Phil Carson: 'Nobody cared at the record company [in the US], to the point that when they delivered the second album, which was Dirty Deeds, they didn't put it out. And they dropped the band.

'I managed to get to Ahmet and Nesuhi Ertegun [the founders of Atlantic] and said, "You can't drop AC/DC. Look, I sold 25,000 records in Europe, it's just started, let's keep it going." And, thank God, they listened. In spite of even the president of the company and his A&R staff not liking the band. I think Jerry [Greenberg] was listening to his A&R people, and fair enough, I think they'd sold 7000 records [in the US], so why would he continue really?'

The Giant Dose tour continued in Tasmania at the end of the first week of 1977 and saw one show only attract about 60 people. Not that they didn't have some serious fans in that part of the world.

Phil Eastick: 'Launceston is the home of some fairly nasty motorcycle riders who absolutely adored AC/DC. As Phil [Rudd] and I were coming out of the gig there, we were confronted by this group of bikies and I thought, we're going to get our arses kicked. No, they'd actually stopped to tell us how fantastic it was and invite us back to a party at their place that got seriously out of hand. The crew car was leaving at about 7.30 or eight o'clock the next morning and I had to beg to get out of there [the party] at 7.15 in order to get the car, otherwise I would have been riding the back of a Harley for the show that night. Phil was still there when I left.'

It was also in Launceston that Eastick discovered first-hand just how wrong some of the media perceptions of AC/DC were.

'A chick got up on stage and was trying to pants Angus [pull his shorts down] and I pushed her off the stage reasonably roughly — I didn't punch her or anything. They were horrified! They'd never, ever seen anyone do that to their fans, because they never needed to. At the end of the show it was like, "Man, why did you have to push her so hard?" Well, she was trying to take Angus' pants off. "Well, yeah, so? He's played with his pants down before."'

Back on the Australian mainland, further problems with officialdom weren't far away. The local council at Warrnambool in country Victoria acted on a number of complaints, which were again based on media reports, and withdrew permission for the band to play at the Warrnambool Palais.

It was the third cancellation of the tour, drawing troubling comparisons with the Sex Pistols' ill-fated Anarchy In The UK juggernaut, which had ground to a halt several weeks earlier in England, with the band having played only three of the 19 planned dates.

But it was time to fight back. In regional Victoria, they'd been threatened with police action for the slightest trouble, so the band decided to make a statement about how they had been treated. After getting word that the police on duty had been called away, the band and the entire crew stripped naked on stage. Mercifully, the tour wrapped up on 14 January at Ballarat's Wendouree Shire Hall and everyone breathed a deep sigh of relief.

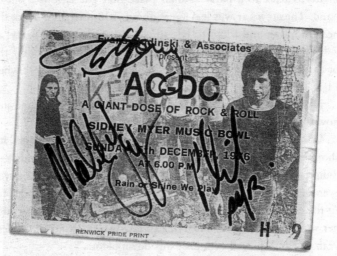

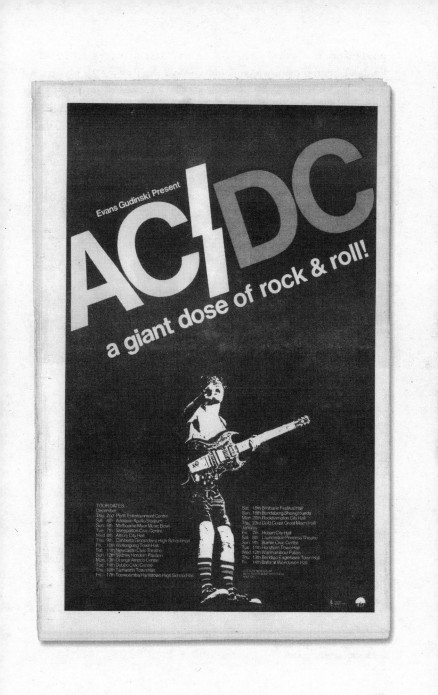

Evans Gudinski Present

AC/DC

a giant dose of rock & roll!

TOUR DATES:
December
Thu. 2nd Perth Entertainment Centre
Sat. 4th Adelaide Apollo Stadium
Sun. 5th Melbourne Myer Music Bowl
Tue. 7th Shepparton Civic Centre
Wed. 8th Albury City Hall
Thu. 9th Canberra Grundnera High School Hall
Fri. 10th Wollongong Town Hall
Sat. 11th Newcastle Civic Theatre
Sun. 12th Sydney Hordern Pavilion
Mon. 13th Orange Amoco Centre
Tue. 14th Dubbo Civic Centre
Thu. 16th Tamworth Town Hall
Fri. 17th Toowoomba Harristown High School Hall

Sat. 18th Brisbane Festival Hall
Sun. 19th Bundaberg Showgrounds
Mon. 20th Rockhampton City Hall
Thu. 23rd Gold Coast Great Miami Hall
January
Fri. 7th Hobart City Hall
Sat. 8th Launceston Princess Theatre
Sun. 9th Burnie Civic Centre
Tue. 11th Horsham Town Hall
Wed. 12th Warrnambool Palais
Thu. 13th Bendigo Eaglehawk Town Hall
Fri. 14th Ballarat Wendouree Hall

1977

Malcolm, Phil, Angus, Mark Evans
and Bon, the Rainbow, London.

chapter 13

LET THERE BE ROCK

*t*he reaction to the Giant Dose tour effectively signed Australia's death warrant as far as AC/DC were concerned. Coupled with America turning its nose up at the *Dirty Deeds* album, the band now — more than ever — had a point to prove: one that they could forcefully stick up the arse of a few people.

In any event, the impact they'd made in the UK and Europe needed to be driven home hard with an album that not only had the physical potential to flatten audiences and critics, but in the process elevate the band into the real heavyweight league.

For that reason, when they entered Albert Studios almost as soon as they arrived in Sydney after the Giant Dose tour, the game plan was to make an album with George and Harry that was a declaration of intent, rather than simply another slice of product. Others could worry about hit singles and airplay on radio.

Malcolm had noticed that some rock acts, particularly those on the American stadium circuit, had realised the power to be had in slightly longer songs and tapping into extended solos and general guitar hijinks. As no-one on the planet did better guitar fireworks than Angus, the temptation to show the competition — the emerging punks on one hand and American soft rock on the other — how rock and roll was really done was too much.

Angus: 'We said, we'll just make a fucking good guitar album! Fuck it!'

The studio set-up at Albert's was perfect for what was planned. All the amps were in the same room as the drums, which were positioned in the corner. The guitar sound spilt over into the vocal and the drum microphones so a perfect precision recording was difficult, but that was part of the charm.

The amps were nice shiny new ones too. While in the UK, the band landed a sponsorship deal with Marshall Amplification, which saw Angus and Malcolm walk away with several Marshall stacks each and Mark Evans some weighty bass gear.

Their old amps were offloaded at almost giveaway prices to eternally grateful members of The Angels. For Angels guitarist John Brewster, it was a simple act that underlined everything that took place at Albert's.

'It wasn't just about AC/DC or The Angels or Rose Tattoo or about George and Harry; it was about everybody. I'm sure we all had our own agendas, but there was this feeling that you belonged in this wonderful family. We all took interest in each other.

'Malcolm used to come to our gigs in the early days, he'd be standing out there in the audience and he'd always talk positive. He'd say, "That song you do where you do that long intro, I love that." The whole thing was just fantastic.'

Using the studios at Albert's had a similar community feeling, a little like doing shift work; there was always someone on the job before you.

Buzz Bidstrup (The Angels): 'You know how they say in submarines that they sleep the guys in rotation? They'd sleep in the same bed so you'd get into a bed and it'd already be warm? Same sort of deal with the studios. You'd get into the studio and it had just had AC/DC in it for 10 hours or something, and the studio would still be warm and still crackling, still buzzing.'

That was exactly the scene each morning after sessions for the *Let There Be Rock* album, which were fuelled by McDonald's. The material was written in the studio and tested on the piano with George.

Time was also of the essence, which suited George and Harry's studio ethic perfectly.

Harry Vanda: 'Spontaneous is basically the word. I suppose if we were talking at the time about no-bullshit rock and roll, we meant it! Balls everywhere! Not like the Americans' no-bullshit rock and roll, which takes two years to record.

'They had very, very definite ideas what it is they wanted etc. And so did we. In that field, you're always looking for bigger and better bass drums, bigger and better snare drums, and as a result everything comes up with it.

'We never worried that much about whether things were that correct as sounds. To us it was always more important whether it had the balls and the atmosphere, you know, whether it had the heart. So if we had to choose between a take which had all the heart and it was farting and buzzing and all that, we'd go for that, because we'd prefer that to the sterile version, which might have been correct but it was boring. On *Let There Be Rock*, we managed to marry a few of those things where the sound was good as well, plus the performances were all there.'

Buzz Bidstrup had seen that theory in practice on several occasions.

'They'd play for 15 or 20 minutes on this riff or feel, play the song a few times, and then George would say, "I think you got the feel there, boys! Feeling pretty good there!" Then they'd put the record button on and record the song.

'And most of that time Bon would be singing in the little side booth and the band would just be in the one studio, and Angus would be doing his solos crawling around the floor and on top of amps. They were pretty wild.'

The album's title track, for which Bon wrote the lyrics in an office in Albert's with the help of a Bible from a nearby bookstore, was Exhibit A.

Angus: 'I remember towards the end [of recording the song Let There Be Rock], the fucking amp was smoking, there was smoke pouring out of the back of the fucking amp! George is fucking screaming, "Don't stop!" I'm there fucking banging away and I could see this fucking smoke filling up the fucking room. It lasted until the end and then this fucking amp, it was just like it gave in, it just went "blaaaaaaah!". It melted. [*Let There Be Rock*] was an album where it was cooking.'

John Brewster from The Angels was a regular observer in the studio and witnessed the song Let There Be Rock being blasted onto tape.

'It was totally exciting watching them in the studio, because they weren't sitting around like experienced session musos with headphones on just going through the motions. They were performing like they do on stage, which is just their natural way of being. Such a total inspiration. I think I recall Angus' headphones went flying off and I've got a funny feeling he finished up on the floor doing his spinning around stuff!'

Let There Be Rock was completed in roughly a two-week time frame — unlike the staggered recording of the *Dirty Deeds* album — and sounded just as powerful as intended.

With it out of the way, the band played a large indoor show as part of the Festival of Sydney on 30 January at Haymarket in the inner city, on a hot, sticky summer night. For some reason, punters were asked to fork out three dollars to see AC/DC, while it only cost a dollar to take in the sweetness and light of the internationally successful Little River Band at the festival.

But the band shone and not just because of Bon's sparkling new set of teeth that he'd had installed while in London, reportedly for a not-to-be-sneezed-at £800, or maybe simply thanks to the English national health scheme. The new choppers were uncomfortable for some time and took a while to bed down, but a very drunk Bon was in cracking form and introduced Can I Sit Next To You, Girl as Can I Sit On Your Face, Girl. There were occasions around this period he also referred to the song as Can I Shit Next To You, Girl.

A small number of other shows in Adelaide, Melbourne and Perth, along with another in Sydney at Hurstville Civic Centre, followed between 12 and 15 February and were Bon's last official, publicised performances in Australia with AC/DC.

Phil Rudd for one didn't have great memories of Hurstville. In fact, his clash with a bouncer the last time the band had played at the venue had left everyone less than enthused about going back. The show itself had the same primal feel to it — both in the audience and from the stage — that had concerned Rudd, although this time there was no trouble, except that the sound system cut out a few times.

Angus took the microphone and the audience by the throat for the opening of TNT.

'Alright!' he barked. 'That's enough fucking around then! Ya alright? Come on! GET IT MOVIN!' he screamed as Rudd kept a steady beat with just his kick drum and hi hat. 'Come on! Oi! Oi! Oi!' he spat, before thinking of a better strategy. 'Fuck! Fuck! Fuck! Fuck! I wanna hear ya!'

Enthusiastic as the crowd had been, it was less than one tenth of the size of the audiences they'd played to in the UK and as such represented much of what was wrong with AC/DC playing in Australia at that point.

It was at least satisfying to find that, while Australia had largely turned its back, the readers of *Sounds* in the UK were still holding a candle. The results of the magazine's annual poll were printed on 19 February, and in the category for best new band, AC/DC ranked at number seven over Thin Lizzy and the Sex Pistols, who were placed at nine and 10 respectively. The readers of the *NME* were less enthusiastic and gave AC/DC the 14th slot in the best new act category.

The rest of the world was clearly beckoning. But that meant fewer good times in Sydney with family and friends at George's home in Epping, where Bon, Malcolm, Angus, and friends like John and Rick Brewster from The Angels, would gather for barbecues.

They were wonderful family oriented occasions that would often end with everyone jamming, or George leading in the singing of songs by Dylan, Little Richard and Fats Domino.

John Brewster: 'George would be on the piano and Angus would always throw himself into it. He's a great character — just so happens he's an unbelievable guitar player as well. And Malcolm's just the same, speaking from a rhythm guitar point of view.'

A single of Dirty Deeds Done Dirt Cheap backed with Big Balls and The Jack had been released in the UK in January to prepare for a February tour. In a pre-emptive 'fuck you!' strike, the tour poster carried a tongue-in-cheek community service-styled warning stating 'All radio stations are banned from playing this record'.

Unfortunately, its content, cartoon cover of Angus with his hands suggestively deep in his pockets, and tone represented an era and character the band had mentally left behind with the recording of the *Let There Be Rock* album. However, *Dirty Deeds* — recorded 12 months earlier but, confusingly, the 'new' album in Britain — was what the UK tour was all about.

The 30 tour dates were splashed across the entire back page of *Sounds* and kicked off on 18 February with a performance at Edinburgh University which resulted in a near riot. During Dog Eat Dog, the band had to stop playing in an attempt to restore some degree of order, when they objected to the heavy handed manner security staff adopted when fans climbed on stage.

In a slight rerun of the fear and loathing of the Giant Dose tour in Australia, three dates were cancelled after local councils, worried about anything even remotely connected to punk, refused to have rock bands of any description on their premises. Of course, having a single with songs like The Jack and Big Balls on it didn't help.

This time, the authorities were taking no chances and, not too surprisingly, the band were refused permission to appear at the Glasgow City Hall, where memories of the trouble at their previous appearances remained vivid.

The band took it all in their stride. They knew that eventually they'd be welcomed back and that revenge was a dish best served cold and very loud.

The show at London's famed Rainbow on 11 March was memorable for two reasons. First, Angus almost physically took apart the guy who spat at him, and second, Doug Thaler, booking agent with American Talent International (ATI), saw AC/DC for the first time.

Thaler already had a history of sorts with the band, having met George and Harry in the late '60s while they were in The Easybeats and he was playing with Gene Pitney.

Doug Thaler: 'I remember George Young saying in that summer [of] '67, "Hey, I got an 11-year-old brother at home that can play guitar better than anybody on this tour!" I thought he was joking. Then, some time in 1976, a promoter from Columbus, Ohio called my attention to a record that was doing really, really well in his market called It's A Long Way To The Top by this group AC/DC. I got a copy of the album sent over and I listened to the track and I thought, "Hey, this is good, I love this, it really rocks."'

Thaler noticed that the album was produced by his old friends George and Harry, and after some digging around got a phone number for Albert Productions in Sydney. He successfully placed a bid to be AC/DC's agent for North America, an association that would last until the end of 1979.

That night at the Rainbow, David Krebs, who at that point was managing Ted Nugent and Aerosmith, was with Thaler. He liked what he saw in AC/DC and subsequently offered to co-manage the band in the US with Michael Browning and split his management share in the process. Browning turned down the offer.

All the while, plans for a live album recorded in Glasgow, and several stops on the last Australian tour, were being talked up, along with the release of the Russell Mulcahy documentary of the Giant Dose tour. Both projects were eventually shelved.

On 21 March, the day of the last gig of the UK tour, both the *Let There Be Rock* album and the single of Dog Eat Dog backed by

Carry Me Home, Bon's harrowing suicide-by-drinking vision from the Vineyard sessions, were released in Australia. The album wouldn't sell anything like *TNT* or *Dirty Deeds* had, but that wasn't the issue.

The much bigger picture was that it represented a total makeover of AC/DC and a massive expansion of their sound. You could almost smell the valves in the new amplifiers burning. The grainy monochrome of the cover art was virtually a direct colour-coded match with the white Marshall logo on black speaker grille.

For Angus, the album was the guitar equivalent of the wild recordings Little Richard had done for the Specialty label in the '50s. Throughout *Let There Be Rock*, he did the rock and roll guitar equivalent of the 'sheets of sound' approach of sax master John Coltrane, with a blur of notes executed at high speed.

For the first time, real women were represented by name in Bon's lyrics. There was Ruby — her real name was Wendy, but she was nicknamed Ruby Lips by Ted Mulry — who was namechecked in the opening lines of Go Down. The band first made her acquaintance after their performance at the Moomba Festival in Melbourne in 1976.

Then there was the legendarily large Tasmanian red-head, Rosie. Bon's sexual expedition of her was celebrated on Whole Lotta Rosie, which was like a reworking of the title of Tennessee Ernie Ford's Sixteen Tons.

Angus: 'Malcolm had the guitar riff and George said, "Why don't we try — a little bit of an experiment — try [inserting] these breaks at the front [of the song]?" Malcolm and Bon were always big fans of that old Elvis Presley song — the blues thing he did early in his career, Misery or something.'

Malcolm: 'We were always big fans of early rock and roll, like Elvis and Heartbreak Hotel, things like that — the stop-and-start things, the dynamics. If anything, for Whole Lotta Rosie we were looking for a feel like Little Richard, a good old steamin' rock feel, and see what we could lay on top with the guitars. It evolved into that, but you're just looking for the vibe, what's exciting, and that's what we were listening to. Simple to put together, but still around like a classic.'

Thankfully, there were no names attached to the blues-based and just plain blue wordplay of Crabsody In Blue, which was a less effective variation on the same venereal theme as The Jack from the *TNT* album. 'Crabsody', of course, was a play on those endlessly itching crabs in the pubic hair, a widespread affliction at the time, as most bands were intimately jumping all over the same circle of ladies.

In a sign of the then prevailing times for the band in Australia, *The Sun* newspaper in Sydney gave *Let There Be Rock* a D-plus, with the cutting headline 'What a bore'.

But the recording elevated AC/DC to the status of an album band, something that had previously been the exclusive domain of the likes of the Stones, The Who and Led Zeppelin. Gone were the cartoon images of power supplies and explosives linked to the band's name, and obvious associations with the schoolboy garb of Angus. Instead, and possibly quite strategically, the live shots inside the sleeve showed Angus either bare-chested or in a striped T-shirt without a school uniform in sight.

Chris Gilbey: 'After the first and second albums I remember thinking we've got to get away from this sort of cartoon thing to becoming more of a serious band, and not appear to be frivolous. That wouldn't have been a word I would have used then, but certainly that sort of sense.'

As had been the case with *Dirty Deeds*, the band were overseas in the lead-up to the Australian release of *Let There Be Rock*, and therefore the cover art had to be sorted out in their absence. Opportunity knocked for Englishman Chris Turner, who at that point was an occasional member of Rose Tattoo, and who in the '60s had shared stages and equipment in London with one David Jones, later known as David Bowie, and Steve Marriott.

Chris Turner: '[Photographer] Colin [Stead] got me up there to the studio and said, "Can you do a run up the neck [of the guitar]?" Which of course I probably could, you know — struggle through it!

So we did the shot, and lo and behold it came out on the cover. But I did hear later on that Angus said you can tell they're Turner's fingers because they're fat! Angus and Malcolm have got really skinny fingers, so I took that in the light-hearted way it was intended.'

Stead recalls that either Malcolm or Angus or both hated the cover at first, thinking it looked too much like some sort of serious guitar tutor record, rather than the rampaging recording it was.

On the other side of the world, AC/DC were preparing for a European tour. Two days before it began, they took time out to film a London performance specially for the 'Countdown' 100th program, which was hosted by Leo Sayer. It was a long, slow day, but alcohol flowed freely from the bar and the timing was perfect for the fierce Dog Eat Dog.

The 12-date European jaunt from 5 April involved supporting Black Sabbath in France, Germany, Switzerland, Belgium, Holland and Sweden. The first show in Paris with their new road crew was a first-class disaster.

The gear AC/DC had been allocated was in extremely poor condition. However, it wasn't until they started the show that they discovered just how lousy it was. The furious band were forced to cut short their performance, but not before Angus led a physical assault on the offending equipment that conjured up visions of The Who at their destructive best.

Angus: 'We got on stage and everything went wrong, all the gear was blowing up. We were playing away and the audience was staring at us — they weren't reacting — and I think we played about 20 minutes, then we just destroyed the stage. It was just frustration that everything had gone wrong. All our equipment, guitars, amps had blown up, so the stage got wrecked, and when we left, the audience erupted! As Malcolm said, they thought that it was fucking Picasso [an artistic statement], it was art!'

The crew looked on horrified. After all, it was their responsibility to have the equipment in working order no matter what the circumstances. But while they braced themselves for a barrage from the band, instead they received an apology. It was an early gesture of loyalty that would come to typify the AC/DC approach.

For all the embarrassment, the explosive onstage retaliation against the equipment generated priceless publicity for the subsequent dates, during which Ozzy Osbourne and Bon traded footwear secrets.

Ozzy Osbourne: 'I remember we did a show in Sweden and I used to wear these brothel creepers on stage, and Bon came up to me and said, "Another sensible guy," and he showed me his. They [the brothel creepers] were great to work with on stage and I thought I was the only guy that wore them. I remember that distinctly.'

According to much-repeated legend, in Sweden Sabbath bassist Geezer Butler allegedly pulled a flick knife on Malcolm, who in typical style retaliated by punching him in the face. This resulted — so the story goes — in AC/DC being kicked off the tour.

Graham Wright, who worked as Sabbath drummer Bill Ward's drum tech, later explained what really happened on BlackSabbath.com.

'The Sabs, AC/DC and their respective road crews were having a drink in a hotel bar in Zurich, Switzerland, after the gig at the Volkhaus. Geezer was playing with a toy flick-knife comb, Malcolm mistook it for the real thing and was annoyed — end of story.'

Regardless, the tour was cut short when the final dates in Stockholm and Helsinki were cancelled. Tension had long been a fuel for the workings of AC/DC. Clashes between band members at a moment's notice were also commonplace. But nothing got in the way of the show.

Back in London after the Sabbath tour, the clash of personalities between Mark Evans and Angus — which had been brewing for some time — came to a head.

Michael Browning: 'I got a call one day from Malcolm and Angus. We were in London, I went round to their apartment and they told me they wanted to get rid of Mark. Him and Angus didn't see eye to eye. They used to have a sort of tit-for-tat thing going, but nothing that I would have ever thought was going to be gig-threatening [a threat to his position in the band].'

Evans was sacked on 3 May: his last performance with the band had been on the Sabbath tour in Gothenburg, Sweden on 22 April. On his return to Australia, he teamed up with Finch and appeared on their 1978 album *Nothing To Hide*, and then after the band changed their name to Contraband, also on their 1979 self-titled effort.

In late 1983, after a stint in The Beast — a trio with Robin Riley, formerly of Rose Tattoo — Evans flew to America to join the Michael Browning-managed Heaven for dates with Black Sabbath, Judas Priest, Mötley Crüe and others.

Auditions for a new bass player for AC/DC began immediately in London. Being off the road and off radar for any period at this point was not an option.

Rumours circulated that former Sex Pistol Glen Matlock was considered to fill Evans' shoes, a move that would have flown wildly in the face of AC/DC's sneering, anti-punk stance, although they did sometimes drink with him.

Glen Matlock: 'They never approached me. Perhaps they were thinking about it, but I was never asked. I don't quite know whether that would have been my cup of tea, to be honest. My knees are too knobbly for that, I think.'

Malcolm and Angus initially hoped to fill the bass position by drawing on their memories. Both had been very impressed with the talents and work ethic of Manfred Mann's Colin Pattenden when they'd played at Randwick Racecourse in Sydney with Free and Deep Purple several years earlier. At one point during the show, Pattenden broke a bass string but didn't miss a beat, while a contortionist roadie somehow managed to replace it.

Browning was horrified at the prospect of recruiting someone so far removed from the look and age group of AC/DC.

Michael Browning: 'He was a good player, [but] it was totally the wrong look. We had lots and lots of things to do in the music industry, particularly in America, and we didn't want to arrive over there with a bloody old-fart bass player. I was just like, you can't be serious!'

Browning's preferred candidate, on the other hand, was Englishman Cliff Williams. The Liverpool-raised Williams was not in a band at the time and unaware he was a marked man, so he was surprised to get a phone call out of the blue asking if he would like to audition.

Other than having Browning's backing, Williams wasn't exactly at any great advantage. He wasn't really a fan of the band — although he liked what he'd heard — he'd only ever seen them perform on television once or twice, and owned none of their records. Browning ordered him a crash course in AC/DC.

Michael Browning: 'I was so worried about them getting this other guy, I literally coached Cliff on what to play, and how to play it, at his audition.'

Williams' audition took place in a tiny, unassuming rehearsal room in Victoria, London. He was nervous but was quickly put at ease by the band, who put him through his paces with blues jams and songs like Live Wire.

Williams, whose easy-going personality was a strong point in his favour, knew from their reaction that he'd done well. But he didn't know exactly how well until Browning called and offered him the job.

Michael Browning: 'He just came in and nailed it and I can remember them saying, "Oh man, he did exactly what we've been looking for!" Oh, really?!'

The irony was that Williams had auditioned for Manfred Mann's Earth Band when it seemed that Pattenden was destined for AC/DC. On 27 May, Cliff Williams officially signed on as a member of the band.

Williams was older than most of AC/DC and brought a quiet depth and enormous experience. Born on 14 December 1949 in Romford, his family moved to Liverpool when he was nine. He got his first guitar at 10 and just two years later was playing the clubs.

Affected by fellow Liverpudlians The Beatles — like almost everyone else on the planet — at 14 he got his first bass and started to play, more out of practicality than any long-standing desire, when a local band put out an emergency call.

Armed with the knowledge he was able to glean from Beatles, Stones and Ry Cooder records, he rounded out his training with a single lesson from a neighbourhood bassist. What he was shown was impressive but of no use in the music he was interested in.

At 16, Williams — whose other great passion was motorbikes — put school behind him and went to work in a local factory. Music soon took priority and the band he was playing in decided to turn professional, a move that initially seemed vindicated by the offer of four shows at a local club.

However, their singer was sacked following the final gig of the engagement and that was that.

After a move to London for an unsuccessful stint with Jason Eddie and his Rock And Roll Show, Cliff hit rock bottom. With no money, no fixed address and certainly no access to hot water for bathing, he was forced to live rough, sleeping in a box.

He went on to play with Delroy/Williams Soul Show and other blues outfits. Williams then worked in a supermarket, a machine shop and even did some demolition work.

In May 1970 he placed an ad in *Melody Maker* and met guitarist Laurie Wisefield. When their first band, Sugar, split, Williams and Wisefield formed Home with scene veteran Mick Stubbs (vocals) and Mick Cook (drums).

In August 1971, their debut album, *Pause For A Hoarse Horse*, was released in the UK and Europe and in November they supported Led Zeppelin at the second Electric Magic show at the Wembley Empire Pool. Argent, the Faces and the Jeff Beck Group were among other acts Home would work with, while February 1972 saw the US release of the album.

By September, the second album, *Home*, was out in the UK and received excellent reviews and continued support from the BBC's John Peel and Bob Harris. *Melody Maker* called it one of the year's best efforts and it would eventually sell 10,000 copies in Britain alone.

A UK tour supporting Mott the Hoople was an ideal promotional vehicle, and their performance at London's Rainbow impressed the *NME*.

'Those who went to see Mott the Hoople at the Rainbow the other week,' read the review on 28 October, 'came back talking about Home, instead.'

Cliff using a violin bow on his bass was always something of a showstopper.

In January 1973, Home was named fifth 'most promising new name' in *NME*'s readers' poll. The latest of the band's BBC recordings followed as did two shows in March supporting Slade at Wembley's Empire Pool. In late July, the concept album *The Alchemist* — inspired by the book *The Dawn of Magic* by Louis Pawels — was released. Although hailed by *Disc* as 'a work of genius', it failed to make an impact commercially.

After Stubbs departed, the band toured the US as Al Stewart's backing outfit in May and June 1974. They split afterwards, when Wisefield was asked to join Wishbone Ash.

Williams stayed in America and formed the short-lived Stars, and, following studio session work, joined the more pop-oriented Bandit in 1976 in London. Their self-titled album came out in January 1977 and was very well received by the British press, but completely ignored in America.

The highlight of the next few months was five UK dates in March and April opening for Deep Purple splinter project, Paice Ashton Lord. But all people wanted to know about by then was the punk movement spearheaded by the Sex Pistols and a much talked about Australian act called AC/DC.

In May, Bandit split, then briefly became the backing band for British rock and blues godfather Alexis Korner. An album was recorded in Wales with Korner, but it was shelved until its eventual release as *The Lost Album* in Germany, when the masters were rediscovered in 1990.

Honour that it was, teaming up with Korner was never going to result in a change of fortune for the bassist, but a phone call he received soon after certainly did: an offer to try out for AC/DC.

Following a successful audition, and after jamming with his new bandmates another three times, Williams hastily tied up his personal affairs as best he could in the short time available. He had to be in Sydney in June to face a professional baptism of fire.

Not only was AC/DC's crucially important first American tour looming on the back of the stateside release of *Let There Be Rock*, but a new album was scheduled to be recorded beforehand. Williams was more than up for it all: for once in his career he was in a band that wasn't just technically razor sharp, but also had power and energy to burn.

With Williams in the line-up, AC/DC had a fresh versatility and an additional backup singer, while Bon was grateful to have someone around who was closer to his own age.

The recording sessions were productive, but in the end only helped to shape what would become the *Powerage* album the following year. Songs that came out of the sessions included Up To My Neck In You, Kicked In The Teeth Again and an early version of Touch Too Much.

Despite AC/DC's growing international work schedule, sex was still not all that far from anyone's mind. Angus explained a particularly harsh assessment process at gigs that was probably more about image than anything else.

'If there's something good lookin' you go straight to bed,' he told *People*'s Jack Mooney on 28 July 1977. 'If there's something ugly, you go out on the town.'

On a night off, Angus and Bon joined Rose Tattoo on stage at the Bondi Lifesaver for searing versions of Chuck Berry's Johnny B. Goode and Jerry Lee Lewis' Whole Lotta Shakin' Goin' On. Angus rolled on the stage just as he always did and ended up in the crowd, somewhere at the end of his extended guitar cord.

Angry Anderson (Rose Tattoo): 'Bon was one of the only singers to ever get up and sing with the band. I was never comfortable with anybody singing with my band. We held him in such great esteem and high regard and affection that he had an open invitation.

'Bon loved Rose Tattoo, and Bon, particularly, and Angus were very, very supportive. They said, "You guys have gotta get a deal and get out of here [Australia]." And we couldn't get signed, I mean, we couldn't get arrested — well, we got arrested all too frequently, which was part of the problem, but we couldn't get a record deal.

'The boys brought George and Harry down, who, as they said, could see past all the other stuff, and see that we were a talented band. Thankfully, they gave us a deal.'

In July, while still on home soil, it was decided to squeeze one more task into the schedule and film a video for Let There Be Rock, which could be put into storage until the double-sided single was released later in the year. The grainy footage was shot in Sydney's Surry Hills in a church that is now an exhibition and function space known as the Kirk Gallery.

In keeping with the biblical theme of the song and their surroundings, Bon dressed as a priest and delivered his lyrics as a sermon, while Angus was done up as a choirboy — or perhaps an angel — complete with a halo that bobbed about with his every manic move.

The resulting video, which was shot at both the church and Albert Studios, had a painful and debilitating conclusion for the singer. When Bon jumped from the altar at the end of the song, he landed heavily on the front pews and tore all the ligaments in one of his ankles. It was just another day at the office for him, really.

There was always something going on with Bon.

That same month, the entire band returned to the Bondi Lifesaver for two performances, which put Williams on public show for the first time and not in the most ideal of circumstances. Problems getting a working visa meant that the Englishman was unable to perform with the band — at least officially.

For that reason, the Lifesaver shows were originally meant to be secret gigs, which were reportedly also to give the venue an injection of financial assistance. However, with their none-too-cryptic billing as 'The Seedies' — as they had become affectionately known — 'Dirty Deeds' and 'Surprise LiveWire International Guest Act', it didn't take a nuclear physicist to figure out who was appearing.

Their crew basically grabbed every piece of equipment they could for the occasion and piled up gear everywhere, including on the bar and outside the venue.

Phil Eastick: 'The place could actually sweat and it was sweaty that night, I tell you. I'd seen probably 100-plus [AC/DC] gigs at that point and it was probably the best thing I ever saw them do. It was just stunning.'

By the second night word had gotten around, and fans lucky enough to squeeze inside were treated to one of the truly great excessive moments in Australian rock and roll.

The Lifesaver had hosted many a memorable AC/DC show, like the time Angus trod on a glass while duckwalking his way along the bar. The soles of his sneakers were obviously too thin to protect him and a roadie went above and beyond the call of duty and bandaged his foot in gaffer tape, while the patient just kept on moving. After the show, he bled all over the dressing-room floor.

Angus: 'I think because of all the adrenalin coming out it looked worse than it was. It was a bit like a movie, you know, it was just spurting out. I think I got [blood on] a few girls that night. They went home with a bit of tomato sauce on them!'

Cliff's second show at the Lifesaver had hardened gig goers standing open-mouthed in amazement, but cheering on the activities anyway. It was all courtesy of a guest appearance by a lady friend of the band.

Fess Parker, from the night's support act Big Swifty, who later evolved into The Radiators, recalls:

'They had a van outside recording it all. There were people standing up on tables, even clinging onto walls. We'd done our set and I came out the front to watch. I was a few rows back and the next minute this girl jumps up on stage, grabs the microphone off Bon and it goes straight up under her skirt! I just couldn't believe it! This is rock and roll! And I was laughing because I was thinking, the sound guy in the recording van all of a sudden must have gone, "Where's all the top end [high frequencies] gone out of Bon's mic? What's going on here?" And she's stuck it right up inside her!

'It was a wild night — it was all going on. There was all this cheering up the back so I went up to have a look, and this roadie had this girl on the table giving her a good serve! And everyone was standing around, standing up on tables clapping.'

Angus: 'It turned into a right Babylon!'

While the shows were a roaring success, Williams' recruitment and the band's increasing popularity overseas drew scorn from some. Many card-carrying members of the Australian punk rock scene, who followed Radio Birdman and The Saints and had initially been attracted by AC/DC's intensity, honesty and sheer energy, had now turned their backs.

Roger Grierson (The Thought Criminals): 'AC/DC became too popular and Birdman were cool because they were underground. By that stage, there was a war on and there were pretty clear guidelines about who was in and who was out. AC/DC were out. Or were certainly uncool to namecheck — as they'd been on "Countdown" and stuff like that. Cliff Williams was a pretty boy and punk had happened, so they'd sold out.

'As Nick Cave says, "1977 was the year we fought the big one," and we didn't see anyone from AC/DC on our side. They failed to enlist for the war against the jive. We needed recruits and they failed to show.'

Deniz Tek (Radio Birdman): 'I recall being envious of the apparent ease with which they garnered success. We thought their music was just more of the same lame early '70s boogie trip that was so prevalent. We equated it with things like Foghat or Lobby Loyde and the Coloured Balls. We were Easybeats fans, but thought that AC/DC only were able to score because of nepotism via the family connection. They were the "enemy" only by virtue of their mainstream status. Not personal.'

Malcolm and Angus could not have given less of a fuck about what anyone, least of all the Australian punk scene, thought of them.

To them, punk rock, even in its broadest sense, which included the MC5- and Stooges-inspired Radio Birdman, was a combination of amateurism and fashion and deserved nothing more than sneering contempt. However, Malcolm later conceded that the movement did serve a purpose: to kill off the hippies.

A tour with a UK act around Christmas was pencilled in, but right now, apart from international scheduling considerations, the band simply didn't need the aggravation of doing battle yet again with ill-informed morals campaigners and unsettled local councils. Besides, they knew from the outset that survival in Australia alone was a limited and limiting prospect because of its size and population.

'We had to go and as soon as we had the money in our hands, we went,' Angus told *Juke*'s Vince Lovegrove (former vocalist with Bon in The Valentines) on 28 February 1981. 'We knew we'd have to start from scratch everywhere.'

1977
Not the Grateful Dead: Bon, Angus,
Malcolm, The Old Waldorf, San Francisco.

chapter 14

THE PROMISED LAND

*i*t wasn't long before sunrise when pioneering Australian radio figure Barry Chapman sat down for a face-to-face audience with Led Zeppelin's Jimmy Page. Towards the end of the interview in the guitarist's American hotel room, Chapman asked who — in Page's opinion — were the big bands on the horizon, acts to perhaps follow in Zeppelin's enormous footsteps.

Page responded by handing Chapman two cassette tapes. One was by The Clash, who had shown signs of being the distance runners of the UK punk pack; the other was by AC/DC. Their taking of America was officially signed off.

The 50 states had never really been an issue when AC/DC started. The images that beamed out of Australian television sets in the '60s and early '70s squarely framed England — the home of The Beatles, the Stones, The Who et al — as the pinnacle of the music market, the place to grab by the throat and be seen worldwide to do so.

That was until AC/DC actually got to the UK and realised, for all their immediate success, that the other side of the Atlantic Ocean was really where they should be focusing their energies. It was, after all, the birthplace of rock and roll and the home of so many of the heroes of Malcolm, Angus and Bon.

Jerry Lee Lewis, Little Richard, Fats Domino, Chuck Berry, Muddy Waters and Howlin' Wolf all had the red, white and blue coursing through their veins, as did jazz greats like Louis Armstrong, Miles Davis and John Coltrane. The US was also home to Elvis and Graceland, Sun and Stax Studios and Chess Records.

For those reasons, going to America was almost a pilgrimage, just as it had been for the Stones the first time. Conquering the US just made sense.

The fact that The Easybeats had only ever made cultish inroads in America was not lost on Malcolm or George and meant that a successful US campaign was all the more important.

The American release of the *Let There Be Rock* album on 15 June had cleared the ground before them and took clear, take-no-prisoners aim at the disco and soft rock that had a stranglehold on the country's airwaves and dancefloors. Atlantic were now more receptive to the band.

Phil Carson: 'I went to John Kalodner [A&R person at Atlantic US] and I said, "Listen, we got this group. Your predecessor didn't think *Dirty Deeds* was a good album, didn't want to put it out. Come to England and have a look at what they do." Which he did, as did Jerry Greenberg [president of Atlantic US], by the way. And they both got it, so they put *Let There Be Rock* out.'

The album came with a slightly revised track listing from the Australian edition — Crabsody In Blue was replaced by Problem Child — and with very different cover art. In addition to a live shot of the band on the front, the American version carried, for the first time anywhere, the band's logo in what would become their signature cold, metal-plate style, courtesy of Atlantic's Art Director, Bob Defrin.

Taken as a whole, *Let There Be Rock* was a perfect statement of intent for AC/DC's opening US assault.

Perry Cooper, who started at Atlantic in 1977 as Director of Artist Relations, recalls:

'Jerry Greenberg gave my former boss [Michael Klenfner] and I a film to look at of AC/DC. We liked what we'd heard of the band, but we'd never seen them. I gotta say my boss didn't even want to look at it, so he gave it to me. And I looked at it and I went crazy. Except for seeing Chuck Berry do that duckwalk, I'd never seen a rock band like that.

'So we decided at that point, "Let's bring them over and get them touring," because the label was thinking of dropping them at that point — at least here in the US. Because they were getting no airplay, their lyrics were dirty, supposedly, and radio just avoided them like the plague in the beginning.'

Like Doug Thaler, Cooper had a previous association with the band. When he saw AC/DC in person for the first time he was struck with a sense that he knew Cliff Williams from somewhere, but couldn't quite place where. Then it hit him.

'I said, "Were you with Al Stewart's band years ago?" He went, "Shhhhh. Don't tell anybody."'

The first leg of the US tour kicked off on 27 July in Texas. As disciplined as the band's touring protocol was, Bon, typically, was governed by his own laws of time, place and direction, as he showed on a couple of occasions prior to the first gig.

He and the band became separated on their way to Texas, after a Mexican woman at the airport had caught his attention so completely that he missed his flight. With time to kill, the pair went to a rough bar where Bon gleefully proceeded to beat all comers at the pool table.

Unfortunately, the friends of one of his conquests, which just happened to be most of the bar, didn't take too kindly to the stranger's winning streak. Bon sensed the shift in mood, strategically lost a few games and then quickly excused himself.

The first show of the 27-date US tour was opening for the hugely popular Canadian outfit Moxy at the World Armadillo Headquarters, a huge barn-like building in Austin. Again, Bon disappeared beforehand.

Ian Jeffery (tour manager): 'We'd been down there rehearsing for a couple of days and the day of the show everyone was there. "Where the fuck is Bon?" All of a sudden, 30 minutes before doors [opened], two hours late for rehearsal etc etc, this fucking pickup truck comes over the hill and there's Bon with a load of Mexican guys. He's been out to the lake partying with them and they decided to bring him to the first gig.'

The show was a baptism of fire. As a rule, fools weren't tolerated in these parts, let alone crazed miniature Australian guitarists in schoolboy gear. Everyone braced themselves for a hail of projectiles or worse. Instead, after a few minutes they were showered in blood-pumping worship.

In all his years, roadie — and subsequently author — Barry Taylor had never seen an audience as wild: '5000 very boisterous Texans in varying states of narcotic and alcoholic decay,' as he put it in his book *Singing In The Dark* in 1990.

Getting such a raucous initial response so far from home was a huge confidence boost; but then confidence was never really an issue. Self-belief wasn't in short supply in AC/DC's ranks. They knew they had the goods, even though Americans were stunned when they met the band that people as small as Angus and Malcolm, in particular, could sound so powerful.

Angus: 'When I first came to America, some of the women that used to come looking for me were like Amazons. I'd open the door and say, "It's okay, I'm just his butler."'

The doors Angus opened weren't exactly the gateways to five-star hotel accommodation. Budgets were tight and luxuries were few and far between, but then going to America was never meant to be a holiday.

Ian Jeffery: 'We were in a 12-foot rider [van] — me and [crew members] Barry Taylor and Keith Evans — and the band were in their station wagon with the guitars. We'd always call in to a Dairy Queen. We had no PDs [per diems: a daily allowance for food etc] then. We'd pool our money together, get an ice cream, fill the car up, fill the van up, go to the next gig.'

AC/DC's modest means of transportation caused problems with concert security, who refused to believe that without a limo they could be part of the show.

Angus: 'We were arriving in an old station wagon and there was many a gig you were spending half your time fighting outside with the backstage security to get into the show. A lot of the bands, they all came in the big limos and stuff.'

Nothing on the tour was left to chance. Barry Bergman of EB Marks Music, Albert's sub-publisher in the US from 1976 to 1982, recalls the efforts that were made to keep the band well away from any situation that might attract the wrong sort of attention.

Barry Bergman: 'There was an incident with a roadie in Texas, where there was some DEA [Drug Enforcement Administration] officer that came into the gig and checked their back room. One thing about this band is as long as I could see, they ran around clean. They drank a lot, except for Angus. I remember there may have been some pot in the dressing room or something, and Michael Browning sent the roadie right back to Australia.

'He was always cautious about the band having a problem with their visas, and God forbid not being allowed to play in the country. He didn't want groupies on buses, he didn't allow drugs in the dressing rooms, and wouldn't allow strangers walking in with stuff and whatnot.

'There was a time where we went to dinner after a show in a Texas city or something, and Angus walked over to a guy by the counter and said, "Can I get some tea?" The guy thought he meant drugs, thought he was talking about pot. And he took him into the back, into the kitchen. When Angus came out, he was fuming. He said, "Do you believe this? All I want is a hot cup of tea and he's trying to give me drugs!"'

The band's engagements in Florida were in a much safer setting on a bill with REO Speedwagon, who were yet to become kings of middle-of-the-road US rock and were firmly rock and roll based at the time. The first night, the pair co-headlined the Coliseum in Jacksonville, AC/DC's strongest fan base to that point, before 8000 people.

It was there, it's believed, that the Australians first encountered some of the famed locals; several members of Lynyrd Skynyrd. The two camps immediately became kindred spirits, sharing an earthy honesty and strong sense of family. Bon and Skynyrd's Ronnie Van Zant had the added bond of being poets of sorts. According to one report, Bon, Angus, Malcolm and Cliff later attended a Skynyrd rehearsal and jammed on Skynyrd's Sweet Home Alabama.

The band encountered some additional Southern hospitality when they teamed with Charlie Daniels for a charity show for muscular dystrophy, titled Day For The Kids, at the Spartatorium in Hollywood, Florida.

In an act that was 180 degrees from their reception by officialdom in Australia, and in a measure of their standing in that area, the band were presented with the keys to the city by the mayor. If anyone could die of smirking, AC/DC would have folded right there and then.

With the following two days off, the ever-gracious Skynyrd offered the band and their representatives from Atlantic who were on hand, such as Perry Cooper, seats on their plane either to see the Southerners' next show or to drop AC/DC off at their own.

Angus was yet to be fully comfortable with the experience of flying, and the lure of a nonstop party was completely lost on the tiny teetotaller. For Malcolm, the proposition was far more attractive and he eagerly accepted.

That was until his girlfriend Linda, who later became his wife, asked that he spend his all-too-brief touring downtime with her. The flight offer was subsequently declined on behalf of everyone.

Meanwhile, Bon was lapping up AC/DC's success: his confidence and his chest seemed to swell that bit more each time he strode on stage. And with good reason. He was born for this stuff.

'Here's one for ya,' he told an enthusiastic crowd at West Palm Beach, 'as soon as Angus gets himself undressed here. Have you ever seen a naked Australian before? You can't see him, he's too small.'

By the time he introduced The Jack, Bon was on a roll.

'Do you get them things out here in America?' he asked. 'Do you get social diseases, do you? Do you get The Jack?'

The audience responded wildly. AC/DC were on a winner.

Striking at regions away from the bright lights of the major cities was a practical strategy based on the fact that much of the early interest in the band was in those areas. And places like Austin, Texas and Columbus, Ohio would soon be stronger AC/DC bases than anything they had generated in the UK to that point.

Doug Thaler: 'First time I booked them there [Columbus], they played two nights at a club and drew about 4000 people, which was pretty serious. Down in Jacksonville, first time in, they played the arena: they did 8300 people in Jacksonville, Florida! Which gives you an idea how strong the audience reaction was to their music.

'I mean, you heard the music, you wanted to see that band and it sounded like it was gonna be an exciting band. And when you saw it, they didn't let you down. If you're expecting it was gonna be good, it was way beyond that — it was great.'

Nonetheless, storming America required a very different strategy from that which was used to tackle the UK and Europe.

Michael Browning: 'In the UK, there's such a concentrated media that you can actually tackle it more from a print media perspective: so you'll do a big gig in London and it'll resonate all over the country and even Europe. But in America you can do a huge gig in Columbus, Ohio, and outside of that radius people never hear about it. So the idea was to go where they had a little bit of airplay happening and build on it from there.

'Consequently, they'd go to a place like Columbus and play to a really enthusiastic audience, go up the road to Cleveland and nothing. Zilch. And then the same in Jacksonville, Florida — their first gig there was sold out [at] the Coliseum and you'd go to a town just up the road, Orlando or something, and play to 20 people. Wherever they received airplay they received massive airplay, because the reaction was so good. So like in Jacksonville, they were probably the most added band on radio, and yet nowhere else.

'I remember we were in Miami at a big show and they were running late and we were actually paid not to appear. That's how much we meant there! Here's $1500 — go away! It was a case of taking your shots where you can get them, then hoping that the next album will take you to the next stage where you start to fill up some of those gaps. Just an evolving process.'

Crucial to the band's early successes in the South was Sidney Drashin, a promoter in Jacksonville and the first person in the States to really jump up and down about the band.

Michael Browning: 'It was there [Jacksonville] and Columbus, two pockets that probably gave Atlantic Records the confidence to see that it could actually work in America. It was very crucial to the group's career.'

The tour continued with dates in the Midwest, where the band alternated between headline shows and opening slots for the likes of Foreigner, Mink DeVille, and by far best of all — as far as Malcolm and Angus were concerned — Johnny Winter.

Winter's album *Nothin' But The Blues*, which featured Muddy Waters and his band, had been released that year, and the Texan had also produced and played on Waters' 'comeback' album, *Hard Again*.

The run also included a spot opening for Santana at Shaumburg, Illinois. Photographer Ed Rottinger was working for Santana at the show.

'At the end of the AC/DC set Angus asked Carlos, who I was standing next to, if they could do one more and he said, "Go ahead, mate!!" and they brought down the house! Carlos loved them!'

On 13 August, three days before Elvis died, *Let There Be Rock* peaked on the US Billboard charts at number 154. It was a modest position, but quite an achievement nonetheless. There wasn't much celebrating at their first date in St Louis. Far from it.

A brawl broke out in the bar after the show; just like the early days on the Australian touring circuit. Bon wanted to keep his expensive new set of choppers in mint condition, but when Angus became a target, as the guitarist's unofficial bodyguard, Bon didn't hesitate, grabbing a chair and bringing the guy down with a thud.

With their credentials proven — one way or another — in middle America and the southern areas, and both Bon's and Angus' face intact, it was time for AC/DC to advance on the big cities. New York was the first in their sights. As it was their debut in the Big Apple,

Atlantic's Perry Cooper decided to give them the full New Yorker treatment.

He arranged a trip to a Yankees game and rented a limo which picked them up at the hotel. On the way out to the Bronx, they literally crossed paths with New York City's most famous couple.

Perry Cooper: 'We were on Park Avenue somewhere and stopped for a light, and there's John and Yoko walking down the block. And they [the members of AC/DC] completely freaked! I mean, I remember the guys going completely crazy.'

The New York show was on 24 August at the Palladium. After all his hard work booking the gig, Doug Thaler was furious to find the band weren't even allowed the basic courtesy of a pre-show soundcheck for their all-important NYC debut.

The Palladium performance was short but typically blazing, which only further frustrated Barry Bergman, who didn't have the success he would have liked in convincing radio station programmers to come down and see the band open for home-city heroes The Dictators.

It wasn't the New York band's first encounter with the Australians, after several regional shows together.

Andy Shernoff (The Dictators): 'They were friendly, down-to-earth guys and totally cooperative to us as an opening act, unlike many bands at the time. I particularly liked Bon; he was very funny and he reminded me of a sailor. Maybe it was the tattoo on his bicep — in those days only sailors had tattoos. Anyway, NYC was our town and they were actually third on the bill. They were great, though I don't recall the audience loving them.'

Angus unveiled his cordless guitar for the first time at the Palladium, which further increased his already breathless mobility on stage and off. In doing so, he was one of the first guitarists to take the wireless guitar technology developed by Kenny Schaffer for a test St Vitus spin.

But he hit a snag when he walked outside, planning to duckwalk triumphantly through the crowd back to the stage. Security wouldn't allow him entry, but changed their minds when AC/DC's road crew made it plain that either Angus was coming in or the security was going out. Angus came in.

At midnight, with their hair still sleeked down by sweat from the Palladium show, the band hit the hallowed punk rock turf of CBGB's as opening act for The Marbles. As if for the occasion, Bon and Angus had been interviewed by New York's *Punk* magazine, which ran the story in its May 1978 edition. The American punk scene was different to the UK chapter in both sound and appearance and had even less to do with what AC/DC was about. But in the *Punk* interview, Bon proved he could outrage as well as any of them.

Among other things, he told the magazine's John Holmstrom that he had a dream he was receiving great oral sex and that it was the first time he 'fucked a lung from the mouth'.

It seemed that some of the Palladium audience who'd retained some type of hearing function, and who could still walk, had followed the Australians down to CBGB's for a final few beers.

'Long live the king, Angus Young!' cheered one woman in a tone that had her message hanging in the air long after it burst from her throat.

'Oh! Those legs!' screamed another. 'Got a match?' yelled someone, no doubt in reference to Angus' matchstick-like legs.

The band showed no signs whatsoever of wear from the Palladium set and opened up as usual with Live Wire, before crashing into a particularly ferocious version of She's Got Balls.

At one point, Angus made the most of his recent lack of cord restriction and walked out of the club and into the street while playing. It wasn't the sort of place he'd want to be seen hanging out in on a regular basis anyway.

Angus: 'It was a toilet — I know that much! We even used it as such. I thought I'd seen them all until I'd been there.'

The head of Atlantic Records, Ahmet Ertegun, was at the show. The story goes that Bon was pissing into a bottle backstage when the regal and much-respected Ertegun appeared.

But it was Angus' brilliance on the guitar that really caught

Ertegun's attention. According to Angus in the years since, the Atlantic supremo has often raised the idea of him doing a solo blues album.

At the time, Browning believed that Atlantic simply didn't realise what they had on their hands with AC/DC.

'I quite honestly don't think the Americans had a clue about the potential of AC/DC at that point and it was really just Phil Carson in London who was a believer. He really was the champion for the group.'

Whatever Atlantic's attitude in marketing meetings, the band left New York smug in the knowledge they had made a very strong impression and left numerous perforated eardrums in their wake. They were absolutely determined to make their own space in a 'soft rock' marketplace focused on the Eagles, Fleetwood Mac and, to add insult to injury, fellow Australians the Little River Band.

They certainly worked in a non-musical sense at separating themselves from that sort of company. At one point they were paid an extra several thousand dollars just to ensure Angus kept his pants up and for Bon not to utter any obscenities.

Los Angeles was next on the agenda and Angus was again horrified to find that some people took his endless energy on stage to mean that he did drugs.

Bob Daisley was in town at the time. He knew Bon from his days on the Australian gig circuit in the late '60s and early '70s and was now playing bass in Rainbow with Ritchie Blackmore.

Bob Daisley: 'I was staying at the Sunset Marquis in West Hollywood. We were sitting by the pool, it was quite hot, and I remember Bon saying he'd love a beer. So I gave him the keys to my room and said go up and help yourself. He came back with a can of cold beer and he was happier then. The thing that made me laugh was that when we went back up to the room, he'd left a dollar next to the fridge for the beer! He was like that. Very polite and nice.'

Work in Los Angeles was three nights from 29 August at the Whiskey on Sunset Strip in West Hollywood. Like the Marquee in London, the Whiskey was a touchstone for American rock and roll, having hosted everyone from The Doors, The Velvet Underground and The Byrds, to tourists such as the Stones, The Who and The Kinks.

Three nights, however, was a big call, as radio in LA hadn't been particularly supportive of the band. But while the numbers weren't great — one estimate put the body count at around 80 the first night — Iggy Pop and Aerosmith's Steven Tyler came to see what all the fuss was about. More significant, in a subsequent business sense, was the presence at one of the shows of a curious Gene Simmons of Kiss, who was enormously impressed by what he saw.

Gene Simmons: 'You know what it's like? It's like seeing an army of soldiers on one end of the hill and you're on the other end. Nothing is going to instil less fear in you than when you see a group of soldiers marching in time and there's nothing going on in their faces — they're just going through the motions. It's paint by numbers.

'But when you see soldiers who are not marching in time — who are just going berserk and beating their chests like barbarians coming down the hill — you get a chill up your spine. You're going, "Oh my fucking God, this is real!" It scares you. They're not just going, "March left, turn right!" No, no. When you see barbarians you go, "Uh oh!"'

Simmons went backstage after the show and later took Angus to Denny's, a 24-hour restaurant just up the street, for some food.

'We sat around and talked and I said, "You're going to make it, this is going to be a big band, and I want to be a part of that. We're going to take you out on tour with us."'

Having witnessed the Kiss experience first-hand at the Hammersmith Odeon in London the previous year, the band knew exactly what the offer from Simmons meant: massive, enthusiastic audiences who liked it hard and loud — particularly in America.

It was at the Whiskey that Bon used a wireless microphone for the first time and designer Kenny Schaffer attended the show to oversee the use of his baby. The need to have the microphone switched off after use was comically illustrated.

Michael Browning: 'Johnny Young [the ever-smiling host of Australian teen talent TV show "Young Talent Time" and scene veteran] was in America driving around the countryside being a tourist. He came to the gig and he came upstairs at the Whiskey to say hello to the band. Bon had left his mic running, so we had Johnny Young talking about what a sore arse he had from driving all around America going through the PA downstairs!'

The wireless technology was slowly adopted by the entire band as the tour progressed. Apart from increased mobility for Angus, the lack of a maddening spaghetti bowl of cords made life a lot easier for the band's road crew and a safer onstage working environment generally.

Angus still had tinglingly vivid memories of a gig a few years earlier, when soaked in sweat and despite his rubber-soled shoes, he was shocked on a stage live with electricity. A roadie, who came to the rescue and grabbed his guitar, was slammed into a wall by the force of the current.

The wireless gear was also a blessing for Bon, who used to carry Angus — with his 100-foot guitar cord — through the crowd on his shoulders. The cable would get wrapped around the arms and necks of fans and generally be a nightmare.

But with Angus able to venture into the audience on his own, Bon could retire for a quick drink or smoke backstage and try to get his breath back. Not that he exactly hated his little expeditions into the crowd with Angus. They did allow him to have a hands-on approach with the women around him and have them blame his tiny passenger.

However, all this fancy new technology wasn't any indication that AC/DC were beginning to live the high life. Their existence was frugal, with no unnecessary or lavish expenses.

Barry Bergman: 'They were very cautious with their money. There wasn't much to spend, but they were very practical, very realistic. Their work ethic was second to none — I didn't know of a harder working band. They were more concerned about the show being great than they were about anything else. They didn't act like big shots, they didn't take limos and all sorts of fancy transportation to get around. In New York, they took a bus or a cab or whatever. They took public transportation.'

In September, around the release of the Problem Child single in America, the band put another major city on notice, with two shows on the second and third of the month at the Old Waldorf in San Francisco. In marked contrast to their engagements at the Whiskey, a more than respectable 750 people came through the doors each night, a sign of the much stronger radio support in the area, with local radio identity Bill Bartlett in a key supporting role.

For the second show on 3 September, the crowd was particularly vocal and were treated to some of the still-unreleased songs the band had recorded before leaving Australia — Up To My Neck In You and Kicked In The Teeth Again. But as enthusiastic as the crowd had been all night, towards the end of the show a seething Angus exploded.

'Come on! Get off your arse and get up!' he screamed with the same aggression that had characterised the show. 'Don't mind these seats here,' Bon added more diplomatically. 'They're for standing on!'

While in San Francisco, Bon, typically, made some new friends who, in a stroke of luck, just happened to distil their own alcohol. Bon disappeared with them for three days. The environment was much less easy going for the tour's final show on 7 September at the 4 O'Clock Club, a Mafia haunt in Fort Lauderdale, Florida that, incredibly, was used for a record company convention and a platform to showcase the band.

Perry Cooper: 'It was ridiculous. It was velvet, posh — it was very Mafia. That's all I can say.'

The US shows were, nevertheless, an unqualified success.

Perry Cooper: 'We started to get little pockets growing, like the Cleveland, Philadelphia, San Francisco area. I mean, they became real big AC/DC pockets. And that's where they started to break out of — there were just certain radio people that locked into them very early.'

By the end of that first US tour, which saw the band travel from one side of the country to the other and back again — often in just a matter of days — they clocked up a staggering 60,000 kilometres. But no-one had any complaints or regrets. It was all a means to an end.

Back in London before the next round of European dates, Bon was staying with his girlfriend, Silver, and was woken one night at three in the morning by two guests of hers: Rolling Stones Ron

Wood and Keith Richards, who were downstairs playing guitars. It would not be Bon's last brush with the Stones.

From mid-September through to early October, AC/DC undertook 14 headlining dates in Scandinavia, Germany, Belgium and Switzerland. There, the quiet satisfaction of the early advances they had made in the crucial US market was stopped in its tracks. In Helsinki, Finland, only a 10th of the venue's capacity was sold, while in Malmo, Sweden, the band faced a mere few hundred people in an arena that could fit several thousand.

But by the last date of the tour on 9 October at Kontich in Belgium, attendance figures were the least of anyone's concerns. The gig was marked by a near-riot when the local police tried to close it down after the band allegedly ignored a strict 11 p.m. noise curfew.

The band either couldn't hear, didn't understand or didn't care about police attempts to stop the show. Maybe all three. Then things got serious. An officer who stepped onto the stage with an Uzi machine gun was pounced on and disarmed by the road crew. From there, according to witness Paul Vinck, Angus, without missing a note, leapt into the crowd with the police in pursuit, but eventually was hit by a cop. There were also incidents between the police and the audience.

The problem was that the venue was in a residential area and beneath a café. Not too surprisingly, there had been complaints about the noise. This was AC/DC after all.

The frustrated police attempted to seize the band's equipment. But when they found that meant stripping the gear down and packing it without assistance from the road crew, they thought better of the idea.

When the band made it to the safety of the ferry for the trip back to England, behind the jokes and bravado everyone was shaking inside. They had had one hell of a scare. Those machine guns didn't have blanks in them.

When *Let There Be Rock* was unleashed on the UK on 7 October, some reacted with heavy handed tactics of their own.

Our Price record store in London's West End marked the occasion with a competition with a prize of a £500 home-music set-up for whoever could bring the biggest piece of rock to the store. Richard Morrison didn't take any chances. At the cost of £200, he had a truck and a small crane deliver a three-tonne sandstone block.

In a promising sign, the album, with the same cover art as the American edition but the original Australian track listing, became the band's first to chart in the UK and peaked at number 75.

Critical response was enthusiastic, although still somewhat patronising. A four-star review in *Sounds* had the headline: 'Body music from Wagga Wagga.'

Angus: '*Let There Be Rock* was really the album that kicked it home for us all over the world, I think. We'd gone into Britain before and we'd done a lot of touring in clubs and bars and stuff and you'd sort of got a cult thing, but it was the first record that really got into the charts.'

The snotty musical subculture of the UK at the time was perfect company for an album like *Let There Be Rock*. The key figures in the punk rock movement — the Sex Pistols, The Clash and The Damned — all released their debut albums that year. Each, like *Let There Be Rock*, was designed not to destroy rock and roll, but to reinvigorate it.

More to the point, Steve Jones, Brian James and Mick Jones — the guitarists in the Pistols, The Damned and The Clash respectively — all had major Keith Richards fixations. And in turn, Richards was, of course, like Angus, a huge Chuck Berry fan.

Even the punks thought they shared common ground with AC/DC.

Steve Jones: 'It was an image thing, though — it was just image. They [AC/DC] were like heavy metal. Even though both the Pistols and them were two great rock bands, know what I mean? They're very similar, really, in one way, but they had the long hair [so] it weren't in the image. Kids didn't see them as a punk band. Musically, they were pretty similar, I thought.'

A triumphant return to the UK saw AC/DC strike like never before with a 17-date tour from 12 October. The fact that Angus was now using cordless gear briefly caused a few problems, as some fans initially thought the band were committing the cardinal sin of miming.

A sold-out return headline show at London's Hammersmith Odeon ended up being something of a reunion with original drummer Colin Burgess, who by then was a member of opening act, the George Hatcher Band.

Colin Burgess: 'It was a huge crowd. They went on and the place was just absolutely shaking; the whole theatre was actually moving. The crowd went berserk.'

Just over a week into the tour, tragedy struck on the other side of the Atlantic. On 20 October, Lynyrd Skynyrd's plane — the same one that AC/DC were offered seats on back in August — crashed near Gillsburg, Mississippi, killing singer Ronnie Van Zant, guitarist Steve Gaines, his backup singer sister, Cassie, and tour manager Dean Kilpatrick. The AC/DC camp were stunned.

Skynyrd's 1976 live album, *One More From The Road*, was the band's strongest possible statement of who and what they were. It was just the sort of record AC/DC wanted to make and with their growing live following and the vivid onstage sound of *Let There Be Rock*, the idea of a live album was again dusted off.

The prospect of documenting a show at the Apollo in Glasgow — which, due to the frenzied enthusiasm of the crowd, they felt was the most important gig in the UK — with a live album was foremost in their minds. The idea was later expanded to include performances from Fort Lauderdale, Melbourne's Myer Music Bowl and Sydney's Bondi Lifesaver. But again, the proposal was quietly shelved for some unknown reason.

Alex Harvey had decided to retire so AC/DC took over the Sensational Alex Harvey Band's slot at London's Golders Green Hippodrome for the BBC's 'Sight & Sound' TV program, with a stereo simulcast on Radio 1.

By the end of the UK tour on 12 November, a total of 30,000 dazed patrons had been ploughed through, although they were not as shell-shocked as AC/DC would have liked. The sound system on the tour had a device fitted that limited the skull-cracking volume.

The second leg of the all-important American tour was looming, but in mid-November Bon travelled to Paris with Silver to meet up with Ron Wood and the Rolling Stones.

The Stones were recording the *Some Girls* album at Pathé Marconi Studios. Bon later told Mark Opitz about the experience.

Mark Opitz: 'They got on really well, hanging out. He might have even done some singing in there; I don't know, who knows? And he looked around the other studios and there was some other band in there and they were doing an AC/DC cover song, and he walked in and it just blew his mind.'

The band was French outfit Trust, who were recording AC/DC's Love At First Feel as their debut single. They changed the lyrics from English to French and called the song Paris By Night. Bon hung out with them for a few days and, typically, didn't forget about his new friends.

The second run at America was a 21-date affair from 16 November. Three of these performances involved opening for Rush followed by four co-headlining shows with the far more rock and roll-oriented and AC/DC-friendly UFO, who Bon took an immediate liking to.

When the opportunity arose, Malcolm visited Skynyrd bassist Leon Wilkeson in hospital where he was recovering from the plane crash. AC/DC had been particularly close to the bassist and, at one point during the visit, it was decided that a drink was the best possible medicine to aid Wilkeson's recovery. The bassist left his hospital bed and with Malcolm made his way to a local bar, where the handicap of Wilkeson's wired-up jaw was circumvented by him drinking through a straw.

Wilkeson later travelled with AC/DC and hung out with them during his rehabilitation.

By December, the band were doing headline dates of their own in the Midwest which were pleasantly interrupted on 7 December by a concert recorded in front of a small audience at the Atlantic Recording Studios in New York City. The event, which was the brainchild of Perry Cooper, was broadcast live over Radio WIOQ in Philadelphia and hosted by Ed Sciaky.

The resulting promotional album, *Live From The Atlantic Studios*, was given to radio stations across the country and became a prized and highly priced collector's item in the years that followed. The band had done similiar sessions in the past but there was a special, even sacred quality about Atlantic Studios.

Angus: 'Aretha Franklin and people had recorded there so we knew it would sound great and that was a plus for us.'

Perry Cooper: 'We did it live and mixed it that same night. The band came back after everybody had left, and I think Jimmy Douglass [the Stones etc] mixed it. And we had it out real quick. There were a lot of radio people there. And the idea was just a real stroke. WIOQ was one of the first stations to play their records, and they were the station broadcasting it live. [It was done] totally live, one take.'

Barry Bergman: 'We were going to the studio that day, and — I'll never forget it — Bon says to me, "Barry, I'm gonna make you a star!" And I said, "Great!" I had no idea what he meant. We were in the studio, there were several hundred people there — that's a big studio. I'm standing on one end, with the audience, and they're in the other end doing their thing, and doing The Jack. And all of a sudden, in the middle of the song when they go, "She's got the jack, she's got the jack," Bon comes running across the whole studio, shoves the microphone in my mouth and says, "Sing it, Barry!"

'Bon was a madman. Bon would sing The Jack and he was running around getting the jack. On a regular basis. They needed a doctor on tour with them, not a tour manager, because these guys were wild. When it came to women, they were wild. But they were gentlemen.'

Two days after the Atlantic Studios performance, it was back on the road until 21 December, opening for Aerosmith, Styx, Blue Öyster Cult and co-headlining with Cheap Trick.

Rick Nielsen (Cheap Trick): 'Harvey Leeds, from Epic, our label at the time, had a brother who worked for Atlantic, and said this group they had just signed from Australia had a guitarist that ran around a lot like me. Harvey gave me a copy of the album and, from the first notes I heard, I've loved these guys ever since. The best rock band, bar none, that I've ever heard. When we toured together, I watched every show from the side of the stage. Nothing fancy, just great playing and great songs. No ballads.'

Then, as Gene Simmons had promised, came the dates with Kiss who were in the middle of the mammoth four-ringed-circus spectacle of the Love Gun tour, which was immortalised on Kiss' *Alive 2* album.

The headline act's attitude towards their guests made quite an impression.

Ian Jeffery: 'The first time we met Kiss was in Louisville, Kentucky. We kept getting messages, "Gene Simmons wants to meet Angus," and Angus would go, "It should be the other way around. I want to meet him, don't I?" We played our set and just before they [Kiss] were going on the messages were still coming over and Angus said, "You sure it's not the other way around?" So he [Simmons] came toddling over, and, you can imagine, seven foot six worth of nonsense decked out in his fucking gear and Angus had just finished and was in his little shorts with a towel around his shoulders. The tour was great. They [Kiss] loved AC/DC and they really looked after us well. Fucking great guys.'

It was a surreal experience. Not only was AC/DC's staging incredibly bare and workmanlike in comparison to the tonnes of amps, flame throwers, costumes and hydraulic lifts that Kiss were using, Malcolm and Angus had only one spare guitar between the two of them. And it was all they needed.

Guy Picciotto, later of Fugazi, witnessed the show at the Capital Centre in Largo, Maryland, on 19 December, two days before the end of the tour. Originally Styx were to open until the local rock radio station announced that 'some punk rock band from Australia called AC/DC' would be taking the slot.

Guy Picciotto: 'We were all super intrigued and a bit scared 'cause punk was supposed to be so over the top but we were psyched too, mainly 'cause we would be spared Styx. The place was just totally smoked out with pot. People were passing joints down the rows and smoking out in the bathrooms. My friends and I were 12 so we were totally digging how debauched the whole thing was. None of us had ever seen footage of these guys or even seen any of their album covers, so when Angus came out in the schoolboy rig we were completely blown away. It just seemed like he was actually insane. Being my first concert, I just couldn't believe how fucking loud it was.'

Picciotto recalls being amazed when Bon took Angus on his shoulders and went into the crowd.

'Probably really dangerous considering the audience was filled with brawling longhairs who probably thought Angus was gay. We had already seen two fights up near us in the cheap seats and had even seen a security guy hit a dude with a wrench down on the floor.

'Kiss played later and were great too. But I remember being so impressed with how AC/DC didn't have anything extra on stage, no production shit at all, but they rocked the place just as hard with nothing but their playing, their energy and their commitment to the moment. It took a long time before I saw anything that was as challenging, frightening and mind-expanding as that concert.'

The strength of AC/DC's performances was beginning to create very real problems. No headline act, many of which were established bands with strong sales and chart positions, wanted to be shown up night after night by the little-known name that came second or even third on the billing.

The knees of American rock, and not just those of Angus, which were always keeping time when he played, were starting to tremble.

Perry Cooper: 'Their performance was so electrifying that bands started getting nervous. Most bands, a lot of bands, were afraid.'

1978
Louder than you'll ever be: Bon and Malcolm,
supporting Ted Nugent at Seattle Coliseum.

chapter 15

POWERAGE

ngus couldn't take it any more and had to put the heckler back in his place.

It took a very special sort of arsehole to force his hand and make him break stage character and at Fresno's Selland Arena one had happily presented himself.

'Here! Oi!' Angus spat just as he was about to launch into the final guitar meltdown that signed off Bad Boy Boogie.

'Out there! Hey, PRICK! Fuckin' come 'ere! If you wanna fuckin' throw things at us, we can fuckin' heave 'em back, alright?'

It was 1978, the year that AC/DC planned to launch a barrage of projectiles at the world.

They had smelt the blood in the water that the *Let There Be Rock* album had produced and were gleefully eager to finish the job. The offensive weapon for that task was to be an album drawn, at least in part, from the songs that had been recorded in July 1977, which, by that stage, they had had plenty of time to sleep on.

The new album was just the tip of the iceberg for the year's proposed schedule. A two-week tour of Australia was to follow in late March and then AC/DC's first-ever performances in Japan. An appearance had also been lightly pencilled in at the prestigious Knebworth Festival in the UK which had hosted what was incorrectly rumoured to be the Stones' final performance in 1976 and in 1979 would host Led Zeppelin's historic 'return'.

The t's were to be crossed and the i's dotted on the band's storming career to that point, with the unleashing of the much mentioned and by now highly anticipated live album and a television documentary. At least that was the plan.

Instead, the first few months of 1978 were an exercise in crashing heavily back down to earth just as returning to Australia from Britain in late 1976 had been.

Cliff Williams' previous immigration problems were now professionally crippling. While the rest of the band arrived back in Australia two days before Christmas 1977, he failed to secure the necessary visa in London and so couldn't enter the country. To add insult to injury, an official told a frustrated Williams that his coming to Australia would put a local musician out of work. The band's road crew from the UK were also wrestling with immigration problems and the Australian Musicians' Union weighed in to attempt to rectify the situation.

AC/DC made no attempt to disguise their disgust in the media at Williams' treatment and the debilitating effect the situation had on their operations as a whole. Securing the necessary paperwork for the entire band to work in the US had been far less difficult.

And the Australian media were now also keeping a strange, sometimes confusing distance, almost as if they had disowned AC/DC in the face of growing international success.

Then there was the smiling face of the taxation department, which hit Bon hard for an estimated 11 years of back payments.

Bunkered down in Albert Studios in Sydney in early January, they could shut out all this. Mark Opitz, who, during this period, had also been helping reshape the sound of The Angels on their second album, *Face To Face*, and would later work with Cold Chisel, INXS, Kiss and Bob Dylan, engineered the sessions that were again produced by George Young and Harry Vanda. In the absence of Cliff Williams, George initially played bass for the *Powerage* sessions with songs yet again sketched up on piano.

Mark Opitz: 'Malcolm would have a few bits and pieces of songs and riffs and stuff and we just rehearsed for a month in Studio B in Albert's in King Street. We'd start at eight o'clock at night and go until whatever in the morning.'

Cliff's absence gave Bon the rare luxury of some pressure-free time to piece together lyrics to go with the rough backing tracks that were put down.

Buzz Bidstrup (The Angels): 'The thing I used to love was finding him [Bon] in one of the offices at Albert's writing some lyrics. I got to look over some of his lyric books and stuff and have a bit of a look at some things, lines he crossed out!'

For Mark Opitz, Bon in lyric-writing mode provided a wonderful snapshot of the singer's character.

Mark Opitz: 'One morning as we were finishing up and we'd recorded a lot of the tracks in terms of the bed tracks and just stupid melody vocals on top, not real lyrics, Bon came up to me and said, "Mate, have you got anything to smoke?" I said, "Yeah, I have." I had this little bit of hash in my pocket. I broke it in half and I gave him some, you know, $10 worth, not a lot. He said, "Fucking great, mate! You saved my life!" And he went off to write lyrics.'

Several months later, Opitz was wandering through the Albert's building and heard someone calling his name. It was Bon.

'He said, "Mate, I've been looking for you for ages!" And he pulls out this massive huge slab of hash and breaks it in half and gives me half. I gave him half of what I had so he gave me half of what he had. It didn't matter that it was like 20 times the size.'

One night Bon, ever the enthusiastic gig goer, went to Selina's at Coogee in Sydney's eastern suburbs to see The Angels, who were starting to pull huge crowds in the lead-up to the release of their *Face To Face* album. Not surprisingly, he ended up on stage with his friends.

John Brewster (The Angels): 'We weren't arseholes but we never let anyone on stage. Never. But Bon just fitted right into it. I don't know how it happened actually, but he got up on stage with us and I'll treasure that memory forever. I tell you, it was frightening and fortunately we delivered too.'

After a few weeks of rough work on the album, everyone breathed a huge sigh of relief when Cliff finally touched down on Australian soil late in January. They could now really throw themselves at the task of the new album.

In the studio, Angus wore and played his guitar everywhere he went, even in the toilet. His guitar work, along with Malcolm's, was again pivotal.

Mark Opitz: 'Malcolm and Angus' right hands [and] the way they hit the strings [was vital]. For example, one thing we used to do was gun the amplifiers nice and loud and hit [the strings] light. That's a trick that I actually used with The Angels as well — the same idea. The guitar sound was very important.'

George and Harry's technique for getting the strongest possible take during the sessions was as much about psychology as it was actual musicianship and skill. The idea was to create an aggressive state of mind and then channel that onto tape.

Mark Opitz: 'To do a take, we'd all come in, throw a cigarette around the room and be sitting there and someone would say, "What about that fucking so and so? What a cunt! Do you know what I mean?" And everyone would go, "Yeah, he's a cunt. What about that other so and so? What do you think of him?" "Ah, he's a cunt." And we'd get into this whole thing, George, Harry, me and the band, just putting shit on someone and then just pouring it on and on and on and on until George said, "Right, do a take now," because everyone is up to a fever pitch. They'd just pick a subject to get aggro on, whether it be a manager, whether it be someone in the industry, someone on TV. They'd pick a point and so with that they'd go in and just thrash down a take. It was just magic the way it worked.

'The intensity was incredible, the whole time, everything was intense. Angus is laidback; Malcolm's very intense; Cliff was the new boy and just wanting to please and do the right thing; Bon was Bon, you know, relaxed character, very Michael Hutchence-like in his view on life, so to speak. But George ... so intense; Harry kicked back but the intensity just from the Youngs was just insane.

'[George] could look at an ashtray and make it move just by thinking about it. He's got that determination. He could play any instrument that he laid his hands on, just pick it up and start playing it.

'Malcolm was the kind of guy who said, "You're the fucking singer; write the fucking lyrics!" So you really can't sit there under that sort of pressure and write the lyrics while they're all standing around. But obviously he [Bon] sketched some stuff in the studio and some stuff he'd get a bit of help on here and there, but primarily he'd go off and do it by himself, come back, then, say, George or whatever would help edit [it] down. Obviously Malcolm would be involved in seeing if it was okay. If Malcolm didn't like something he'd go, "That's fucked! What's that?" And off he'd go again and do something [else]. Malcolm definitely held sway in the band. But I don't think a lot of people realise that. I think most people look at it and think it's Angus' band.'

Some of the songs that were lined up for the *Powerage* album were first aired during the sessions for *Let There Be Rock*, Riff Raff believed to be among them. Opitz recalls Angus standing next to him, thanks to a cordless guitar, and tearing off the song.

'We did a lot of solos in the control room and for me to be sitting at the console while Angus is right behind me, right on my shoulder, just pouring out a solo on Riff Raff that's still there [on the album], it's legendary stuff, stuff that's printed for all time, and I'm there and I've got my hair standing on the back of my neck as he's just ripping this fucking thing to bits. Again, first or second take.'

Not everything that was recorded made the final cut. Like *Dirty Deeds*, the *Powerage* sessions stretched over a period of something like eight weeks — in addition to the time spent in the studio in July 1977 — with as much as a week or two between sessions. After a while, keeping track of what was in and what was out began to be a task in itself.

Maintaining a good supply of cigarettes was almost as challenging. At least two packets of Benson & Hedges per person were mandatory, not to calm nerves but to participate in another of the rituals that took place after a take or when a break was called.

Mark Opitz: 'Everyone would come and sit down and talk for a bit and Malcolm would come and sit down, you know, okay, well, you know, fuckin' this and fuckin' that. He'd pull out his cigarettes and he'd just toss everyone a cigarette in the room and you'd smoke. So any time anyone got a cigarette out it basically was the unwritten law you just tossed everyone else a cigarette. I know it's hard to imagine but little things like that did build up this sort of bond. [You] just didn't ask for a cigarette, you weren't asked if you wanted one, it just got tossed to you. So you'd usually end up smoking about a million cigarettes in a day.'

There were relaxing moments outside the studio, too.

On one occasion when a session finished at eight in the morning, Opitz, Malcolm and Phil Rudd hired a little runabout boat and went out into the middle of Sydney Harbour with a couple of six-packs of beer. It was a weekday morning so there were commuters on ferries on their way to work, while the band members were sitting back in the morning sun, fishing.

It was during the *Powerage* sessions that Atlantic Records in America made the first moves towards what it believed would ensure AC/DC cracked the US market sooner rather than later. The band's US agent, Doug Thaler, met with George and Harry when he came to Sydney.

Doug Thaler: '[Atlantic] realised they really had something and they were wondering how to take the next step, and, as it happened, I could speak openly with George and Harry, and they were indeed interested in giving up the reins; they felt that they'd done everything they could do for the group up to that point.'

In the meantime, Bon and Angus were non-performing special guests on Australia Day, 26 January, at Williamstown Rock Festival in Victoria, with Rose Tattoo, Skyhooks and Dragon among others. The pair arrived by helicopter and were interviewed live by

Melbourne radio station 3XY, a move that some, not unreasonably, saw as a promotional exercise for an upcoming tour.

Rumours flew around Melbourne that the band would almost certainly perform at the Eureka Hotel in Geelong on 14 March as a warm-up for a run of dates. But, with their schedule blown out by Williams' delayed arrival, the entire Australian tour, including the supposed Eureka show and an advertised appearance for the opening of Melbourne's cavernous new venue Bombay Rock on 17 March, evaporated.

The forced cancellation of the tour only added to the perception in some quarters that the band were using Australia as little more than a refuelling station between overseas tours. Basically, they were. Australia had had its chance. At least for the moment.

Powerage was completed in March. Rather than being the American-radio-friendly album that Atlantic were hoping for, though, it had an even greater, more ferocious sense of attack and aggression than *Let There Be Rock*. Worse still, at least from the Americans' standpoint, it had a deliciously muddy, primal sound, and Atlantic didn't think the album contained any potential hit singles.

Michael Browning: 'It was an important record because the group had achieved a fair bit in England and Europe and needed to get it happening in America. But I seem to recall feeling very flat about that record. I'm trying to remember why. I didn't think it lived up to what we'd hoped for in terms of the record that was going to crack America.'

In a bid to rectify the situation, Rock'n'Roll Damnation was recorded at the request of Phil Carson after the album had been completed and submitted to Atlantic, in the hope that at least this song would make it onto radio and become a hit. For this reason, the first pressings of *Powerage* in the UK didn't contain the track.

This desperate search for a hit single was strange, given that plans for an Australian greatest-hits-type album called *12 Of The Best* were well advanced by that point. But, like the previously proposed live albums, it was ultimately shelved, even though album and cassette sleeves had been printed. The band hadn't sanctioned the project and Malcolm was firmly against the idea of an AC/DC greatest-hits album, a position he has maintained throughout their career.

By April, AC/DC were back in the UK and after two days' rehearsal in London began storming through a tour that, due to demand, expanded from its original eight or nine shows to a total of 24 from 27 April. Although it had only been five months since their last British dates, the tour would sell out with the exception of just two shows.

Audiences only thought AC/DC had been loud on previous tours. This time they presented another dimension of volume again, one that made not just the ears ache but the face sting as well.

There was no better snapshot of that take-no-prisoners ethic than at the Apollo in Glasgow — or 'the Shrine', as Ian Jeffery called it — where on 30 April the band finally came good on Angus' earlier desire that the venue host the recording of an AC/DC live album.

It was an ideal choice. The show had sold out in a single day and the stage that towered four metres above the fever-pitch home-town audience not only forced the first 10 rows to crane their necks to see, but made the band look as though they were delivering a very loud sermon from on high. Such was the excitement of the crowd that they made the upstairs balcony move up and down a foot in mad worship.

Coral Browning: 'The Scots go crazy at concerts, so they built the stage up really high so the kids couldn't get on it. But at the AC/DC gig they made a human pyramid to get up to the stage. And they lit fires under the seats. It was pretty out of control!'

As Ian Jeffery put it, 'It was mental, mate. Mental.'

Seizing the sense of occasion, for the encore — a rendition of the Scottish-flavoured Fling Thing that led into Rocker — the entire band returned wearing the uniform of the Scotland football team that had just qualified for the World Cup finals.

The Apollo erupted, little knowing that if things had panned out a bit differently 15 years earlier, Malcolm Young could perhaps have been part of the country's side, if he'd pursued a football career.

While the scorching recordings that night would later make up the majority, if not all, of the *If You Want Blood You've Got It* album, the entire event was also caught on film and was later the basis for a 35-minute promotional feature for television that was shown in Europe.

Fan Brian Carr was at the show and recalls: 'The "Angus" chant [before Whole Lotta Rosie] came up a few times during the show. During the soundcheck, they played Rock'n'Roll Damnation, Gimme A Bullet and then they filmed a promo for Rock'n'Roll Damnation. Malcolm told me they filmed the whole show, as they heard the Apollo was closing down and wanted to get on film one of the last great rock venues. Even back then he said it probably never would get released.'

The Apollo show wasn't the only performance that made it to tape during the tour. A total of four of the UK performances would be recorded for the live album and it was planned to document an additional three in the US.

Powerage was dropped on Britain on 5 May and was followed two weeks later with the single Rock'n'Roll Damnation.

Malcolm: 'I know a lot of people respect it [*Powerage*]. A lot of real rock and roll AC/DC fans, the real pure rock and roll guys. I think that's the most under-rated album of them all.'

The most real of those pure rock and roll guys was the Rolling Stones' Keith Richards.

'The whole band means it,' Richards told Paul Elliott in *Kerrang!* on 30 January 1993. 'You can hear it, it has spirit.'

For some unknown reason, the version of *Powerage* released in the UK and Europe was slightly different from that available in the US, Australia and the rest of the world. The British/European album was partly remixed with different versions of Rock'n'Roll Damnation, Down Payment Blues, Gimme A Bullet, What's Next To The Moon, Gone Shootin' and Kicked In The Teeth with an added track, Cold Hearted Man.

When later issued on CD, the album mirrored the contents of the Australian/US version.

The show at London's Hammersmith Odeon didn't need the release of *Powerage* to elevate it; it had sold out two weeks before, although Angus needed the assistance of a harness to fly through the air during the encore. The theatrical days of 'Countdown' maybe weren't that distant after all.

The UK tour concluded on 29 May with two shows cancelled and rescheduled in early June after Angus fell ill.

Atlantic's call paid off on 10 June when Rock'n'Roll Damnation peaked at number 24 on the British charts, AC/DC's first Top 40 single there. This meant the band were invited to appear for the first time on 'Top of the Pops' which, under sufferance, they did on 8 June.

The promotional blitz continued in Australia where *Powerage* was released on 19 June; Angus arrived in the country late in the month to talk up the album. The pinnacle of his visit was an appearance on 'Countdown' as guest host, a role the wee guitarist sailed through thanks to his razor-sharp comic instincts and an ever-present prop: his gleaming new teeth at the reported cost of $2000, which he gleefully flashed at the cameras like a blade.

The business of the week was broken by Rose Tattoo's invitation for Angus to join them on the Tuesday night at the War and Peace disco in Parramatta in western Sydney, a venue that was a clash of several cultures. On one hand, there was the elevated dancefloor which was colour-lit from below and looked like something straight out of *Saturday Night Fever*. On the other was the dark, brooding presence of local chapters of several of Sydney's most serious bikers.

Amazingly, Angus was able to walk about in virtual anonymity. Not a soul among the 200 or so people in the small venue bothered him while he was standing at the bar with Angry Anderson after Tattoo's first set. It was only when he relieved Tattoo's Mick Cocks of his red Gibson SG at the start of the second set that it clicked with the crowd who the little guy was.

Over the next 15 minutes and through a sound system typical of Rose Tattoo — large and loud enough to be comfortably used outdoors — the extended band blasted through a slow blues and then a frantic take on Little Richard's Keep A Knockin' that had

Angry screaming the song on his knees while bent over Angus who had typically found it more comfortable to spin around on the stage than stand on it.

Angus then made his move onto the still sparsely populated dancefloor where he was met with a strange mix of grins and curiosity. The smile of one girl quickly disappeared after Angus got down on his knees before her and tried to inspect what was under her skirt. He was just trying to be friendly.

AC/DC repaired to Miami for a two-week holiday before they launched into another conquest: a massive 63-date tour of America where *Powerage* had been released on 25 May. But the downtime just bored them. AC/DC didn't relax well.

Audiences on the first leg of the US jaunt from 24 June until 3 October were served with the full force of that pent-up emotion.

The first four shows were opening for Alice Cooper on the East Coast, which coincided with *Powerage* peaking on the Billboard charts at number 133. The assault continued until late July with alternating headline shows in Texas — their performance in San Antonio was recorded — as well as Indiana, California, Utah, Oregon, Missouri and, for the first time, Canada, supporting Molly Hatchet (who, with a similar earthy spirit to Lynyrd Skynyrd, would become close friends), Ronnie Montrose, and Aerosmith.

Bon hung out more with support act Yesterday & Today than AC/DC during their time together, as they were a little looser than his band in their discipline when it came to sex, drugs and rock and roll.

With the tour came an appearance at the Texxas World Music Festival, a huge five-day affair in various venues in Dallas, featuring Aerosmith and Ted Nugent. AC/DC opened for Mahogany Rush at the Fairgrounds Complex on the second-last day of the event.

It was during the dates with Aerosmith that future AC/DC manager Peter Mensch, then tour accountant with the Boston outfit for Leber-Krebs management, first encountered the Australians. He was absolutely amazed with what he saw.

And it wasn't only Mensch's jaw that was on the ground watching AC/DC.

Joe Perry (Aerosmith): '[They were] one of the few bands that opened for us that I would go down and watch play almost every night. It would be like, hey, Angus is doing that fryin' bacon thing again on stage! They were great. They reduced the elements of rock and roll to the basics and they didn't pull any punches, and that was it.'

While in Los Angeles, the band finally made it to the stage of the Starwood for a sold-out show, with Australian guitar hero Kevin Borich opening.

Future Mötley Crüe singer Vince Neil was in the crowd that night.

'Bon was great. He was just phenomenal. A great singer and really raw. I dug it.'

It was then back to the big rooms, opening for Aerosmith and a prized opening slot for Aerosmith, Van Halen, Foreigner and Pat Travers as part of Bill Graham's third Day On The Green festival at Oakland Stadium on 23 July.

This festival was where the big boys played and were made, and AC/DC had arrived at this point with minimal to non-existent radio support.

Graham was a giant among promoters. Feared and respected in equal proportions, he had established the Fillmore East and Fillmore West venues in New York City and San Francisco respectively, the major dates on any band's American tours in the late '60s and early '70s, and worked with virtually every major act there was from The Grateful Dead, Janis Joplin and Miles Davis to the Sex Pistols, the Stones and Led Zeppelin.

And he liked AC/DC.

Angus: 'He fucking hyped the fuck out of us before we'd even come there.'

Doug Thaler: 'Bill Graham was really supportive of that band; [he] treated them like gold.'

By the time AC/DC walked on stage at 10.30 in the morning to deliver a scorching set, an estimated 65,000 people had already arrived.

Angus: 'It was just ... magical. You could feel this magic ... Bon said it was like the fucking Christians going to the lions. Graham had hired all these fucking lizards and, like, zoo iguanas, the big ones

— one might have even been a Komodo dragon or something — and fucking Bon's got them all over him! But it was one of those sorta magic things.'

Not everyone was pleased that AC/DC were on the bill. The Foreigner camp didn't want to play anywhere near the competitive Australians, a situation Michael Browning argued heatedly to sort out for much of the morning.

Van Halen, on the other hand, were more amazed and admiring than fearful.

'I was standing on the side of the stage thinking, We have to follow these motherfuckers?' Eddie Van Halen recalled years later on Van Halen's website.

Mark Opitz: 'They were very aggressive; it was similar to the way before we recorded takes. Similarly on tour, they used to say that, whoever they were supporting, the whole aim was to blow these fuckers off stage. "This is it! We're going to kill! We're going to kill!" And that's why you hear all those stories of main acts having the lights turned on AC/DC to get them off stage and taken off tours, because they were just killing. They were very aggressive towards the main act in a sense of wanting to play better, rock harder and be stronger, and not putting up with shit.'

After AC/DC played, Bon disappeared. Ian Jeffery was desperately trying to find him for a 12.30 photo call but Bon hadn't gone far.

Ian Jeffery: 'He was lying in this fucking pool with the iguanas, a bottle of Jack, and he's lying with all these animals! He's having a great time, oblivious to everything.'

The next problem was that, because the band had played so early in the day, by mid-afternoon they were itching to do it all again. Thanks to the exposure at Day On The Green, the next gig and much larger ones weren't too far away.

Angus: 'Hell, we didn't even have a record in the Top fucking 50! The buzz and the feedback off [the Day On The Green] was great and it was good because a lot of the bands that had the big number-one records and stuff were freaking when they heard we were on the show.'

While in San Francisco, Bon decided to increase his tattoo count.

Angus: 'He [Bon] said to me, "There's this guy up the road. Ang, if you want a tattoo, this guy's fucking magnificent! He does it all in one hit, like a brand!" He was going to get his colours re-inked so they glowed a bit better, so he went in and he had a few done. He [already] had one down here [Angus motions to an area well below his belt line]. I said, "Fucking hell, Bon, you're brave! Going in there and getting that done."'

While the ears of those who saw the band at Day On The Green were still ringing madly, a few days later Angus again raised the subject of a live album in an interview with the prophetically named Boni Johnson in the *Star News* in Pasadena on 29 July.

'A live thing could catch us where there's all the people and energy and the women to look at; where I could make the guitar lethal.'

A further run of dates with Aerosmith followed, including a spot opening at yet another major event with Foreigner and Van Halen at Chicago's Comiskey Park for the Summer Jam festival.

The appraisal of Peter Mensch from the Aerosmith camp was typical of the assessment of AC/DC at that point.

'People came to see Aerosmith,' he told Frank Watt in *Metal Attack* in 1985, 'but were leaving being blown away by AC/DC.'

The tour saw the band operating at the absolute peak of their blistering onstage powers before large and increasingly receptive audiences. At least part of the fuel for the journey to that point was the often fiery relationship between Malcolm and Angus. They loved and greatly respected each other but that also gave them plenty of latitude to make a point physically when it was necessary.

Doug Thaler remembers receiving a call from a promoter in Allentown, Pennsylvania, the day after AC/DC had passed through.

'He goes, "Whoa, what a band, they were great!" They sold out two shows. He said, "But it got strange; I mean, the end of the night, there's the two brothers, and they got an encore, and they were arguing backstage before they went back on about what they would play for an encore, and one brother knocked out the teeth of the other brother!" I went, "Well, sounds like the fighting Young brothers!"'

Wisely, however, no-one ever took on Bon. He would have been horrified and hurt if anyone in the band he loved so much had done so.

Malcolm: 'We were all quite fiery guys in those days and we'd all have our share of getting one too many drops down our necks and things, but generally I don't think I punched Bon because Bon would have fucking punched me back and I would remember that. I mean, I've punched other people. Bon's punched other people.'

The rest of August was taken up with supporting former Ten Years After guitarslinger Alvin Lee, Rainbow, Savoy Brown and Ted Nugent, as well as co-headlining with Cheap Trick, tickets for which were a mere three dollars.

Chris Gilbey: 'Michael Browning's great theory, which proved to be true and I think was one of the critical reasons why the band broke, was touring, touring, touring, touring. You've just got to keep working the band live. That's it. Don't rely upon the record company. Just work the band live, build the following live and eventually people will start buying the records. And that's why that band broke in America.'

Bon's old mate Vince Lovegrove caught up with the band in Atlanta on the dates with Cheap Trick while he was working on a documentary on Australian rock.

Vince Lovegrove: 'Bon was on the balcony of this particular theatre. The whole crowd was pushing down to the front of the bottom floor and looking back up and the spotlight's on Bon standing up on the first floor of the theatre with Angus on his shoulders. It was just such a magic memory, such a snapshot memory.'

When the tour hit Jacksonville, the gracious Cheap Trick suggested that AC/DC close the show in what had become the Australian band's heartland, despite the fact that it was scheduled to be Cheap Trick's headline.

Rick Nielsen (Cheap Trick): 'It was the first co-headline kind of tour we'd ever done and we did flip-flop dates with those guys and I think they got a little more popular than we did, but we got along good. They'd make us work hard every night and we'd make them work hard every night. They are what they are and we are what we are and together it was a pretty good package.'

During the mid-August dates with Rainbow, the Young family's fighting spirit was again on show but this time directed squarely at hecklers at the show in Calderone, Long Island.

Malcolm was a strong believer in never letting anything disrupt the show but even that creed had its limits.

Angus: 'Some guy hit me with one of those orange drink cans. It didn't hurt, but he went on from there and started throwing any other thing he could grab. So I went across to Malcolm and Malcolm used to always say, "Ah, ignore it." But this guy kept it up all night. I said, "Stuff this; either he goes or I go," and took off the guitar and went for it. The trouble was, I didn't see the full height of him. When I saw the size of the guy, I wasn't going to tackle him!'

A bouncer fixed the situation on behalf of Angus, beating the shit out of the guy and then showing him the door.

Angus: 'But the rumour came out. This had happened on a Saturday and by the Monday, I think, when we were playing in the Palladium [in New York], there was like a couple of hundred people all waiting to see me come out and chin anyone that blinked.

'I remember the time there was a series of hecklers. It was weird. They were like fans but they used to just come and heckle me because they said they loved heckling me "because he looks great when he gets so upset"! I got helped once too, I remember, by a heckler. I cut my leg and this guy had been giving me a hard time all night and then afterwards he came up and drove me to the hospital.'

Doug Thaler was in Calderone for the show with Rainbow and saw a quiet class war between the haves and the have-nots.

'Rainbow's manager, Bruce Paine, comes over to me and goes, "Who are these guys?" I said, "What?" He says, "Well, they walked into Rainbow's dressing room, and just started eating their catering!" And when somebody said something to them they went, "Well, this looks better than what's in our dressing room so I think we'll have this!" And it was just matter-of-fact stuff! They didn't think, like, they did anything wrong. Nobody's gonna tell them they're doing anything wrong; they just went about their business.'

A week later, the tour wound its way to Boston and the show at the Paradise Theatre was broadcast on WBCN. Angus pulled out all stops. The story, and it's a beauty, goes that not only did he walk out of the theatre and into the street during the solo in Rocker, but he jumped into a cab and was taken to the radio station in Boston's Prudential Building. When the elevator doors opened on the building's 50th floor, he was still ripping into his fretboard.

The momentum around the band was now so strong you could almost touch it. For that reason, a proposed event in Australia, being put together by Vince Lovegrove, that involved the television and radio broadcast of a reunion concert of bands like The Easybeats and The Valentines was simply out of the question. Bon had enough on his plate. The show was subsequently cancelled, anyway.

An indication of just how fast things were moving — apart from the ever-increasing rise in embarrassing worship from their record company, which AC/DC loathed — came on 2 September with a return appearance at the year's second Day On The Green festival at Oakland Stadium with Ted Nugent, Journey, Blue Öyster Cult and Cheap Trick; a far better proposition than accepting another slot on that year's Reading Festival in the UK.

Once again in the wake of Day On The Green, the subject of a live album drawn from a number of US dates, including Texas, as well as Glasgow, London and Australia was teasingly, even strategically, raised.

Then, on 6 September, an appearance on the legendary 'Midnight Special' on the ABC was taped. They played two songs, although only Sin City was aired. Guest hosts Ted Nugent, who had taken the liberty of renaming the night 'Extravagonzo' in his own honour, and Aerosmith's Steve Tyler almost got into a shoving match, albeit a light-hearted one, while giving AC/DC an enthusiastic introduction.

The rest of September was spent opening for Blue Öyster Cult, UFO and Thin Lizzy, as well as headlining spots of their own, including a show at Vet's Memorial in Columbus, Ohio, before a wildly receptive audience.

'Our albums are all rock and roll and here's one that's really rock and roll!' Bon yelled by way of introducing Bad Boy Boogie and then invited the crowd down to the front of the stage.

Unfortunately, the response to Bon's call to move forward was far stronger than expected and he was forced to make an urgent plea after the song was finished.

'We don't want to see you hurt 'cause we're with you. So please, if you can, back off the orchestra pit 'cause it'll collapse and you'll get hurt, man, you'll get hurt.'

When enthusiasm overtook common sense and security moved in to herd fans from the area, the rest of the audience booed. Bon just glared down at the bouncers and told the crowd, 'They're not our friends either; don't worry.'

That us-and-them attitude was on high beam in a legendary incident when the band warmed up for Thin Lizzy in Detroit. The incident centred around a strict decibel limit, which was ironic given that Detroit is the historic birthing place of some of rock's loudest acts such as Ted Nugent, Grand Funk Railroad and The MC5.

Lizzy guitarist Gary Moore took in the opening exchanges from the balcony while AC/DC were doing soundcheck.

'The promoter goes up and he's pissed off at them because they're playing too loud, so they have a huge row on the stage with the promoter and I think it was either Malcolm or Angus — at that time, I didn't know their names — and I hear one of them go, "Why don't you fuck off and jerk yourself off in the fuckin' alley, you cunt! That's the end of the soundcheck, yeah?"'

Round two came during the show that night.

'Halfway through the fucking set, the guy comes up with a couple of bouncers and he pulls their sound guy off the board and pulls the faders down and stops the gig. So we're in the dressing room — of course we've heard all this now, of course they think we've done it [to sabotage their gig] so they want to have a big fight with us, but of course it's nothing to do with us and Phil Lynott's getting really pissed off because he thinks, in his fucking wisdom, that they've come all the way from Australia to support Thin Lizzy. He said, "If these fucking guys don't get paid, we're not going on!" So we're trying to help them but they think, like, we're the enemy through this whole thing.'

Ian Jeffery was doing sound for AC/DC at the time and it was he who was dragged away by security after trying to reason with a city official.

'I took the two masters [which controlled the volume from the sound system] and pulled them down and said, "This is not me [that can be heard now]. That's them." He said, "I don't care, it's still too loud, turn it down." "Okay. There is no PA. Can you hear the singer?" He said, "I can hear him a little bit." I said, "That's because it's the [stage] monitors essentially. There's nothing else on, mate. That's them [just the band with no PA] coming off the stage."

'Next thing I knew, I'm physically lifted up by the security guys and carried into the foyer. Show's over for us, right? I run down the outside of the theatre and go back in and I'm on the side of the stage and I'm waving, trying to get Malcolm's attention, and Malcolm turns around and does a double-take. He looks at me like, what the fuck are you doing here? You're supposed to be out front! He wanders over and I said, "They've thrown me off; too fucking loud."

'So they stop playing and [he] threw his guitar and walked over and threw these monitors in the orchestra pit, and all of a sudden you've got these sound guys who they were using at the time for their PA — they grab Malcolm; I get them off Malcolm. We go back to the dressing room and Malcolm says, "Show me the cunt! Who's the fucking cunt? Who's the promoter?" I said, "It's not his fault, Malcolm." He said, "Yes it fucking is!" There's no reasoning, right? So we got to the front office and Malcolm just lays one on the promoter. Then there were police and everything called.'

When possible assault charges were waved about by the promoter, the band cancelled out the threat with a bill for almost $20,000 for equipment damage, presumably for the stage monitors although Malcolm's fist and the promoter's face were also worse for wear.

Mark Opitz: 'The tales that he [Malcolm] would tell on tour of just, you know, getting physical with promoters ... After Malcolm's hit the promoter a couple of times on some midwestern American gig, the promoter's going to call the cops on him and he [Malcolm] said, "And who do you think they're going to believe? You who's six foot eight that me at four foot nothing is beating the shit out of you?" Stuff like that.'

Gary Moore: 'The next night in Cleveland, they went out and they blew us [Thin Lizzy] off the fucking stage, because they got to play their full set and they fucking killed us that night. They were trying to psych us out the whole time, like Angus wouldn't look you in the eye and they were definitely out to get us.

'On the last night — it was Chicago; we did really good there because Thin Lizzy were very big in Chicago — our manager did a really nasty trick because he knew the drummer in AC/DC had gone for a shit — he saw him going to the toilet — so he said "House lights!" and the guy had to come running out with his pants hanging down; he's trying to pull his pants up in the middle of having a shit and jump straight on the drums. So there was all kinds of shit going on between the two bands just for those three days. It's a good job we didn't tour [for longer] because we'd have killed each other, I think.

'Bon used to come in the dressing room and pretend he liked us, you see, to get all the free beers. He'd drink their booze then come and drink what was left of ours because we weren't big beer drinkers. So he'd come in, "You know what? I didn't think I'd like you guys but you're okay." It was all this bollocks just to get our free booze!

'The last time I saw Bon he had a letter from his wife or something and he looked really sad and I just remember him standing against this wall outside the gig looking really, really sad. But they were fantastic! What a great band! Angus was fucking unbelievable. There were trails of snot hanging from his nose the whole time. He was like fucking epileptic up there, man. And Bon couldn't speak because he was that drunk but he'd come over to the monitor desk and sort of *blu blu blu* and go straight back out and start singing totally coherently. Really strange. Very impressive!'

The final dates supporting Aerosmith, or Hairy Smith as Malcolm at least semi-affectionately had come to refer to them, were 2 and 3 October and the last shows on the US tour.

The entire exercise had been an unqualified success and AC/DC, on occasion, had begun flying from gig to gig, due to the sheer size of the country. But they'd still only just scratched the surface of what was potentially a massive audience. Nevertheless, sales of *Powerage* were now tipping the scales at 200,000 copies, more than the combined figures for *High Voltage* and *Let There Be Rock*.

There were other telltale signs of their success in terms of the number and calibre of females who began to hover about. But the women and their shallow star-fucking agenda did nothing for Malcolm and Angus and neither, typically, did most of the acts they saw, heard and dealt with. The pair couldn't understand why some of the bands used such a low onstage volume that they then massively amplified to the audience with a towering PA system. To them, bands like the hugely successful Boston and Foreigner seemed like they were scared to get their hands dirty.

'They're not taking control of their own sound,' Malcolm told Phil Sutcliffe in *Sounds* on 11 November 1978. 'The Dictators were the only band we saw really working ... It's them who should be given the breaks.'

AC/DC had led by example on stage and it was now time to unleash that much-talked-about live album as a take-home slice of what a live, sweating, bleeding-eared rock and roll show should really be all about.

Tapes of shows from all over the planet had been piling up for some time.

Mark Opitz: 'It was amazing to listen to all of it. I basically sat there and just mixed everything, every title. I don't even know what mixes of mine got used in the end and what didn't. My brief was, "Okay, you've got the studio from eight o'clock at night; here's all the tapes; just do it."'

For all the excitement of working with the tapes, Opitz was very much aware of the great expectations of his mentors.

'The only thing in the back of my mind was fear, abject fucking terror that I couldn't do a good enough job! We all would take turns at doing stuff, like I'd do mixes and mixes and George and Harry would come in and do mixes and mixes and we'd do mixes together and whatever. But it was just me trying to do a good job and sitting there and playing stuff to George and just hoping he fucking liked it. It was always the way.'

The bulk, if not all of the album, was made up of the recording made in April at the Apollo in Glasgow. The cover art was from a shoot done back in August with Atlantic Records' staff photographer Jim Houghton before the show at Boston's Paradise Theatre, the idea for which came from Atlantic's art director, Bob Defrin.

Bob Defrin: 'The photographer got theatrical blood which we brought up with us. We had a guitar altered. I think we had the neck cut off so that it would look like he [Angus] was impaling himself. He was really into it.'

The album's name, *If You Want Blood You've Got It*, was an extension of Bon's response to a journalist at the Day On The Green festival in July who asked what they could expect from the band.

Angus: 'He was asking Bon, "What can we expect from you?" And Bon said, "Blood."'

In the UK, where *If You Want Blood You've Got It* was made available first on 13 October, the patronising Australiana references that had plagued the band since they first arrived in the country continued with the review of the album in *Sounds* on 28 October under the heading of 'Billa Bong! Boomer Anngg!'

Interestingly, while the album showed AC/DC in full balls-out rock flight, their UK punk contemporaries from 1976 and 1977 had all gone off on other tangents. The Sex Pistols had imploded 10 months earlier in America and John 'Rotten' Lydon had re-emerged in July with Public Image Limited, who owed far more to The Stooges, Krautrock and dub than Chuck Berry licks. The Jam, on the other hand, had reached a level of sophistication on the *All Mod*

Cons album, as The Clash, to a much lesser degree, were about to with their second effort, *Give 'Em Enough Rope*.

On 10 October, AC/DC returned to Europe for a 15-date tour. In Paris, Bon remembered Trust, the band he met while visiting the Stones, and, even though they didn't have a record label at the time, organised for them to open at AC/DC's first headlining show in Paris at the sold-out Le Stadium.

During the 17-date UK tour that followed until 16 November, AC/DC had the honour of being the first to sell out two consecutive nights at the Mayfair in Newcastle.

The tour began with a special gig at Colchester's University of Essex organised by the BBC for the program 'Rock Goes To College' which was an amazed Brian Johnson's first sighting of the band that would quite literally change his life in the years to come.

In Glasgow, after going outside for some air during a break, Bon was denied re-entry by security staff and had to have a merchandise worker vouch for him in order to get back inside the venue.

The tour culminated in two sold-out shows at the Hammersmith Odeon. A poorly timed reception was held after the first show that roared on until the early hours, which left Bon very much worse for wear but, as usual, he came through for the second show that night.

Record Mirror's Steve Gett took in not one but the pair of the Odeon shows. While hugely impressed on both occasions, Gett wrote on 25 November that the band now had to ensure that their next studio album was a killer, given that they now no longer had a statement as strong as a live album in reserve.

He was dead right, although *If You Want Blood* was one hell of a stop-gap. It was released in America on 21 November and Australia on 27 November, just as the band arrived home. In something of a marketing gift, TV audiences across America were treated to vision of the tiny Australians behind the album's monstrous racket when their performance on 'Midnight Special' was finally shown, two months after it was recorded in September.

Two days before Christmas, the album peaked on the US Billboard charts at number 113. Not a perfect position but a promising one.

In AC/DC's absence during the year, Australia's pub-rock scene had exploded with bands like Cold Chisel, Midnight Oil, The Angels and Rose Tattoo all playing most nights of the week — sometimes across the road from one another — to ever-increasing crowds.

In particular, AC/DC's friends and label mates The Angels, with the perfectly in-sync twin-guitar machine-gun attack of John and Rick Brewster and the energetic, literary theatre of singer Doc Neeson, had grown to be a huge drawcard. Their breakthrough effort was that year's *Face To Face* album, which had been producer Mark Opitz's other project around the time of *Powerage*.

John Brewster: 'When AC/DC went overseas, that left us, and we rose to the top. We were the fucking number-one band in this country. We were putting people in rooms on Monday nights with 500 people outside trying to get in.'

But missing some perceived boat in Australia wasn't a concern for AC/DC and neither was taking an extended break. Time off was something other folks had and on 2 December, just two weeks after arriving back in the country, the band were back in Albert Studios in Sydney recording with George and Harry and engineer Mark Opitz.

Now, more than ever, discipline and focus were paramount. The next album had to be the one, the knockout blow.

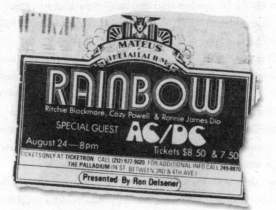

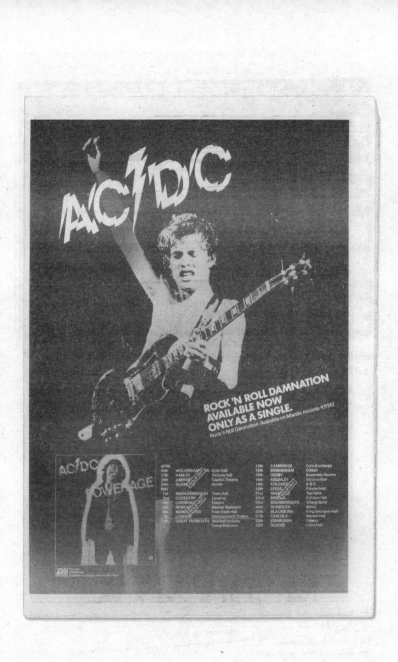

1979
The great outdoors: Malcolm,
Bon and Angus, Wembley Stadium.

*i*n 1926, when US Highway 666 officially came into being, the name of the strip of tar that would stretch across four states reflected nothing more than a simple, sequential reality: US 66 now had a sixth offshoot.

But with its three-digit tag, which corresponded, according to the Bible, with the feared coding mark that would identify the Antichrist or 'The Beast', the highway cast an inky black shadow.

The local Native Americans were troubled by the satanic connotations while others pointed to the number of fatal car accidents hosted by the roadway. And other people, also of a superstitious nature, believed that those who mocked their concerns, made light of the name, or simply stole one of the highway signs, as happened countless times, were tempting fate and fucking with forces that were best not fucked with. The highway to hell had to be respected.

On the other side of the planet, however, some seemed to be tempting fate.

Angus: 'There was a lot of buzz about us and a girl asked me, "Well, what would you call the tour?" And I said, "It's a fucking highway to hell. It's an AC/DC tour."'

The sessions for AC/DC's new album, which had only begun in early December, had spilt over into the new year. Bon wasn't altogether satisfied with his efforts on *Powerage* and felt that the lyrics of songs like Gone Shootin' were simply too serious. This time he wanted to lighten up and songs like If You Want Blood were just the style he was after.

Atlantic Records in America still wanted to make some changes themselves. *If You Want Blood* stood poised to outstrip the US sales of *Let There Be Rock* and *Powerage* combined. Clearly, AC/DC's position in the States was escalating but Atlantic wanted more marketplace bang for their buck from the band — they wanted an album that was a big seller right across the country, spearheaded by a hit single. And they wanted that breakthrough now.

The previously flagged issue of a new producer with fresh ears and ideas rather than the usual partnership of George Young and Harry Vanda was now seen as critical in this process. So serious was the situation that Atlantic vice-president Michael Klenfner travelled to Sydney to meet with the band and George and Harry.

When Klenfner arrived, he was given a run-through of what the band had assembled by that point. Drummer Ray Arnott, who had done numerous sessions for Albert's with George and Harry and performed with Stevie Wright, was sitting in for Phil Rudd at the time.

Ray Arnott: 'I went into the studio one night, just banging around with them to show this American guy some of the licks they'd been working on. He was there to check they weren't sun-baking!

'We called him Tons of Fun. That's all I remember him as, Tons of Fun. I can remember going out to a restaurant one night and the Yank ordered some wine and I think it was about $80 a bottle, this red. Bon said, "That's what you put in your fucking fish and chips, lad!" And the next bottle Bon bought was about $300. But the Yanks were paying for it. We had a good night.'

For Arnott, it was a big week. He was soon to be married and a buck's night was held in his honour.

Ray Arnott: 'It was me, Malcolm, George, Angus and a couple of other guys and we went to this club down the end of George Street in Sydney. They wouldn't let us in; they said, "You look too rough and ready," and they were playing AC/DC on the fucking disco! We were all looking at each other pissing ourselves laughing.'

But behind the scenes the situation was anything but humorous.

Being told what to do was bad enough but what really pissed off Malcolm and Angus was they felt that George was being treated disrespectfully by Atlantic, like an amateur with no great track record when it came to production, even though he and Harry had scored a Top 10 hit in America only a few months earlier with John Paul Young's Love Is In The Air.

Then there was George and Harry's Flash and the Pan, a hugely successful studio-only exercise that never toured, but enjoyed considerable chart success in Australia, Europe and the US.

A spokesman for George and Harry papered over some of the cracks by telling *Juke* that the possibility of an external producer had been 'on the cards for some time'.

Malcolm seemed less pleased with the situation and went so far as to tell Radio 2JJ in Sydney that the band had been virtually 'forced' to go with an outside producer.

Losing Harry was one thing. Losing George was almost literally like losing a sixth member of the band, and much more.

Michael Browning: 'George and Harry were pretty honourable about it. They could have been outwardly sort of pissed off; I'm sure they were. For an American record company to say to you you've got to change producers when they're sort of revered in their own country was a little bit of a slap in the face, I suppose. So it was very, very difficult. Malcolm and Angus didn't like it at all; they were very pissed off. They were very unhappy about it.'

Browning, however, believed that the shift to a different producer and one familiar with the machinations of American rock radio was, at that point, vital.

'As much as I think Vanda and Young were totally crucial in the role of creating the sound and developing the music and bringing the best out in Malcolm and Angus and Bon, as good producers as they were, they weren't switched on to what American radio was sounding like. You had to be in America to really understand what the mentality of the kids was, the listeners and their programs. We just reached the stage where you can have all the attitude and all the vibe but you've got to disguise it as something slicker with a more full production. But it had to happen, it definitely had to happen. Atlantic were 100 per cent right.'

Atlantic's choice of producer was Eddie Kramer and he was no new kid on the block. His early work history included David Bowie, The Kinks, The Beatles, the Stones and The Small Faces. But what really carved out his name was his landmark recordings with Jimi Hendrix on the *Are You Experienced?*, *Axis: Bold As Love* and *Electric Ladyland* albums. His later work with Led Zeppelin and Humble Pie on their live classic *Rockin' The Fillmore* further strengthened Kramer's standing.

For Atlantic, it was his output over the past five years with Kiss on recordings such as *Alive!*, *Love Gun* and *Alive II* that made him the man for AC/DC.

Meanwhile, the expense of transporting the band's by then sizable touring set-up to Australia was given as the reason for not playing in the country. Bon, only half seriously, would tell *RAM*'s Stuart Coupe on 9 March, they were 'too drunk, too stoned, too fucked' to tour their homeland.

While Bon promised that when they did eventually hit Australian stages it would be the greatest rock and roll show on earth, in reality, touring Australia, or anywhere in the world for that matter, wasn't a priority at the time. Touring had gotten them to where they were. It was now time to slam the right album in the barrel to get the job finished.

When Eddie Kramer arrived in Sydney, he met with George, Harry, Ted Albert and Michael Browning and then bunkered down with the band at Albert Studios to do some demos.

The band's power and strength of character collectively and individually were immediately obvious and backed up everything Kramer had seen and heard on video back in New York. More to the point, as a rock band, they compared more than favourably to a number of Kramer's previous studio charges, albeit with one glaring difference.

Eddie Kramer: 'Obviously a much rougher, tougher, grittier, simpler kind of vibe. I mean the two brothers were just really calling the shots and I thought that they had it down and with that singer, Bon Scott ... Jesus, he was just bloody amazing. It was just incredible.

'You get a great singer and a cool-sounding band. They were different than Zeppelin, for obvious reasons. They're a simple, raw, basic, to-the-point rock and roll band, a fundamental rock and roll band that is hard to find, and is hard to find today, for God's sake.'

That said, for Kramer there were no parallels with the band that had been a huge influence on AC/DC from the beginning of their career.

Eddie Kramer: 'The Stones had a much higher level of sophistication than these guys. Different sort of animal.'

With the demos completed, the band packed up and prepared to shift to Miami, just as Bon had casually and light-heartedly prophesied in late 1977, for the recording of the new album at Criteria Studios in February.

Somehow, in between all this, Angus, George and Harry joined Jimmy Barnes, John Swan, Rose Tattoo's Peter Wells, Warren 'Pig' Morgan and many others on the first of Ray Arnott's two albums for Albert's, *Rude Dudes*. Vanda and Young were production consultants on the album, now an extremely rare item, which was released in November 1979 in Australia only.

Ray Arnott: 'With Angus it was just blues, just basic sort of slow 12-bar and he just ripped it apart; played like a champion.'

Angus: '[Ray] was in the office and I came through and he said, "Hey, while you're here" ... I didn't think I was going on tape. It was done in five seconds.'

As an unintended send-off before leaving for America, Angus, Malcolm and Bon took to the stage of the Strata Motor Inn at Cremorne in northern Sydney for an impromptu performance with George on bass and Arnott again on drums. It was to be Bon's last live appearance with Malcolm and Angus in Australia.

Ray Arnott: 'There were three or four suckling pigs on a roast and everybody had a good feed and a good drink and then a guy came running in and said, "Do you want to have a blow?" And we said, "Yeah!" So we jumped up and the audience just went bananas. One part was the club and the other side was the restaurant half, which they shut during the day. So we were partying in the restaurant and threw the door open and went through and got up on stage and played.'

For the next half an hour the stunned audience was treated to five or six songs, including Baby, Please Don't Go and Let There Be Rock.

Bon and Angus weren't strangers to the Strata where they would sometimes go along to see the jaw-dropping guitar fireworks of The Emmanuel Brothers — Tommy and Phil.

Phil Emmanuel: 'Greg Johnson, the manager of the Strata, came over and said, "Would you like a drink?" Yeah, yeah. So he went over to the bar and got two double Jack Daniel's and Coke for me and Tommy and I think Angus had a lemon squash or something, and he just looked at Bon and said, "The usual, mate?" And Bon said, "That'd be great." He came back with a big glass of ice and half a bottle of Johnnie Walker Red Label for Bon. And in the time it took us to drink our drinks, Bon had just about downed the whole bottle. Never seen a man drink like him. Bloody amazing and he could handle it really well, too.'

The trip to Miami was delayed by a day or two after it was discovered, when the band assembled at Sydney Airport, that a very drunk Bon, thanks to yet another triple Scotch and Coke, was ironically the only one to have his visa in order.

Bon was in fine form at the airport, making the most of every photo op with the women around him. He even went so far as to compliment a female friend of music journalist Stuart Coupe on her figure and offered his phone number in the event that Coupe didn't respect her body as Bon felt he should.

Once they finally arrived and settled in Miami, rehearsals with Kramer began around noon each day, sometimes earlier. It wasn't an hour that the band, who usually worked in the studio from late at night until early morning, were used to.

But it wasn't the working hours or the shoestring living budget that were the problem.

The band had become used to working up songs in the studio with George rather than arriving with completed material ready to record, which was more along the lines of what Kramer was expecting.

Eddie Kramer: 'They were a very independent bunch. Obviously they were very talented and I thought we could make a really good record here. But I think the problem that I had with it was that the material wasn't quite ready and the way they worked was in a sort of strange manner, I guess. It was kind of, "Oh, we've got these songs," and Bon Scott was having problems with the lyrics and problems with drinking and everything else.

'In retrospect, he was such the prototypical tough-guy rocker and his image in terms of drinking and carousing and being completely out of control ... that was his style and I was not used to dealing with that.'

Kramer didn't think the members of AC/DC were too interested in his professional experiences with many of their heroes. Or maybe they didn't want to seem to be interested. He may not have been the enemy personally but he was put in place by those who the band felt definitely were, so he was an adversary by association. To show a lack of interest in him as a professional would have been a powerful weapon.

Kramer wasn't unsympathetic towards AC/DC's situation. He knew he had been virtually forced on them and understood a certain degree of their resentment. But that didn't make things any easier.

Basically it came down to a clash of agendas.

Malcolm: 'Eddie, we soon learned, was just a good sound man. He'd get good sounds but he was too ... This guy walked in and he played us a Rolling Stones track and he played us another track from someone else and said, "Put that verse together with that chorus and I've got you a hit." We just went, "Fuck off!" That's the end of that. It wasn't going to work out.'

Eddie Kramer: 'That's a given with me. I like to hear hit songs. I think that's really important. But, once again, that was not the way to do this band.'

It was painfully obvious to all concerned that the project was doomed when, three weeks into the Miami exercise, they were not even getting past rehearsals.

Eddie Kramer: 'I think that band required a specific type of handling which I had no idea how to do at that moment in my career. I was used to working with Kiss, who were rough and ready in a different sort of way. I had a rapport with Kiss which I didn't have with this band and, you know, there were some problems.'

The mission was terminated after Malcolm rang Michael Browning and told him to get them the fuck out of Miami.

Browning felt that Atlantic had misread the situation in relation to both George and Harry and Kramer.

Michael Browning: 'They underestimated the musical arrangement and sort of role that George had played in terms of being [the band's] musical conscience or whatever, just keeping the direction sort of honest and just being their mentor — their musical mentor, I suppose. [Kramer] was obviously very talented at pulling good sounds but the other half of it was completely missing. He had them in a rehearsal studio in Miami and they hated every second of it. The straw that broke the camel's back was that his idea to break the group was to do a cover version of Gimme Some Lovin'.'

Kramer had no recollection of that at all.

'If I did make that suggestion, what a dumb thing to say.'

While no songs were completed in Miami, some ideas did pop up, like Angus' title Love Hungry Man and the original germ for the song Highway To Hell. Angus came up with the halting opening riff and Malcolm leapt behind the drums to provide a backbeat.

The story goes that for some very strange reason they then allowed a studio technician to take home the cassette recording of the session, where, to his horror, one of his kids happily pulled metres of the tape out of the cartridge. Thankfully, Bon was able to rescue the tape's content.

Malcolm: 'There were hundreds of riffs going down every day, but this one [Highway] we thought as we did it: that's good, that one — we'll get back and listen to that. We kept moving on because we're on a bit of a roll and something else might come along. We got back to it the next day and it just stuck out like dog's balls.'

The collapse of the relationship with Kramer was a double-edged sword. Firstly, it had proven what the Youngs had suspected — that someone outside their circle would not work successfully with them. Secondly, the band now had to attempt to bond with another figure foreign to them, and the clock was ticking.

At the time Malcolm's pissed-off distress call came through to Browning, he happened to be sharing a house in New York with producer Mutt Lange and his manager, Clive Calder.

Michael Browning: 'I just turned round to Mutt virtually as I had Malcolm on the phone and said, "Mate, you've got to do this record." That was it.'

Doug Thaler had an existing business relationship with Calder and played a role in securing Lange's services from Atlantic's end.

'I brought up Mutt Lange's name. Atlantic Records was pretty hot on Mutt Lange; they were trying to do a deal with Clive Calder to have Mutt produce exclusively for them by then. So this kinda fell right into place, something that the label could embrace.'

Lange was supplied with a tape of six roughly recorded song ideas that AC/DC had put down with Bon on drums underneath Kramer's radar — they told him they were having a day or two off to go to the beach — and the deal was done.

The Miami fiasco meant that the band's upcoming timetable was blown clear out of the water. Having calculated that the album would be completed by early March, they were scheduled to play three dates in Japan for the first time from 7 to 12 March. But as soon as AC/DC's entire crew landed in Tokyo, they were told that the band wasn't coming. The official reason given at the time was that Bon had contracted bronchitis but, in actual fact, some visas couldn't be secured.

They were only three months into the year and they'd already blown substantial sums on costly studio time, travel and flying their crew and gear to Japan for a tour that didn't happen. Financial losses for absolutely no gain were the last thing they needed.

While attempts were made to reschedule the Japanese tour in May, all current touring plans, including some tentative dates in America, such as an appearance at the California Music Festival and a support slot for Aerosmith at Los Angeles Coliseum in April, were put on hold to concentrate on the album.

Next stop, freezing cold London.

While Lange had cut a name for himself with his work with The Boomtown Rats and Graham Parker, his was a client base that didn't, at that stage, boast the legendary status of many of Eddie Kramer's charges. But something sparked with Lange and AC/DC immediately and work on the new album, which would be called *Highway To Hell*, could finally get under way.

In the English winter, heat was exactly what the band needed during the two weeks they spent rehearsing and shaping the new songs.

Doug Thaler: 'They're rehearsing in this place and they had a dirt floor ... and they were wearing their winter coats — it was the dead of winter — and they had this construction heater that ran on kerosene; that was the only thing that kept the room warm while they were rehearsing in it.'

By then, after sessions firstly in Sydney and then Miami, the band had enough material for four albums.

In a first, the songs were firmly in shape before they went into London's Roundhouse Studios in March to record, even though Bon was typically still scribbling down notes during the sessions.

The album they wanted to make, which they knew at the same time would shut Atlantic the hell up, began to materialise. Lange's input and influence touched everything, even Bon's vocals, although the producer felt that AC/DC were so powerful rhythmically and instrumentally any singing almost detracted from it.

Michael Browning: 'I can remember some conversations that went down with Mutt Lange where Bon was kind of describing himself to Mutt Lange as sounding like a weasel on heat. That was Bon's perception of himself, based on what somebody had written about him somewhere.'

Lange showed Bon how to breathe so he could be a technically better singer on songs like Touch Too Much for which Bon had the basic melody, or at least was as melodic as he got.

Bon didn't always appreciate Lange's direction. His voice had served him well for more than a decade and he didn't enjoy someone who had known him for five minutes telling him what to do with it. But what he didn't know, until he found out the hard way, was that the bass-playing Lange had been a trained singer in South Africa before he moved to the UK.

Ian Jeffery: 'A couple of times Bon would come in and say, "Okay, you cunt! You think you can fucking sing it? You sing it!" And Mutt would just sit there and sing it in his seat because he's a trained singer. Bon would stop in his tracks and say, "Okay, cunt, I can do it."'

Bon was philosophical in his general approach to singing. Yes, what came out could sometimes make him cringe, but that was no reason to not keep at it.

'We're all capable of making mistakes and blunders,' he told Pam Swain of 2JJ in September 1979. 'It's just a matter of letting yourself go. If I drink a bottle of whisky, I have no problem letting myself go then!'

Lange's other vocal ideas included the introduction of harmonies, even if they did sound like a sound grab from a riot at times. For those moments, he would arrange a choir from people in the studio, and, if additional voices were needed, he himself would step up to the microphone. The problem was that his voice was so distinctive that half the time he would have to move to the other side of the studio so it didn't drown out everyone else.

Probably the oldest song on hand during the sessions was Night Prowler. The title was about two years old and four unsuccessful versions had been recorded on previous occasions. This time it positively bristled. The song's rhythmic stride and pace were perfect and Angus provided a searing demonstration, as he had on The Jack and Ride On, that, for a schoolkid, he sure knew a hell of a lot about blues guitar playing.

Mixing engineer Tony Platt was the ideal choice to work on the album with Lange. He had been at Island Studios in London in the heyday of Island Records with bands like Free, Spooky Tooth and Traffic, as well as others such as the Stones, Thin Lizzy and even Bob Marley.

Platt immediately had respect and affection for AC/DC.

Tony Platt: 'They come from the tradition of musicians that I grew up with when I first came into studios. People that had a good time, played hard, worked hard and got on with it. They put in what they expected to get out.'

Platt only went to a couple of the recording sessions which were getting a bit of a panicked atmosphere about them because of lack of time. But that only served to galvanise the band to get the job done.

With the body of the recording done, additional sessions took place at Chalk Farm Studios and in April it was off to Basing Street Studios to mix the album. There, Bon did the vocals for Night Prowler, including the two startled-sounding chill-factor inward breaths at the beginning — maybe nothing more than an innocent, if hurried, last steadying smoke — as well as the odd backing vocal and a couple of guitar grabs.

Tony Platt: 'We did the backup vocals for the single Touch Too Much during the mixing time, and I remember sitting there and going, "Fuck, this is going to be huge! This is going to be a massive single!" And when it wasn't, you go, "That's really, really annoying!" That [song] always just stuck out for me. And Highway To Hell — that's just right out of the box. The first time I pushed the faders up on that I thought, this is a classic song! In the same way that [Free's] All Right Now was. Obviously there are slight comparisons that can be made there but it just had that rawness. It was so raw you could taste it.'

In something of a record, in just over a week the mixing was done and the *Highway To Hell* album completed in late April. Of greatest significance was the fact that Malcolm was won over by the results. He had learnt a lot from the experience with Lange, including the importance of being prepared before going into the studio. Most important of all, he had learnt to trust his own good instincts rather than simply look to George.

With the newfound energies and additional confidence that the *Highway To Hell* exercise had injected into the band, they launched into the first leg of their US assault, a 53-date run from 8 May. The lengthy tour opened with 23 shows with UFO with AC/DC supporting on all but one date in Columbus and then headlining shows of their own in Tennessee and Georgia.

AC/DC were now like a brain-crushingly loud paramilitary machine with a large-scale stage production. They were simply untouchable when it came to power and intensity.

The broadness of Bon's chest and shoulders seemed to have increased and his stage patter had been distilled down to little more than brief song introductions.

Angus had mastered a sullen, unsmiling (he never smiled on stage, anyway), give-it-your-best-shot-type look.

'I used to try and come on as tough as I could,' he told Neville Marten in *Guitarist* in April 1991. 'I'd put a cigarette in my mouth, walk on stage, stub it out on the floor and hope nobody would call my bluff!'

And the movement of everyone on stage, with the exception of Angus, had been honed into almost a soul-revue discipline where everyone had a place on the stage and kept to it. Malcolm and Cliff would move forward from the back to sing a chorus and then retire again to the semi shadows.

Although AC/DC had not toured America since October, they had lost no ground. Quite the contrary. They were in devastating form, which made a performance in late May supporting Boston and The Doobie Brothers at Orlando's Tangerine Bowl that much more of a dominance-and-submission exercise.

Ian Jeffery: 'Nobody wanted to play fucking after us, I can tell you that.'

Bon likened the band's too-loud-is-never-too-much approach to performing to bringing down the walls of Jericho.

'We just want to make the walls cave in and the ceiling collapse,' he had earlier told David Fricke in *Circus* on 16 January 1979. 'We all have always shared a common belief that music is meant to be played as loud as possible, really raw and raunchy and I'll punch out anyone who doesn't like it the way I do.'

A support spot for Heart, Nazareth and UFO at John O'Donnell Stadium in Davenport, Iowa, for the Mississippi River Jam II festival made for a healthy drinking posse given the already solid relationship AC/DC had developed with UFO and the fact that Nazareth were fellow Scots.

Angus came close to ending up behind a different type of bar when he teasingly dropped his shorts during the show. Only the fact that his shirt covered his tiny bum saved him from trouble with the law.

The US sales of *If You Want Blood* now tipped the scales at the 250,000 mark, the band's biggest unit mover to date, and it showed no signs of slowing down. Atlantic had noticed this and arrived at the Tower Theater in Philadelphia. UFO were opening and after their show went to wish AC/DC well, as the Australians were up next. One of the heavies from Atlantic, thinking UFO singer Phil Mogg was Bon, congratulated him on the night's performance which, of course, was yet to take place.

When it did, it was even more memorable than usual after someone in the audience threw a firecracker that set a curtain alight. In keeping with Malcolm's rule that nothing interrupts a show, the band didn't flinch.

When they hit Texas, they tore it up with that little extra something they always seemed to save for the Lone Star state. Bon's partying reputation preceded him.

Jim Heath (aka The Reverend Horton Heat) was mock horrified when he found that his sister went one better than his playing AC/DC records in his bedroom and was actually hanging out with Bon.

'She partied with him one night when they came to Corpus Christi. I was mad! [Assumes his best Texan yell] "I can't believe you went and hung around with that dang rock and roll band!" Nah, I knew who they were. I wasn't like that. But I was going, "Damn, Patty. You're running with a pretty fast crowd, hanging around with Bon Scott from AC/DC." She didn't date him or anything.'

On 1 July came a whole new chapter in the band's career, at least in a business sense, when they signed with the powerful management firm Leber-Krebs.

Michael Browning found himself out in the cold just before the album that could really launch AC/DC globally was released.

Michael Browning: 'It was more a case of like if you're married and you meet someone else who you think you like better, you'll find a million reasons all of a sudden why your present wife is no good. It was pretty much that. Then a bunch of just silly things — minor sorts of things — were blown out of proportion, I suppose, and that was it.'

The situation dated back to early May when Browning entered into a partnership with US promoter Cedric Kushner to co-manage the band, a situation AC/DC weren't at all keen on.

Doug Thaler: 'They [AC/DC] were starting to meet with other managers. The person that I favoured — that'd been the most supportive of my efforts, and I'd thought would do a great job for them — was David Krebs.'

Leber-Krebs was, at the time, the biggest management company in America. Steve Leber and David Krebs had started as music agents at the William Morris Agency in the late '60s, where their clients had included the Rolling Stones. In 1972, they formed Contemporary Communications Corporation, a company that included a music-management entity, Leber-Krebs.

Their first signing was the New York Dolls, followed later by the then unknown Aerosmith. By 1979, their roster included the enormously popular Ted Nugent.

Thaler took David Krebs to see AC/DC at their show in Poughkeepsie in June. Krebs had expressed interest in managing them two years earlier and had been instrumental in putting them on their biggest US tours so far with Aerosmith and Nugent.

Ian Jeffery: 'I remember Malcolm and Angus saying, "Alright, mate, you put your fucking money where your mouth is and we'll sign to you," because he promised them a million dollars for a summer's worth of work and we were a $1500 or a $5000 or $6000 opening act in clubs and things.

'We'd met all these managers who were fucking pathetic in Malcolm and Angus' mind, and they said to Leber-Krebs, "Okay, you guarantee us that, we'll sign with you." All of a sudden we were playing all these Day On The Green in San Francisco — all these huge festivals — and getting like 25 to 50 grand. It was like, what the hell is going on here?'

But Leber-Krebs was a major organisation and a busy one and Malcolm didn't want AC/DC to be lost in it. He wanted a point man who would also have to move to London with the band. To Leber-Krebs' amazement, Malcolm wanted Peter Mensch, who was still a tour accountant with the organisation. Mensch had befriended the band during the 1978 Aerosmith tour, and had wanted to manage them himself but didn't have the structure or clout that Leber-Krebs offered.

It was a speedy transition and with the ushering in of Leber-Krebs came the level of business that AC/DC had loathed for so long, but which was vital to take on the world.

Within days, it was back to business as usual. Five promotional videos were shot for songs from *Highway To Hell*, including one for Shot Down In Flames with Angus in a Japanese school uniform specifically for that market. Then it was out supporting Cheap Trick for five dates although the opening show on 4 July produced the wrong kind of fireworks.

Rick Nielsen (Cheap Trick): 'AC/DC opened for us near our home town of Rockford, Illinois. We had 40–50,000 fans, and, when they were on, some idiot threw an M-80 [a powerful firework] and Phil's drum tech got his eardrum blown out.'

A more warmly memorable moment of the tour came on the last night in Omaha, Nebraska, when Malcolm, Angus and Bon joined the headliners during their encore for a version of Sin City and Chuck Berry's School Days. Rick Nielsen perched himself on a roadie's shoulders and hammered away at his guitar in homage to Angus' usual stage practice of sightseeing from atop Bon.

In the middle of the US tour they flew to Europe for a one-off show for Veronica TV in Arnhem, Holland, at the Rijnhallen, where Angus met Ellen, his future wife. Holland was strong AC/DC territory — Whole Lotta Rosie had been a Top 5 hit there the previous year — and part of the concert aired in August on national television.

They were back across the Atlantic to resume the US tour from 19 July supporting Mahogany Rush and headlining their own shows. That leg of the tour included an incredible third appearance on 21 July at Bill Graham's Day On The Green festival before 60,000 people at Oakland Stadium. The show placed the power of their new management in plain view, as the entire festival consisted of bands managed by Leber-Krebs — Aerosmith, Nugent, Mahogany Rush and St Paradise.

Six days later, on 27 July, *Highway To Hell* was released in the UK. The review of the album in *NME* was glowing. But once again the press couldn't help but sarcastically qualify their praise of the band as if they were still wrestling with the fact that something of such power and quality had come from Australia courtesy of five little guys who just looked like your average rock fan. The headline over the review screamed: 'The greatest album ever made' in a large uppercase type, and much smaller underneath appeared '(in Australia)'.

The album was a refinement of their previous recordings but struck a smart balance between polish and AC/DC's gritty firepower.

While *Highway To Hell* was wowing everyone in the UK, the band's focus of assault remained in America where on 28 July they supported Aerosmith, Nugent, Journey and Thin Lizzy in front of 80,000 people at the Cleveland Stadium for the World Series Of Rock festival.

The lead-up to the show wasn't pretty. Several thousand camped out overnight to ensure they secured tickets, only to be terrorised by local gangs. According to reports, one fan was shot dead, four wounded by gunfire, nine stabbed and many beaten or robbed during the night. The concert itself was, thankfully, relatively unaffected by violence.

A working association with Nugent followed with six dates, including AC/DC's first appearance on the stage of New York's Madison Square Garden on 4 August, the second-last date of the US tour. By the end of Nugent's set, the seats that had been gleefully torn up had been thrown together in a pyramid-shaped heap of carnage.

Bon was jubilant. This was everything that he had ever wanted, and more. He had just never dared dream of it.

'This is gonna be one of the biggest bands rock's ever seen,' he told Andy Secher in *Hit Parader* after the show. 'Give us a year or two, and we'll sell this place out ourselves. We've got the talent, and we work harder than anyone.'

News of worldwide sales of *If You Want Blood* tipping 500,000 copies gave the occasion an added sweetness and sense of triumph. But an endless stream of hotels, admittedly of increasing quality, rather than plush mansions were still the band's only homes, as life on the road continued. It was exactly the sort of situation that George, back in the band's earliest days, had wanted to have AC/DC hardened and prepared for.

Highway To Hell was released in America on 3 August as the title cut was released as a single in the UK. While the cover of the album and its title had slipped in almost unnoticed in Britain, things had been very different in America. For a start, Atlantic had firmly opposed the title *Highway To Hell*. There were serious concerns that it would be considered a direct affront to those people in the so-called Bible Belt in the southern states of the US. Sales would suffer if stores in those areas refused to stock the album and concerts were picketed.

Highway To Hell's original cover art was actually an illustration of good versus evil, with AC/DC framed as the nice guys. The initial design bathed the band in an angelic white light on a lonely road at night, dead in the sights of a car driven by a demonic creature. The band rejected the idea as being too arty, although the photo on the back cover of the final version of the album came from that same night-time session in Staten Island, which involved a location van, makeup people, the works.

The front cover showed Angus with a forked tail and horns, among his relatively innocent-looking bandmates.

As it happened, Atlantic's worst-case-scenario calculations weren't wrong, just about five years premature. With the *Dirty Deeds* album not available in America, Atlantic had yet to feel the heat of fans mischievously dialling the 'telephone number' in the title song, so they suggested that *Highway To Hell* be titled as a phone number.

The band were appalled.

Back in the UK, Atlantic's Phil Carson attempted to get the band on the bill at the Knebworth Festival where Led Zeppelin were headlining. It would have been an excellent promotional exercise for the new album but he ran into some opposition.

Phil Carson: 'Robert [Plant] didn't like the band ... I really wanted AC/DC on the bill, and Robert wasn't very keen. He thought they were a bit derivative, you know, which is a fair comment, really; I mean, they are.'

It didn't matter: they were hardly short of work.

The band headlined the first day of the Bilzen festival in Belgium. Then they were part of The Who And Roar Friends festival at Wembley Stadium in London on 18 August, along with Nils Lofgren and The Stranglers.

Malcolm and Angus were huge fans of The Who and to be asked by the band to be on a bill with them was an enormous honour. AC/DC were on second before The Stranglers but the massive audience was theirs from the opening bass lines of Live Wire.

Maddeningly, the PA system failed during Whole Lotta Rosie with Angus in mid solo. But they didn't stop playing and a huge roar erupted when the sound finally burst back into life halfway through Rocker.

J.J. Burnel (The Stranglers): 'They were awesome. And it was solid-packed. It was like 80,000 people, capacity audience. I just remember seeing a huge fight while we were playing, a huge punch-up in the middle of the stadium with Stranglers' fans having a fight with mods, I think. Punks versus mods! There you go! Classic!'

On 25 August, during five dates in Dublin and Belfast where the band were wildly received and Aix-les-Bains, France, *Highway To Hell* peaked at number 17 on the US Billboard charts and at number eight on the UK charts at the end of that month.

While in Germany they performed the song Highway To Hell live on TV show 'Rock Pop' and during rehearsals the previous day jammed with Rick Nielsen from Cheap Trick.

Another major festival appearance followed on 1 September at the Open Air festival at Zeppelinfeld in Nuremberg where the dark spectacle of the Nazi mass rallies of the 1930s had been held. As if to underline the horrors of the Third Reich, it poured rain for the show that saw AC/DC join Cheap Trick and the Scorpions to again support The Who in front of 60,000 people. While AC/DC's set was delayed, Angus stood side of stage for The Who's performance, transfixed by guitarist Pete Townshend who had previously tipped his hat to the power and raw energy of *Let There Be Rock*.

After the show, all the bands met up in the bar of their hotel.

Angus: 'Townshend came in and he said, "Oh well, you've done it again, you fuckers! You stole the show!" And Bon said, "That's right, Pete. So what the fuck are you going to do up there? Fucking sleep?" Which was mighty brave. He's a big guy, Townshend, you know, and then [Bon] walked up to him in the bar the next day at the hotel and said, "Here, Pete, buy me a drink!" Because he knew Townshend at the time, I think, was on the wagon, so he was just rubbing it in.'

With the Highway To Hell single released in the US, from 5 September the band embarked on the second leg of the American tour, 37 headline dates in all. By this point, there was nothing too hellish about the transportation on the tour. The band's coach seated 18 with beds for up to 12. Apart from a toilet there was also the luxury of not one stereo but two. There was also television and a video player plus incidentals, such as whatever Phil Rudd's great passion was at the time, and other comforts — basically, the little things to make an endless life on the road a little more enjoyable and home-like.

But that relative luxury wasn't quite what it seemed despite the band's commanding onstage status, rabid reception from audiences and increasing album sales. When they were in headlining mode, there was a total of 25 people in the band's entourage, all of whom had to be paid, fed and accommodated. That personnel, which of course included the band, travelled in two coaches, while up to three huge semi-trailers filled with lights and sound equipment rumbled along in their wake. The economics were simple: to keep a juggernaut this size rolling, it was necessary to cram in as many people as possible at each show. Not that this was a problem.

Accordingly, money was a constant sword hanging over their heads.

'This tour should just break even,' tour manager Ian Jeffery told Pam Swain in *RAM* on 6 October. 'You hope all those people go and buy the record so the next time round you can move to bigger halls and make some money.'

There were other financial considerations.

While it was tough to put a dollar figure on the cost of Angus bloodying his knees each night, the price of the wear and tear on the band's gear was very real. If, for example, any of AC/DC's wireless equipment became troublesome, its creator Kenny Schaffer would, at the band's expense, have to fly to wherever in the world they were to fix it.

Time to get faulty gear back in working order was an issue in itself, as the equipment was needed almost every night. And chances of getting enough downtime to service anything were becoming more remote by the day with the increasing momentum around the band.

The American tour took them back to Texas for four shows with Southern buddies Molly Hatchet. The two bands often travelled in each other's buses between the five gigs in the Lone Star state.

While in Dallas, Angus did battle with a heckler, not at the gig, but when the band appeared at a record store. But by the next show in San Antonio, humour was the order of the day and in a demonstration of just how close the AC/DC and Hatchet camps were, Hatchet guitarist Dave Hlubek took to the stage in a school uniform during AC/DC's set.

Further proof that the South was gonna rise again, at least for AC/DC, came in late September when they headlined the Coliseum in Charlotte, North Carolina, before 13,000. It was a feat they near repeated three days later on 2 October at the Coliseum in Knoxville, Tennessee, in front of 12,000, an attendance figure that beat the record held by the Rolling Stones at the venue.

But Bon clearly hadn't forgotten where he came from. In Towson, Maryland, he found himself not only performing but also monitoring the activities of overzealous security staff. After Shot Down In Flames he made his first plea to the crowd.

'I don't know why these guys are throwing people out down the front here but please don't get thrown out because we want all of you to be here for our concert.'

A few songs later, as he introduced The Jack, it was clear he'd had enough of the bully-boy tactics of security.

'Here's a song we'd like to play for the security because they're such a pack of arseholes.'

Still the trouble persisted and he let fly.

'You're all enjoying yourselves tonight, huh? You're all having a good time? So we'd like the security down the front here to fuck off! We're having a rock and roll concert and they,' he spat slowly and deliberately, 'ain't rock and roll.'

When one of the guards took exception to his remarks, Bon just met him with a steely gaze and bristled, 'I don't care what you think.'

By that point, plenty of people in America were onside with Bon and the band.

The Mutt Lange shaping of *Highway To Hell* was starting to produce clear dividends with radio finally throwing some weight and air time AC/DC's way. Combined with the feverish gravitational pull of fans to the band's live shows, sales of the album were now strong enough for it to be certified Gold in the US for sales of 500,000 units.

There was plenty to celebrate and after the tour the band flew to New York for a presentation and lunch with some record company executives. The presentation wasn't without its irony.

Doug Thaler: 'There was another executive there at the time, who will remain nameless, who [had lobbied] Jerry Greenberg [president of Atlantic US] heavily to just drop them from the label. Interestingly enough, in late October 1979, when it was time to present the band with their first Gold record, it was that particular executive that had wanted to see the tail end of them in 1977 who was there presenting the plaques!'

The awards almost had to be accepted by someone else on the band's behalf after an incident the night before.

Perry Cooper (Atlantic Records): 'We got a little crazy in the hotel. Well, we moved some furniture around. When I went to check out in the morning, the police had been called and so I was dressed in a suit so I didn't look like I was part of the band, and I remember checking out and getting to a phone and calling Ian [Jeffery] and telling him, "Get the guys outta there quick!" And fortunately they got out of there.'

Rising popularity and the cartoon horror of *Highway To Hell*'s title and cover art drew an offer of a starring role in a movie called *Dracula Rock*. Not too surprisingly it was turned down and was subsequently offered to Queen, who also declined.

Within days of the American tour, it was back to the UK for a 13-date run from 26 October with future Mutt Lange studio charges Def Leppard as support. The tour covered smaller venues than those in America but the excitement of audiences was exactly the same. Although the first date of the tour in Newcastle was cancelled due to a fire erupting in the venue while the band was doing soundcheck, it was anything but a bad-luck sign with four sold-out shows at the Hammersmith Odeon a highlight of the schedule.

Leppard drummer Rick Allen's 16th birthday was on 1 November and Bon, who wished the young Sheffield act luck each night of the tour, led the toasts and speeches after the show.

Bon had always been generous no matter what he had in his pockets and now he was in a reasonably comfortable position was more happy than ever to assist those in need. One night on the tour, Leppard singer Joe Elliott was one such beneficiary when he needed £10. Bon had also extended his generosity to former Rose Tattoo guitarist Mick Cocks who was in London at the time. He offered Cocks a seat on the band's tour bus for the dates with Leppard.

Malcolm had his own reasons to smile. While in Glasgow, the band managed to see the crucial Rangers vs Celtic derby match. It would have brought back fond memories for the Young brothers of their family's long-held passion for the Rangers team.

Highway To Hell was released in Australia on 8 November. The cover art for the Australian album was slightly different to the UK and US editions and showed the band engulfed in flames. Depicting the band in an inferno on one version of the album and not the others was an eerily similar scenario to the reissuing of Lynyrd Skynyrd's *Street Survivors* album without flames licking at the band on the cover — as had been the case previously — after the Southerners' tragic plane crash in October 1977.

Touring continued on 11 November with a 28-date European run with openers Judas Priest.

Rob Halford (Priest singer): 'I was on the stage as often as I could every night just to watch the band, just because of their energy and their power and their love of what they did.

'It was just before we started to record the *British Steel* record. We would bale after every show because we were all crammed in a little van and the only way we could get to the next gig was to leave straight after the show — either spend the night in a lay-by or get a cheap hotel and pile six into a room. And AC/DC thought we were being a bit stuck-up. They thought we were taking off in our big tour bus, but of course we had absolutely nothing. We were barely making money to pay for petrol and a bit of food. And when they found out about that, they generously offered their tour bus [with its comfort and accommodation] which we gladly accepted on occasion.'

In France, which was not AC/DC's favourite touring location after several incidents in the past, such as the faulty equipment they'd been provided with which marred their Paris show opening for Black Sabbath in 1977, Bon teamed up with his friend from Trust, Bernie. The pair took the usual step of travelling about by train for the entire tour.

Bernie was amazed when Bon threw down three double whiskies before midday on one occasion. But Bon was just being Bon. He was having a ball and his mood was infectious.

By the time the tour hit Paris, Bon had lost his voice.

'They had to call a doctor to see him,' Bernie told Francis Zégut on radio station RTL in November 1997. 'Then when the doctor left, he took a glass of whisky and Coke and said "Doctor Whisky!"'

Thankfully, it was the last week of the tour, but on 9 December AC/DC had to play two sold-out shows on the same day at Pavillion de Paris. Angus could imagine what French fans must have been thinking.

Angus: 'They [the French] thought, "These guys are going to get on and sweat their balls off for four hours [over the two shows]," and I think that's what really sort of made it even more exciting.'

That excitement touched all levels of French society.

Angus: 'Even clothes designers were standing there [at a concert], even Yves Saint-Laurent was there!'

Although both shows were filmed, the second show, which was in the evening, would later be released as the feature movie *Let There Be Rock* and screened in theatres around the world.

Film-makers Eric Dionysius and Eric Mistler originally intended just to make a promotional video. The band's management asked to see some of the pair's previous work to support their proposal and that posed a problem.

Eric Dionysius: 'We hadn't done much at all. So we bluffed and told him [Peter Mensch] that all the films we'd done were overseas and the only thing we had left at the time was a short clip on [French band] Bijou. We sent the small three-and-a-half-minute clip, which they liked. About a week after that they said okay. They assumed we wanted to do a full feature movie! So we said [to each other], "Let's try to finance a full feature movie." We borrowed all over the place.'

With that, the task expanded to not just capturing the band's searing live show on film but also behind-the-scenes footage on what was AC/DC's most successful tour to date.

Dionysius had never seen AC/DC before and wanted to get a feel for what it was he would be shooting. So, two weeks before the concert in Paris, Dionysius and Mistler went to Ludwigshafen in Germany to film the band, just on an amateur VHS camera.

With an understanding of their subject under their belts, they started to put together a team in Paris and began shooting in the other French cities the band were playing — Metz, Reims and finally Lille — three days before the Paris shows.

The interviews were done in Metz in the band's hotel rooms, but for some reason the footage of the relaxed atmosphere of their tour bus where the band were playing poker, talking and watching television wasn't used.

In Reims, the pair caught the band on film in the champagne cellars and Malcolm indulging in his other great passion: playing soccer.

It was in Metz where what would eventually be the movie's introduction was recorded — basically Angus walking around the empty venue with his guitar, checking the sound.

Eric Dionysius: 'We thought we'd never have the time to do it in Paris, and of course his wireless guitar didn't work in Paris. But I thought that sound was great, it's like [he's playing] in a cathedral.'

Like Malcolm, other members of the band were shown indulging in favourite pastimes. For Angus, it was drawing — slightly provocatively — a devil.

The scenes with car nut Phil driving the Porsche and Cliff seeming to fly the World War I plane were filmed at la Ferté Alais, a small airport in the south of the French capital.

Come the day of the shows in Paris, a film crew of 40 were at work.

For much of the team, who had never previously seen the band perform, the first show in the afternoon was virtually a rehearsal for their filming of the second performance that night.

The second show was shot by five cameras but it wasn't documented in its entirety. Dionysius and Mistler didn't like the song TNT so simply didn't shoot it.

A week or two after the concert, when the films were processed, Dionysius and Mistler discovered that certain parts of the film were either not of satisfactory quality or missing due to unavoidable technical issues such as operators having to change film during the shoot.

It was decided that they would go to Le Mans in January 1980 to fill these holes but in the meantime it was off to Versailles to shoot Bon's individual scenes where, almost typically, there was a near tragedy.

Eric Dionysius: 'We wanted to film a sequence with a motorbike for Bon because he was a motorbike fan. Unfortunately we couldn't get the bike delivered, so we made him dance on the lake. The lake was frozen and the ice was cracking under his feet! Imagine, if he'd fallen in the water through the ice, he would have died! He wasn't too thrilled about it. I did test the ice. It was solid, but you could hear it crack and you'd see long crackles start where you'd walk. It didn't move, just crackled, but the noise was impressive. Also, to get warmer at the same time, Bon had lit a joint.'

The film-makers ended up with something like seven hours' worth of film, which, combined with interviews, gave them approximately 10 to 11 hours of footage, which was edited down to 95 minutes for the screen.

France's apparent curse on the band continued when Bon pulled a muscle in Nice after clowning around with a roadie, although he did the show anyway. The injury came back to bite Bon early in the batch of four UK dates between 17 and 21 December. The show on 18 December at Southampton had to be rescheduled for 27 January.

Back once again at the Hammersmith Odeon, the crowd was treated to It's A Long Way To The Top and Baby, Please Don't Go, which hadn't been played since 1976 and 1977 respectively. Probably not wanting to deal with the problems he had with the bagpipes on previous occasions, Bon didn't play them in It's A Long Way To The Top. Instead that role sounded as if it was handled by a synthesiser.

AC/DC's set lists were usually pretty much set in stone and departing from them was extremely rare. It was almost as if the band was giving those songs, and even the era they were from, one last airing before closing the door on that period of their career permanently and moving forward.

In any event, Bon was enjoying the ride now, after 15 years, more than ever as he was finally making a few bucks and getting some long-overdue respect.

'I'm 33,' he told Michel Embareck in *Best* magazine. 'You're never too old to rock and roll.'

And for Bon, AC/DC was the perfect vehicle for that exercise and he was enormously proud to be on their front line. The band members were all like brothers to him and he had the greatest respect and admiration for each of them.

His dedication to AC/DC was complete and beyond question.

Peter Wells (Rose Tattoo): 'Some French designer came up with these jeans with round holes in both cheeks of your arse. Bon was going to get a pair of pants and cut the arse out of them and get "AC" tattooed on one side and "DC" tattooed on the other. He never did it but he thought it was a great idea for about five minutes.'

Bon once best summed up his feelings about the band in *Juke*.

'Don't mention other bands around us, okay? We're the kings of the scene; no-one else fucking matters.'

As he always did when he could, Bon came back to Australia for Christmas to catch up with family and friends and to relax. Among those he looked up was Peter Head.

While Bon revelled in being a rock star and the adulation that was rightly coming his way, he also longed for a more settled life, as he told Head.

Peter Head: 'We went out, bought some booze, got some dope and went to a party in Stanley Street [Sydney]. It was a wild party — the next morning we both woke up in adjoining rooms in bed with women whose names we couldn't remember, and then he suddenly got up, walked out, and I never saw him again. During the night, he had started to tell me that even though he initially had really loved the period of being enormously successful, what he really wanted now was to settle down and have kids, and felt that this was far more rewarding than superficial success as a "rock star".'

The plan for the new year was to conclude the *Highway To Hell* tour in the UK, where they would do the next album, have it wrapped up by March and possibly commence touring again in April or May in Australia, before mounting an assault on the rest of the world. Within the next year it was anticipated that AC/DC would be the biggest rock act on the planet. Bon's long, patient wait to be in the penthouse suite seemed close to being over. Unless, as he joked, fate stepped in.

'Hopefully the band's still alive then,' Bon had told Bill Scott of Radio WABX in October with a laugh. 'We might all die from malnutrition and exhaustion.'

1979
Last laugh: Bon, Lille, France.

chapter 17

TOO CLOSE
TO THE SUN

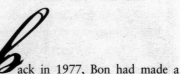

ack in 1977, Bon had made a dramatic announcement while he was in the band's booking agency in Melbourne. According to a tarot reader, by 1980 he would be dead. It was almost an eerie licence to continue to live life to its fullest.

'He went to a tarot-card reader,' Malcolm told Francis Zégut on RTL in October 1997, 'who told him he would meet a blonde, get divorced, meet a dark-haired girl, and he'd have a short life.'

It was a Tuesday night in the middle of January 1980 and there was a reasonable crowd at the Family Inn in western Sydney. Swanee, fronted by John Swan, was headlining with the Lonely Hearts in the opening spot. It seemed like any other night until halfway through the Hearts' set when singer John Rooney noticed four very distinct individuals arrive and position themselves near the bar that ran along the back wall.

John Rooney: 'When we finished our spot, I went down to the bar and realised that the person that was sauntering over the back of the dancefloor for the Lonely Hearts was Bon Scott. He was there with some girl whom I don't know and the other person was Jimmy Barnes and his wife. Bon was classic because he had these jeans on that were painted on — that's how tight they were — and he had boots on and a midriff top and a waistcoat. I'd never seen him before in regards to a close-up and thought, "Gee, he's quite tiny and completely out of it!"'

Swanee delivered a typically powerful set and for the encore was joined on stage not only by Barnes, who was Swan's brother, but also Bon. The trio proceeded to roar through three songs including Led Zeppelin's Whole Lotta Love and Chuck Berry's Back In The USA.

They signed off with a salute to the audience, with Swan in the middle, Barnes on his left and Bon on his right, all brandishing the microphone stands above their heads.

John Swan: 'The energy that was on the stage was fucking tremendous, an unbelievable amount of energy.'

John Rooney: 'It was phenomenal! The power of Bon Scott over the top of those two guys which is saying something! It was just sheer power! After the show, my brother ran into him backstage — in the toilet actually — and Bon said, "Good band [the Lonely Hearts], mate! Good band! Good stuff!" And my brother was obviously chuffed about that. He [Bon] was very, very polite. Completely out of it but very polite.'

For Bon, Barnes and Swan, the night wasn't a one-off; the trio were often out together when Bon was in Australia and no-one could party like they could. January 1980 was no exception.

John Swan: 'Jim, Bon and myself were the three best drinkers I knew. We used to fucking drink all night and maybe two nights, three nights, but don't forget we were taking speed as well. So if you were a normal drinker and a hard man you would still go to sleep at two o'clock in the morning because you were drunk. We were drunk but we wouldn't go down because the fucking speed would make us rattle all night. So you would continue with copious amounts of alcohol, and of course when you had more alcohol, somebody would come in with some speed.

'[On one occasion] Bon, Jim and myself were sitting down on the cliffs where the surf club [at Bondi] is. We'd been up for two or three days and I was feeling really hungover and really fucking rotten, and Bon's gone for a run along the beach and I thought he was going to have a fucking heart attack! He's a maniac.

'When he was with you, Bon was your best pal. You talk to anybody about Bon, and no matter how out of it he was he could still be the most charming man in the world.'

A few days after the Family Inn gig, Bon was back in France and the UK for the final shows of the *Highway To Hell* tour and to begin work on the new album. There he looked utterly invincible, even immortal, in the shot by photographer Robert Ellis from the *Highway To Hell* tour that appeared on the single of Touch Too Much. Released earlier in the month, the photo framed him perfectly: bare-chested in a denim vest with the sleeves torn off, a large belt buckle, skin-tight jeans and his head thrown back with one leg propped up on a monitor at the front of the stage. It was the sort of photo that Bon could have handed out as a business card. The image showed exactly what he did for a living; he was a rock and roll singer in the world's best rock and roll band.

The final date of the *Highway To Hell* tour was the rescheduled show at Southampton Gaumont on 27 January, which Ian Jeffery believes was the sole occasion Bon drank prior to performing. A symbolic moment in more ways than one, although he was simply continuing on from the night before.

The *Highway To Hell* tour had, in every respect, been the band's biggest to date and there was a feeling of quiet excitement for what the future held.

All the white-line fever they had suffered through due to countless hours on the road since they first left Australia in April 1976 was finally paying off in exactly the right type of dividends: growing album sales rather than just the increasingly wild scenes at venue box offices.

Bon took time out to see his friends UFO at one of the shows of their three-night stand at London's Hammersmith Odeon on 3, 4 and 5 February. He had loved the earthiness of the English outfit and their rock-solid onstage attack ever since they had first toured together. The fact they liked a party as much as he did wasn't lost on Bon, either. For several members of UFO, that party involved dabbling with heroin, as Pete Way told Geoff Barton in *Classic Rock* in February 2005.

'Now we as UFO were on substances, right? If you've never done heroin before — and we were doing heroin after the show like we always did — and you drink, the odds are that at some point you'll fall asleep and you'll choke and you'll die.'

Meanwhile, even though AC/DC were officially off tour, there were still a few promotional matters to deal with.

On 7 February, they appeared on the UK's 'Top of the Pops' and performed Touch Too Much. Playing before studio cameras was never their situation of choice and, to make matters worse, on this occasion, to their amazement, in a flashback to Elvis Presley's historic first appearance in 1956 on 'The Ed Sullivan Show', Angus was told that he would only be in shot from the waist up.

Attitudes were very different two days later with their first Spanish TV appearance on 'Aplauso' in Madrid, where they ran through Beating Around The Bush, Girls Got Rhythm and Highway To Hell then faced a press conference the next morning.

Bon was enormously excited about AC/DC's next album and spoke enthusiastically about it to almost anyone who crossed his path. Like some sort of rock and roll coronation, it was his time, his moment, after all these years. And his lyrics on *Highway To Hell* showed he was about to really hit an unmatchable stride this time around. He was probably smiling that sparkling, impish smile in his sleep.

At one point, Bon, during one of his regular visits to Jeffery's flat, left behind a folder of lyrics in progress for the next album which provided a fascinating insight into the singer's working methods.

Ian Jeffery: 'The lyrics were sketchy but that's the way Bon did it. It was like a little fucking notebook that he'd flip over and make a few notes, scribble one or two lines, cross them out, add one thing

— sometimes one word would change — or he'd write two words on one page.

'Bon was quite organised. He had a folder with all [his potential lyrics] inside, believe it or not Bon used to come to work with a folder and he'd leave with it — that was his life. That was Bon. And he'd have postcards in there that he was writing to people. He was the best communicator in the world.'

With his time his own again for a few days, on 13 February Bon was in the studio with his French buddies Trust while they were recording their *Repression* album in London. Together they jammed on a version of Ride On that would later surface on a promo single for the band. It would be Bon's last-ever recording.

'A few months before, we [had] talked about doing something together,' Bernie from the band told Francis Zégut from RTL in November 1997, 'and the first thing he told me when he came in was that he [had] worked on the lyrics [of the English version of Trust's album] and that he had seven or eight songs. I was thrilled.'

Tragically, Bernie never got to see the lyrics.

Meanwhile, Angus — who had recently married — and Malcolm were working in the E-Zee Hire rehearsal studio in London on riffs and songs for the new album and Bon called in to check on their progress sometime between 12 and 15 February. The Young duo had been shaping two new songs, Have A Drink On Me and Let Me Put My Love Into You, when he arrived. Rather than grabbing a microphone and running through some of the lyrics he'd been piecing together, Bon made a beeline for the drums, which suited Malcolm and Angus just fine.

Angus: 'He said, "Let me bash away," which was great for me and Mal because every now and again it would help, especially if we were writing songs, because otherwise Malcolm would get behind the drum kit and I would do all the guitar work and/or bass or Mal would get on the guitar and I'd try my hand at the kit.'

Bon's drumming skills from childhood and from his days in The Valentines had been sharpened over the years watching and, indeed, physically feeling the simple beauty of Phil Rudd's playing during AC/DC's performances.

Now he was able to thump out an opening passage for Let Me Put My Love Into You, which delighted Malcolm and Angus.

It was another sign that everything was falling into place. The next album would be the one to really grab the world by the balls and squeeze. The band and everyone around them could feel it.

When word came through on 14 February that *Highway To Hell* had sold one million copies in America, the success of the next album, even though it was only in its early stages of construction, seemed almost a foregone conclusion.

On 17 February, Bon took part in what was his usual Sunday ritual — lunch at Ian Jeffery's place with Jeffery's wife, Suzie, and her friend Anna, whom Bon was dating at the time.

Ian Jeffery: 'Every Sunday it was a ritual — they'd come over about 11 or 12 and my missus and her friend would make Sunday dinner, and me and Bon would go to the pub. We'd meet a few other friends — the crew guys that used to be with [Rick] Wakeman [from Yes] and a few of our crew guys and sometimes Malcolm and Angus would come as well. We'd have a few bevvies and go back home at two o'clock. The footy would come on the telly so we'd have our Sunday dinner and watch the football and maybe have a little kip. Then, nine times out of 10, we'd go back to the pub in the evening.

'That particular night I was really tired and I wasn't feeling that well, so Phil Mogg and Pete Way [from UFO] — they used to live really near me — called up and said, "Come on! Are you going to the pub tonight?" So Bon said, "Yeah, we'll go to the pub." In the end, I couldn't be fucking bothered. They went up the pub like they normally do and then they went on to the Camden Music Machine after that, which was a Sunday-night haunt. I spoke to Pete afterwards and he said, "We got hammered and we were going home and Bon didn't want to go — he wanted to carry on drinking."'

The next day, 18 February, Bon had planned to spend the evening with his friends from Trust, but they'd received their first Gold record that night and their record company had other plans for them. At a loose end, Bon made two calls that evening. The first was to Coral Browning in Los Angeles. She wasn't in. The other was to his former girlfriend Silver Smith, who was living in London.

Although Bon was due in the studio with AC/DC the next day, he wanted to hit the town, but Silver wasn't interested.

Alistair Kinnear, a former flatmate of Silver, then called her. Kinnear had been invited by Zena Kakoulli to the Music Machine for the launch party of Lonesome No More, an outfit fronted by Kakoulli's sister, Koulla, which also included Billy Duffy, who later became the guitarist in The Cult. Silver suggested that Kinnear take Bon so, with his plans for the night now set, Bon called Trust's Bernie to let him know he'd be at the Music Machine at about 11 p.m.

According to Kinnear in the *Evening Standard* on 21 February 1980, Bon was well into party mode when Kinnear arrived to pick him up, and at the Music Machine was downing four shots of whisky per glass.

AC/DC's original drummer, Colin Burgess, and his brother, Denny, were also at the Music Machine.

Burgess has a very different recollection of Bon's condition.

'I remember us leaving and he was alright ... like he wasn't drunk at all. Absolutely perfect. And we went home [Bon didn't leave] and next day he's dead! I cannot imagine how he could be so drunk to have that happen to him ... To me, it's just a really, really strange thing ... I can definitely say, to this day, that when we left he definitely wasn't drunk at all.'

Kinnear did his share of drinking at the Lonesome No More show, but managed to drive Bon home to Ashley Court in Westminster when the night drew to a close. Towards the end of the journey, he became aware that Bon had passed out.

'I left him in my car and rang his doorbell,' he told Maggie Montalbano in 2005's *Metal Hammer and Classic Rock present AC/DC* magazine, 'but his current live-in girlfriend [Anna] didn't answer. I took Bon's keys and let myself into the flat, but no-one was at home. I was unable to wake Bon, so I rang Silver for advice. She said that he passed out quite frequently, and that it was best just to leave him be to sleep it off.'

But sleep where? It was by now very late and freezing cold, a stark contrast to the heatwave conditions that met AC/DC when they first arrived in the UK in 1976. He decided on Plan B: drive Bon back to the flat on Overhill Road in East Dulwich where Kinnear lived. But once he'd pulled up outside, he found that Bon's soundly sleeping body was a dead weight — too much in Kinnear's party-weakened condition to shift. Kinnear had now run out of options.

'I put the front passenger seat back so that he could lie flat,' he told *Metal Hammer/Classic Rock*, 'covered him with a blanket, left a note with my address and phone number on it, and staggered upstairs to bed.'

Kinnear had been asleep for about six hours when a friend woke him around 11 a.m. Kinnear was feeling the full effects of the big night before and asked his friend to go down to the car and look in on Bon, whose hangover had to be at least as bad as Kinnear was experiencing. His friend reported that Bon had gone, and so, thinking the singer had decided to make his way home to his own more comfortable bed, Kinnear drifted back to sleep.

Band rehearsals continued for a second day without Bon. No-one knew where the hell he was. But it had happened before and no alarm bells rang. Bon would be there when it really counted.

That evening, at about quarter to eight, Kinnear was bewildered to discover that Bon was in the car just as he had left him. (His body was not bent around the vehicle's gearstick as was later reported.) This confusion turned to horror when he noticed Bon wasn't breathing.

Kinnear rushed him to King's College Hospital but he was pronounced dead on arrival.

For someone who once gleefully said that he worked for the women, the whisky and the glamour, it was a decidedly unglamorous and lonely way for Bon to go out — dying in a car parked on the side of a south London street in the freezing cold.

The hospital contacted Silver after Kinnear gave them her details. Angus received the news via calls from two women, presumably

Silver and Anna, just as he got back from rehearsing that night. The normally subdued Angus was confused and horrified and made a hurried call to Malcolm, who in turn phoned Ian Jeffery.

Ian Jeffery: 'I got a call at three in the morning from Malcolm, actually, and my first comment to him was, "You're joking!" He said, "Would I fucking joke about a thing like this, you fucking cunt!" I called Peter Mensch and he said the same thing to me: "Don't fucking joke! Don't wake me up to tell me this fucking shit!" I said, "I'm not fucking joking!" I called Jake [production manager Jake Berry] and he came around, and I called Malcolm back and went down to Mensch's and then went down to the hospital to identify the body.

'At six-thirty, seven, in the morning, we got to the hospital and it was chaos with all the emergency stuff from the night before. This person met us and took us with them and we turned this corner and I couldn't fucking hear anything — the chaos that was going on! I said to Mensch, "He's in that fucking room there." And, sure enough, we got to the room and there he was. I got up to the window, looked through and saw the fucking slab — I saw the sheet — and I said to Mensch, "It's him! I'm not going in!" Mensch said, "Come on, you've got to come in," and I said, "It's him; it's Bon! I'm not going in!"'

Malcolm had the grim task of calling Bon's parents in Perth in an attempt to save them the horror of hearing of their son's death on television or in the newspapers, or, worse, being advised of the tragedy by a reporter expecting a comment from them.

At first, Bon's mother mistook Malcolm for Bon making one of his frequent calls to check on his parents and bring them up to date with all his news. The couple was devastated when Malcolm explained the reason for his call.

The headline posters for Sydney's *Daily Mirror* on the evening of 21 February spelt out the unthinkable, and the news bulletins confirmed it: Bon was dead. Roger Crosthwaite, then a journalist with Sydney's *Daily Telegraph*, who once had a very-late-night run-in with Bon at Chequers (Bon had been just about to punch him before he was restrained), recalls the reaction to the singer's death.

'Apart from Johnny O'Keefe, he was the first Australian rock personage to die, and it was big in that way because it was kind of a shock. Like, our people didn't die; your overseas loonies died. And he seemed so indestructible — he was such a strong character.'

John Swan: 'How many people that were affected was fucking unbelievable. John Lennon's death had a great effect on a lot of people, but Bon's death actually changed a lot of people, too.'

Ozzy Osbourne: 'I wasn't a chum of Bon Scott's, but I used to see him from time to time. I was trying to kick the alcohol and I know he had an alcohol problem, and when he died it gave me the shove I needed ... It was so fucking sad because Bon was a great singer — Bon was just made for AC/DC.'

'The guy already died a couple of times before anyway,' Phil Rudd told VH1 in March 2003, 'so we all expected him to sort of turn up for practice the next day. Things were going so well.'

The inquest into the death was conducted by Sir Montague Levine, the Assistant Deputy Coroner for Inner South London, on 22 February. According to Professor Arthur Mant at the inquest, Bon had consumed half a bottle of whisky in his final hours.

One rumour that circulated briefly was that Bon's death had been caused by a punctured lung, an injury he sustained after wrestling with a roadie, and that, in turn, was exacerbated by his reported asthma and, of course, his drinking.

There was an element of truth in the story — Bon had indeed hurt himself horseplaying with a member of the crew in Nice back in December. But the official cause of death was recorded on the death certificate as 'Acute alcohol poisoning', 'Death by misadventure'.

On 29 March, Dave Lewis reported in *Sounds* that the autopsy rated Bon's overall health as 'excellent', the condition of his kidneys and liver included, even given his legendary passion for partying.

The generally accepted belief was that Bon had been lying in a position that obstructed his airways and, when he went to vomit, he choked. Jimi Hendrix had died under similar circumstances.

Angus had seen Bon put away extraordinary amounts of alcohol in the past and then fall asleep wherever he was. The next day he would always be ready to take on the world again.

'I remember he was somewhere one night,' he told *Sounds'* Dave Lewis, 'and the people he was with filled him full of dope and things, and he was really drunk then, too. But fortunately they took him straight to hospital, and they kept him in for the day and he was alright then.'

Given the reported circumstances of Bon's death, suddenly his light-hearted party expression 'Straight booze gets you drunker quicker' took on a grave weight he'd never intended, as did stories about him shouting entire bars and drinking aftershave.

His reputation for drinking certainly preceded him.

Peter Wells (Rose Tattoo): 'I remember he walked into the Largs Pier in Adelaide one night when we were playing over there. He'd just ridden over on a bike from Melbourne, speedin' off his tits. He was, like, wired to fuck, you know, and he was drinking these things — a jug of gin, port and Coca-Cola.'

Barry Bergman: 'I remember at Marks Music we gave [AC/DC] each a quart of good Scotch for a gift, and, before they left the office, Bon's quart was already finished. Before they left the office! They were there maybe for an hour. His philosophy was he's living for today. He was never concerned about what would be; he was concerned about living now and living for today. I had discussed it with him a bunch of times; we talked about the alcohol, the drinking, the problems and whatnot. For him, it didn't seem like a problem.'

A report in *Juke* on 1 March said that George Young and Harry Vanda had planned to speak to Bon about his drinking when AC/DC toured Australia in April.

The same article reported that overseas touring partners Cheap Trick warned during their Australian dates that the singer was headed for an early grave unless he took action.

But, over the years, particularly since the early '90s, questions have arisen as to whether there was more to the official story about Bon's death than had been reported at the time.

Bon had passed out on previous occasions and drinking too much seemed in character; however, it seemed strange that someone with a proven cast-iron constitution could simply die in a parked car with such a relatively small amount of alcohol — half a bottle of whisky wasn't much for Bon — reported to be in his system.

During a 1980 interview for a US magazine, a band member was quoted as saying that the coroner found Bon's death had resulted from choking; the band member added that the violent reaction had been triggered 'by certain things they didn't release'.

It was a stunning admission that, at least on the face of it, seemed to go some way towards supporting the view that substances other than alcohol were involved in Bon's demise. However, the possibility of other health-related issues also being a factor shouldn't be entirely discounted. After all, the 33-year-old singer had been pushing his body hard for the best part of almost two decades, both privately and on stage.

In any case, rather than set the record straight, the reported comment raises more questions than it answers.

Firstly, it hardly seems likely that the authorities would have failed to disclose, or tried to mask, all of the contributing factors. Secondly, and most importantly, AC/DC were not in a position in early 1980, if indeed anyone ever is, to wield the type of power that would allow them to dictate what was officially recorded on a death certificate.

Malcolm: 'There was a cover up, I'd read at some point. Gee, I thought, how could us guys command that type of power, to go in and take over the British laws and everything that's involved in dying? It's incredible.'

In essence, if Bon was a casualty of anything, it was simply the times. Life was more easy-going and less restrictive. Partying hard with no thought about tomorrow, until the sun rose — sometimes long after it did — was the order of the day, as Rose Tattoo's Peter Wells sagely explains:

'It was pre AIDS and pre drink driving and pre dirty drugs. For all those reasons, people probably just lived it up a bit more. Like the end of [Bon's] career. We had a lot of nights like that. It was bad luck, nothing else. Like anybody else you could have died a hundred fucking times.'

Regardless of the details, Malcolm and Angus were devastated by the loss. According to Ian Jeffery, it affected the brothers differently.

'The same but totally different, if that makes sense. Malcolm was more angry and Angus was more "I can't believe this!"'

Angus, who had always been more sensitive than his brother, was crushed. It felt like a member of his family had been cruelly snatched away. And family was everything. But he was slightly comforted by his final vision of Bon behind the drums in the studio a few days before his death.

'Probably the first time I saw him and the last time I saw him he was playing an instrument he loved.'

Bon had disappeared before, but losing him permanently just didn't make sense.

Angus: 'I felt horribly grown-up in a way because, when you're young, you always think you're immortal, and I think at that time it [Bon's death] really sort of spun me round.

'He'd always been quite wild but, because I think we were young, that's the last sort of thing you think of someone because up until that time we steamed through everything. A lot of times we didn't even think.'

'He was really close to me,' Angus told Stephen Blush in *Spin* in February 1991. 'I really came to realise how fragile life can be, and how quickly you can lose it all.'

It also most likely confirmed in the mind of the teetotalling Angus that the straight and narrow — apart from cigarettes, of course — was the best path.

'I think a lot of people sort of think I'm a chronic alcoholic or something. Usually when I say I don't drink, they think I'm lying. When I was a teenager, it was like that was the thing to do — you had to hit the pub ... At the time I always thought, well, okay, been there, seen that, done that, now what else? I thought to myself I didn't want to be hanging around a bar all my life.'

For Leber-Krebs, it was, in a way, a case of tragic déjà vu. They were managing the New York Dolls when drummer Billy Murcia died in London in 1972, just as the Dolls were on the cusp of really making an impact. Now the same thing had happened to AC/DC.

In the wake of Bon's passing came the sombre task of sorting out the singer's affairs. Giving Bon a dignified and affectionate sendoff under difficult circumstances was part of that process.

Ian Jeffery: 'We came to this quick decision that we put Bon in this rest house — if you want to pay your respects, you go there, etc. And [Bon's girlfriend, Anna] sat vigil out there, just because of the hospital thing, the police thing and everything else.'

Still haunted by the dreadful vision of Bon at the hospital, Jeffery, one of the few — out of practical necessity — who had access to the singer's flat, picked out some more friendly and familiar clothes for his good friend.

'I remember seeing the sheet [in the hospital] and saying, "There's no fucking way my mate, the band's friend, is going to be shrouded in that fucking shit," and I picked up a pair of jeans and his white T-shirt which he used to love to wear.'

Bon was going to go out with the same swagger that he had in life.

A stark reminder of all that the band had lost and just how much their dreams had been dashed came within days of Bon's death, when they were presented with a preview of what would be the *Let There Be Rock* movie. Bon himself only ever saw a very rough mix of the movie, just for the synchronisation with the images. They sat uncomfortably through the rushes, made a few remarks and then left quietly. They were crushed all over again.

On 28 February, Bon's body was repatriated to Australia, with the entire band in tow as a mark of respect.

Jeffery had one major responsibility on the trip.

Ian Jeffery: 'I mean, Angus is so sensitive, right? The record company's flying us first class and it was like, "We're not fucking sitting in first class with our mate underneath us." A big thing with Angus was to make sure that Bon was on a different plane to us. So I guaranteed him that. But we get to Perth and we're ready to leave the plane and I'm looking out the window and I see this fucking box coming down. It was like, I gotta make sure Angus doesn't see this! No hearses at the airport or anything like that — it'd totally freak him out! I promised him it would be on a different plane. It came down the same fucking escalator thing, the same thing as the bags came down, and there I was looking at it!'

Bon was cremated on 29 February and his ashes interred in the Fremantle Cemetery's Memorial Garden, near Perth, in a quiet ceremony on 1 March.

The funeral service was a low-key affair with no mass outpouring of grief from hordes of fans. Only a few milled around and were reserved and respectful. It had been two and a half years since AC/DC had played on an Australian stage and despite the fact that a funeral notice appeared in the *West Australian* newspaper, sadly it seemed to be a case of out of sight, out of mind. Neither the media nor the heavyweights of the Australian music industry, apart from Albert's, were represented.

Jeffery recalls how surreal it was after the cremation seeing a peg in the ground outside, marking where Bon's ashes were to be placed. That was what the enormous character and spirit of his friend was reduced to.

In the years that followed, a bizarre ritual grew which involved fans spending the night on Bon's grave. According to local myth, any women who did so woke the next day with love bites on their necks.

The horror of losing her son had only really struck Mrs Scott the day before the funeral when the band went to the Scotts' home on arrival in Perth.

Ian Jeffery: 'There was all sorts of shit going on the radio and in the press — drug overdose, suicide, the whole crap that was going around him. I'll never forget, mate, walking in the house and — the usual thing — [Mrs Scott's] got sandwiches, the whole thing. She could have been your mum or my mum. She was so fucking glad to see someone who had been with her son, who had been close to Bon, and knew what the fuck was going on, so we walked in the house. She said, "Come on and sit here," and she'd got fucking five chairs out and she fucking lost it. It was the first time I really think that she knew then that it was true. And that, to me, was one of the worst moments.'

In Australia, *RAM* magazine's 21 March issue carried a classic live shot of Bon on the front cover with the words 'Tribute to a fallen warrior'. Inside was a four-page feature by Vince Lovegrove plus a stark, graphic-free, full-page advertisement that simply read:

A great singer, a great lyricist, a great friend, one of a kind, we'll miss you — Harry and George.

In that same issue of *RAM*, Kristine Leary, a fan from Tasmania, had written to express her sorrow about Bon and to thank him for the card and autographed picture he had sent her. It was classic Bon.

Trust dedicated their hugely successful 1980 second album, *Repression*, to Bon, while Cheap Trick, who had often played Highway To Hell at their gigs, included a song on their 1980 album, *All Shook Up*, titled Love Comes A'Tumblin' Down, as a tribute.

Rick Nielsen (Cheap Trick): 'While we were doing the *All Shook Up* album sessions with George Martin, I got two phone calls in one day on Montserrat. The first one said that a third of my house had burnt down, and the second was that Bon had been found dead. My family was with me, so I knew no-one was hurt at my home, but the loss of Bon was, and still is, one of the saddest days in rock.'

Nielsen had had big plans with Bon.

'I had wanted to use Bon, Alex Harvey, Steve Marriott, Roger Chapman [Family], Freddie Mercury, and [Cheap Trick's] Robin Zander for a project I was thinking of doing. I asked Bon and he asked me, while we were on tour together, to be on each other's future solo projects, if or when we had some time.'

A saddened Joe Elliott from Def Leppard felt a twinge in his hip pocket when he heard the news.

'I still owe him 10 quid. I never got the chance to give him his tenner back. In fairness, if he was still alive he wouldn't have it either. He should have known better than to lend me £10!'

Even in death Bon seemed to live on. In the weeks after his passing, Christmas cards he'd sent to friends, which had been lost in the mail, finally arrived. Atlantic's Perry Cooper was one of those who received an unexpected communique.

Perry Cooper: 'He'd sent it [a card] to me and it just took a long time to get to me, and he'd already died by the time I got it. It was just weird. He wrote, "I didn't know who to send this to, and, once I read it [the printed message on the card], I immediately thought of you. Bon."'

Bon had always been a conscientious dedicated correspondent.

Vince Lovegrove: 'He used to write letters to everybody he knew during the '60s and the early '70s as he was travelling around the world — to all the friends that he made during that time. He never forgot them and always kept in touch with them, either by letter or by phone. He was a great letter-writer, Bon.'

Ian Jeffery: 'A lot of times we'd be checking out [of hotels] and one of Bon's first questions to the girl behind the desk would be, "You got any stamps?" so he could send a postcard sometimes to people he only met once, twice or whatever. He was just that kind of guy. Just a genuine fucking diamond.'

Rose Tattoo's Angry Anderson saw Bon as something far more colourful and romantic than simply a dedicated correspondent.

'We were the last of the rock street poets because that's the way we saw ourselves. We wrote poetry and put it to music. It just happens to be violent poetry and put to [sometimes] violent music. We saw ourselves as the last of the gypsy vagabond devil-may-cares in the Errol Flynn mode — Captain Blood, buccaneering Genghis Khans. And that I think even now.'

Only AC/DC knew the real tragedy of it all. Bon had been starting to really get somewhere, after almost two decades of back-and gut-grinding, not to mention at times soul-destroying, work. Now he had been ushered out just as his powers were seemingly about to peak. The next album, Angus told *Sounds*' Dave Lewis on 29 March, 'would've been the crowning glory of his life'.

And Bon would have been more than happy to share the glory.

Angus: 'He was not an ego guy. I think, because he was a drummer, he always thought like a band [rather than about himself]. He never used to put himself in front or above, and he would always grab me and shove me forward and go, "Come on, they want to see you, Ang." He didn't sort of subscribe to that school of fame that is vain. That, I always thought, was his greatness.'

Angus has gone so far as to liken Bon to Hendrix and Chuck Berry in terms of stature.

Angus: 'Chuck Berry's got the gift of it all — great songwriter, player and innovator. It's the same thing, I think, with Bon. But in terms of what the world would call a loss, I would say he ranks as good as any of those that people have said are worthy to be remembered. I think Bon is up there with all the big ones. Even with Presley, I rank him. Even more so. He didn't possess the smarmy bullshit.'

Sure, Bon pushed the envelope, but he seemed to know where the line was and, if he did cross it, he did so on his own.

Angus: 'He always said to me, "Whatever I do, don't follow." He would always make that clear. Sometimes he'd arrive someplace and didn't know how he got there. He just knew that he'd been partying for a few days somewhere. I remember that somebody told me they went down to the airport in London to collect Bon and he arrived [three days late] with hardly any clothes on; he just arrived with a pair of pants on. He walked through Customs with a pair of pants and a pair of sunglasses and nothing else — no shoes, shirt, socks. Nothing. All we knew was his mother had seen him off from Perth Airport in Australia days earlier. When he showed up, he didn't know where he'd been or what!

'[On another occasion] I remember he was scrambling up the PA system, and he could really climb — he was good at that. He used to never wear shoes and a lot of times he'd get on [stage] and perform in bare feet. So he scrambled up this PA system that was about 60 feet high. I was on the other side and he's going, "Now we'll jump!" I said, "You're on your own here, buddy!" But he did it! He was brave; he had no fear of things like that.'

Like, as Peter Wells recalls, practising his diving technique back at the Freeway Gardens Motel in Melbourne in 1975, just because of a foolish dare.

'He used to come out on the balcony and dive into the fucking pool pissed — from the second floor! That blew me out. He used to give it an awful big nudge and be pretty crazy. You always knew he was about. They'd lock you up [for that sort of stuff] these days. A lot of the anecdotes — some of them are true, probably some of them aren't, and there's other ones that you probably couldn't talk about that are bigger than all of them!'

1974
Glitz and glam: Brian Johnson in Geordie, Chequers, Sydney.

chapter 18

NOT THE MOST AMBITIOUS LAD

*d*uring the 4 March flight back to London following Bon's funeral, the issue of new singers was raised, but Malcolm, the band's razor-sharp business mind and unspoken leader, was dismissive. He was yet to get his head fully around the situation.

But, according to tour manager Ian Jeffery, there was never any doubt the band would go on, just as Bon's dad had encouraged Malcolm to do. It was just the operational fine print that was the problem.

'The first thing was: we're going to continue. There was never any [doubt]. Never, never a fucking minute. They were shocked at first … [but] we were moving on from day one. How were we going to achieve it? We had no idea.'

That was Malcolm's dilemma.

Simply calling time would also have been a slap in the face of the tough, hard-working character the band represented, and that was never going to happen. It was a matter of commitment, just as it always had been.

After a few days back in London, the work ethic that had gotten the band to where they were slowly began to kick in once more. Malcolm and Angus had never been good with downtime.

Malcolm, perhaps initially for the simple therapy of a familiar routine, if nothing else, got the itch first and picked up a guitar again, something he hadn't done since Bon's death. He wasn't going to sit around brooding for the rest of his days. It just wasn't his style. He called Angus and asked if he wanted to get together and look over the songs they had been working on.

Angus welcomed the distraction from the horror of Bon's passing and the pair shut out the world as they immersed themselves in the rehearsal room at E-Zee Hire Studios.

Of course, the magic between them hadn't diminished and the new songs were smouldering like hot coals. The future of the band, or at least what they would be playing, slowly became more clear.

Besides, as Angus told Penny Harding in *Juke* on 27 September, 'Bon would have kicked us all up the arse if we'd split.'

Angus: 'As soon as we said we were going to go on, people were saying, No, this isn't going to happen, that was them finished. You had pressure too from your record company coming at you, you had everyone, but the only ones that were really cool and calm was the band at the time.'

Announcing the decision to continue didn't solve their central problem.

Malcolm and Angus knew how Bon would have treated the new material they were forging, but it was difficult if not impossible to imagine how another party would tackle the songs. They had to try and find out, though.

First, there were their dream candidates: Steve Marriott and Slade's Noddy Holder. Both names were briefly thrown about, a surreal situation given that the brothers were contemplating employing one of their heroes.

They had seen Marriott's Small Faces in Sydney with The Who in 1968 and George knew the raspy throated singer from his days in England with The Easybeats. The tiny East Londoner certainly fitted the band's unspoken height requirement, but as with Holder there were concerns that such well-known names would attract an enormous amount of attention for a project that was already certain to come under plenty of scrutiny.

Gary Holton, formerly of the Kids or Heavy Metal Kids, and Terry Slesser, who did time fronting Back Street Crawler and had a future gig waiting with a band called Geordie, were considered more actively. Both Holton and Slesser had been Atlantic label-mates of AC/DC, so their candidacy most likely came out of them being known quantities. Tragically, Holton would be dead five years later.

Then there was the Australian contingent, from which many thought Cold Chisel's Jimmy Barnes was an obvious contender. Angry Anderson — who'd played in Buster Brown with Phil Rudd — seemed another. Like Marriott, he was a similar size to the rest of AC/DC, had a good relationship with the band, and sounded like a roughed-up Rod Stewart at his very best.

But it was the dark horse, John Swan, who was said to be the quiet favourite. Not only was he a Scot and an ex-boxer and drummer, but he was warm, good-humoured and blessed with one of the best rock, soul and blues voices in the world.

John Swan: 'I would say it would have been a definite maybe. But, my honest opinion in my heart and soul, I don't think they would have been in their right minds to take me, because they would have had another Bon on their hands. I say that with great respect because I was doing speed, coke, Christ knows what else, plus I drank 24–7.

'I would love to blow my trumpet and say, "Yeah, I was this and I was that," but the boys never walked up to me and said, "Swanee, would you consider joining the band?" I heard it all going around, I heard the wind blowing, but they'd be taking a big fucking risk, taking another one on.'

It was decided to cast the net more widely and one applicant each night was brought to Vanilla rehearsal studios in London. There was a snooker table downstairs where the crew settled the applicants when they arrived. They then took them upstairs, when the band were ready, where a tape recorder was set up out of view.

Malcolm and Angus were patient and did their best to make the hopefuls feel at ease, though they themselves were still quietly struggling with exactly what it was they were doing and why. But they knew one thing: they didn't want an imitation of Bon. And as it happened, absolutely none presented themselves.

For the most part, the applicants were average at best, surprisingly so given the calibre of the gig they were shooting for.

Ian Jeffery: 'The band would chat to them [the applicants] for a couple of minutes and say, "What do you want to do?" Ninety per cent of the singers blew themselves out of the water because they wanted to sing Smoke On The Water. They were history! They were gone! They'd grab the microphone, wrap their leg around it like fucking David Coverdale.'

One candidate from left-field stood out. His name was Gary Pickford Hopkins, one of the singers on Rick Wakeman's *Journey To The Centre Of The Earth* project; a connection no doubt made through Jeffery's links with the former Yes keyboard man.

Ian Jeffery: 'He had a good chance because they brought him back twice. They liked his voice, but it just didn't have the edge.'

It was during this process that rumours about the possibility of another Australian candidate surfaced: former Easybeat Stevie Wright.

'Stevie's Just Right For AC/DC' punned 'Countdown' host Ian 'Molly' Meldrum's Humdrum column in *TV Week* on 15 March, while the headline 'Grieving AC/DC may have found Mr Wright' topped Dave Dawson's Rock Beat column on 11 March in Sydney's *Mirror*.

The talk was subsequently picked up by *Melody Maker* in the UK and run in its 15 March issue. In *Juke*, an Albert's spokesperson flatly denied that Wright was a contender and added that approaches had been made to nine singers.

While the prospect of Wright sounded great on paper, the fact was that he was still taking things relatively slowly was after a well-documented drug problem and in no shape to spearhead the virtual relaunch of a band on the brink of massive global success.

Back in London, the selection process continued. Mutt Lange and Tony Platt, who had worked so successfully on *Highway To Hell*, had already been earmarked for duties on AC/DC's next album. The regard in which they were held by the band gave them a degree of input in the recruitment process.

Lange suggested Brian Johnson, the former singer with Newcastle's Geordie. Johnson was of ideal working-class stock and perfect for AC/DC.

Born in Dunston, Gateshead — in the northeast of England — on 5 October 1947, he was one of four children and grew up in Preston Village, North Shields in a home finely dusted in soot from the coal trains that rumbled past. Brian's father, Alan, was a sergeant major in the British Army who'd fought in Africa and Italy during World War II. Later, working in the mines played hell with his lungs.

On Brian's ninth birthday, BBC Radio played Johnny Duncan and the Blue Grass Boys doing Last Train To San Fernando and his life was suddenly mapped out before him.

He soon discovered he could hold a note or two and became a choirboy, which provided something to line his pockets with. The choir master gave him some singing lessons and he appeared for three years with the scouts in their Gang Shows.

Brian left Dunston Hill Secondary School at 15 to begin an apprenticeship as a fitter and turner and studied engineering at Gateshead Technical College. No coal mines for him, thanks.

Within two months he was gigging with his first band, The Gobi Desert Canoe Club, with some friends from the factory where he was working. Brian was a singer by default: he simply didn't have the money for a guitar or drums. The first song he sang in public was Buddy Holly's Not Fade Away. That night, Brian walked out of the youth club in Newcastle with £7 for his efforts with the band. It was a pivotal moment.

He was a changed man and grew his hair and updated his wardrobe to reflect the current trends. Not long after, an under-aged Brian got himself into Club A Go Go in Newcastle to see The

Animals and was spurred on further when he bought his first record by the Paul Butterfield Blues Band.

Soon he began to snap up albums by The Animals, the Yardbirds and BB King, the less fashionable the better as far as he was concerned. But it was the godfather of British blues, John Mayall, who was really the catalyst for Brian's musical aspirations, and he didn't pass up the chance to see Mayall and later meet his legendary guitarist Peter Green when they came to Newcastle.

At 17, Brian joined the army and was sent to Germany for two years with the Red Berets parachute regiment. Planes had long been a great passion and being a paratrooper was one of the great joys of his life. After leaving the army at 19, Brian became a draftsman but the job drove him crazy and after three months he again began to feel the magnetic pull of playing music at least part-time.

He played in dozens of bands in the '60s and in 1971 teamed with Brian Gibson (drums) and Tom Hill (bass) in Buffalo. A year later, the trio joined forces with Vic Malcolm in a band curiously called USA, and Brian decided to become a professional musician.

The first USA gig was on 1 February 1972 at Thornley Working Men's Club in Peterlee, and in May they signed with Red Bus Records in London, in a deal that effectively gave Red Bus total control of the band.

No-one was too impressed with the name change in June to Geordie, least of all the fans, but the band didn't have many other options under their restrictive contract. Times were very hard and they were, almost literally, starving. Maybe a new name might spark something.

The band went to London for their first recording sessions for Red Bus in July, and then late in 1972 relocated permanently to the capital, where they found the going even harder than in Newcastle. To survive, they used to loiter about restaurants and, when someone walked out, grab whatever was left before the waiter cleared the table. Another tactic was to get up before dawn in the freezing cold and steal milk as soon as it was delivered by the milkman.

Relief came in the form of their first single in the UK, Don't Do That, which was released on 29 September. BBC Radio latched onto the song and their support formed the basis for the *NME*/Red Bus Free Road Show which ran from 17 October until 3 November and included a date at the Marquee.

Tony Tyler in *NME* on 28 October 1972 liked what he saw in Brian:

'Perhaps the strongest character on stage is vocalist Brian Johnson, whose looks and zaniness quickly establish rapport with audiences.'

By November, Don't Do That had reached a point where the band landed their first TV appearance on 'Top of the Pops' and the song peaked on the UK charts in early December at number 32.

That wasn't to say that they were rich: the band lived on $60 a week and on tour usually slept in the van. However, things were looking up. Geordie landed an opening spot for the remnants of New York's Velvet Underground — minus Lou Reed — at Newcastle's Mayfair in the first week of December.

A month later came a crucial support spot for Slade's two gigs at London's Palladium. Geordie's mix of flamboyance and raucousness was perfect for the occasion, and within a few months they would be likened to Slade, largely because of the similarities between Brian's voice and that of Noddy Holder.

'We like to get a pub atmosphere,' Brian told Michael Benton in *Melody Maker* on 14 April 1973. 'All our songs are simple, nothin' complicated about us.'

A scheduled support for Chuck Berry at Frankfurt's Festhalle fell through, but they eventually opened for the rock and roll elder statesman on two other German dates.

The *Hope You Like It* album, which had been recorded in just 48 hours, came out on 2 March and later that month their second single, All Because Of You, peaked at number six on the UK charts and would eventually sell one million copies worldwide. A second appearance on 'Top of the Pops' drew the priceless attention of The Who's Roger Daltrey.

'He came up to us and told us that he liked what we did,' Brian said to *Melody Maker*. 'He's invited us to use his recording studio — that's an offer we're bloody accepting.'

All this, plus a gig supporting The Sweet at London's Rainbow on 30 March: it seemed that Geordie were finally onto something. And no-one was more surprised than the band at how quickly it had happened.

'Little over a year ago,' Brian told *Melody Maker*, 'we were playing the pubs and clubs around our home town of Newcastle under the name of USA ... takes a bit of getting used to.'

Come April, Geordie were supported by Australian band Fang, which featured Bon Scott, at two gigs, Torquay Town Hall and Plymouth. At Torquay, Bon was impressed by Brian's hellish performance. What no-one knew was that Brian was seriously ill. He eventually passed out in the middle of the show and spent the night in hospital with suspected appendicitis, which turned out to be food poisoning and exhaustion.

Brian (self-mocking tone): 'Fucking good singer! I was in fucking agony!'

In Plymouth, Geordie had the relative luxury of staying at a cheap bed and breakfast. The woman who ran the place wasn't a fan of men with long hair and Fang, with the added disadvantage of being broke, were pointed towards their freezing bus for the night.

Brian wasn't having any of that. Once the landlady was out of sight, he and the rest of Geordie smuggled the Australians in through a window, and they spent the night in front of a gas heater with a few beers. The next morning Fang's bus, which had broken down, was towed away and Brian never saw Bon again.

In May came a headline at the Newcastle Mayfair where Geordie were supported by Supertramp, a proud homecoming for the Newcastle ambassadors.

'It's like they just walked off a factory floor,' said James Johnson in *NME* of the show on 26 May. 'Geordie are loud and crass and very straightforward. What they have going for them is an incredible rough energy.'

Tours of Europe got a similarly enthusiastic crowd reaction and the Can You Do It single hit the UK Top 20 in June. Despite this success, concerns began to emerge within the band that their entire fan base was very young kids who just screamed, only wanted to hear the hits and pull their heroes into the audience and tear off their clothes. In a perilous echo of The Easybeats, Geordie wanted to be more than that.

Meanwhile, their light was fading. When the album, *Hope You Like It*, and the single, All Because Of You, were released in the US, both sank without a trace. Meanwhile, UK sales of *Hope You Like It* were also low.

The cancellation of a free concert at Newcastle United's football stadium, the 60,000-capacity St James' Park, was possibly a blessing in disguise. To add insult to injury, in August a planned US tour with Uriah Heep also fell through.

But there was a new album to do that month and an opportunity to show what they could do outside of pop singles. Unfortunately, for all his enthusiasm Roger Daltrey was too busy to help with the recording.

Geordie were ranked number 10 in the 'brightest hopes' category of *NME*'s annual readers' poll, but while the Electric Lady single peaked at number 32 on the UK charts in late August, it would be their last charting single in Britain.

In early October, the band completed recording sessions for the second album, and in November did more than a week of dates in Germany supporting Slade.

Plans were discussed to play their ace: a live album recorded at Newcastle City Hall later that year. But first there was the cultural shock early in 1974 of spending two weeks in Japan doing promotional work, and then in February a tour of Australia.

The two weeks of Australian dates ballooned into six in the late summer heat and took in remote places that Brian was sure weren't on any map. Then there was the accommodation. If Geordie ever rode a highway to hell, as far as Brian was concerned that tour was it. A stop-off in Alaska on the way back to London was as close as they ever came to going to America.

After months of delay their second album, *Don't Be Fooled By The Name*, was finally released in April and followed *Masters Of Rock*, a compilation of their hit singles.

Their popularity in the UK had waned considerably but they had a sizable audience on the continent, particularly in Scandinavia and Germany, where they opened for Deep Purple.

In early 1975, guitarist and main songwriter Vic Malcolm left. Then, it was Brian's turn to call it quits mid-year. The push for hit singles, which became all audiences ever wanted to hear (their albums never made it into the charts), and fights over stage presentation — Brian just wanted to wear work clothes rather than boots and satin — were the nails in the coffin.

He had had enough of working his guts out for little, if any return, while it seemed that those closer to the bright lights of the big city had everything handed to them whether they deserved it or not. Brian couldn't even afford a car.

In late 1975, he recorded a solo single, I Can't Forget You Now/I Can't Give It Up, which EMI released on 9 January 1976. It sank without a trace. In fact, the only copies which have ever been seen are promotional versions. The single may never actually have been commercially available.

Within two years of its release, Brian had the performing bug once more and formed Geordie II, with Derek Rootham (guitar), Dave Robson (bass) and Dave Whitaker (drums). The singer was smiling again and wore his soon-to-be-signature cap on stage for the first time at the band's debut gig at the Western Excelsior Club.

His brother had given him the cap to keep the glue he used at work — at Newcastle's Top Match car roofing and windscreen repair business — out of his hair.

Fun as the band was, it was also frustrating. When they played, venue owners more often than not simply wanted background music between games of bingo, despite the big crowds Geordie's racket attracted.

It was during this period in 1978 that Brian first heard AC/DC, when he was played the *Let There Be Rock* album. Brian loved

Whole Lotta Rosie and when a band member arrived at rehearsal with a tape of the song it was decided to include it in their shows, where, to their amazement, audiences would chant for some guy called Angus.

With his curiosity aroused, a few months later Brian noticed that AC/DC were to appear as part of a live UK concert television series called 'Rock Goes To College'. He was puzzled because the series, to that point, had involved more serious, highbrow bands. Brian tuned in that night anyway, and was delighted to see AC/DC tear the place apart.

The singer loved Geordie but was keeping his options open, and in November he auditioned to replace Ronnie James Dio in Rainbow, though he was unsuccessful. Brian almost became a member of Uriah Heep and Manfred Mann's Earth Band as well.

It didn't matter. Geordie were earning decent beer money and his business in Newcastle was ticking over comfortably.

Legend has it that Brian came under AC/DC's radar after a fan in Chicago pitched the idea, which seems an unlikely and simplistic scenario given the stakes were so high. He wasn't an unknown quantity to Malcolm, Angus or Albert's, anyway.

With their steel-trap-like memories, not only did Malcolm and Angus more than likely remember Brian from when he toured Australia with Geordie, but Albert's had organised the tour and were handling the band's publishing. Bon had also spoken of him in glowing terms after they'd crossed paths in the UK, and felt that Brian was up there with Little Richard when it came to really belting out a song.

According to Ian Jeffery, Malcolm wasn't initially sold on Johnson as a candidate. He didn't think much of Geordie.

'Malcolm's first thing was, "That fucking cunt? That fat cunt?" Mutt's going, "I think you're getting confused with the guitar player — this guy is a wiry kind of guy." Malcolm was like, "You're fucking speaking out your arse, mate!" He wasn't going to have it.'

Unbeknown to Malcolm, during the second week of March Jeffery called Brian in Newcastle, where the singer was staying at his mother's place. It was almost midnight. He didn't tell him who the gig was for, only that it could be well worth his while.

Brian was unmoved: he was quite happy with his lot. However, his curiosity was sparked. The problem was he didn't really have the money to make the trip to London, but after scraping together some cash and getting a loan and some encouragement from a friend, he hired a car and drove down to the capital.

Then, between Newcastle and the rehearsal studio he disappeared, or so it seemed. Jeffery asked if one of the crew, Evo or Malcolm and Angus' nephew Fraser, who was working in the city and spending some time with his uncles, had seen Brian.

'I asked them, "This Brian Johnson, has he turned up?" He [Evo] said, "We were playing pool with a guy, but he's in the bog at the minute." This guy comes out and he's been playing pool with them for 20 minutes, after he'd just walked in and not introduced himself. I said, "What's your name — not Brian Johnson?" He said, "Yeah it is." I said, "We need you upstairs!" He thought they were the band he was playing with! So we went upstairs and he walked in and he said, "Is this who I think it is?"'

Brian, wearing his trademark cap, was met with a Newcastle Brown Ale, which delighted him and he was immediately put at ease.

'I really felt as though I could go out and have a pint with 'em and I wouldn't have to prove anything,' he told Dave Lewis in *Sounds* on 19 April 1980. 'Once you step inside their door and meet these lads, the bullshit stops right on the doorstep.'

Brian was stunned that the band had more sound gear in the rehearsal room than he used for gigs. He asked if anyone minded if he smoked, which got him onside with Malcolm immediately, while Angus was twitching with nerves, eager to play.

After talking for a few minutes, it was reckoning time. Malcolm asked what songs Brian knew and, to the amazement of both him and Angus, the singer called for Ike and Tina Turner's Nutbush City Limits — a welcome rhythmic change from Smoke On The Water. And in a key — at Brian's request — that forced his voice to reach and demonstrate his range. Additional points from Malcolm for

Brian, and there were even more when Brian opened his mouth to sing and could be heard over the band.

For the first time in the entire audition process, Angus came to life.

Ian Jeffery: 'The first fucking strain [the first few lines of Brian's vocals] you could feel the hairs on the back of your neck stand up. Angus gets out of his seat from his cross-legged position and his right leg's on the go. We're off and racing!'

They then did Whole Lotta Rosie and a few Chuck Berry songs. By then, the band were performing rather than just rehearsing. After they finished, Brian felt confident enough to point out that they hadn't played Rosie properly — it wasn't fast enough.

A relaxed Brian was pleased with his efforts but philosophical about the exercise. If he missed out, he could always tell his mates at the pub about the experience. He might even get a few extra pints to retell the tale.

Nevertheless, he was unable to stand around and talk. After about 15 minutes he excused himself, explaining he had gig commitments back home with the latter-day line-up of Geordie.

'Heaton Buffs [a venue in Newcastle] has always been a good pay,' Brian told Tyne Tees television in 1983, 'I think, about 120 quid between the four of us, which was like a big pay night.'

Malcolm was the first to admit he had been wrong about Brian. He and Angus knew they didn't want to see anyone else — Cliff and Phil were also impressed — but they worked through the list of other applicants over the next few days just in case.

Three days later, Jeffery called Brian to see if he could come back the following Monday or Tuesday. In another fine show of working-class character, Brian said he couldn't as he had his business to deal with and that was his livelihood. Besides, he had a lucrative weekend of gigs with Geordie.

Ian Jeffery: 'I said, "We're going to fly you down etc — whatever you're getting paid, we'll pay you." He said, "Let me check then." So even then he wouldn't commit to it. So I said, "Okay mate, I'll call you back in 10 minutes." I called him back and he said, "Aye, that's alright."'

But again punctuality was a problem, as Brian was two hours late getting to the audition on 25 March. His day had simply gotten more complicated than he expected.

What no-one knew was that, after being contacted by Jeffery, Brian had received a call out of the blue for another gig; £350 to sing on a TV commercial for Hoover, which featured John Cleese. He innocently thought he could fit recording the ad and a second audition for AC/DC neatly into one day.

Ian Jeffery: 'The band at that time were really fretting. "Fucking hell, do you think he really wants this? Does he like us? Is he not coming?" The coin had completely turned. It was like, we need him.'

All was well again when Brian arrived and explained the situation. For round two, the band played some riffs and asked Brian just to make some words up on the spot to go with them. One was Given The Dog A Bone.

Again, it was huge grins all round: but this time Malcolm wasn't going to let the singer run off so quickly. By the end of the week Brian had to go home — weekend gigs were waiting — but he knew he had done well, even though he hadn't been offered the job.

No-one was more surprised by the turn of events of the previous few weeks than him. He thought he'd had his moment — such as it was — with Geordie the first time around and he'd come out of that experience disillusioned and penniless. Now he was being at least considered as the new frontman for a band that only six weeks earlier was poised to grip the world. But Brian doubted himself.

'If you can understand,' he told Capital Radio on 17 November 1980, 'I'm not the most ambitious lad in the world, and the thing is, I'm not the most overconfident person in the world.'

To cushion the blow of possible rejection, he figured that, as AC/DC had been auditioning for several weeks by that point, he was simply one of the last names that came up and not necessarily a certainty for the job. This was confirmed — as far as Brian was concerned — when the NME's 29 March issue carried a report that Allan Fryer from Adelaide's Fat Lip had been appointed as AC/DC's new singer.

Like Stevie Wright, Fryer fit the profile well — perhaps even more neatly. Glasgow born, and later to front the incredibly loud Heaven, Fryer loved a drink and the ladies and possessed a raw, raspy voice with a range of several octaves. He seemed ideal.

Allan Fryer: 'I heard through the wires that AC/DC were going to carry on, and I spoke with George [Young] and he suggested I come to Sydney and talk. To cut a long story short, we went into the studio and laid vocals on Whole Lotta Rosie, Sin City and Shot Down In Flames: we took Bon's vocals off the masters and I sang on the tracks.

'After I finished, George was really impressed with the tracks and he wanted to get them off to the boys in London. A week later, I heard I was the new singer. It was in *New Musical Express* and *Melody Maker* in Europe and on various TV shows in Australia.'

Brian knew it made sense that the band would get an Australian to fill Bon's shoes. Besides, Brian had Geordie and had also been rehearsing with another Newcastle band, a covers outfit called Skinny Herbert.

Then, on 29 March, his phone rang. It was Malcolm, wanting Brian to come back a third time. He explained that the *NME* story was bullshit and pressed Brian to return — they had an album to do.

So, a puzzled Brian asked, I got the job then?

After Malcolm confirmed he had, Brian asked him to call back in a few minutes so he could settle down and get his thoughts together. He then paced the empty house hoping he hadn't dreamt the call, but itching to tell someone anyway. Malcolm called back as requested and Brian celebrated by drinking an entire bottle of whisky. His young brother thought it was an April Fool's joke until the singer got his sign-on cheque.

It wasn't just Brian's hurricane of a voice that landed him the job, or his love of soul and blues belters like Eric Burdon, Ray Charles, Tina Turner, Howlin' Wolf and Joe Cocker, although both those factors certainly helped. His no-bullshit earthiness and wonderful sense of humour, plus the fact he liked a pint, played darts and was his own man, were also key selling points.

The most important was the fact that Brian was a personality — even if a language barrier presented itself when he spoke too quickly or got excited — which was exactly what Malcolm and Angus were after.

'We wanted someone who could do what Bon did and was a real character,' Angus told Penny Harding in *Juke* on 27 September, 'but we didn't want someone who was just a perfect imitation of him.'

On 8 April 1980, it was officially announced that AC/DC had their new singer.

Brian was put on a £170-a-week retainer but was still under contract with Red Bus Records, so Atlantic advanced him a small fortune to buy himself out of his contract. However, he still had to record a solo album for his old label.

Brian: 'Joining AC/DC was a bit of fucking luck, really. Everybody gets a break in life, I suppose — you've got to get a hold of it with both hands and use it, you know?'

While the situation seemed like an enormous stroke of good fortune for Brian, the luck cut both ways.

Ian Jeffery: 'There was fucking many moments of doubt when we came back from Bon's funeral watching these fucking prats coming through [during auditions]. They just didn't get it. Thought we were never going to find a singer. It was like, "Why can't we find someone like Noddy Holder or like Steve Marriott?" It was great that Brian came so early as well, because if it had gone on for a few weeks ...'

1981
Brian, Forest National, Brussels.

chapter 19
BACK IN BLACK

alcolm wasted no time introducing Brian to AC/DC's number one philosophy: we do what we do, we play what we play and what critics think doesn't matter a fuck. No discussions. End of story.

It took a few days for the situation to fully register with Brian. He had big shoes to fill.

'I'm going to be nervous at first, no doubt,' he told *Sounds*' Dave Lewis on 19 April 1980, 'but I'll give it my best shot, you know ... I just hope they give us a chance.'

Brian's last gig with Geordie had been on the weekend of 21 and 22 March at the Heaton Buffs in Newcastle. They were delighted for him, although typically he felt guilty that he was effectively putting them out of work for a few weeks until they got another singer. But when he was able, he made sure that things weren't too bleak for them financially, as did his new employers.

'AC/DC said, "Yeah, we understand,"' Brian told *The Interview* in November 1980, 'and made a lovely little gift to the boys in Geordie ... and some money, until they got a new singer.'

When the March issue of French magazine *Best* hit the stands, its readers' poll results must have been dizzying for Brian. They read as if it had been completed exclusively by AC/DC fans, with best singer going to Bon, best band to AC/DC, best live band, AC/DC, and best musician, Angus.

That year, The Angels did two European tours with Cheap Trick, and through their gigs in France were able to confirm the poll results first-hand.

Angels guitarist John Brewster recalls:

'We did Nice and went down a storm, but it was a very aggro, very male-dominated audience — they go berserk in France. Cheap Trick came on and they got pelted with cans and things. It was heavy stuff, and it was looking really dangerous.

'They didn't know whether they were going back on stage or not, and then one of them turned around and said, "Would you guys come back on with us?" So we all went back on stage and we did Highway To Hell. And fucking hell! We tore it up! The crowd went bananas. There was like 10 of us on stage — four guitarists, two bass players, we just plugged in to whatever we could find. Robin Zander could sing Bon Scott type of stuff brilliantly.'

Rehearsals, which began in April at London's E-Zee Hire Studios, were originally to run for three weeks but were cut to just one when an opening came up at Compass Point Studios in Nassau, in the Bahamas. The Bahamas move was partially tax related and partially due to a lack of studio availability in the UK, their preferred working environment. Polar Studios in Sweden — owned by Abba and once used by Led Zeppelin — was an option at one point, but Abba were using it and AC/DC didn't have the time to sit around and wait until it was available.

Work began in the Bahamas in the middle of April and ran until May, with the *Highway To Hell* team of producer Mutt Lange and engineer Tony Platt.

The band had never been to a place even remotely like the

Bahamas, where many of the locals were lizards and frogs and a decent beer was something in a travel brochure. The locals, meanwhile, probably wondered what these five pale, slightly built, little guys had to do with the sun and sand.

But the weather wasn't exactly tailor-made for the beach when the band arrived. The area was being lashed by tropical storms, so the most basic of necessities — like a regular, ongoing supply of electricity — was a problem for much of their first week. And of course, with no power, they couldn't make any noise; at least not the level of noise they came intending to blast out in the serene environment.

Being unable to work lessened the frustration of their guitars being impounded at Customs for several days and having to wait for their other equipment to be freighted over from the UK. But it wasn't just officialdom and the elements that had the band in their sights.

There was the large, intimidating woman who ran the less than five-star accommodation where AC/DC were staying. There were also her warnings about thieving by locals and she provided spears that were used for fishing just in case things got a little rough with the natives.

Brian had fears all his own. All the band knew of him was from a rehearsal room, and working in a high-tech studio he wouldn't have the same racket to hide behind — everyone would be able to hear his every breath.

The song titles were all pretty much in place. What Do You Do For Money Honey, for example, was a title George Young had come up with during the *Powerage* sessions. Apart from that, all the band had were riffs; there were few songs as such, just ideas that Malcolm and Angus had been working on before and since Bon's passing.

Apart from the week's rehearsal in London, the band hadn't had a chance to work on the material as a unit: there simply hadn't been time. Now there was even less, and any lyrics that were written while they rehearsed in London and on the way to the Bahamas had to be completed in the studio.

To his amazement, Brian was given first crack at them, although he knew full well that they would be subject to input from Malcolm and Angus. He was honoured, but it was just one more additional pressure.

Angus couldn't think of anything worse than attempting to gain mileage from the death of their friend by looking to the lyrics Bon had been forging for the new album. It was a simple matter of respect to Bon and courtesy to Brian.

Phil Carson: 'Bon didn't write any of it. Malcolm and Angus did what they always did, and write the riffs and the basis of the music, and they would generally leave it to Bon to write the lyrics and come up with the melodies. And that's what they did with Brian. Brian came up with every single melody and every single lyric.

'If you look at the lyrical content of Brian Johnson-AC/DC, it's maintained the direction of where Bon was, but takes it to a new level. Brian has got an incredible sense of humour, and he's able to use double-entendre lyrics — little bit tongue-in-cheek with some of his stuff, even the song titles are a little tongue-in-cheek — but he's able to do that without coming off being at all cheesy.

'Please don't listen to anybody who says anyone else wrote those songs — Brian Johnson wrote those songs. I was the A&R man, I know who wrote the songs. So, that's it.'

Brian's nerves were calmed the night before they were due to start work, but not initially with the most pleasant of sensations. He woke in a cold sweat and sensed Bon was standing looking down at him. Something reassuring passed through him: maybe it was just a dream.

Once they settled into the studio, there was a quiet excitement and optimism. The rough songs had everyone pumped up and the general mood was that a truly great album was within reach. And absolutely nothing less than a landmark recording was what was needed.

With Bon, the band had been on the brink of something huge, but if this didn't work, if whatever they came up with wasn't readily accepted as the next step in the band's career, they were facing extinction. You're only as good as your last album, and that last album had involved a man who was not only irreplaceable but had been on his way to becoming a legend globally.

If this was to be the last thing they did as a band, it had to be the strongest possible statement: there could be no excuses and no second chances. But rather than be a negative, the situation made for the perfect team-building formula.

Tony Platt (engineer): 'These are not people that get tense in the way that normally people get tense. They kind of focus it towards getting the job done. It really was like a load of mates going to make an album and everybody [in the band] was in roughly the same situation — of course, they'd not made a whole mess of money out of *Highway To Hell*, because at that point in time it really hadn't sold a lot of albums.

'Everybody was on the same per diem and we all kind of just tried to eke it [the budget for the album] out and make it last and so on. So there was a real sense of camaraderie about it and it was very close.'

Platt had to deal with the fact that Compass Point, like the Roundhouse Studios back in London where *Highway To Hell* had been recorded, was sonically 'dead' and so employed the same techniques to rectify it as he had for that album.

'The thing about AC/DC — or the thing about Mal's approach to the sound of the band — was that he really didn't like big echoes and stuff like that. I think possibly because they wanted to put some kind of clear blue water between them and bands like Zeppelin. They wanted it really dry and in your face. So this technique of using a roomy kind of ambience really worked very well on their music.

'Having kind of debuted that on *Highway To Hell*, when we went in to do *Back In Black* I'd got a clear idea of how I wanted to go about recording things, and I made a point of recording quite a few ambience tracks.

'When we were putting the tracks down, I made sure there were a couple of room microphones out there so that when you listened to the album, you felt like you were in the same space as the band were when they played it.'

Malcolm had been a student of sound, song and rhythm for a lifetime himself, and the tutoring of George, along with the confidence he had gained by doing *Highway To Hell* without his older brother's direct input, was all coming to the fore. Although he respected Lange and Platt, Malcolm stamped that authority on the sessions right from the recording of the first song, You Shook Me All Night Long. He was not at all impressed with the changes to the rhythmic accents in the song.

Tony Platt: 'We recorded the choruses of You Shook Me All Night Long and I can't remember exactly how the emphasis was, but we hadn't recorded it as "You" — bomp — "shook me all night..." It wasn't quite like that. There was a slightly different accent that we put onto it, and then Malcolm heard it and said, "No, the way I'd heard it was that there was that space in there." So we had to go back and do those again.'

On Let Me Put My Love Into You, the band were concerned that the original last line in the chorus lent itself too much to a pre- or post-sex cigarette. It was simply too explicit — the result, no doubt, of the magic rum and coconut milk elixir, the fuel of choice for the album sessions — and had to be changed.

On the other hand, there was nothing lighthearted or ribald about Hells Bells, with its Old Testament doom and destruction imagery. It first surfaced during the rehearsal sessions in London, partly courtesy of the title of Bob Dylan's 1975 Rolling Thunder Revue and then sealed by the storms in Nassau.

The tumbling phrasing and timing of Brian's vocal on Back In Black was styled on jazz singing and the riff was something Malcolm came up with during the *Highway To Hell* tour. Using an acoustic guitar, he had recorded it onto a cassette and, unsure if the song was any good, gave it to Angus to see what he thought. Unsurprisingly, his younger brother gave it the thumbs-up.

Rock And Roll Ain't Noise Pollution was the last song to be recorded. The title was believed to have been based either on a line that Bon threw at a furious landlord during an argument over the volume of his stereo, or came from an expression Angus used back in 1976 in London during the band's days at the Marquee amid environmental concerns about the noise. In any event, Malcolm casually threw the song together sparked by a riff Angus came up with when they found they needed an extra track.

Tony Platt: 'Mal stayed behind at the studio when we all went out to dinner that night, and the assistant engineer — a big black guy called Benji — played drums while Mal was knocking out a few ideas. When we came back again they played us this thing that they'd put together and everybody just went, "Whoa! That's it!"'

Brian's opening vocal on Noise Pollution also captured a loose jazz feel out of him searching for a groove and quickly finding one. He sounds like a man of the cloth giving a sermon. What's that sound right at the start? It's Brian having one last drag on his cigarette before he begins.

Throughout the entire sessions, Brian sang like a man possessed; someone who, like legendary 1930s blues artist Robert Johnson, had traded his soul for a supernatural lung capacity and octave range. But he found, just as Bon had, that when it came to vocals, Lange was an absolute perfectionist.

Tony Platt: 'Mutt is very, very particular about getting every line of a vocal to be absolutely spot on. And quite rightly so, because when you've got something which really just consists of two guitars, bass, drums and a vocal, every single thing that happens has got to count 110 per cent.

'And it was very important to get these vocals to just sit absolutely right. When you're singing in a band that's got Angus playing guitar, you've got to make your vocals as exciting as his guitar playing, and that's a real mountain to climb for anybody! So it was as much a matter of Mutt being very exacting about virtually every syllable that got sung — and making sure it was exactly the way it should be — and at the same time making sure that it was exactly the way that Malcolm had it in his head.

'By the same token, from Jonna's [Brian's] point of view, every single note of that is right at the edge of anybody's range. And it isn't just that it's sung up high, it's sung up high with all of that power and excitement at the same time. And I think that's what set it apart — every line is just absolutely there!

'And obviously [there's] the whole thing of getting that voice to be at the right level and the right height [in among the rest of the band's sound] and making it work for Brian, rather than Brian trying to just be another Bon.'

Occasionally, there was the odd guest to witness these various processes — just one of the curious locals. Lange heard it before he saw it. It sounded like someone was tapping their feet, and he wound the band up so he could listen again. Nothing. The band started playing again and Lange again yelled for them to stop. He had found the noise; a large crab shuffling across the wooden floor of the studio.

Bon would have found a way to write Crabsody In Blue Part 2 after the visitation. He was never far from anyone's thoughts. Platt recalls a conversation he had with Malcolm:

'It was just something that's always stayed in my mind. Malcolm said something along the lines of the strange thing about Bon was that he would always be disappearing here and there. There were all sorts of stories about him disappearing at the end of one gig and then not pitching up until the soundcheck for the next one. He said this was the thing about Bon — he'd always turn up on time eventually and Malcolm said it's just getting used to the fact that he ain't going to be turning up any more. I thought that was a very poignant thing to say, because I thought that very much summed up the way that the band were.'

But while the album was being recorded in the shadow of Bon's death, some light shone through during the sessions when Malcolm's wife had a baby. It was like a good omen, a sign of rebirth. Proud and usually teetotal Uncle Angus toasted the new member of the Young clan in uncharacteristically big style with a bottle of whisky.

'Downed half of it in one swallow,' Brian told Richard Hogan in *Circus* on 31 December 1983. 'By God, I couldn't even keep up with him, and I like whisky. He just collapsed afterwards. We had to carry him to bed.'

Fortunately for Angus, the next day wasn't the one they went deep sea fishing, an exercise not for those who lack a lump of lead in their stomach, let alone those unused to suffering from a vicious hangover. When they did hit the high seas, they returned with a catch of tuna and some dolphin fish. The tuna was passed on to the cook at the place they were staying, who prepared it and put it in the freezer.

Unfortunately, during the night one of the chunks of tuna fell off the top shelf and pushed the freezer door open. By morning, and with the heat of the sun, the tuna was all over the floor in a rancid, partly liquefied heap. The place reeked so much they had to move out for a few days.

Ian Jeffery hadn't travelled to Nassau for the sessions and was taking care of business back in the UK. He received a phone call from Malcolm and Angus with an unusual request. They wanted a bell and Jeffery was off to Loughborough to find one.

Ian Jeffery: 'I went to the lighting company and the people who make all the props and things and they said, "We can make it like this, look exactly and look as heavy [as a bell]," and I said, "What don't you get? We want a real bell! We don't want something that looks like it — we want a real fucking bell!"

'I did a load of research on it and found this company which make all the church bells. It was like going into a shop and ordering a TV. What size screen do you want, sir? What size bell do you want? Somehow in their minds they had a one-ton bell. They said, "Oh, we do a one ton, it's this size." So I had to take a photo of the bell and put it next to something that they [Malcolm and Angus] could relate to. I forget what it was, I think it might have been a car, so they could see the size of the bell and say, "Yeah, that's what we want."

'Then they [the people at the foundry] said, "What do you want it tuned to?" I said, "No fucking idea, mate, I want a one-ton bell." Then the next thing was, "What do you want on it? Do you want two circles on it? Three circles on it, to go around it?" I said, "Actually no, I want 'Hell's Bell' written on it and 'AC/DC'," and then their whole parameters switched, because they didn't know if they could put the word "Hell's" on a bell, right?!'

Before the mixing process began, and with little more than a few backing vocals to finish, Platt flew back to England. The idea was to record the bell so the bell the fans saw and heard on the forthcoming tour was the same bell that was on the album.

As it happened, the foundry hadn't finished making it and suggested Platt record one that was hanging in a nearby church. Microphones were placed on and near the bell, only for Platt to discover that there were birds living inside.

Tony Platt: 'Every time we hit this damn bell, all you heard on the microphones was a flutter of birds going, "Oh shit!" and disappearing very quickly. So it was a complete washout. It was like, "Oh no! What do we do now?" So they kind of brought forward making the bell. The bell had been cast, but because of the amount of metal in it, it takes a long time to cool down — they can't hurry that up. So we cut it very fine to take the bell out of its mould and hoped that it was as tuned as it could be. As it happened, it was perfectly tuned when it came out of the cast. So I then went back up with Ronnie Lane's mobile [studio].'

Once it was recorded, they sorted through the best hit of the bell and the best microphone positions, then slowed that down to half speed to take it down to the pitch they wanted. Then they dropped it in one hit at a time onto the song Hells Bells.

After just seven weeks, which was longer than the band had originally planned to spend, the *Back In Black* album was completed and was mixed in New York at Electric Lady Studios.

Returning to Newcastle and putting in a few windshields, just as he had done before the madness began back in March, Brian couldn't believe it had all happened so quickly. He didn't hear anything and just hoped he had done well and that the album would do the job. But his guts began to churn: he knew what the next phase was.

Doing what he had done in a studio in front of the band, some crew, Lange and Platt was one thing. Performing those tracks before an AC/DC crowd, not to mention singing Bon's songs and all the while somehow being himself on stage, was a big ask. His doubts crept in again.

Atlantic had concerns of their own. They were stunned the band were demanding a plain, all-black cover for the album, with AC/DC and the title embossed and buried in that blackness. From their standpoint, it was a potential sales and marketing nightmare. The band stood firm, but allowed Atlantic to print a thin grey line inside the band's logo so it could be read.

Lange had also been concerned that the title of the album was too bleak.

Angus: 'He [Mutt] asked me what we were going to call this record. I'd said, "Well, *Back In Black*," and he said, "You don't think that's morbid?" I said, "No, because it's for Bon, it's our tribute to him and that's what it's going to be!" And he was a bit taken aback.

'I'd said to him, "Mutt, listen. When we did *Highway To Hell*, you were freaking out. You were saying American radio won't play it [and] the Midwest, you said they're very religious, they won't play this record." And I said, "Mutt, they were the first people to play it." I said the only thing I know is we go out there and play in front of people and so at least allow us that factor. This is what we were built for, to go on a stage. This is what we do best. At least allow us the courtesy of trusting our judgment on this.'

Rehearsals for the tour began in June at London's Victoria Theatre, but not without some difficulties.

Ian Jeffery: 'The stage was below ground height, if you know what I mean, and the load-in door was on the side of the street. You ramped things down but there was nothing that would take a one-ton bell. So we had to hire this fucking crane with a huge boom [arm] and stop the traffic for 20 minutes to pick it off the truck, swing it across the street, lower it into the theatre and lower it onto the stage, where we'd built a special place with a support, so it could land on the stage until it was time to [hoist it] in the air. It was just fucking huge! Central London coming to a standstill for this bell.

'Malcolm brought us a tape so we could listen to the album and I remember we were all in the balcony where the mixing desk was. We were sitting, going, well this is totally different, because it was, but it was fucking amazing! Just from the tape through the PA it was fucking amazing. And it really, really brought Malcolm's rhythm playing out, because Malcolm's probably the best rhythm guitarist in the world. It was monstrous, the fucking guitars were monstrous. We sat in the balcony in disbelief.'

After a few weeks of rehearsal, from 29 June until 6 July the band did six warm-up dates in Belgium and the Netherlands, but without the bell.

Brian's debut was in Namur, Belgium. They had wanted to play a small venue to start with, but the fans had other ideas. On the day of the show it had to be moved to a larger venue, then to a third. The crowd was enormous, to the point where the promoter commented that it seemed all of Europe had come to take in the event. Angus was particularly nervous, while Brian just walked around the dressing room psyching himself and the band up.

The full emotional weight of the show was brought home to Brian when a fan with a tattoo of Bon on his arm approached him and wished him the very best.

'I just stood there shaking,' Brian told Robin Smith in *Record Mirror* on 26 July 1980, 'I mean, what can you say when people are prepared to put their faith in you like that?'

But when the band took to the stage at midnight, three hours later than scheduled, their reception took some of the edge off Brian's nerves.

'I was really shitting myself,' he told *Juke*'s Christie Eliezer on 13 July 1991. 'But I went out, they gave me this fantastic cheer, and I saw these banners "Welcome Brian", and I was chuffed.'

Fan Pierre Grandjean was among those who attended the show:

'The crowd was packed at the entrance of the Palais Des Expos [in Namur], the glass doors were bending under the pressure, ready to break in. The sound was horrible — they didn't have the time to do a soundcheck.'

The show itself was a very loud, very rough but spirited affair, and there were the sort of mistakes that could be expected so early in a tour.

Overall, it wasn't a memory Brian will treasure. He had been learning so many songs that they had started, quite understandably, to bleed into each other in his mind.

'The second song we did was Shot Down In Flames,' he told *Juke*, 'and the third one was Hell Ain't A Bad Place To Be, and I sang the same lyrics for both.'

Few in the crowd probably noticed, but Malcolm, of course, picked it up and gave Brian a 'what the fuck do you think you're doing?' glare. There were no such problems in Deinze, also in Belgium, on 1 July and if Brian still had any nerves that night, a huge response to a spirited delivery of Highway To Hell elbowed them aside.

AC/DC were back, but there had been more changes than just the singing role. With Bon, the band had been a two-man circus, a rolling rock and roll tag-team act between the hugely charismatic singer, the overdrive antics of Angus and the comic talents of both. Now Angus was the star attraction with Brian in a strong supporting role.

And the almost-choreographed precision that had come to mark AC/DC's latter-day performances with Bon had gone up another level, as did the band's volume. Brian's between-song banter was kept to an absolute minimum: there was no storytelling or dedications to fans or friends and no wasted words.

With Bon's occasional waywardness out of the frame, it was now possible to really tighten up the operation. And they did.

Perry Cooper (Atlantic Records): 'I think the Bon thing shook them up a lot. And I mean, I don't think they were drinking as much or doing, you know, things like they used to.'

Meanwhile, in the lead-up to its release, work associated with *Back In Black* continued out of sight of the band's major markets. In early July, audience-free promotional videos for Hells Bells, Back In Black, Rock And Roll Ain't Noise Pollution, What Do You Do For Money Honey and Let Me Put My Love Into You were filmed in Breda, Holland by Eric Dionysius and Eric Mistler, who had shot the *Let There Be Rock* movie. Dionysius recalls the band arrived at 6 p.m. instead of noon, so they had to work until 1 a.m.

Finally, on 13 July, with a red dot painted on the Hell's Bell, so Brian knew exactly where to clobber it for maximum effect, the singer went in at the deep end with a 64-date North American tour that ran until 11 October. Between 13 and 28 July they played an unprecedented 11 dates in Canada, the first country to award *Back In Black* Gold record status.

AC/DC were largely supported in Canada and the US by such bands as Gamma, with former Edgar Winter guitarist Ronnie Montrose; Humble Pie, with, of course, Steve Marriott; Def Leppard; Johnny Van Zant, the brother of late Lynyrd Skynyrd singer Ronnie Van Zant; Blackfoot; Saxon; and Krokus, who would later be one of the leading acts to shape themselves in AC/DC's own image.

Some home comforts were installed in the band's backstage area, including an English pub complete with dartboard and all the trimmings. But there was nothing relaxed about the merchandise situation at the sold-out first show of the tour in Edmonton, Canada.

Ian Jeffery: 'We imported about 200 grand worth of T-shirts and the merchandise company said, this is going to be fucking huge, right? I've still got one and it said "Back and Black". We had to fucking can them all! We couldn't sell a T-shirt at the first gig because they all had "Back and Black" on them!'

The tour was a great culture shock for Brian, who thought AC/DC were essentially an English and, naturally, an Australian phenomenon. He had no idea they were so popular in America.

Atlantic's Perry Cooper was taken to a show in Calgary to see Brian for the first time and loved what he saw.

'I got a kick out of him 'cause I couldn't understand a fucking word he was saying! I still can't at times! And he was just one joke after the other, and with that accent, although it's gotten better in the last few years, but I kept going, "What the fuck are you talking about?" I mean, it was just funny. But he fit in so perfectly — they couldn't have found a better person personality-wise, vocal-wise, just everything. It was amazing.'

Angus was hugely impressed by Brian's professionalism and that he was able to concentrate on his singing while the guitarist was running around him like a madman creating all manner of distractions.

Angus: 'You didn't know how everyone was going to look at us. Brian had to go out there and fill pretty big shoes. When you'd meet some people they'd always sort of say, oh well, it's not even AC/DC, you know? So my hat goes off to Brian in a little way because he did take a lot [of flak], especially in the beginning. But he stood his ground and he's as big a fan of Bon as anyone.'

The tour was tough going for Brian. It had been many years since he'd worked so hard, and even then never on a scale remotely like this.

'It was so frightening,' Brian told Jonathan Gross in the *Toronto Sun* on 28 July 1980, 'I felt I was in the middle of a World Cup soccer game. And I'm in such poor condition after so many years of inactivity that they have to have oxygen on stage during every concert.'

Brian was sometimes physically sick after the show with the strain of it all, and his signature cap, which became a cloth ambassador for Newcastle, did just as much moving as poor Brian's stomach muscles. It wasn't his fault: as soon as the music began, his head started to nod and his cap would fly off.

Final judgment day came on 25 and 31 July, with the release of *Back In Black* in the US and UK respectively. The album was a revelation.

It seemed loud even when it wasn't played at top volume and sounded glorious when it was. The guitars of Malcolm and Angus seemed to explode from the speakers. The rhythm engine room of Phil Rudd and Cliff Williams pushed the air from your chest, and that voice: Brian sounded as if he had been buried alive for decades and had finally burst free.

In years to come, studios in Nashville, the country music capital of the world, would use *Back In Black* as a means to check the acoustics of a room, while Motörhead would use it to tune their monstrous sound system.

It was also a landmark album in that it summoned strength through adversity and then channelled it into an enormously powerful expression of mourning and respect for Bon, with Hells Bells and Back In Black specific nods to his passing.

The solemn statement of the cover art said more than any sleeve note dedication ever could. Besides, this was AC/DC. Hearts and flowers would have been inappropriate.

'We all decided that it was a far better tribute to call the whole thing *Back In Black*,' Angus told Steve Gett in *Melody Maker* on 30 August 1980. 'That way, the album is dedicated to him rather than just one little line on the back of the sleeve — it goes a lot deeper than that.'

Some felt that given the circumstances of Bon's death, a song called Have A Drink On Me was in poor taste. But it was simply continuing the same theme that Bon himself had written about for so long.

After the album was released, Brian ran into some old friends in Newcastle who were surprised he was singing so high — too high, they believed — and felt that it wouldn't work for him or the band. He thought about what they'd said and was depressed for a few days. Maybe he had made a huge mistake. But by 9 August, Brian would have the last laugh on his mates when *Back In Black* topped the UK charts for two consecutive weeks.

It was early in the morning in Norfolk, Virginia when the band received the news. America was the major market to crack, but there was something special about taking England. To celebrate, the road crew bought all the booze they could, then went to the beach and sat chanting, 'We're number one!' for the mystified locals. They were just grateful to have come through such an impossibly difficult time so commandingly.

Malcolm: '*Back In Black* is the album we're proud of, because we thought it was the end of the band, to be honest. Me and Angus had been together two weeks jamming [on ideas for the album] and after [Bon's death] we thought, well, this is it really. I just can't see David Coverdale singing with the band, you know what I mean? Nothing [in the way of singers] looked appealing out there. There was no incentive. We were all quite shocked about it.

'But after a couple of weeks of sitting around, we just had to do something — you're sitting at home all the time doing nothing. So we decided to get back to these couple of riffs that we'd put together and we just carried on through that. But because Bon wasn't there, it gave us so much more determination. We had to do something, you know, you had to get your energies out.

'It was a real gut-wrenching thing, the whole episode, and we didn't still know what was going to happen. You were sort of in a limbo world and I think that came through in all the stuff we came up with on that record. We always thought that Bon was with us in that too, you know what I mean? He was a big part of what we were doing, and his spirit was all over it because a lot of the energy was coming from Bon. So that's a special album.'

Being number one in the UK was only part of it. The success of *Back In Black* meant that AC/DC were the first band since The Beatles to have four albums in the British Top 100 simultaneously — *Highway To Hell*, *If You Want Blood* and *Let There Be Rock* having all re-entered the charts.

America wasn't too far behind. On 16 August a court order was required to allow the band to perform at the Cincinnati Riverfront Coliseum. City officials had attempted to block the show, arguing there would be too many people in the area because an exhibition game of pro football was scheduled for the same evening in nearby Riverfront Stadium. The following day was the Toledo Speedway Jam 2, where AC/DC were second on the bill to headliners ZZ Top and positioned over Sammy Hagar and Humble Pie, plus, according to the posters, 800 kegs of beer. It would be more than 20 years before they again raised the curtain for another act.

On 22 August, a single of You Shook Me All Night Long backed with Have A Drink On Me was released worldwide, and the following day *Back In Black* entered the US Billboard charts. You Shook Me All Night Long would be their first Top 40 'hit' in the States, peaking at number 35.

In Houston, Angus was involved in a minor car accident and injured his hand. But despite it swelling up like a balloon, after some painkilling injections the Houston show went on — twice — with a later low-key gig at the 1000-seat Agora club, much to the owner's disbelief.

By the time the band arrived in Palm Beach, Angus' hand had healed, which was a good thing, as he needed it for more than just playing guitar. He decked a fan who threw a beer over him, in a simple case of degrees of justice — either he hits the guy or a man-mountain security guard does. Angus just gave him the easy option.

By September, global sales of *Back In Black* were soaring, while spurred on by the band's new profile, their back catalogue also picked up numerous sales awards across the world.

The pressure was beginning to show, as Ian Jeffery found when the band were in Nebraska. It was four in the morning when his phone rang. It was Phil Rudd.

'He [Rudd] said, "Can you come to my room? There's a load of people here and I want you to get rid of them." I said, "Sure, no problem, mate, I'll be there." And there was a lot of noise going on, right?'

What amazed the affable Jeffery when he got up to the floor Rudd was on wasn't the fact that there was so much racket, but that there was none. Not a sound.

'I go into his room and he'd left the door ajar. And there's nothing [no people in the room], nothing at all. And he pops out from behind the curtain and I said, "What the fuck are you doing? I thought there was a party going on here." He had his ghetto blaster there, which was switched off at the time, I guess that's what it [the noise Jeffery had heard on the phone] was, right? I said, "Where is everybody?" And he got a glass of water from the side of his bed. And he said, "See? They didn't even fucking finish their water before they left!" I thought, holy shit! What have I walked into here?

'It was then I realised how strung out he was etc etc, so we sat and we talked for a while and I said, "Phil, there's nobody here, mate," and he admitted it in the end and he started crying and everything else and he said, "Don't tell Malcolm — for fuck sake, don't tell Malcolm."'

None of this pressure and success counted for much to some of the people AC/DC encountered in Kalamazoo. After the show, the band went back to their hotel and decided to have a drink in the bar where a jazz combo was playing. AC/DC were refused service — they clearly didn't fit with the collar-and-tie dress code — and all hell broke loose.

Malcolm, who had never been one to take a backward step, decided that actions spoke louder than words. He strode up, snatched an instrument from one band member and furiously thrashed the small stage with it. Rough translation: they wanted a drink. The police arrived soon after.

Meanwhile, the accolades kept coming. In Detroit, where only a few years earlier Malcolm had battled a promoter over the volume of their show, AC/DC outpolled Bob Seger as most popular rock act, which was like outvoting Hendrix in the guitar legend's home town of Seattle.

In the final weeks of the tour, the band began to include The Jack in their shows. Brian, out of respect for Bon, had been reluctant to do so, but after a few showings it was obvious that audiences were anything but offended by Brian's treatment of the song.

In Rochester, the singer cheekily got into the swing of things. 'I want you to sing along with this one,' he told the audience. 'This is a story about a young chap from Rochester who had a drip on his pecker.'

Brian: 'I feel very close to [the sentiment of Bon's songs] actually, because I went through the same thing meself trying to get a band started — sleeping in the back of vans, the highway to hell bit, you know? When's this fucking road going to fucking finish? Where's the gig? Not getting paid, stealing milk bottles off people's steps in the morning just to get something in your stomach, you know?

'I feel very much the same way. I mean, I canna go through his own personal things he went through, but I can understand everything he says. He was a great communicator, I believe. He could communicate exactly what he thought and put it down in song, which is a hard thing to do.'

The mood had darkened considerably by the time they reached the Nassau Coliseum in Long Island five days later, during the last week of the American tour. Representatives of Atlantic were coming late in the afternoon to present the band with a sea of sales awards, and a party was to be held after the show in New York.

The trouble began when Rudd showed up two hours late. Malcolm was furious and Jeffery had to step in and calm things down. Round two was still to come.

Ian Jeffery: 'Unfortunately, Phil carried on in his own little world without anybody knowing — me or anybody, right? And he actually couldn't play the last song of the encore and fell off his fucking stool, so we had to abandon the show going into the second song of the encore. I went to the dressing room to see what was going on, and just as I was walking in Malcolm went over and just wellied him, laid one on him.'

A week later *Back In Black* reached Platinum sales in the US — one million copies — and by the end of October, *If You Want Blood* and *Let There Be Rock* had each moved 500,000 copies. US radio had finally swung in hard on the back of the multitude of calls they received for the band, and when they began giving AC/DC airtime tapped a huge, previously unrecognised level of interest. The bittersweet irony was that while the powers-that-be had murmured about the quality of Bon's voice, Brian's own throat at times was more an instrument in its own right than an articulate channel for the English language.

Michael Browning: 'The Bon version of AC/DC was always going to be hard going for the American psyche to really get into. Not as obvious as the AC/DC part 2.'

Even former detractors were forced to stand up and join the line for a few minutes of the band's time. Brian loved to hate *Rolling Stone* magazine — to him they represented 'serious' critics who overintellectualised and politicised everything — and took great delight in them being forced to cover AC/DC now they were so hugely popular. The band warmly welcomed the reporter the magazine sent along, but they were stunned to hear that when he'd been briefed, *Rolling Stone* had said they couldn't guarantee his safety. AC/DC were to be feared, not just loathed.

Brian's first gigs with the band in the UK were from 19 October, a 24-date tour that included three shows at the Hammersmith Odeon and three at the Victoria Apollo, all sold out. The singer had a ball at his triumphant homecoming at the Newcastle Mayfair, even if everything was so loud that it was impossible to know what was going on.

The Hell's Bell was unable to appear at Newcastle, Bristol or Leicester as it was simply too heavy for the venue's structure to handle. But this problem would be corrected next time. AC/DC weren't about to fade away, not with worldwide album sales now at the 10-million mark.

On the last night of the UK tour, AC/DC's road crew had a gift for the tour's openers, the Starfighters, featuring Stevie Young, a nephew of Malcolm and Angus. Halfway through their set the crew lowered a tiny bell down from the roof behind the singer's head.

That was America and Britain dealt with. Now it was time for Europe, and the first leg of the tour kicked off on 19 November, 24 dates in all, with the exception of Italy. The country's political situation at the time — with a spate of kidnappings — meant Italy was not the sort of place a high-profile rock band wanted to be, thanks all the same.

As it was, an appearance at a US Army base in Germany the day after John Lennon's murder was disturbing enough. The band's head of security, Big John, decided to have the local police search fans as they entered the venue. The contraband they seized was frightening: more than 20 knives and a handgun.

During the tour, while the band flew from city to city, the car-loving Rudd drove his newly acquired Ferrari, the first tangible sign of the fruits of AC/DC's success and perhaps, for the drummer, an indication that he was functioning on another level to the rest of the band. Or perhaps one all of his own.

While in Paris, they visited the Pathé-Marconi Studios, where they planned to record their next album. As if to coincide with the visit, on 10 December AC/DC The Film — *Let There Be Rock* was released in France.

Back in April, the band had turned down the original sound mix and asked that it be redone by Tony Platt.

Tony Platt: 'They'd set up a special screening for me, but they hadn't done it in a viewing room — they'd done it just in a cinema. So I sat in the pitch black trying to make notes. Because they couldn't actually set up for me to mix it to visuals, I was kind of mixing it by memory really, and from the notes as to who was doing what, or who was on what side of the stage at what particular point.'

The film was an enormous success in France and did a million dollars of ticket sales in Paris, while 300,000 people across the country also saw it — an almost unprecedented response to a music movie. It cost roughly $100,000 to make.

The second leg of the European tour began on 8 January, a 14-date run which included the band's first-ever dates in Spain, where the wait was clearly well worth it for all concerned. Twenty-eight thousand fans poured into one show, a figure that smashed Led Zeppelin's not inconsiderable record at the venue. Not surprisingly, *Back In Black* hit the number one position on the Spanish charts.

On the final night of the tour in sweltering heat at Brussels Forest National, the band brought on a special guest. In his introduction, Brian mentioned the individual's association with acts such as Led Zeppelin, which drew a huge response from the crowd who might have thought they were about to witness Jimmy Page on stage with their heroes. But it was Atlantic Records' UK head Phil Carson, who had signed AC/DC to the label in the first place, who was ushered out to play bass on a rough version of Little Richard's Lucille.

With sales of *Back In Black* now at three million copies in the US, Brian received his first royalty cheque. It was for £30,000. The singer had a mortgage and was constantly driven crazy by the building society, so he took great delight in paying them a visit.

'The guy at the building society, he was a complete git,' he told

TOP LEFT Young Brian Johnson in Dunston, 1950s

TOP RIGHT Geordie: Brian Johnson, Brian Gibson, Vic Malcolm, Tom Hill, London, late 1972

LEFT Rawing glory: Brian, Birmingham Odeon, October 1980

BELOW Noise pollution: Angus, Dallas Convention Center, August 1980

LEFT Cliff, Dallas Convention
Center, August 1980

BELOW Brian at one of his
first AC/DC shows – Deinze,
Belgium, July 1980

BOTTOM Phil during the
1980 US tour

On the best seats in the house: Angus, Orpheum Theatre, Boston, October 1980

Celebrating their first 10 million album sales worldwide with manager Peter Mensch, Cockney Pride, London, November 1980

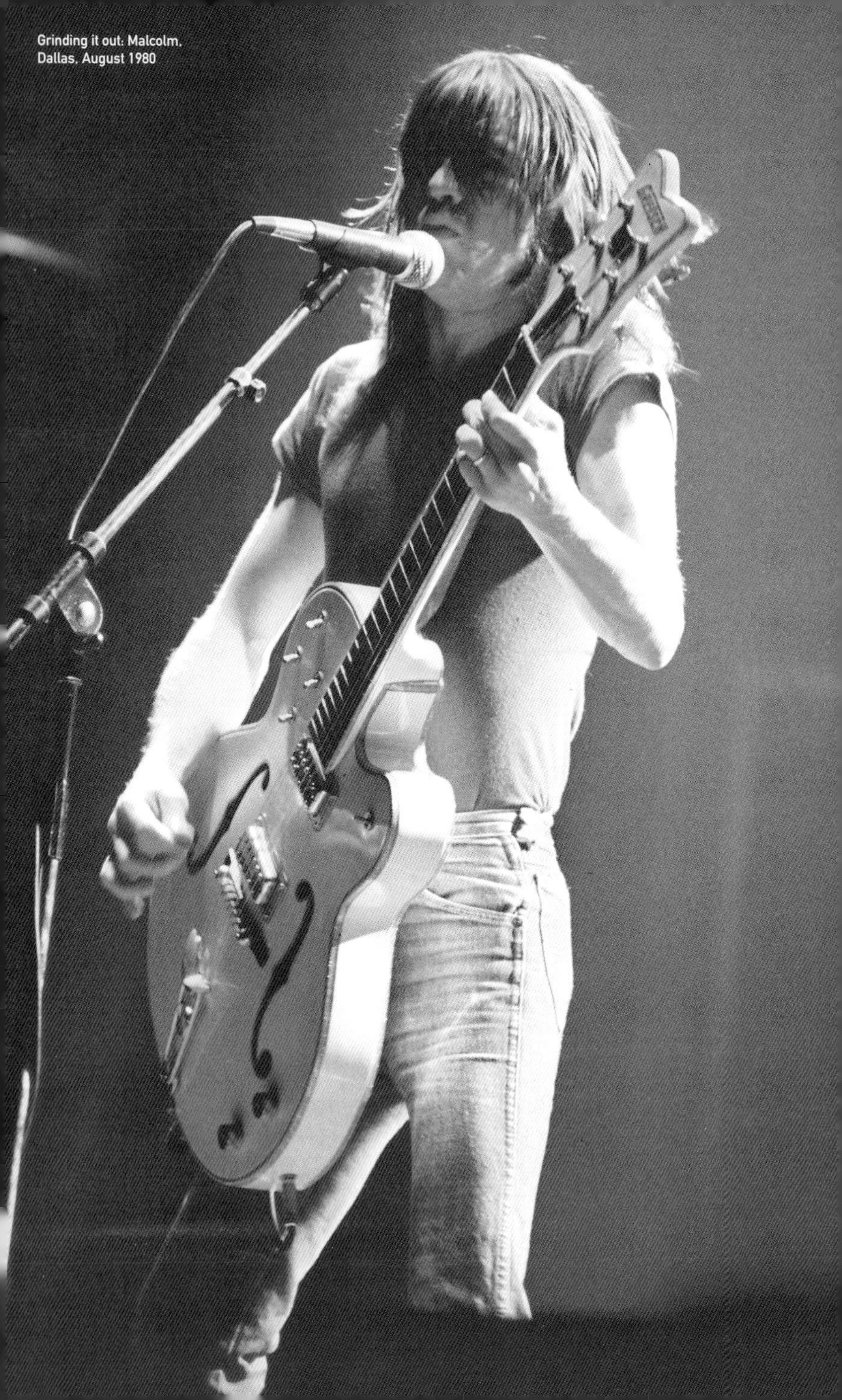

Grinding it out: Malcolm,
Dallas, August 1980

LEFT Shorts as loud as the guitar: Angus, New York, December 1981

TOP The French connection: Angus jamming with Bernie from Trust, Rose Bonbon, Paris, December 1982

ABOVE Switch flicking: Cliff, Brian, Angus, Malcolm, and Simon Wright, US 1983

Top of their game: Wembley Arena, October 1982

Guitar size does matter:
Angus. Blossom Music
Center, Cleveland,
September 1986

TOP LEFT Cliff, Ernst-Markt Halle, Hamburg, January 1986

ABOVE Pressing the flesh: Brian, Cleveland, September 1986

LEFT Simon Wright, Hamburg, January 1986

BELOW LEFT Malcolm, Sporthalle, Cologne, January 1986

BELOW Blow up that video! Angus, Australia, February 1988

No cap gun: Brian, Hamburg, January 1986

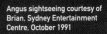
Angus sightseeing courtesy of Brian, Sydney Entertainment Centre, October 1991

THIS PAGE AND OPPOSITE
Sydney Entertainment Centre,
October 1991 (clockwise
from top left) Malcolm,
Angus with 'Rosie', Chris Slade,
and Brian beats the hell out
of the Hell's Bell

TOP LEFT AND ABOVE Malcolm and Cliff, Castle Donington, August 1991

LEFT Pushing it out: Brian, Wembley Arena, London, April 1991

RIGHT AND BELOW Geniuses at work: Brian and Malcolm at Warehouse Studios, Vancouver, August 1999

BOTTOM AC/DC – Let there be lights: Australian tour, February 2001

TOP LEFT **Extra MSG:** Angus
at Madison Square Garden,
New York, May 2001

TOP RIGHT **Cool as Keith:**
Phil, Circus Krone, Munich,
June 2003

LEFT **Brian,** Geordie II reunion,
Heaton Buffs, Newcastle,
October 2001

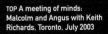

TOP A meeting of minds:
Malcolm and Angus with Keith
Richards, Toronto, July 2003

ABOVE Completing the circle:
Angus and Malcolm jam
with the Rolling Stones,
Enmore Theatre, Sydney,
February 2003

LEFT Game on: Angus and
Brian, Le Stade de France,
Paris, June 2001

A man and his aura: Angus,
Le Bourget, Paris, December 1982

VH1 in March 2003, 'and he was always on us. I'll never forget, I took the money into his office, cash, and laid it on the table, and went: "You never phone me again, you piece of shit."'

A four-date February tour of Japan followed, the band's first visit to that country, and the Tokyo show was recorded for radio and TV, the only concert of the tour to receive such treatment.

It was then time for Brian's final and greatest hurdle — a tour of Australia, the band's homeland, where Bon was virtually a national icon and *Back In Black* had been released on 11 August and sold by the shipping container load since. He need not have worried.

The five-date visit — the band's first Australian tour in four years, from 13 to 28 February 1981 in the middle of the country's scorching summer — was an overwhelming success, with a sound system and staging on a level that was a long way from the last Australian appearances at the Bondi Lifesaver in July 1977.

Opening the shows were The Angels and Swanee, led by John Swan, who became very tight with Brian during the tour.

John Swan: 'There was a good reason — because I was close to Bon. I can't remember who it was — Angus or Malcolm — walked up and said, "Do us a favour, have a talk to him [Brian] because obviously he's a bit intimidated, he's in Australia, it's Bon's territory, he doesn't know anybody." I can't remember which one of them it was, but that was the sort of scenario. So I walked up and I said, "Do you want a drink?" Aye, we had a drink. "Don't play darts, do you?" He said, "I do." Set up the dartboard, had a game of darts.

'We became instantly as good friends as if we'd been brothers all our lives. When I first got sober and AC/DC came back, there would be a phone call from Brian and it would be, we're having dinner tonight and we'd like you to be there. I wouldn't take the phone call because I didn't want to go to dinner because I was frightened I wouldn't be able to drink, because I had no confidence without a drink in me; couldn't go outside the door, couldn't answer the phone, couldn't speak to my mates.

'Brian persisted and persisted and persisted. He'd ring me during the day to see if I was alright: aye lad, how you doin' then, eh? You alright, boy? I drove in to the Regent where he was staying and he had his wife there. He was a real sweetheart and he got lunch for us and he got the guy to bring tea — he didn't have a drink, she didn't have a drink. The loveliest people you could possibly ask for.'

The tour opened in Perth and it was a tall order for Brian: his first show in Australia and in Bon's home town. It conjured up a lot of deep emotions, particularly as it was just one week shy of the first anniversary of Bon's death. Brian met Bon's mum — his dad didn't attend the show — and dedicated High Voltage to her. Her warm wishes meant the world to him.

The band hadn't lost its keen sense of class warfare — it was still a case of us and them. Away from the stage and the fans, they were still considered second-rate citizens, as shown when they weren't allowed into the bar of the hotel where they were staying. Angus was furious. AC/DC were by now making money for the first time and could easily have bought not just the bar, but probably the entire hotel.

There were other logistical problems, again due to the sheer weight of the Hell's Bell.

Phil Eastick: 'The bell, I gotta tell you, was a monumental pain in the arse because nothing would support it. It actually had to be suspended from a crane. It had to be on the boom arm of a crane with a hole cut in the roof [of the venue] to lower it because there wasn't a roof anywhere that would actually hold it. We ended up moving it [by rolling it] around the stage on a bunch of two-inch galvanised pipes because it was so heavy [to lift].'

In Adelaide, where Bon had first met the band just over six and a half years earlier, it seemed a fitting mark of respect that the show generated noise complaints from 15 kilometres away. And little wonder.

Phil Eastick: 'That was the wall of Marshalls era where they had the 60-feet wide Marshalls, which actually were fake. While it appeared to be literally a wall of Marshalls side by side, most of it was just the logos with an incredibly loud monitor system. It was stunning.

'I lived in the States for quite a long time and ran a tour and logistics company in San Francisco. Probably the last act I did there was one of the Van Halen tours, and I remember going to the production meeting before the tour started and saying, "What do you guys want?" They said, "Whatever AC/DC put up, we want twice that." I had to say to them, "Well, in most of the places we're going to play, guys, that's going to be physically impossible. There is no way to put more than they put up. It can't be done. You can match it but you can't beat it."'

The performance at the Sydney Showgrounds, where Malcolm and Angus had seen Led Zeppelin nine years earlier, was postponed twice due to rain — a decision the band agonised over — and finally took place on 23 February before 30,000 fans.

John Swan: 'I think the first gig was washed out and we might have been there most of the fucking time playing darts and drinking. Then we went back to the hotel, drank some more and partied and I think he [Brian] finished up getting me a dentist at about 12 o'clock at night. The sweetest man. And, I think, the perfect replacement for Bon, because he wasn't similar to Bon in any aspect, shape or form.'

It was said to be the last show at the venue, as local residents were up in arms about the noise and had lobbied hard for rock acts to be banned. The band got wind of this and are thought to have strategically unveiled an unrehearsed Rock And Roll Ain't Noise Pollution to mark the occasion.

AC/DC's volume made a mockery of the anthem. The sound reportedly went into the red at a staggering 130 decibels, almost 30 per cent over the showground's prescribed limit, drawing complaints from residents kilometres away.

But as US rock magazine Creem once reportedly wrote: AC/DC are everyone's band, even the deaf.

There were predictable media reports of fights, seven cars left burnt out, 10 fans landing in hospital and, on a more surreal level, even a person on the rampage with a syringe.

After the show, in a large tent behind the stage, the band were presented with 27 Gold and eight Platinum albums by Ted Albert, with guests naturally including George Young and Harry Vanda, as well as friends such as Lobby Loyde, Angry Anderson and Peter

Wells. Angus didn't stay around for the presentation. He was completely drained and, after drinking buckets of tea, as he did after each show to stop dehydrating, went to bed.

The all-important night in what was seen as AC/DC City had been everything that everyone wanted it to be, but it had been enormously stressful.

'Angus is fucked tonight,' Brian told Kent Goddard in *RAM* on 3 April. 'He was so built up doing it. The tension in that man before we went on tonight was unbelievable.'

Victorian police wanted to have the second show cancelled after the first was marred by the attendance of a fleet of 20 police vehicles and, subsequently, 30 arrests. It was also reported that railway staff were up in arms after well fuelled fans fought on their way home. All too obvious headlines, such as 'Rock Riot', only compounded the poor perceptions. And there was talk of trouble after the second show nonetheless.

Sales of *Back In Black* rose to meet the tour, and it peaked in Australia at number two after spending six months in the charts with 300,000 copies sold. While the response was heartening, it wasn't lost on anyone that some of the media who now wanted to talk to them were the same people who wrote the band off a few years earlier.

Meanwhile, the plaudits continued to roll in from the rest of the world. *Back In Black* was voted second-best album of the year by *Creem* and the number two album of 1980 by the readers of *Musik Express* magazine in Germany.

The acclaim and the sales figures moved Atlantic in America to once again push for the release of the originally rejected *Dirty Deeds* album, something they had been itching to do since March 1980, a few weeks after Bon's death. This time AC/DC relented, but demanded the sleeve carry a sticker specifying that the line-up 'Young-Young-Scott-Evans-Rudd' recorded the album, and that it be sold at a 10 per cent discount.

Accordingly, on 27 March 1981, *Dirty Deeds*, which in comparison to *Back In Black*'s polished wallop sounded all the more rough and ready, finally saw daylight in America, where sales of *Back In Black* were now tipping the scales at four million copies. *Dirty Deeds* reached number four on the US charts and would sell two million copies before the end of the year, quite an achievement for an album deemed not commercially viable by its label five years earlier.

Phil Carson: '*Back In Black* sold millions and millions of albums and I think it was one of the first albums that became multi-Platinum as quickly as it did. By then Jerry Greenberg had left Atlantic and Doug Morris had become the president.

'He called me up one day — I guess it was towards the end of 1980 — and said, "Look, I found there's a record there that we never put out, it's called *Dirty Deeds*." I said, "Yeah, it got turned down by the Atlantic A&R department at the time." He said, "There's a hit on it." I said, "There's always been at least one hit on it, Doug — there's a good record, but nobody cared." He said, "Yeah, but we should put it out now." I said, "Are you fucking out of your mind? You can't follow a Brian Johnson-led AC/DC with a Bon Scott-led AC/DC! What are you thinking?" And we had a huge argument.

'I said, "If you put this out, yeah, it'll sell two million, but all the nine million people that have found AC/DC [through *Back In Black*] who don't know about Bon Scott are gonna think this is the next album, this is the future of the group. And it's not! He's dead! Where you gonna go from there?"

'And I said, "I'm resigning if you do that. I'm gonna leave Atlantic Records." Somehow [Atlantic supremo] Ahmet Ertegun talked me into staying, which, you know what, I regret. I wish in a way I'd left Atlantic right then, and got more involved with AC/DC, which they [the band] wanted me to do at that point.'

The belated release of *Dirty Deeds* wasn't the only blast from the past that ended up back on the agenda. To finalise his contract with Red Bus, Brian was to record his still-outstanding solo effort in Sydney with Malcolm acting as producer. Nothing eventuated and, as it happened, didn't need to.

Red Bus, cashing in on AC/DC's huge success in Europe, had issued an album of old Geordie recordings and released it as Brian

Johnson and Geordie. Somehow, this legally saved Brian from recording a real solo album, which he'd never wanted to do in the first place.

Meanwhile, the band were voted most popular act in the readers' poll of French magazine *Best* for the second year in a row. In the singer category, Bon came first and Brian third, and they also landed best band, musician, live act, album and movie.

Then came the holy grail of sorts with the announcement that AC/DC would headline that year's Castle Donington Monsters Of Rock festival in August, their only UK gig in 1981.

Donington was the flagship of the English heavy metal and hard rock movement and the sheer power of AC/DC saw them placed at the very top of that mountain, just as their intensity and attitude originally saw them lumped in with the UK punk movement. A 'heavy metal' tag would follow the band for the rest of their career, much to their annoyance.

Malcolm: 'Bon used to call it "tin foil". Heavy metal was always to us studded belts and leather and makeup and streaks in their hair and spandex. Heavy metal was always trash! It was Uriah Heep and stuff like that. They got the wrong end of the stick on their influences. They'd been influenced by the wrong players or whatever, but real feel never entered their vocabulary!'

Angus: 'I always looked at the metal thing more as music by numbers. It's been devoid actually of a lot of feeling. It's more concentrating on technique. Like now you see a lot of them going at it fast and furious. Like Brian Johnson says, it's like they're all out there to catch the 3:04.'

The band's alleged metal content was confirmed in June with the first issue of new British magazine *Kerrang!* which plastered Angus across the front cover. The readers of *Sounds* — which had spawned *Kerrang!* — also voted Whole Lotta Rosie the number one heavy metal song of all time. Black Sabbath and Led Zeppelin must have been stunned.

Harry Vanda wasn't at all surprised.

'It's just one of those flowing rock riffs. Angus has got a talent for that. If you write a riff you better go check with Angus, because chances are he'll already have one exactly like it!'

By now, *Back In Black* was nothing short of a phenomenon. Sales had reached a staggering seven times Platinum in the US, quadruple Platinum in Australia and Canada, Platinum in France and Germany, Gold in Belgium, Holland, Spain, Switzerland and England, and Silver in Portugal.

No-one was more pleased and relieved than Brian.

'I always had the thought in my mind,' he told *Hit Parader* in August 1980, 'that if people don't accept the band now, I'll be the one responsible.'

The release of the *Let There Be Rock* movie in Germany in July brought the band's past with Bon swelling back, as did *High Voltage*'s entry into the US Billboard charts. It seemed it was simply impossible to get too much AC/DC.

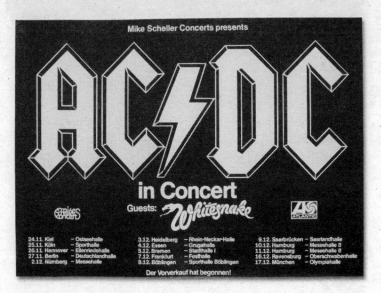

1982
Cocked and loaded: Forest National, Brussels.

FOR THOSE ABOUT TO ROCK

chapter 20

On 22 August 1981, AC/DC headlined the second Monsters Of Rock festival at Castle Donington Park in front of an unexpectedly enormous crowd of 65,000 people. Also on the bill were Whitesnake, Blue Öyster Cult, Blackfoot, and, probably much to Brian's amusement, Slade, the band in whose shadow Geordie had struggled for so long.

Police concerns about the crowd killed off plans to do a video the day before the show. It wasn't a good omen.

The rain tumbled down on the festival, just as it had the previous day, and AC/DC took the stage over an hour late. To make matters worse, half the sound system collapsed before the band even walked on.

Ian Jeffery: 'Fucking total disaster! And all because of the BBC. They had all their trucks and things there and it was pissing with rain, right? And what they did was they pulled out one of the mains of electricity and plugged their fucking thing into it and blew all the bass end of the PA. Nobody knew it. This was just before we were

353

going on — there was nothing you could do about it. So they played the whole show with whatever was left of the mid and the top — there was no fucking bottom end of the PA. We drove to the back of the track and it was like listening to fucking somebody with a comb with a bit of toilet paper on it.'

While the sound was mediocre at best, so was the band's performance — and they knew it. It was their first show in six months — time spent writing new songs — and they performed the same set that most of the crowd would have heard on the *Back In Black* tour. There was simply no new completed material to show off. The entire exercise was a rare and major miscalculation.

But shitty sound, rain and a less-than-explosive performance or not, doing Donington was a big deal. It was the culmination of years of hard work and the horrific expense of losing Bon. Ian Jeffery, who as tour manager had been through it all with the band, burst into tears.

That achievement aside, the real problem was that, although it had been on their schedule for some time, Donington took the band and their focus away from recording what would be the *For Those About To Rock We Salute You* album in Paris, a process that was already proving difficult enough without added distractions.

Malcolm and Angus had begun to write and rehearse the material back in May, but getting the right studio had been a nightmare. The band had begun work at EMI Pathé-Marconi Studios in early July with producer Mutt Lange, but were unhappy with the sound and left after just two weeks.

Jean Louis Rizet from Studio Ramses, who had worked on the soundtrack for the *Let There Be Rock* movie, was then contacted but his studio wasn't available. Eventually the band opted to record basic tracks in an old warehouse on the outskirts of Paris with the Mobile One studio, with vocals later recorded at Family Sound Studio, and overdubs done at HIS Studios.

All this stress was in addition to the already huge pressure of having to come up with an album to match the enormously popular *Back In Black*. The problem was that they no longer had the same level of gut-wrenching emotional fuel from Bon's passing to drive them on.

Some were handling the pressure of success and expectation from the record company differently than others.

Ian Jeffery: 'Phil was off buying 90-grand Ferraris and driving them down the Champs Elysées at 150 miles an hour.'

Meanwhile the entire band were living in apartments in Paris that they hated. It wasn't the most ideal environment.

The recording sessions coincided with television broadcasting the sights and booming ceremonial sounds of the marriage of Lady Diana Spencer to Prince Charles. When the cannons exploded in an act of royal salute, the hair on the back of the neck of everyone in the studio stood up. Malcolm got to thinking.

By September, the *For Those About To Rock* album was finally done, while the services of manager Peter Mensch had been dispensed with, although the band remained with the management firm Leber-Krebs.

By that time, the movie *Let There Be Rock* was being shown in selected theatres in the US. For future Nirvana drummer and Foo Fighter Dave Grohl, it was a life-changing experience.

'When I was in the fifth grade, I guess I was 10 years old, my best friend and I went to see that movie, *Let There Be Rock*. I had never been to a rock concert or seen a rock movie and that fucking movie changed my life, man. They had a PA system in the theatre that was the same size as the PA system in the local Coliseum. It was the first time I'd ever had the feeling of getting up and playing air guitar and killing my teacher, smashing the chairs in the movie theatre, whatever. Total adrenalin. It was so loud that you couldn't even understand what they were saying when they interviewed the members of the band.'

The Stones offered a million dollars to have AC/DC do the opening honours on at least one vast stadium date of their 1981 North American tour. But the band had learnt from their past mistakes, such as playing at Donington months after the *Back In Black* tour finished rather than staying focused on the next album, and decided to stick to their own schedule, tempting as the offer from their heroes was.

Over and above that, Malcolm simply didn't want AC/DC to be anyone's opening act.

After five days of rehearsals at the Palladium, the site of their New York debut in 1977, the focus was on the first leg of their own 28-date US and Canadian tour from 14 November, which saw the band headline in arenas all over the country for the first time.

The success of *Back In Black* pumped this tour into something gigantic in terms of staging. The Hell's Bell, the focal point of the *Back In Black* tour, was now joined by 12 mock cannons on each side of the stage, which thunderously punctuated the song For Those About To Rock.

As far as Malcolm was concerned it was all about sound, not theatre. The bell had chimed for the tragedy of Bon's death, and its presence solemnly represented the difficulties of making the *Back In Black* album.

Malcolm loved the sound it made when Brian belted it each night. It was the same with the cannons.

'I don't give a toss about cannons or the flames coming out of them,' he told Dave Lewis in *Sounds* on 2 January 1982, 'I just want the bangs. Their sound's like an instrument, like the bell.'

It was obvious early in the tour that the interest in the band had escalated rather than levelled off since *Back In Black*. Exhibit A came on 19, 20 and 21 November with three sold-out concerts at Chicago's Rosemont Horizon to a total audience of 52,800 people. The next day, the legendary Muddy Waters and Rolling Stones show took place at Chicago's Checkerboard Lounge, while AC/DC were in Minneapolis. Malcolm and Angus would have done anything to be in Chicago that night instead.

The Rolling Stones then followed AC/DC and played at the Rosemont themselves, but as an indication of where AC/DC ranked at the time, even the Stones' run couldn't better AC/DC's three nights.

It was on 20 November, during their Rosemont dates, that the *For Those About To Rock We Salute You* album, with its unique catalogue number of 11111, was released in the US, and then in Europe on 23 November.

While Angus did a rough sketch of an idea for the cover, once again Bon's presence hovered over the album, but this time the more studious side of the man that few saw or knew about. Knowing that he was interested in history, the singer had once given Angus a book called *Those About To Die Salute You* about the brutal and bloody theatre of the gladiators of ancient Rome. Angus eagerly devoured the book and, as was the case with anything he felt significant, filed the title away in his mind.

The album had some of the power of *Back In Black*, particularly the anthemic title track which was designed to be a showstopper, but the time it took to make robbed it of any continuity.

'By the time we'd completed the album,' Malcolm told Mark Blake in *Metal CD* in November 1992, 'I don't think anyone, neither the band or the producer, could tell whether it sounded right or wrong. Everyone was fed up with the whole album.'

Meanwhile, the growth in audience size compared to the *Back In Black* tour was obvious everywhere. When the band had last hit Indianapolis, they'd pulled something like 4000 people. With Brian still trying to learn the words to the new album, this time around 17,000 came to the show.

But crowd figures were not the problem.

No-one had ever taken military hardware on the road, let alone actually fired it.

In Hartford, the crew were advised — right before the encore in which they were to be featured — that if they used the cannons, the police would arrest them.

The threat was one big red rag to a tiny Scottish bull. Malcolm instructed the crew to fire them anyway, little knowing that those in charge of the cannons, along with Ian Jeffery, had been handcuffed just in case.

The artillery remained silent, although in defeat it was unlikely Malcolm did.

Around the same time, the Moral Majority began to picket the band's shows in the belief that rock acts such as AC/DC were corrupting young people.

In Cleveland, there was trouble when fans objected to the moralists' picket.

The irony was that the band — whose only vices were countless cigarettes, a few drinks and the buckets of tea that Angus absorbed post-gig — were far more disgusted with the campaigners than the campaigners were with AC/DC.

All this was swept away on 2 December, with AC/DC's historic first headlining show at Madison Square Garden in New York. Unfortunately, they weren't given the red carpet treatment: security didn't recognise Brian and, thinking he was just another fan trying to get backstage, threw him out.

The same thing had happened to Malcolm on a previous occasion, and while it was the price to be paid for not looking or acting like a rock star, the misunderstandings weren't always easily forgiven or forgotten.

The situation eventually prompted the reluctant decision to travel to gigs in limos with security, so someone else could look after any access problems.

As if issues with the cannons, the Moral Majority and overzealous security weren't enough, a couple from Chicago demanded $250,000 in damages because they'd been receiving obscene phone calls on 36–24–36, the mythical 'phone number' in Dirty Deeds Done Dirt Cheap.

The band's sanctuary from it all was backstage, though not because it separated them from the fans who had paid to see them. It was where they could relax and play darts in a mock establishment they named the Bell End Club (in honour of the business end of the penis), and even the road crew had to be financial members. But the set-up wasn't without its stresses for darts players desperate to make it to the final round.

'At $10 a head [the fee each participant had to pay],' Brian told Tommy Vance on BBC Radio in December 1981, 'that's £200 — the winner gets 200 quid ... I mean, the gig's important, but by God, your darts!'

On 7 December, *For Those About To Rock* was released in Australia, while two weeks later it hit the number one spot on the US Billboard charts where it stayed for three weeks and went double Platinum. In the UK, it peaked at number three.

It was the signal to crank up the promotional machine and two dates at the Capital Centre in Largo, Maryland on 20 and 21 December were recorded and filmed. An edited 35-minute edition was later serviced to TV stations and aired all over Europe, and the live versions of For Those About To Rock and Let's Get It Up were used as promo clips.

That hot, sweaty and very, very loud setting was a long way from an earlier proposal to do a large-scale video for the album's title track, complete with gladiators, in a Roman coliseum setting. The band laughed the idea out of the room. AC/DC might have had an enormous stage show in enormous venues, but Malcolm was still keen to keep the essence of what they did on as intimate and club-like a level as possible — which would be tough in ancient Rome.

'I wanted to go back to the Red Cow or the Marquee,' he told Dave Lewis in *Sounds* on 2 January 1982, 'and just play with eight lights and two speaker columns.'

There wasn't much chance of that.

Before the end of December, *For Those About To Rock* was certified Platinum in France, with 400,000 units sold just two weeks after its release.

In January 1982, exactly what the term 'rock' meant was thrown wide open when AC/DC were nominated for the best rock band at the American Music Awards, only to have super-sweet Australian soft-rock duo Air Supply take the honours. Being voted number one band in *Hit Parader*'s annual readers' poll went some way towards righting that curious wrong.

On 17 January, the second leg of the US tour kicked off with 28 dates and included four shows at the Seattle Coliseum, two at the LA Forum and three at the Cow Palace in San Francisco.

AC/DC's biggest tour to date just kept getting bigger, and three days in, *For Those About To Rock* was certified Platinum in the US with one million sales.

In February, Brian and Malcolm spent an evening with John Belushi. A few weeks later, the comedian and *Blues Brothers* star was dead. The incident brought all sorts of memories flooding back, but the AC/DC juggernaut rumbled on.

In the same month, they took out the best band, second-best album and second-best guitarist awards in *Kerrang!*'s readers' poll. But while Britain clearly remained a staunch fan base — even if the review of *For Those About To Rock* in *Sounds* showed a shot of Brian without his cap screaming his tits off, with the headline 'For Those About To Yawn' — Brian had to make some hard decisions about his situation there.

He had struggled to make a living with Geordie, but was now experiencing enormous success with AC/DC. That meant he was in a much higher income bracket, and with the UK's crippling top-end tax rate of something like 83 pence in the pound, something had to give.

'It's ridiculous having to go out and do a whole American tour and sell about a million records just to pay tax,' he told Simon Tebbutt in *Record Mirror* on 10 February 1982.

The fans didn't care about why the band were on tour; they were just glad that they were.

For the third year in a row, they were voted number one band in French magazine *Best*'s readers' poll, with Angus voted number one musician again, while *For Those About To Rock* landed the number one album slot. In an eerie twist, Bon was voted number one singer, two years after his death.

On 7 May, after a major legal battle over distribution rights, the movie *Let There Be Rock* finally opened at theatres across the US, re-released by Warner Bros. It would eventually open in 49 cities across America.

Typically, Brian, with his heart on his sleeve, was out for blood when a writer from *Rock en Stock* magazine allegedly accused him of trying to stop the movie, quite ridiculously because he wasn't featured in it. The singer confronted another of the magazine's writers and gave him a blunt message to pass on: he was going to kick the guy's arse.

Early June saw the band back in Japan for four dates and severing ties with management firm Leber-Krebs when their three-year contract expired. Long-serving tour manager Ian Jeffery, whose diligence and loyalty were well established, became their de facto manager. Jeffery was taken aback by AC/DC's request — he told them he wasn't a manager as such but, as always, was quite happy to do what needed to be done for the band.

A European tour was lined up with big outdoor festival dates in Germany and France during July and August, but was postponed and then inexplicably cancelled. Rumours of trouble within the band were rampant in the press and not without some foundation.

They finally hit the UK with a sold-out 19-date tour that kicked off on 29 September and included four consecutive nights at the Hammersmith Odeon. For these shows, the band added some real Civil War memorabilia in the form of two actual cannons they had retrieved from Tennessee.

Some reconditioning was required but they were the genuine article, unlike Brian's 'solo' album, *Strange Man*, which, to his disgust, was released in the US and Germany and was made up of material he'd recorded with Geordie between 1972 and 1975.

After the British tour came a 10-date European jaunt from 26 November, and in Paris fans were fainting from the heat faster than they could be pulled out of the crowd. The band did it even tougher under the heat of the stage lighting, and at the end of the show it was difficult to tell who was in the worse shape: them or the audience.

The day after their show at Le Bourget was spent with the members of Trust, Bon's old friends. They played cards and relaxed at AC/DC's hotel until around 2 a.m. when there was some interest in a drink at the Rose Bonbon, where, as it happened, an AC/DC night was being held. At the last minute, Angus, who rarely socialised, decided that he'd come along.

A few members of Trust got up on stage to jam, which was too much temptation for Angus, even though by now it was four in the morning. But if Bernie from the French band hadn't been so close to Bon, he would never have left his seat.

'For an hour and a half we had Angus Young,' Trust's singer Bernie told *Rock* in February 1983, 'just like in front of 15,000 people, sweating, running all over the place ... we couldn't believe it.'

They tore through versions of AC/DC's Live Wire, Ride On and Problem Child, along with Eddie Cochran's Twenty Flight Rock, Jerry Lee Lewis' Great Balls Of Fire and Chuck Berry's No Particular Place To Go.

Before the year was out, AC/DC were voted number one band, number one live act, number one single, number one guitarist, number one bass player, number two drummer and number three singer in *Kerrang!*'s annual readers' poll.

A proposed live album to capture the sheer power of the *For Those About To Rock* tour was planned but eventually shelved, with a new album considered a better option. But with total worldwide sales of the band's albums now at 25 million copies, Brian's hand was forced, and, like it or not, he had to leave the UK and the country's gutting tax system.

By early 1983, he was calling Hawaii — where Cliff Williams was already settled — home. For Brian, it was like going back to the Bahamas. Unfortunately, others were having trouble finding the line in the sand.

1983
Turned on: The Forum, Montreal.

chapter 21

FLICK OF
THE SWITCH

*I*n March 1983, after a few months writing back in Australia, four weeks of rehearsals took place on the Isle Of Man off the English coast for what was to be the *Flick Of The Switch* album. By April, the band were back at Compass Point Studios in Nassau in the Bahamas where *Back In Black* had been recorded.

They would produce this album by themselves, largely Malcolm with some help from the 'Dutch Damager' and 'The Gorgeous Glaswegian' (alias Harry Vanda and George Young), while Tony 'Have Ears Will Travel' Platt would engineer and mix the sessions. A total of 13 tracks were recorded, three of which remain unreleased, two being Out Of Bounds and Tightrope.

After the initial mixes the recording sounded too similar to *Back In Black*, so Malcolm again gave a very firm brief as to what he wanted the album to be — bare, raw and stripped down. To illustrate, he pointed to Frankenstein by Edgar Winter and Muddy Waters' Mannish Boy from the 1977 album *Hard Again*.

Tony Platt: 'I think there was a general feeling [within the band] that *Back In Black* was the pinnacle of how produced AC/DC should ever be. *For Those About To Rock* was a bit overproduced in terms of what the band were about. There was a genuine desire to get back to the basics with *Flick Of The Switch*.

Tony Platt: 'There was a general kind of consensus that we needed to find some way of moving on a little bit. You know the Johnny Winter version of Muddy Waters' Mannish Boy? Where they're all shouting in the background? Basically what Mal had said was that he wanted to try and get that feeling of being in the room with it all happening. I don't think it really worked entirely.'

There had been other movement since the band were last in the Bahamas, and not much of it very comfortable.

Tony Platt: 'It was an unhappy album to be making, ironically slightly more unhappy than *Back In Black* because *Back In Black* was fuelled by determination. *Flick Of The Switch* was sort of slightly undermined by some disillusionment in some respects.'

On the upside, Brian was well established and respected in his role, and the band that just three and a half years earlier was on weekly per diems was now one of the biggest acts on the planet. But everything had caught up with Phil Rudd.

The pressure and workload had been on the increase since *Highway To Hell*. Then came Bon's death, which affected Rudd perhaps more deeply than it did Angus, a burden he carried through the massive *Back In Black* and even bigger *For Those About To Rock* tour.

'The whole thing literally drained me,' Phil told Phil Lageat in *Rock Hard France* in June 2001.

At Nassau, Rudd, as usual, played like a freight train — he was one of the finest and straightest time-keepers since the Stones' Charlie Watts — and quickly nailed all his drum tracks.

His musicianship, however, wasn't the problem — a messy personal situation that involved someone in the Youngs' circle was, for Malcolm at least. For him, it was the last straw. He and Phil clashed heavily over the issue in Nassau in May and this time the guitarist wanted him on the first plane out the next night. That was that.

Angus was devastated.

Ian Jeffery: 'It was an absolutely stupid thing that finished it, but it had been brewing for a long, long time. But it was the culmination of things in Malcolm's mind, because you've got to remember then as well, Malcolm was pretty heavy on the sauce [drinking a lot].'

Another factor, kept quiet at the time, was revealed by the band years later.

'He [Rudd] got into the drugs and got burned out,' Malcolm told KNAC.com on 30 August 2000.

'We were due to start in the States straight afterwards,' Angus told Howard Johnson in *Kerrang!* on 29 September 1990. 'He would have gone overboard and done something drastic to himself or to someone else.'

How a band as disciplined as AC/DC, and run with such an iron fist by Malcolm, allowed the situation to blow out to the point it had was a mystery.

Back in the Bahamas, when things had calmed down, the severity of the situation kicked in: AC/DC had no drummer. With a US tour looming, the band made use of the fact that all this had taken place largely out of the public eye and used their location to keep a lid on things.

Several drummers were quickly flown in to audition. Showing his love of old-school musicians and strong memory yet again, Malcolm was optimistic that former Procol Harum drummer B.J. Wilson would be the band's new beat-keeper. But while Wilson jammed with the band as the overdubs for the album were being taken care of, he didn't do any drum tracks on the recording, and wasn't hired to fill Rudd's position.

More unsuccessful auditions were held in New York while the album was being mixed. When the band arrived back in London, they decided to advertise the position. Simon Kirke of Free and Bad Company fame was a contender but again, disappointingly for Malcolm, who was a huge fan, he turned out to be not quite the right fit. Paul Thompson, formerly of Roxy Music, became the main hope for the job and rehearsed with the band for 10 days. But again something fell short.

Ultimately, the successful applicant after a reported 400 auditions in America and 300 in the UK ended up being Simon Wright.

Wright had answered the band's anonymous but large ad in *Sounds*, which called for a 'Hard hitting rock & roll drummer ... any other crap need not apply'. He had no idea he was applying to join one of the biggest bands in the world. In fact, when he first auditioned at Nomis Studios in London, the band were nowhere in sight.

Simon Wright: 'The audition was with the drum tech, Dickie Jones. The drum kit was set up, and you had to play to three songs. I think it was like Led Zeppelin, ZZ Top and AC/DC. And luckily for me, I'd been playing a lot of these songs. I sort of figured it might be a good gig because of where it was being held, 'cause it's quite a fancy rehearsal studio.

'There wasn't much reaction really. I just finished and Dickie Jones — he's been with AC/DC for years — he said, "That's great, we'll definitely be in touch with you." And I think a day later, they got in touch and said, "You wanna come back and play?"

'I didn't know what band it was for. So I go back and I'm walking down the corridor and there's flight cases with AC/DC all over ... and I'm like, "Oh my God! You gotta be kidding! It can't be them!"

'And I get shown in and say hello to Angus and Mal and Cliff. Brian wasn't there. I mean, I was shittin' myself, you know? But they were really nice, they were great, made me feel comfortable. And we just played and that was it really. I got a call a couple of days later.'

Like Phil Rudd, Wright was a no-frills, meat and potatoes type time-keeper.

'If we'd heard him back when we were first forming,' Angus told Todd Everett in *Record Review* in February 1984, 'he would have been a contender to be our drummer then.'

On 5 August 1983, an Atlantic press release officially announced that Wright had joined the band.

Born on 19 June 1963 in Alden, near Manchester, Wright had begun teaching himself drums at the age of 15, while working during the day as a bricklayer.

His first band was at school with future Thin Lizzy member, Darren Wharton. He then formed Tora Tora, before joining AIIZ a year later who split shortly after releasing the single, I'm The One Who Loves You. After cutting a demo-single with Aurora in 1982, he joined the promising New Wave Of British Heavy Metal (NWOBHM) act Tytan, but during Wright's time in the band in 1983, their entire work schedule consisted of a gig in Belgium and recording one track for the album *Rough Justice*, that wouldn't come out until 1985.

Wright had a few of AC/DC's albums and had seen them on the *Highway To Hell* tour. Now he could watch them every night from the best seat in the house, even if it was at the back of the stage.

But while the drummer situation had been sorted out, the uncertainty and tension that had been part of the album's sessions flowed over into other areas.

For a start, the US tour that was scheduled to start on 28 August was postponed. Then there were internal issues at Atlantic. Few of the people who'd championed the band in the late '70s were still there: Jerry Greenberg was gone, and Phil Carson was busy guiding Robert Plant with his new solo career.

The view was that the new album was neither a *Highway To Hell* nor a *Back In Black* in terms of sales potential. As such, it wasn't considered a priority when it came to budgets or marketing.

Perry Cooper: 'I don't think *Flick Of The Switch* was one of their greatest albums ... What could be on a par with *Highway To Hell* and *Back In Black*? I mean, it's like, how does Led Zeppelin outdo Stairway To Heaven?'

There were also arguments about the cover art, which included a simple, pencil-drawn picture of Angus that he himself had originally sketched out to reflect the simple, raw approach of the album.

It was all a frustrating and slightly puzzling situation for a band that only two years earlier had been the toast of Atlantic Records.

Losing key members like Bon, and then Phil, in just three years was a devastating blow and, coupled with having to do battle with Atlantic, the band were quietly disoriented.

Ian Jeffery: 'They had all sorts of fucking problems with *Flick Of The Switch* from the record company not wanting to recognise the record; they didn't like the record at all. Then Angus had wanted the album [graphics] to be embossed like *Back In Black* was. He wanted *Flick Of The Switch* to be the same way and they [Atlantic] didn't want to spend the money because they didn't think the record was … again, they thought there was no fucking single etc etc.'

On 19 August, *Flick Of The Switch* was released in the US and Europe with the Australian release on 23 August. The album, which included Bedlam In Belgium — inspired by the near riot in 1977 — received mixed reviews and minimum promotion. But it did represent AC/DC exactly as Malcolm wanted: loud, raw, and effect- and technology-free, with drums that sounded like drums, not studio-treated cannons.

It was a grand 'fuck you' statement to deliberately separate AC/DC from other rock acts, who were desperately falling over themselves and smoothing off their sound in order to cater to MTV and have themselves beamed into living rooms across America.

Malcolm: 'It was thrown together real quick. I wouldn't say it's a great album but …'

Despite all this, *Flick Of The Switch* eventually peaked at number 15 on the US Billboard charts and reached number four in the UK, though it would only sell half a million copies in the States.

In October, tour rehearsals took place in Los Angeles, during which videos for Flick Of The Switch, Nervous Shakedown and Guns For Hire were shot in the aircraft-hangar-sized area the band were using. Malcolm's instructions to the film crew and director Paul Becher were as to the point as his brief had been for the album: you have a day, get the band on film.

It was the stripped-down live environment fans knew and expected, rather than the spectacular multi-million-dollar video efforts by artists such as Michael Jackson. Eleven different pre-show dressing-room clips — grabs of a minute — were shot later while on tour in Denver and compiled as introductions to the videos.

A three-month US and Canadian tour kicked off in Vancouver on 11 October with a travelling entourage of 30 people. Going on the road for the first time without Rudd was a huge psychological test, but from the first show it was clear that all would be okay.

Simon Wright: 'The place [The Coliseum in Vancouver] was just going nuts — this huge, massive place. But I mean, I was just terrified, it's unbelievable. But I got through it and I did it — there wasn't any mess-ups or anything. That was a big relief, getting that first one out of the way, you know. And it just rollercoastered after that. It was great.'

While the album itself didn't generate too many screaming headlines, the antics of some fans did. In what could have been a horrific twist of fate, a soldier was charged after he shot flares into the roof of the Tacoma Dome when the band were playing This House Is On Fire from the *Flick Of The Switch* album.

The tour was hardly a complete sell-out. In cities where they'd done two or three shows the previous tour, they found themselves playing just one this time, or performing to a half-empty hall on the second night.

Phil Carson: 'I came to a show in Nassau Coliseum where on the previous tour it had been sold out, and on this tour there was half a house, 8000 people. But they came out and they played like it was packed to the rafters.'

Two shows in Detroit's Joe Louis Arena on 17 and 18 November were caught on camera, and a 45-minute film was serviced to European TV stations. They also shot a second video for their next single Nervous Shakedown at the same venue. On 19 December, the tour wound up at New York's Madison Square Garden. Despite the downturn in crowd numbers, there were still enough fans wanting to see AC/DC to have the new drummer in awe.

Simon Wright: 'We were, like, playing three nights sold out [at] Madison Square Garden, I think, just these outrageous numbers of people ... I was totally out of my element. I mean, the guys were good, they kept an eye on things for me. They're always good to be around, 'cause they keep you grounded.'

But by then, as if the year hadn't been difficult enough, another major grounding presence within the band's circle, who had been trying to make things work in difficult circumstances, had been shown the door. With Ian Jeffery now manager, the buck and the blame for the band's circumstances stopped with him, at least as far as Malcolm was concerned.

Ian Jeffery: 'From my point of view, it was very sad. When the tour was getting together, Malcolm turned on me, like, "You're supposed to be on our side, you fucking cunt!" etc etc. I said, "I am! Where there isn't two shows, there isn't two shows! There's one show. We're trying to be realistic here."

'Then it all came to a head just out of the blue. We were supposed to be playing Hartford, Connecticut, and Malcolm called up one day and said, "Are you in your room?" And he walked in and said, "We don't need you any more." I was gobsmacked. Did he really walk in and say that? What am I? Am I sacked? Am I . . . what? I don't know.'

Phil Carson: 'Certain members of the band had personal issues. And those personal issues caused a great deal of paranoia. And they fired crew members, Phil Rudd went . . . It all went a little bit pear-shaped for a while there.'

It was just one more reason why Europe and the UK wouldn't see the band until eight months after the US tour. Curiously, between January and June 1984 time was spent writing, rehearsing and doing pre-production for the next album when only North America had seen the band perform the last one.

Meanwhile, Crispin Dye, a former Albert Productions executive in Europe, was appointed as the band's new manager.

During that non-touring period, Cliff Williams found time to record demos in Hawaii, then put a project together with former Home bandmate Laurie Wisefield and John Andreoni to play the material. The 11-song album was pitched at Atlantic but was rejected, and remains unreleased. During the same period, he played on Adam Bomb's first effort *Fatal Attraction*.

Finally, in July, the band did three weeks of rehearsals for a European tour in Norfolk in England, in what was actually the turret of a castle.

The tour included a series of eight headline performances as part of the huge Monsters of Rock festival from 11 August in Spain, Sweden — where, for some reason, there was no light show at all and the bands played in daylight — Germany, Italy and the UK, with the band's second appearance at Castle Donington on 18 August. Other acts on the Donington bill were Van Halen, Ozzy Osbourne, Mötley Crüe, Gary Moore, Y&T and Accept.

In Mötley Crüe's book, *The Dirt*, Nikki Sixx tells of the Crüe's then pastime of biting people. He thought he'd chewed on Angus at some point, and Malcolm marched up to Mötley's dressing room and confronted the much-taller Sixx.

Nikki Sixx: 'He was talking some squawk — I can't even remember exactly what happened and I kind of got in his face. Not really fair in size, is it?'

But at Castle Donington, AC/DC showed size doesn't matter with a powerful performance before 75,000 people, although, as with their previous appearance at the festival, the band were less than satisfied with their show.

It was at one of the Italian Monsters of Rock shows that [the band's former US agent] Doug Thaler saw that the lukewarm reception of *Flick Of The Switch* wasn't all the band were wrestling with.

'I'd gone into AC/DC's dressing room and had a Scotch with Malcolm and Jonno while Mötley Crüe played. When AC/DC went out to take the stage, Malcolm had clearly had too much to drink. And they were playing the song that Angus used to do his guitar solo and strip to, and Malcolm would just keep a steady rhythm — he couldn't even do that. And he fell into the drum kit, and I thought, "Oh boy, this is not headed any place good."'

Neither were the band's French shows, which followed the Monsters dates. At the last gig of the tour in Paris, the band only drew 6000 people to the Palais Omnisports de Paris-Bercy, an 18,000-seat arena. France once again had a black mark against its name — a history that dated back to an April 1977 Paris show with Black Sabbath that was derailed by poor equipment and an apathetic crowd — and it would be avoided during the next world tour in 1986.

Dropping their guard was rare for AC/DC, but the general position they found themselves in with *Flick Of The Switch* prompted some open-hearted admissions from Angus to Terry Whitfield in *Hit Parader* in October 1984.

'I understand some of the criticism people have made about it [the album],' he said.

He also acknowledged in the interview, perhaps for the first time, that AC/DC were part of a community, rather than being a dominating force of one. He was pleased that bands he liked such as Def Leppard were going so well and said, 'We've had our time in the spotlight' and '[we] have no trouble sharing it [the spotlight] with newer groups'.

It was startling stuff, but these weren't easy times.

Tony Platt: 'The thing is, with a band like AC/DC, if they appear slightly apologetic about something, then people are going to take that as the lead. When they went out and toured *Back In Black*, they were just committed 110 per cent and that's what really took it to great heights. You take a great album like that and you go and play it with that amount of commitment, then people are going to sit up and take notice. With *Flick Of The Switch*, even the tour was sort of hampered by all sorts of bits and pieces going on and the fact that Phil wasn't there — everything had changed.'

But on 19 October, everything seemed right again, even if momentarily, with the US release of *'74 Jailbreak*, a mini-album consisting of Australian-only released tracks, which featured not only Phil Rudd, but Bon as well.

One was resting and the other just sleeping.

1986
Sweating it out: Angus, Sporthalle, Cologne.

chapter 22

FLY ON
THE WALL

*W*hen serial killer Richard
Ramirez was arrested in September 1985, it seemed that the door had
finally closed on one of the most gruesome chapters in American
criminal history. But when Ramirez claimed that AC/DC's song Night
Prowler, from the *Highway To Hell* album, made him commit the 16
murders, that door was kicked wide open again. To make matters
worse, a cap bearing the AC/DC logo was found at Ramirez's
apartment when he was arrested.

It was just what the band's detractors had been waiting for and
the media, especially in America, immediately seized on the case.
Wild accusations that AC/DC were, in fact, devil worshippers were
bandied about. First, the gut-grinding difficulties of the *Flick Of The
Switch* album and tour, now this.

The year had begun on a more impressive note than the band had
experienced since the days of *Back In Black* and *For Those About To
Rock*. Simon Wright only thought that playing Madison Square Garden
was a baptism of fire: it was January 1985 that was the real deal.

AC/DC took three weeks off from recording what would be the *Fly On The Wall* album and headlined two nights at the 10-day Rock In Rio festival in Rio de Janeiro, Brazil, which also featured Rod Stewart, Queen, Yes and Iron Maiden. The band appeared before 50,000 people on 15 January with the Scorpions, and then in front of a staggering 250,000 on 19 January with Whitesnake, Ozzy Osbourne and the Scorpions.

Despite the excitement of playing to such a huge crowd, Angus, for one, hated his time in Brazil. Not the beautiful country or the people, but the fact that so many had been reduced by poverty to begging. The trip was an enormous cultural shock and he hardly left his hotel room the whole time. It was all just too troubling.

The sessions for *Fly On The Wall* had begun in Montreux, Switzerland at Mountain Studios in late October 1984. Malcolm and Angus were producing the recording and work resumed when they returned from Brazil.

The album's backing tracks and vocals were done in a casino ballroom where the legendary Montreux Jazz Festival is held, and where prior to a legendary fire during a Frank Zappa show, Deep Purple had planned to record their *Machine Head* album.

Simon Wright: 'The place we recorded in was amazing. It was this huge casino on Lake Geneva. And there was smoke on the water [just as in the lyrics of the Deep Purple classic]. That's the same one. It was a huge round room and it was all sectioned off with little huts and stuff where they'd put the amps and isolate [the various sounds for recording purposes]. To get up to the control room there was this section of stairs like a fire escape kinda thing.'

Work was completed by late February, and in March *Fly On The Wall* was mixed in Sydney.

It was then that wild rumours began to circulate that Brian was about to do a solo album and had left the band, or been sacked during the *Fly* album sessions.

Juke magazine's Christie Eliezer called Fifa Riccobono from Albert Productions to see if there was any truth in the rumours. She denied the reports but Eliezer persisted. Riccobono calmly repeated that Brian had not left the band and finally, in exasperation, told Eliezer to wait for a moment.

A minute or so later, a voice boomed down the line. 'Christie, me son, what's the problem?' cackled Brian, who had been in her office the entire time.

Five promotional videos for *Fly On The Wall* were shot at the World's End Club in New York's Alphabet City, with the band in their onstage element. The deliberately seedy setting came complete with a compere who could have doubled as a used-car salesman. The whole thing was like a snapshot from the band's early days on the Australian pub circuit, which may well have been the whole idea. But no-one was very happy with the results.

On 28 June, the *Fly On The Wall* album was released worldwide. Although nowhere near as strong as the allegedly weak *Flick Of The Switch*, it contained several classics, including the brutal riffing that opened the title cut, as well as Sink The Pink and Shake Your Foundations. It was rough, gritty and loud, and more than ever the band sounded like a Nuremberg rally on a Saturday night after the pubs had closed.

The concept for the album's art — like the line in the lyrics of TNT — again recalled an Australian TV commercial for fly spray and an unpleasant cartoon fly. Atlantic just had to grin and bear it.

In July, the *Let There Be Rock* movie was released in the UK on video. Everything was ticking away reasonably well, and by early August *Fly On The Wall* had reached Gold sales status in America. Again, in terms of the numbers, it wasn't exactly *Back In Black*. In France, for example, *Fly On The Wall* eventually sold a mere 70,000 copies, whereas five years earlier *Back In Black* had sold one million.

But it would have been a brave soul who pointed out that it had been a downhill slide, as far as sales were concerned, since Mutt Lange produced *Back In Black*. Pumping up Lange's influence made Malcolm and Angus bristle, although the stats were hard to argue with. Everything would have been cleaner and more polished on *Back In Black* if Lange had been given his head, they argued.

'We had to do a lot of battling for what we wanted,' Angus told Harold De Muir in *Aquarian* on 14 August 1985. 'And Malcolm took care of a lot of the songs on that album, because Mutt didn't really understand them.'

On 5 August, *Fly On The Wall* was released in Australia around the same time as a single was issued in the UK titled Geordie Aid — Try Giving Everything, which was aimed, like Live Aid, at helping with the situation in Ethiopia. Members of Lindisfarne, The Animals and players from Newcastle United Football Club were involved on the song by John Mayall.

Brian was less than impressed, and not just because of his all-too-brief appearance — he only sang a single line. Not only did he think the song was lousy and had more of a political overtone than he was comfortable with, but many of the major celebrities from the region who could have really attracted some support for the project and made a difference were absent.

Maybe they should have recorded a version of AC/DC's Whole Lotta Rosie, as that same month the 1977 song was again voted best ever by the readers of UK heavy metal bible *Kerrang!* in their third Hot 100 poll. It was a jump from being third a few years earlier and a return to the top spot it had occupied in 1981.

In the latest poll, it was kept company by no fewer than seven of the band's other songs. It was the good news before an almighty shit storm.

At first it all seemed like just another tour, although now with new manager Stewart Young and Part Rock Management. That was until serial killer Ramirez's arrest.

The 42-date US tour was scheduled to kick off at the Broome County Arena in Binghamton, New York on 4 September after two days of rehearsals and just days after the authorities seized Ramirez. With their alleged gruesome connection to Ramirez, the band were sitting ducks for the media.

The lyrics of Night Prowler were carefully analysed and some newspapers attempted to link Ramirez's Satanism with AC/DC's name, somehow arriving at the conclusion that AC/DC actually stood for Anti-Christ, Devil's Child. For the band, the media frenzy was far more disturbing.

A photo of Angus at a birthday party was wildly distorted into 'proof' of him attending a black mass, simply because of the glow of a few candles.

'What they can't see is that Night Prowler is just about creeping in at night on a couple of old girlfriends and doing the business,' Malcolm told Mark Putterford in *Kerrang!* on 9 January 1986.

Nevertheless, the situation spiralled frighteningly out of control and went right to the top in America, where a US Senate Committee began hearings on the possibility of regulating rock lyrics. The Parents Musical Resource Center, headed by Susan Baker, wife of Treasury Secretary James Baker, and Tipper Gore, wife of Tennessee Senator Al Gore, strongly backed lyric regulation. As far as they were concerned, AC/DC was public enemy number one of moral values.

The band were largely unconcerned, at least publicly, at the possibility of censorship, and just sneered at it all with added venom. Plenty of other acts had more to lose than them.

Brian later gave *Musician* his full and frank take on the censorship issue to Charles M. Young in the magazine's April 1991 edition. The matter of 2 Live Crew — who at the time were being hammered by moralists for their lyrics — was raised. Brian had little sympathy for them or heavy metal bands with gory attention-seeking lyrics.

When asked what separated AC/DC and songs like Sink The Pink from those other acts, Brian replied that AC/DC used the art of the double entendre. Young then wondered if 2 Live Crew should be behind bars for the crime of not being as smart as AC/DC.

'They fucking deserve to go to prison!' Brian roared. 'If they haven't got the fucking brains [to use words cleverly]!'

Out on the road in America, the political and media frenzy translated into something that couldn't be so easily shrugged off.

Simon Wright: 'It was a bit frustrating, you know. Nothing really changed within the running of the band or anything. We got followed around once, I think, at an airport by a camera crew. We [did nothing more offensive than drink] cups of tea and stuff [but were] being portrayed as these devil worshippers. Cup of tea and a cigarette, that'll do us, you know.'

Under pressure from church groups, which objected to the band's 'satanic' and 'lewd' lyrics, city officials decided to bar the band from playing in Springfield, Illinois.

'They're immoral, they're very suggestive, they have satanic connotations, they're destructive, they're lustful, they're lewd,' Springfield's Rev. Robert Green said in an article in the Melbourne *Sun* on 19 September 1985.

But as far as AC/DC were concerned, it was the band who were being discriminated against. Where was their protection of free speech under the First Amendment? Enough was enough and AC/DC returned fire with a million dollar lawsuit, which magically cleared the way for the show to go ahead: although they still had to sit low in their seats when their bus approached the venue.

'They thought they were in 18th century Salem and above the law,' Malcolm told [the Australian newspaper supplement] *Good Weekend* in February 1988. 'The State Governor was so embarrassed that he sent us in with the State police for protection.'

An out-of-court settlement was arranged but the church groups had the last laugh. They managed to convince local hotels to close their doors to the band. As a result, AC/DC and their entourage were forced to spend the night before and after the show a hundred miles away in St Louis.

It didn't end there. In Houston, city officials attempted to devise a rating system for all local concerts and exclude children under the age of 12 from those deemed offensive. And in Dallas, fire officials refused to let the band use its pyro effects for the cannons during For Those About To Rock.

To top it all off, the band's set list on the tour had its own teething problems, with some songs, like Danger from *Fly On The Wall*, failing miserably live and being forever banished.

There was some light relief on 5 October when Brian celebrated his birthday on stage in Kansas City and received his birthday cake in the face. But it was back to migraine time when a show at the Pacific Amphitheater was cancelled.

Press reports suggested it was due to a combination of poor ticket sales, local residents' complaints over noise, and general adverse 'Night Stalker' publicity surrounding the band. The fact was that another homicide had been committed in California a week earlier by someone else wearing an unfortunate fashion accessory: an AC/DC cap. Accordingly, all local radio stations refused to be associated with the promotion of the concert and it died on the vine.

But it wasn't all bad news. The American tour was extended with 14 additional dates from 5 November. Obviously many people wanted to see what 'devil worshippers' actually looked like.

In December, the band were back in the Bahamas at Compass Point Studios to record Who Made Who, D.T. and Chase The Ace, with George Young and Harry Vanda as producers.

The following month, it was announced that AC/DC were to record the soundtrack for American horror writer and arch AC/DC fan Stephen King's debut as a movie director. *Maximum Overdrive* was based on King's short story *Trucks*, which was part of a collection called *Nightshift*.

AC/DC doing a soundtrack album was quite a leap. The idea broadly ran against the band's long-held belief that a) rock and roll and embarrassing C-grade movie scripts were no good in bed together, and b) reselling fans music they already had in the form of a greatest-hits-type album was flat out wrong.

But the King project, for some reason, just felt right. Besides, the author had made no bones about his admiration of the band and included grabs from the song Dirty Deeds Done Dirt Cheap in his book *Skeleton Crew*.

'We ended up doing everything,' Angus told Sylvie Simmons in *Metal Creem* in January 1987, 'all the horror noises and everything. All the Hollywood stuff!'

The New Year had kicked off with an eight-date, sold-out UK tour and was immediately followed by 17 dates in Europe, which ran until 16 February.

Then the results from various polls from 1985 began to appear, and to the band's amazement, after more than a decade of nonstop touring and recording, the readers of US magazine *Circus* voted AC/DC number one 'comeback of the year'. Almost as curious was US gossip magazine *People* picking *Fly On The Wall* as the best album of 1985.

On 25 and 26 February, the video for what was to be the title track of the album *Who Made Who* was shot at the Brixton Academy in London with a multitude of Angus clones. Something like 300 members of the band's fan club, and others who had simply heard about the event on radio, came from all over the country and even slept out in the freezing cold to take part.

The shoot was directed by David Mallet, who'd previously done such large-scale efforts as Queen's Radio Ga Ga and Mick Jagger and David Bowie's Dancing In The Streets. It was Mallet who showed AC/DC that maybe videos could work after all.

The *Who Made Who* album, the soundtrack for the Stephen King movie, was released in the US on 20 May and on 27 May in Europe. It pooled together the songs recorded with George and Harry in the Bahamas, along with their remix of Shake Your Foundations, as well as classics such as You Shook Me All Night Long, Sink The Pink, Ride On, Hells Bells and For Those About To Rock. The title track was praised by critics and was the band's most successful single in years, with the album peaking at 33 on the US Billboard charts and number 11 on the UK charts.

Over three days in June, a new video for You Shook Me All Night Long was shot to go with the album, which was released in Australia on 23 June.

The Stephen King movie was unveiled on US theatre screens on 4 July only to crash spectacularly at the box office and gross a mere $US7.5 million. The band only got to see the movie just before it was released. It had looked promising in the planning stages when they were working on the music, but something got lost in the translation of the idea onto the screen.

It was a favour to King in the first place but once was enough: no more soundtrack work.

At the end of the month, rehearsals were held in New Orleans at the Lakefront Arena in preparation for a 42-date US tour which kicked off on 31 July, supported by Queensryche.

It had been a tough year on the touring circuit, but in a sign that the band might finally have put the horrors of the *Flick Of The Switch* album, Phil Rudd's traumatic departure and the moralists behind them, the tour was completely sold out and became one of the most successful of the year in America.

It included, in August, the band's first-ever performance in Las Vegas. It took some talking to finally get them there. For Malcolm, particularly, the place had too many cabaret connotations that had absolutely nothing — with the sole exception of Elvis — to do with rock and roll.

Later in the tour, at the Nassau Coliseum in Uniondale, half-a-dozen Angus clones took to the stage to open the show. Probably none of them had been through what the man himself had in the previous five years.

'It's assumed there's all sorts of drugs and women,' Angus told Mikael Kirke in *Faces Rocks* in March 1984. 'Now we've seen our share of all that — but we've also seen deaths, and people with ruined lives.'

1988
Making a point: Brian, Australia.

chapter 23
BLOW UP YOUR VIDEO

*t*ony Platt, who'd engineered *Highway To Hell*, *Back In Black* and *Flick Of The Switch*, was working on a Cheap Trick album in Electric Lady Studios in New York City when some of the studio assistants dragged him out into the corridor.

Tony Platt: 'Rick Rubin was producing The Cult in Studio A and we [Platt and the studio assistants] stood in the airlock just outside the studio. A snatch of *Highway To Hell* would get played and then a snatch of *Back In Black* and then a snatch of Led Zeppelin, and we thought, "What the hell's going on there?" [A studio assistant] said, "Well, he's getting the guitar sounds from *Back In Black*, the drum sound from *Highway To Hell* and the voice sound from Led Zeppelin!" Literally, as he was mixing he was getting a guitar sound on The Cult and then comparing it directly with the guitar sound that he wanted to get from *Back In Black*. The same with all the other instruments.'

The Cult's subsequent album, 1987's *Electric*, was the most high profile of a multitude of AC/DC copyists who had been growing in number for several years. None were real contenders; just worshipful clones. During Jason and the Scorchers' Australian tour in April 1987, the Nashville band stumbled across one of the parties that inspired that homage.

Malcolm and Angus were in Sydney continuing a relaxed process of working up ideas and doing pre-production for what would be the *Blow Up Your Video* album. It was a welcome change from the album, tour, album pressure cycle of the previous few years.

On a night off, Angus, who rarely ventured out to see other bands, went to St George Sailing Club in southern Sydney to check out the Scorchers.

Warner Hodges (the Scorchers): 'I had just shown up for soundcheck and was about to head to the stage, when to my surprise I saw a rather small guy out of the corner of my eye. I'll be damned! Angus Young in the Scorchers' dressing room!'

Jason Ringenberg (the Scorchers): 'What impressed me most about him was how he talked about getting up that morning at 6 a.m. to work on songs. I'd never heard of any rocker with that kind of work ethic. He said he wouldn't stay long because he was going to do the same thing again the next morning!'

By July, the raw material from Malcolm and Angus' writing sessions was ready to be knocked into shape with the entire band at rehearsals in London's Nomis Studios. Within a fortnight, they were ready to record. The idea was to pick up where *Who Made Who* left off, which wasn't a bad idea given that the song itself had been voted second best track of 1986 by the readers of *Hit Parader* magazine.

The song was a rallying call to get back to basics again and so George Young and Harry Vanda were enlisted to handle the album's production.

A crop of hungry young contenders who couldn't easily be waved away had emerged at AC/DC's heels since *Fly On The Wall*.

There was the West Hollywood-spawned Guns N' Roses, whose debut album that year, *Appetite For Destruction*, would be an era-defining statement that brought a bottle of Jack Daniel's down hard on the musical establishment. They drank, cursed, bristled, swaggered, oozed a sense of cool mystique, and played rock and roll like no-one — with the exception of AC/DC — had in many years. And they could do a more-than-passable version of Whole Lotta Rosie.

At the other end of the scale were pretty bands with big hair and spandex pants like Bon Jovi and Poison. Between 1986 and 1988, Bon Jovi had the world in the palms of their hands with the phenomenally successful *Slippery When Wet* album and its follow-up *New Jersey*. Their popularity was such that a competition with the childhood home of singer Jon Bon Jovi as a prize received literally millions of entries.

It was absolutely crucial that AC/DC now come back with all cannons blazing.

Ironically, the studio decided upon for the task of taking on the likes of the Jack Daniel's-swilling Guns N' Roses was built in a 12th-century chateau on a secluded vineyard in the south of France. For all its history and picturesque setting, conditions were crude although the food was excellent.

There was no air conditioning and their beds were little more than mattresses placed on the floor, the lack of elevation making it that much easier to get bitten by bugs and scorpions. When a local asked if the 'white lady', the ghost who hovered through the premises, had revealed herself it was decided to look for alternative accommodation.

Sixteen tracks were recorded between August and September at the Miraval Studio in Le Val in Provence in the south of France, with Brian again doing the lyrics. Almost 10 years on, he still found Bon a hard act to follow as a lyricist.

The album was mixed in New York over two weeks between mid-October and November. Meanwhile, tickets went on sale in Australia for the band's February tour. There was mayhem.

Australia had suffered an AC/DC drought with no visits for the *For Those About To Rock*, *Flick Of The Switch* or *Fly On The Wall* tours. Now they were finally coming back for the first time in seven years and no-one wanted to miss out.

Fists flew among overly enthusiastic fans — some of whom had reportedly lined up for two weeks — outside the box office at the

Perth Entertainment Centre. Sixty-one people were arrested on minor charges, while there was also trouble in Melbourne and Adelaide but on a much lesser scale.

Meanwhile, the video for Heatseeker was shot at Cannon Studios in Elstree, near London, under the direction of David Mallet. Its title was the kind of wordplay Bon would have been proud of.

The *Blow Up Your Video* album, with its name aimed at the growing subculture of rock bands making inoffensive film clips in order to secure promotion on MTV, was released on 18 January in Australia, 29 January in Europe and 1 February in the US. Unfortunately, it was more a reflection of the times than a stand against them as the *Flick Of The Switch* album had been.

The world tour began in Perth just four days after the album was released in Australia and ran into 22 February. The 16 dates were hugely successful with five sold-out shows in Melbourne and six more at Sydney's 12,000-seat Entertainment Centre. Angus emerged each night from a rocket in a strange rewind situation to their days on 'Countdown'.

Thirty-three people were arrested in Adelaide and 60 at the Myer Music Bowl in Melbourne, trumpeted the media once again.

'In Melbourne, we were just about to go on stage and up on the news flashed "Full scale security alert going on at the AC/DC show tonight,"' Angus told Mary Anne Hobbs in *Sounds* on 9 April 1988. 'I thought there was a war on!'

The band had planned to play It's A Long Way To The Top in Melbourne until some of the local crew mentioned that national pop hero, and one-time singer for Australian soft rock outfit the Little River Band, John Farnham, had recently performed the song on TV. That was that.

During the tour Malcolm caught up with his old friend Herm Kovac in Sydney and gave him the news that he was no longer smoking dope, as, to Kovac's horror, he had in his days in the Velvet Underground.

Herm Kovac: 'He said, "You're going to be proud of me." I said, "Why?" He said, "I'm not a hippy any more." He gave it up, but he was still drinking.'

Given that *Blow Up Your Video* had hit the number two spot on the British charts, a small, six-date UK tour from 6 March — supported by Dokken — seemed strange. They played in only two cities, London and Birmingham, where live footage was shot at the NEC for the video for That's The Way I Wanna Rock And Roll. An extra date at Wembley was eventually added for 13 April, due, not surprisingly, to overwhelming demand.

For Malcolm, the relatively small-scale tour was something of a blessing, if not a necessity. He had become aware that his drinking was now a problem and he needed time off the road to look after his health.

The talk that was being bandied about in relation to a possible live album would have given him some breathing space, as it involved much less work than recording a studio album. But it came to nothing.

With the UK fans satisfied, at least for the moment, it was off to Europe for 20 dates from 15 March. While in Holland, Angus took time out to visit his wife's parents before the Berlin show. Not long into the return flight, the small plane was struck by lightning. Angus thought his time had come.

Near-death experiences on the tour were really nothing new to the guitarist. At a show in Frankfurt, Germany, the Hell's Bell fell from the ceiling and its massive chain came close to crushing him. From that point on, a different, lighter bell was used, just in case.

At another gig, some genius threw a mortar shell on stage. Thankfully, it didn't explode, although its weight caused some damage. A stun grenade, however, was about to explode.

On 21 April, Atlantic issued a press release announcing that Malcolm wouldn't take part in the next US tour: he needed some rest. He had made it through an Australian, UK and European tour, but at that point America was a mountain he didn't feel ready to climb.

Angus, for one, certainly didn't want what had happened to Bon to happen to his brother. Malcolm decided to stay at home, look after his health and attend AA meetings, while Stevie Young — a gun guitarist formerly of Starfighters and a nephew of Malcolm and Angus — would handle the US tour.

Given that Malcolm was the band's brain and unofficial leader, Angus' mentor, and the other great rhythm guitar player on the planet — next to Keith Richards — it was an unsettling move for all; but unfortunately, a necessary one.

Malcolm: 'Just a case of rock and roll. The lifestyle. I'm just a little guy, like five foot three, you know? I was trying to keep up with the big guys. It just got to me. People can't depend on you any more. So it was just a matter of cutting it [alcohol] right out.

'When you've got an alcohol problem, you don't see it like ... Of course, when you've sobered up [and are thinking more clearly], lots of thoughts would go through your head like [the alcohol-related death of] Bon and lots of other things you might have messed up here and there. It was a combination at the end where you just need help, basically. You can't do it yourself. Especially when you've done everything yourself in the past and along comes this little thing that's snuck up on you. It's a whole different thing.'

Simon Wright: 'I think it's safe to say we all sort of noticed a change in the way he was and his character. He had a lot of problems. It just kind of escalated, really. We finished a show and he just said, "I can't do this, I just can't do this." And we all felt so bad for him. If there was anything we could've done to help him ... he's tough, you know; he's a tough guy, Malcolm, and he made the decision to stop and get himself sorted out, and that's just more power to him. He's an incredible guy. And I have nothing but admiration for him for doing that and actually having the balls to do that.'

In late April, while Malcolm was at home recording demos, handling the vocals himself and experimenting with keyboards and guitar samples, the band was in Boston rehearsing with Stevie Young who, as a rhythm guitar player, Angus likened not only to Malcolm but masters like Richards and Ike Turner.

After just 10 days, AC/DC was ready for the US.

The combined American and Canadian tour was huge and no-one could possibly have blamed Malcolm for not taking part. It ran for a mind-crushing six months from 3 May until 13 November and was supported by White Lion, Cinderella and LA Guns, who took over the opening slot early in the tour that Guns N' Roses were originally scheduled to handle.

Gruelling as the tour was, it was also one of the most successful of the year in the US and one on which the band started to notice there were much younger people in the audience, along with the more customary crowd. A generational crossover was starting to take place.

Given the fact that Malcolm had generally led the band from the back of the stage and that Stevie's playing style was very similar to that of Malcolm, most fans probably didn't even know he wasn't there. Angus, of course, did.

Simon Wright: '[Stevie] did a great job. He was very together, and he played great. I found his playing really cool. Big shoes to fill, but he did it pretty well.'

Perry Cooper: '[Stevie] was fine. I mean, it was weird having him there. It was very weird. Malcolm ruled the band. I was shocked. But they went on, as they did when Phil left, you know; as they did when Bon died. This is a band that never stopped. They had a few hiccups, but they never stopped.'

Malcolm went to see one of two shows at the Long Beach Arena in LA and, like some sort of strange out-of-body experience, watched his double from the side of the stage.

'It was a pretty weird feeling,' he told Howard Johnson in *Metal Hammer* in November 1992, 'but they were having real sound problems that night, so I was kind of glad that I wasn't up there.'

He was probably just as glad he didn't play in Shreveport, Louisiana, on 2 August because, like something straight out of the Old West, the band were literally told to get out of town by the local sheriff after Angus dropped his pants and mooned the audience. The locals were so incensed that they were prepared to make citizens' arrests.

AC/DC made a dash for Dallas after calling in at their hotel and hastily packing up their belongings.

Not that the band couldn't have afforded legal assistance to get themselves out of trouble: the US tour grossed $20.1 million and covered 110 shows in 105 cities.

Finally, things were looking up.

1991

In full flight: Monsters Of Rock, Castle Donington.

chapter 24

THE RAZORS EDGE

*W*ith the discipline that had long been the hallmark of AC/DC's career, Malcolm had successfully quit drinking, quietly with zero fuss and publicity, and resumed working with the band in late 1988 after several months off.

Angus was delighted to have his brother back and marvelled at how he had functioned as well as he did while he had been drinking.

Simon Wright: 'It was just like, "Welcome back, mate. You all right?" It wasn't really a major thing; there wasn't like a big grand entrance and he comes back, you know. I'd call him up and ask him how he was. He said he was doing fine. It just slowly went back to the way it was — us being a band together again.'

Some of the ideas that Malcolm had been working on while off the road were thrashed out with Angus over Christmas and by early 1989 were firming strongly, with the pair taking full charge of the songs and lyrics.

The songs were usually formed in three stages. Firstly, on acoustic guitars, then on electric guitars with a drum machine as a rhythm guideline if a drum kit was unavailable, and finally the entire band.

As an indication of just how rejuvenated Malcolm was, he also found time to co-produce a demo for Stevie Young's new band, Little Big Horn.

Around the same time, Simon Wright was having trouble sitting still, impatient about the lack of activity within the AC/DC camp. Between tours the pace of their schedule dropped enormously. So in January 1990 after more than a year of downtime he accepted an offer from his friend former Rainbow singer Ronnie James Dio to play on his album *Lock Up The Wolves*. Dio was an AC/DC admirer from back in the days of the conflict with Ritchie Blackmore over his remarks about the band back in 1976.

During the recording, Wright decided to join Dio on a permanent basis.

Simon Wright: 'It was a gradual thing. I was becoming bored. I mean, everything was great. I kinda got complacent about the whole thing, [the situation] seemed like ... more time off, you know? I wanted to play more. I gotta say it was a hard decision but I think it was a mutual thing, so I did the album with Ronnie and just basically stayed — never left.'

Wright would only stay with Dio for a year. He then recorded an album called *Pain* with uncanny AC/DC sound-alikes Rhino Bucket in 1994 and later joined AC/DC's old mates UFO. Eventually he re-joined Dio in 2000.

AC/DC needed a replacement for Wright and extensive auditions were held.

The band might have been loud and attracted a 'heavy metal' tag, but drummers of all persuasions knew that no-one, with the sole exception of the Stones, was more precise in their beat-keeping than AC/DC. For that reason, they came from far and wide, among them master English drummer Simon Philips who'd played with a who's who of the music world and later joined Toto.

But it was Chris Slade who made the cut and his recruitment was yet another example of Malcolm's vault-like memory; he had seen

Slade when he was with Manfred Mann and played in Sydney with Free and Deep Purple.

Born on 30 October 1946 in Wales, Slade's credentials were nothing short of stunning.

It was 1963 and he was 16 when he heard that Tommy Scott and the Senators were in need of a drummer. The following night, the band went to his home and he auditioned by playing The Ventures' Walk Don't Run. He was in. The band's singer was later better known as Tom Jones.

Slade's first professional appearance was with Jones at Beat City in London as opening act for the Stones. Slade later played on the demos of what would eventually be the solo singer's signature tune, It's Not Unusual. He also appeared on several tracks of a 1967 album with Jones called *13 Smash Hits*, with John Paul Jones, later of Led Zeppelin fame, on bass.

The Tom Jones connection didn't harm Slade's career prospects on other fronts either. On one occasion in Hawaii, Elvis came to see the Welsh star perform.

'Apparently he liked my style,' Slade told Phil Lageat in *Rock Hard France* in June 2001. 'Since I was about to finish the tour with Tom, Elvis was planning on working with two drummers, Ronnie Tutt and myself.'

The problem was that Slade was unable to go to the early rehearsals with Elvis, so the gig of a lifetime didn't materialise.

Later, Slade received a call from Manfred Mann from the English outfit of the same name. Along with bassist Colin Pattenden, Slade went on to record nine albums with Manfred Mann between 1972 and 1978, with a version of Bruce Springsteen's Blinded By The Light a huge hit worldwide in 1976.

After Manfred Mann split the band in late 1978, Slade subsequently joined Uriah Heep for one album, *Conquest*. He went on to work with Gary Numan on the *I Assassin* album, and then teamed with former Mott the Hoople and Bad Company guitarist Mick Ralphs in 1983. It was while working with Ralphs that Slade got a call from Ralphs' friend David Gilmour of Pink Floyd with an offer to go on tour. The obstacle of him already having obligations to Ralphs wasn't an issue as Ralphs was also involved.

Slade was beside himself until later that afternoon when the phone rang again. It was Jimmy Page. He was putting a band together called The Firm and wanted Slade to be part of it. Not knowing whether to laugh or cry, Slade apologised to Page and said that he had only just signed on with Gilmour and would be unavailable for several months. Page, to Slade's disbelief, said he was happy to wait.

Slade went on to do two albums with The Firm (Page, Paul Rodgers and Tony Franklin), their self-titled debut and *Mean Business*. The project never really took off and Page disbanded the group in 1986.

As fate would have it, in 1989, Slade was working with Gary Moore, who was also managed by AC/DC's management organisation, Part Rock. Malcolm saw him play and Slade subsequently stormed through a successful audition for AC/DC.

With Slade now in the band, although at the time only on a temporary basis for the making of the next album, the new material was rehearsed in a tiny farmhouse in Brighton.

As always, the vast majority of the new songs didn't make the cut: AC/DC tunes had to be instantly recognisable as such. They had to have a certain lyrical and rhythmic magic that was uniquely theirs.

Meanwhile, AC/DC provided some sonic artillery when Panama's dictator General Manuel Noriega holed himself up in the Vatican Embassy in Panama City to escape the American military. Helicopter gunships and tanks blasted recordings of AC/DC and various metal bands at the compound 24 hours a day in a bid to flush him out, or at least give him a brutal dose of sleep deprivation.

'We were just glad to be of service,' Brian told Liam Fay in *Hot Press* on 18 October 1990.

In late February, the band relocated to Windmill Lane Studios in Dublin, Ireland, where they spent a total of five weeks.

The album was supposed to be produced by Harry Vanda and George Young. As it turned out, George did the early recordings on his own without Harry Vanda being involved. Then, he had some personal issues crop up that required his attention and in April the band relocated to Little Mountain Studios in Vancouver with producer Bruce Fairbairn and engineer Mike Fraser in charge of the sessions.

Malcolm and Angus had had their shot at producing their own work but recognised once again that an outsider's ears were crucial.

Initially, there were concerns that Fairbairn might push the band in a more pop direction along the lines of his work with Bon Jovi on their hugely popular 1986 album, *Slippery When Wet*, which sold 14 million copies. But it was soon obvious that Fairbairn was a huge AC/DC fan who simply wanted to experience first-hand the band in all its raw and roaring glory.

There was certainly nothing pretty about his approach to the vocals. Brian was put in a soundproof room where he could yell and scream to his heart's content so he would be ready to step up to the vocal microphone when it was time to record.

Everything felt comfortable and having Fairbairn — who quickly won the trust of Malcolm and Angus — at the controls freed the pair up to do what they did best.

Having one less task to handle also allowed them to relieve Brian of the burden of writing the lyrics. Brian had been concerned that he was letting the side down because he was being kept busy with personal problems and felt slightly guilty that he had run out of ideas by that point anyway, so it was an opportunity for Malcolm and Angus to restamp their authority on the band.

It was during the recording that Chris Slade was asked to join on a permanent basis.

He was constantly amazed by the honesty of what took place around him during the sessions. They recorded together as a band, not individually in separate areas, and they had visual contact while they did so, unlike most acts.

'It's inconceivable, say, [for] Angus to stop by [at the studio] two weeks after the rest of the band to record his guitar parts,' Slade told Phil Lageat in *Rock Hard France* in June 2001. 'And they always keep the first takes. On every track of each AC/DC album, there's always some element of a first take somewhere.'

Which is a good thing. Multiple takes of a song like Thunderstruck, which was based on Angus' near-death air experience during the 1988 European tour, with its complicated and lengthy central guitar passage, would have been torture for his fingers.

On songs like Mistress For Christmas and Moneytalks, Malcolm and Angus showed their working-class roots, despite multi-million-selling albums, by taking aim at the high flyers in the business world. They hadn't forgotten where they came from.

By May, after seven weeks of work, *The Razors Edge* album was completed, and, as thanks and in a mark of respect, Fairbairn was presented with a copy of Malcolm's guitar, The Beast.

In August, the video for Thunderstruck was again shot at the Brixton Academy in London under the direction of David Mallet.

The album was released on 24 September in Europe and the following day in the US and Australia. It sold quickly in America. Within two weeks of release, and just as sales of *Back In Black* were certified at a staggering 10 million copies in the States, *The Razors Edge* had entered the Billboard charts and peaked at the number two position with US sales eventually exceeding three million. The album did similar business in the UK, where it reached number four on the charts.

AC/DC was back with a vengeance.

In early October, with total worldwide sales now between 50 and 60 million units, rehearsals began in London for their upcoming tour. Preparations later continued in New York with a full stage rehearsal late in the month at Worcester Centrum. When all was ready, the 34-date first leg of the US and Canadian tour kicked off on 2 November.

Brian's pre-show warm-up was always the same.

'I usually go into the toilet and give a big scream and a yell and a shout. And when I come out they go, "You alright, Jonna? We thought you were being fucking mugged in there!" "Nah, nah, lads, just clearing the tubes!"'

The band's entourage was now huge, with 30 tonnes of equipment handled by a road crew of 50, which included Keith Richards' former guitar tech Allan Rogan, who was now working with Angus.

In the first week of the tour, on 6 November, the video for Moneytalks was shot at the Spectrum in Philadelphia at a pre-concert taping before 200 fans. Additional scenes were filmed during the actual show.

Throughout the tour, the song peaked with the audience being showered in dollar notes that carried an image of Angus.

Brian: 'I think we get about a million at a time [of fake dollar notes] and just blow it out [into the audience]. Usually lasts for a week, a million dollars. Sounds pretty good, eh? Ah, but a million a week I go through [on tour]. I'm just that kind of guy!'

The fake currency caused problems in England but not because of its nightly distribution to thousands. A £2000 fine was levelled at the band for illegally depicting currency with Angus' head instead of that of the Queen on the cover of the single of Moneytalks.

The second leg of the US and Canadian tour kicked off on 9 January and ran for 28 dates. It brought with it every performer's worst nightmare.

Just over a week into the tour, on 18 January, three fans were killed in a crush towards the stage during the band's performance at Salt Lake City's Salt Palace Arena. The dead were all teenagers: Jimmie Boyd and Curtis Child (both 14) and Elizabeth Glausi (19).

Brian was so racked by the sheer horror and helplessness of it all he couldn't sleep for a week afterwards.

The incident became a major issue in the US media, and again, through no fault of their own, AC/DC were under siege. Exactly what happened during the crush was the subject of some argument. Some witnesses stated that, despite a chant to stop playing, the band continued on with the show.

The band members were stung by the accusations and said that they stopped as soon as they knew there was a problem. AC/DC issued a statement that offered 'heartfelt sympathy' to the families and friends of the victims.

By now the Gulf War had begun and, as the American tour continued, some believed that Angus dropping his pants to reveal stars-and-stripes underwear was his comment on the conflict. In fact, it was just part of the show, and a nod to the country the band were in at any given time. Jerry Lee Lewis didn't make social or political statements and neither did AC/DC.

But Brian, a former parachutist in the army, was quietly concerned by talk that ex-servicemen may be called up for duty.

On 20 March, a 26-date European tour began. Shows in Glasgow, Birmingham, Dublin and Belfast were recorded for a future live album, and it was lucky for Angus that there were no cameras rolling during the show in Northern Ireland.

Angus: 'I was taking off my jacket and I had my shorts on. Normally I sort of pull my shorts off and show another pair under them that I stick a flag on or something. This night, when I pulled the top shorts off, the shorts underneath ripped and I didn't know. I turned around to the guys and they're going, "Ang! Ang!" but I was in my own world. As Brian said later, "I turned around, and there was your wedding tackle hanging out!" I was lucky. The audience was good about it, and, as Brian said, I've got nothing to hide!'

Such was the success of *The Razors Edge* that, on 23 May, the 36-date third leg of the band's US and Canadian tour began. LA Guns were the opening act, as they had been on the 1988 North American run while Malcolm was resting.

Tracii Guns, a founding member and namesake of Guns N' Roses, recalls just how good the headline act were at tackling the songs of their heroes:

'I remember soundchecks. They would always play Rolling Stones songs. And they were so good at playing Stones it was unreal.'

Guns was involved in a surreal incident when the tour hit Vancouver when he, fellow LA Guns guitarist Mick Cripps, Angus and Malcolm went to a bar called The Club Soda.

Tracii Guns: 'This guy comes up to the table and starts screaming at me, like, "Who the fuck do you think you are, hanging out with these legends?" And little Malcolm — he's so little — got up in the guy's face and says, "Why don't you go fuck yourself, and when you're done fucking yourself, why don't you go kill yourself?" That's the best kind of validation a musician could ever have in their life —

to have somebody like that stick up for you and at the expense of losing a fan. They were very dedicated to us. Mick Cripps got married on that tour and Angus got Mick a limousine — a private limousine — for a week for him and his newlywed wife. They were very good to us.'

And the American concert-going public was very good to AC/DC. *The Razors Edge* US tour grossed $17.8 million, making it the sixth-biggest tour of the year.

But it had been hard work. No-one in the band was 19 any more and Brian worked out several times a week to keep himself in shape for the shows, which were now clocking in at 135 minutes, half an hour longer than the previous tour.

But his admiration for Angus far outstripped his own aches and pains.

'I've seen the lad where the doctor's come in and shook his head at what he's seen and Angus just says, "Aaah, fuck it, I'm going on." We've never cancelled out,' Brian told Stuart Coupe in *Hot Metal* in August 1991.

It was during this period that the band was dismissed as a co-defendant in the $10-million wrongful-death lawsuit brought by Bruce Child, father of Curtis Child — one of the victims of the Salt Lake City accident — against the band, arena managers, security firm and others.

But the memories of the horrific incident didn't go away.

Against that tragic backdrop it was a difficult time to play large festivals, but from 10 August the band headlined the European leg of the Monsters Of Rock/Rock Around The Bloc festival tour with Metallica, Mötley Crüe, Queensryche and The Black Crowes.

AC/DC had by now created a separate zone towards the front of the stage to avoid people being pushed and trampled, which, from then on, was adopted on all major 'festival seating' (seating on the floor of venues) concert events.

Rich Robinson (Crowes guitarist): 'We immediately gravitated towards AC/DC, this rock band. Watching Metallica with 60,000 kids going nuts, I remember the first night going, "Man, that's just weird how many people were into Metallica. I wonder how AC/DC will do." Then it was on Thunderstruck, I think Angus would start with that and then the whole crowd would just go fucking nuts! We're like, "Alright, that's AC/DC. No-one even comes close!"'

For Mötley Crüe, the tour was also heaven.

Doug Thaler: 'Mötley Crüe had huge respect for them; Tommy Lee was just a huge, huge fan. And I don't know what AC/DC thought of them. I thought they looked at them like they were probably a bunch of young kids. They didn't short [change] your sound; they didn't short [change] your lights. [It was] like, "Go ahead, give it your best, do the best show you can. We're gonna follow it and kill you, but, go ahead, take your best shot!"

The 20-date tour from 10 August included playing for the first time in some countries — Poland, Hungary and Russia — that had, until recently, been behind the Iron Curtain. It was quite an experience for a band such as AC/DC, who had never had the slightest interest in politics or political causes, and a revelation for audiences, many of whom were seeing their first big international rock band.

In Poland, the concert drew 40,000 people while in Copenhagen and Barcelona 25,000 and 45,000 respectively came to worship.

The show in Yugoslavia was cancelled due to political turmoil as was another in Luxembourg after the promoter disappeared with the advance-ticket-sales monies.

The Gelsenkirchen show in Germany was cancelled after a local lawyer somehow, and for some reason, lobbied the city council to have the concert banned. Two other shows were then added in nearby Dortmund.

Rich Robinson: 'In Dortmund they [AC/DC] were on stage and we would sort of hang out and watch them do shit. And Angus was up there playing slide; it was just like, "Damn! What a fucking cool thing!" I think he had a lighter. He was just playing [slide guitar] with a lighter.'

At one show, during Dirty Deeds Done Dirt Cheap, a couple was sighted by a spotlight crew member doing it doggy style to the tribal thud of the song. A video camera was turned on the pair and their images were beamed onto screens around the massive stadium. They didn't flinch, probably fearful of losing their rhythm and she sang the song's words the whole time. It was official: AC/DC was the international language of lust.

But on 17 August, AC/DC's power extended far beyond the active promotion of sex when they were headlining the Monsters Of Rock festival at Castle Donington in the UK for an unprecedented third time before 72,500 people.

Fifteen-year-old fan Dan Brooks from Bedford, who had lost the hearing in his left ear in a rugby game, had it restored after standing near the towering PA system during AC/DC's performance.

Even 'Satanists' can work miracles.

Although it was their third appearance at the event, it took George Young to calm a nervous Brian. No matter how many times they played Donington, it still got the pulse racing.

He had no need to worry. By the end of the show, he was in stitches anyway at the sight of a cameraman — one of 20 to shoot a forthcoming video — gliding past, seemingly without assistance, just as he was inhaling to belt out the opening lines of For Those About To Rock.

For Malcolm, the Donington experience felt flat, just as it had done on previous occasions. He didn't feel that any of the band's performances at the event had been once-in-a-lifetime type gigs.

Doug Thaler, on the other hand, was just delighted to see that the band was back at full force.

Thaler: 'Malcolm was sober; I don't recall that everybody was sober but if there was any drinking going on by anybody, it was pretty minimal. It was like that stage was over and they'd gone on, and they were their great, tight, amazing selves again.'

As big and prestigious as Donington was, it was just the opening act for the main event of the tour, if not AC/DC's entire history: Moscow on 28 September 1991.

The only real way to get any sense of the number of people was to get on stage and look for the lighting at the edges of the crowd at

Tushino Airfield on the outskirts of Moscow. The official attendance figure as AC/DC headlined a bill featuring EST, Pantera, The Black Crowes and Metallica was 1.2 million people, although getting anything like an accurate count must have been virtually impossible.

The city of Moscow itself was reportedly drained of anyone under 30. Not surprising given that after the fall of communism, the most sought-after items in Russia were anything by AC/DC — the universal party language — The Beatles, Depeche Mode, and, of course, jeans.

As music critic and writer Andrei Orlov told the *New York Times* on 29 September: 'AC/DC is written on every wall.'

The show was held at the official invitation of the Government of the Soviet Union and the City of Moscow and was sponsored by Time Warner. It was planned after thousands of fans trekked to see AC/DC in Warsaw, Poland.

The free event was only given the official go-ahead two days before and was held just a matter of days after a failed coup attempt by the communists.

Two Antonov planes, the largest air carriers in the world, brought the 250 road crew and 30 semi-trailers of gear from Spain. The chaos began the moment the band arrived at the airport.

Brian: 'I heard, "Brian! Brian! This is for your birthday. Happy birthday!" He [the person calling him] didn't know if it was my birthday or not but it was a bottle of vodka with writing on it. And I got a beautiful canvas with the Angus dollar on it [dollar notes carrying Angus' image showered audiences during the tour in the song Moneytalks] handpainted by this Russian kid. All he'd seen it [the dollar note] on was TV, western TV, on the videos and it was perfect. On the bottom of it it said, "We will never betray you. We will be loyal to you forever. This is my address. Please send me anything from the AC/DC from the west."'

Brian sent both fans a tour program when he got home.

When the band arrived at the site of the show, the immensity of the event kicked in.

Brian: 'A crowd at eye level is just a crowd but when we got up on the stage and saw the depth of the thing I think that's when we started shaking a bit.

'Boy, were we nervous. There weren't any change rooms. There were just these army tents with duck boards on the bottom of them. We were just pacing up and down and taking a quick leak round the back of the tent. Every time I went out to take a leak, there'd be CNN or the BBC saying, "What do you think of this?" "What do I think?" I said. "You've got to be kidding. I'm not thinking anything at the minute. I just want to get on [stage]."'

This was no time for Brian's usual impersonations of the characters from his beloved 'Fawlty Towers' or 'The Young Ones'. As it turned out, there wasn't too much to laugh about anyway.

What was meant to be a reflection of the social and political reforms of Russian President Mikhail Gorbachev and a gesture of thanks for resisting a coup attempt turned into chaos.

While the spectacle of the show was amazing and the band performed strongly, culturally Moscow wasn't prepared for anything like this and certainly not a concert on this scale — not the fans and certainly not the huge security presence provided by the Russian military and police, between 20 and 50,000 of them. As a result, there was tension between overexcited partying fans and overzealous security that eventually exploded.

Jason Newsted (Metallica): 'The guards were beating up the kids pretty bad, actually really beating them up! Throwing them in the back of trucks and stuff like that. That was one of the worst things I've ever, ever seen.'

In the end, AC/DC's own security contingent had to step in and try to calm the situation.

Soviet newspapers reported that 76 people were injured during the event, many of them suffering fractured skulls after being struck by flying bottles. The media compared the concert to a battle between drunken fans and the security.

'The Monsters of Rock concert had put an end to short-lived post-coup euphoria and the illusion that we are united at last,' said Russia's national newspaper, *Komsomolskaya Pravda*.

In the lead-up to the Australian and New Zealand tour in October, which wound up the mammoth, year-long, 153-date *Razors Edge* world juggernaut, Brian was in more light-hearted form than he had been in Moscow. When asked if he was planning on one day airing with AC/DC the boots, glitter and striped-pants outfit that he once wore on stage with Geordie, he hooted with laughter.

'I think I'm half the size I was then. I was a fat little cunt then! I think I've lost a size. I also think somebody burned it as a ritual once. I've still got my old Geordie shirt; I keep that as a memory to the little band.'

The respect and affection that his legendary predecessor had received since his death was still a sore point with him more than two decades on.

'I said I was annoyed that Bon wasn't given the respect he was due at the time he was alive. That's a bloody awful thing to happen, you know. It just makes us mad more than anything. The guy deserved a lot more. He was such a talent, such a talent. It's not fair. He was always brilliant, he was always great. And the Aussies knew, the Aussies knew. They saw him come up from the clubs with the boys. They knew all the time.'

AC/DC's Australia and New Zealand run was a 15-date affair from 14 October. At the start of the tour, a media conference was held at Sydney's Entertainment Centre. Several huge semi-trailer prime movers acted as the backdrop behind the band with the Hell's Bell overhead and two cannons on either side of the stage. A huge speaker cabinet stood menacingly with the words 'AC/DC artillery' stencilled on it.

While Brian's father had once said he hadn't heard anything as loud as an AC/DC concert since the war, few media conferences were as quiet as this. Several hundred members of the media seemed to be dumbstruck by the home-town heroes' very presence.

Forced questions broke several long silences, with the band looking confused and uncomfortable, until someone asked for their thoughts on the version of Let There Be Rock by Henry Rollins and Sydney outfit The Hard Ons. The laughter cut through the strange tension.

The final shows of the world tour in New Zealand were anything but a celebration and played into the hands of those who saw AC/DC as some sort of social evil.

The performance at Wellington Athletic Park was postponed until the next day after the roof of the stage collapsed while the band's equipment was being set up. Then, when the concert did take place, it was marred by incidents mostly outside the venue. Unruly fans smashed cars and many fights erupted. Two people were stabbed and police arrested 57 others.

The situation was, if anything, worse at the final date of the tour in Auckland on 16 November, where the band had never previously played. A policeman was stabbed outside the stadium during heavy confrontations with ticketless fans who were trying to force their way in. Seventeen arrests were made.

One fan at the Auckland show who didn't need to gatecrash to get inside was Phil Rudd, who had lived in New Zealand for several years. Afterwards he hung out with the band backstage until the early hours, just talking about old times over a few beers.

Rudd was a great admirer of Chris Slade and liked the way he locked in with the band and could tell that they worked well with him. There was no window of opportunity, as far as he could see, but he made an open-ended pitch to Malcolm anyway, just in case. At least, he thought, Malcolm would know he was interested if anything changed.

The *Razors Edge* tour had arguably been the band's most successful since *Back In Black* with 10 million copies of the album sold worldwide. Three-quarters of a million copies were snapped up in Germany alone, a figure which surpassed the figures for *Back In Black* in that country.

All of this success hadn't just fallen in their laps, of course. As Brian told Christie Eliezer in *Juke* on 13 July 1991, 'Malcolm and Angus are real workaholics. As long as you pull your weight, then you're okay. Once you become lightweight, then you suffer the wrath.'

Malcolm just wished that AC/DC toured with some rock and roll bands that were more in line with what it was AC/DC did, like The Black Crowes.

During the course of 1992, the year that saw Nirvana explode around the world with *Nevermind*, the band worked on a live album, which was mixed with some guitar and vocal overdubs, at Little Mountain Studios in Vancouver with producer Bruce Fairbairn. They worked through tapes of some 30 shows from the *Razors Edge* tour and it was mainly recordings from Castle Donington, Glasgow, Moscow and Edmonton that made the final cut.

If the album was designed to kill off bootlegging, it was perfect timing. According to an August 1992 report in *Billboard*, an estimated 250,000 AC/DC bootleg CDs had been sold in Germany alone during 1991–92, largely due to a temporary loophole in German law. There were more than 200 AC/DC bootlegs released worldwide between 1979 and 1992.

The AC/DC *Live* album and *Live at Donington* video were released on 26 October in Europe, 27 October in the US, and on 6 November in Australia. The album would go on to sell two million copies in the States. The video of the band in all their glory before a massive bouncing crowd was screened at various movie theatres in London, Germany and Australia.

Even though it was more than a decade since Bon had passed away, the band were mindful that some might feel the album was disrespectful to his memory, with Brian belting out many songs that were so personal to the former singer. However, the fact was that it was a document of a hugely successful tour, which for many had been their introduction to AC/DC, anyway.

Malcolm believed that Brian had been doing a great job under all sorts of pressure, but still had a soft spot for the *If You Want Blood* album over the new *Live* set.

'I personally still prefer the old album,' he told Howard Johnson in *Metal Hammer* in November 1992. 'We were young, fresh, vital and kicking ass ... Our live performance has always been very strong because I've always thought that, underneath it all, we're a pretty average band.'

Angus' own favourite live albums were nowhere near as loud as what AC/DC was pumping out.

Angus: 'The Allman Brothers Band at Fillmore East — that's a great live album. There's a couple of great tracks on *Woodstock*, like The Who doing their version of Summertime Blues. The other live album by The Who, *Live At Leeds*, is great, and so is BB King *Live At The Cook County Jail*. Another great one for me was a Muddy Waters thing. Just after he passed away, they released a live album with Johnny Winter doing a lot of the guitar, and there's some great stuff on there, too.'

By December, *Live* had sold 600,000 units in France, which made it AC/DC's bestselling album in that country since *For Those About To Rock*.

By then, the band, along with the venue, promoter and security company, had settled out of court the lawsuits related to the Salt Lake City accident and agreed to pay an undisclosed sum to the families of the three victims.

It was a closure of sorts for everyone, but it couldn't change the horror and loss. The biggest era in AC/DC's history since *Back In Black* was again about quiet mourning.

1996
And another thing! Brian and Angus at Wembley Arena.

chapter 25

BALLBREAKER

*t*he middle-aged man dressed in a business suit in the bar of the Boston hotel decided it was now or never. He walked up to the members of AC/DC and politely introduced himself. His two teenage kids, he explained, kept hounding him to take them to a rock show. He had therefore decided that their first experience had to be one that could not be bettered.

So the three of them came to see AC/DC.

Early in 1993, another fan was given the opportunity to live out his life's dream. Rick Rubin was known for his opposing connections to, on one hand, the rap music of Beastie Boys and Run-DMC, and the onslaught of metal kings Slayer and AC/DC stylists, The Cult, on the other.

Rubin had longed to produce an AC/DC album and asked to work with them on *The Razors Edge*, but the band was already contracted to Bruce Fairbairn.

Rubin's first venture with his heroes was a one-shot test drive for both parties via a song called Big Gun, which was recorded for the soundtrack of Arnold Schwarzenegger's *Last Action Hero*. Its spare sound earned Rubin his stripes for much greater field time in the future.

The video for the song was shot at Van Nuys Airport Hangar 104E in Los Angeles with the movie's star as special guest. Originally, Schwarzenegger was only going to be available for half an hour. That was until he got there, received a wild response and had the time of his life with the band, including extensive instruction on how to do the Chuck Berry duckwalk that Angus had popularised.

The *Last Action Hero* soundtrack, which also included acts like Alice in Chains and Megadeth, was released on 8 June in the US and reached the Top 10. It was released in Europe on 12 July.

On 27 June, Big Gun was unleashed in the US and became Billboard's number one rock track and hit number five on the Canadian charts. A promising reaction. It was released in the UK a day after the US, and in early July in Australia.

It was around this time that Dweezil Zappa, son of the legendary Frank Zappa, wrote to Angus asking if he would be interested in taking part in his project What The Hell Was I Thinking?, a continuous 75-minute piece of music, thought to be the longest instrumental ever conceived.

Frank Zappa had seen AC/DC in Australia early in 1976, and he had spoken about the band over the years with his son who, as a guitarist, no doubt already had his antennae up and tuned in to them.

'His [Dweezil Zappa's] father said, "If you wanna know about guitars, here's some AC/DC records,"' Angus told Phil Lageat in *HM* in December 1996. 'For us that was a huge compliment, because Frank Zappa was such a great musician.'

Angus didn't feel right leaving Malcolm out of such a special moment, so they both went to the sessions in Los Angeles during the first half of the year. They were honoured to be involved with the Zappa family, and by working with Dweezil they were also paying homage to his father.

'He [Frank Zappa] was still alive at the time, so it was also our way of paying our respects,' Angus told *HM*.

Unfortunately, the tapes were lost or stolen, so the fruits of the collaboration have never been released.

Late in July, AC/DC began work on their own new album in London. As usual, their music was grounded in and inspired by the gritty groove and feeling of old Muddy Waters and Elmore James albums. The songs were initially worked up as a trio, with Malcolm on bass, Angus on rhythm guitar and Chris Slade on drums.

The fact that the Brothers Young could so easily swap and interchange instruments like that further underlined what had long been a complementary, even psychic, relationship.

Malcolm: 'We can bounce off each other — that's the good side of it. And guitarwise we know each other. We've been playing together longer than AC/DC has been around, as far as knowing what each other does and how to play guitar with each other. That's the thing that's just evolved from being brothers. At the other end of it, basically when we're out on the road and recording we're working together as well as being brothers, so it's a typical brotherly relationship, I guess. We know the band's bigger than anything. We always call musical differences small because nothing's worth ending everything over. So we'll never bother; we'll get over it quick if we have it out or whatever. When it happens, we usually know we'll sort it out. After 20 years, I think you've got to do that.'

Meanwhile, Phil Rudd's open-ended offer about rejoining the band, made back in New Zealand in November 1991, the first time they had seen him since he left AC/DC, had been bouncing around in Malcolm's mind. The band had never really been the same since he left. He decided Rudd should come to London to see if the old sparks could be rekindled.

Rudd was surprised and excited when Malcolm rang to put the idea to the drummer. Just as Brian had felt after Geordie, Phil quietly believed he had had his moment in the sun and the band was now on a steady course without him.

While Rudd had been out of the limelight, he had been anything but idle in Rotorua, New Zealand, where he had settled.

while he hadn't counted off a beat on his hi hat, struck a snare drum, or hammered a kick pedal with his foot for six years after leaving the band, he'd happily busied himself flying helicopters over the breathtaking New Zealand landscape, immersed himself in his long-time passion of car racing, and had even won some hand gun shooting competitions.

His blood really started flowing again when he built The Mountain Studios, which rekindled his interest in playing once more. He allowed local bands to use his facilities, with him acting as engineer.

An album's worth of material by a band he put together was caught on tape as well, and things looked promising for the project. But then came a fit of déjà vu.

Rudd knew only too well what was next: touring, promotion, and all of it centred on his past involvement with the biggest rock band on the planet, eight years earlier. It was a horse he didn't feel comfortable mounting again just yet.

Over time that resistance softened and, by the time AC/DC hit New Zealand on the *Razors Edge* tour in 1991, he was raring to go.

When he sat down behind the drums in London with the band for the first time in 11 years, it was immediately obvious that the chemistry between them was still magical.

'He's the one who set the drumming style of the band,' Angus told Tony Power in *Guitar* in November 1995.

The problem was that AC/DC now virtually had two drummers. Malcolm put in a call to Chris Slade to let him know that Phil was back and that he'd let Slade know shortly what the future held.

'"Can you wait for a few days?"' Slade recalled Malcolm saying, when the drummer spoke to Phil Lageat in *Rock Hard France* in June 2001. 'But days turned into months.'

Slade grew tired of waiting for a decision about his future role in AC/DC and gave notice that he was leaving. He had been honoured to be part of the band but was gutted it had come to this.

'I was so disappointed, disgusted, that I didn't touch my drum kit for three years,' Slade told *Rock Hard France*.

In August, after talking it over with his wife, Phil Rudd officially rejoined AC/DC.

'I always fired up best when I was playing with these guys,' Phil told Matt Peiken in *Modern Drummer* in August 1996, 'so I really couldn't see how I wasn't going to do it.'

No official announcement was made, however, the band's preference being to quietly re-establish their relationship with Rudd without external scrutiny.

In October 1994, AC/DC began recording at the Power Station Studios in New York, with Rick Rubin producing. They had eight songs in hand and an excited Rubin had a video camera in his to document the experience.

Rubin's and Malcolm's vision for the album was very much the same: get back to basics, in the same style as the band's early recordings.

Malcolm had been a student of that style for almost 30 years. Much like his heroes, Keith Richards and John Lee Hooker, he was keenly interested in what made a piece of music actually move, what made it swing and what, quite literally, made it rock and roll.

Getting Phil Rudd back was a major part of the process of sharpening their rhythmic attack and regrounding their classic sound.

Malcolm: '[Having Rudd back was] pure magic again, you know? We'd become so self-indulgent and just had to get pure AC/DC back. I think once we really thought about it, we thought if we're going to do this right we should look at Phil ... Probably it's a bit late but it seems the right time now!'

Despite the best-laid plans, the room at Power Station Studios was wrong for the old school feel that Malcolm had in mind for the album, and getting the drums right proved impossible. Rubin tried isolating the drums in a tent in the studio and lining the walls and ceiling with material to soak up the extra sound the room generated, but it was all in vain.

The problems underlined the fact that AC/DC songs and the process of recording them only seemed simple, when really it was a very exacting process with Malcolm's razor-sharp ear directing traffic.

Angus: 'I remember many years ago there was a guy doing a thing about Chuck Berry and he thought, oh, Chuck Berry, he's so straight-ahead. It's the same licks. But, when he listened, he found each time it was different and then, when he started really getting into it, he started to see other pieces of the puzzle. Because in Chuck there's jazz, there's country, there's the blues element and, of course, he's got that rock and roll. Then the great thing is he always knew when to play and when not to, and he'd pull it back ...'

Berry had taught Malcolm and Angus well.

After 10 weeks in New York and a reported 50 hours of material on tape, AC/DC finally decided to cut their losses and move to Los Angeles' Ocean Way Studios early in 1995.

Memories of the difficulties of finding the right studio to record the *For Those About To Rock* album and the fear that history might be about to repeat itself were stirred, but in LA it was a whole new ballgame.

Everything felt and sounded better almost immediately. Maybe the recent earthquake had cleared the air and not just parts of the landscape. After all, if the studio was good enough for Phil Spector, who was next door, it was good enough for AC/DC.

Malcolm: 'We hoped we could do the album in New York but, after I think about 10 weeks in the studios there, we came out with three or four tracks and decided we'd call it a day. We took a couple of weeks' breathing space and found a studio in LA. After we started working in LA, the sounds were just a little bit more real and there was just more coming off the tracks we recorded there. So we virtually started again and re-recorded three or four of the tracks we thought we already had. So we basically just did a whole restart.'

One night, before their usual midnight start, Angus went to see veteran blues guitarist Buddy Guy at the Roxy on Sunset Strip and met him afterwards.

Angus: 'I was speechless. I couldn't find the words. Actually, he was really good with me. He was a very humble guy, for all that he's done. He started himself very young playing with Muddy Waters and stuff. And it was just great to see him play.'

Henry Rollins got a call from Rubin asking if he wanted to come down to the studio to watch the band work.

Henry Rollins: '[Rubin said] "You've got to come down here, man! Come down here and just watch Phil Rudd. If nothing else, watch Phil Rudd!"'

Mötley Crüe's Tommy Lee had jammed with Brian at a club on Catalina Island in California and his dream gig was to be Rudd.

Tommy Lee: 'We played some AC/DC songs and, dude, just for a fucking minute there I felt like I was in AC/DC! I was in heaven! We were playing Back In Black, or some shit, or Hells Bells, and just for a minute I was like, yeah! I'm Phil Rudd! I was fantasising heavily.'

Rollins, who with his tattoos and physique cut an imposing figure, was stunned by what he saw when he arrived at the studio.

'The room is so thick with smoke, a huge studio. They're all bunched in one room. They look like they're from 1977. I met all of them; they're super cool, tiny, I mean like, hey, Angus, I didn't want to break him [when shaking hands] and he said, "We heard that song Let There Be Rock with The Hard Ons," and I'd forgot I'd done it and I was like, "Oh yeah," thinking they're going to go like, "That sucked, mate!" And they're like, "We really loved it!" I'm like, "Great!" "And looking at you now, if we didn't like it we would never tell you!" They were so cool. They were like five roadies. Zero pretension, kind of like, "Hey, you got a light?" That's how they are.

'Hung out with Brian Johnson for well over an hour. He sat down with me and Rick and told us stories, and in every one of his stories he's always the butt of the joke. He's like, "And then, fuck me, I couldn't find my fucking way out, I'm a stupid cunt!" What a cool fucking guy. The best. And he was singing really hard. So he's in there singing Caught With Your Pants Down — they do the whole thing live — and he's like, "Caught with your paaannnntttsss!!!!!!!!!!!!!!!" Screaming! And he came out to take a break and his voice was a little patchy and I said, "Do you ever use herbal tea?" He goes, "No." So

I made him up a cup of herbal tea. He goes, "Hippy tea! All right, mate, thanks!" And he's drinking his hippy tea.

'The best moment was they were all just sitting there [waiting to record] — this horrible posture, smoking endless cigarettes — and Rick goes, "Okay, you guys. You guys ready?" They're like, "Yeah right." And they get up [to play]. No warm-up, no nothing. Rudd sits down behind the drum set and looks like he can't even pick up the sticks! He's like cigarette dangling and it's like, "Ready?" Tape's rolling. Counts it off and then he hits the hi hat, that *ch ch ch*! And everything turns into a goosebump! I go, "My God! Fucking AC/DC!" With that hi-hat thing it's like on the beginning of [the song] Back In Black; your hair stands up! You could set your watch by that band!'

When the song was recorded, on the second take, the band clocked off and disappeared like ghosts.

'I didn't even see them put the instruments down. They were gone! I go [to Rubin], "So how does this work?" He goes, "We come in at four in the afternoon and we work on all the guitars and we get everything perfect. They walk in, they hit it, they leave. That's it. They don't fuck around. They sit and wait for you to tell them when it's time to play. They warm up by smoking cigarettes and shooting the shit."

'I'd never seen bands that can play in the studio like that. It was just what they do. It was watching genius at work.'

It wasn't always as easy as Rollins had observed. For some songs, Rubin, who meditated in the studio, demanded endless takes, up to 50 in some instances. In others, like Hard As A Rock, which dated back to the sessions for the *Who Made Who* album, it came together in just two attempts.

These methods generated concerns that the endless takes removed the spontaneity, and sometimes, not too surprisingly, sparks flew between Rubin and Malcolm, who knew only too well how AC/DC should sound, thanks very fucking much, and wasn't easily talked out of a position.

The suggestions going around that Rubin was often absent from the studio and left the band to their own devices while he reportedly saw to the recording of the Red Hot Chili Peppers' *One Hot Minute* album at the same time hardly helped any tension that may have existed, and Mike Fraser's eventual credit on the album as co-producer would appear to speak volumes.

After five months in LA — something of a record for AC/DC — the *Ballbreaker* album was done and so was the band's association with Rubin. What had seemed to be a good idea panned out to be anything but.

'Working with him was a mistake,' Malcolm told Bruno Lesprit in *Le Monde* on 31 October 2000.

In February 1995, *Kerrang!* announced that Phil Rudd was back in AC/DC but no official statement was issued.

Rumours were also aired that the band was a strong contender to headline that year's Donington festival, which was reportedly to be their last-ever UK performance, as part of a farewell world tour for which Angus would abandon his signature school suit.

It was just speculation but, on the face of it, the band calling time didn't seem impossible.

Brian, for one, had been doing his own thing during the year. The singer, who was by now living in Florida, had recorded a number of demos with local rock band The Naked Schoolgirls. He also co-wrote a song with them called Deadly Sins, which would later be recorded by another Florida act, Neurotica, and included on their debut album produced by Brian.

But, as always, the speculation about the band calling it quits was left to simmer in its own juices.

On 22 August, the video for Hard As A Rock was shot at Bray Studios at Windsor in the UK before an audience of excited but respectful fans. The shoot was Phil Rudd's first performance with the band in front of a crowd of any description in 12 years and many called out his name in encouragement when he appeared.

He was quietly delighted and smiled nervously.

AC/DC had attracted a whole new generation of fans in his absence, yet he was still obviously warmly remembered.

Angus? He'd had better days; hanging on a wrecking ball high in the air wasn't his idea of fun.

Angus: 'I was a little bit green that day. Especially when you're hanging 40 feet in the air. I was lucky; I only had to get up, I think, four times in different things. They had a stunt guy and he was showing me all what to do and I said, "That's great but I'm only a guitarist, you know."'

On 22 September, *Ballbreaker* was released in Europe and Australia and on 26 September in the US. The album entered the charts at number four in the US and would reach Platinum sales status before the end of the year.

The title once again was classic AC/DC double entendre. If they had written a musical — like *Cats* — there would be no prizes for guessing what they would call it.

More than ever, the album was a gritty example of the fact that what AC/DC did was not as simple as it seemed.

Malcolm: 'It's not easy making the records. It's hard work, especially when they've all got to sound the same! It's hard to make them all sound the same when they're different. I mean, I've even read Paul McCartney interviews [where he says] that rock and roll are the hardest songs to write — good rock and roll.'

While the album was classic AC/DC, it also featured what could be considered the band's very first social statements.

Burnin' Alive was written about the cult followers in Waco, Texas, who were burnt to death in 1993 during a raid by the authorities. Then there was The Furor and Hail Caesar, two more very uncharacteristic social-commentary shots from a band that had built a career out of ignoring such things. And typically they didn't care what anyone might think.

Malcolm: 'I think: stand up and be counted. If there's anyone that takes it like we want to promote a Nazi regime [in songs like The Furor] or something, these usually are the ones that want to promote a total Christian regime. I don't like this politically correct thing on the planet at the moment, to be honest with you. I don't mind it if it doesn't interfere with you on the street, but the day they screw around with your cigarettes and everything else — and there's a lot of cigarettes smoked in AC/DC in all that music you hear — it might not be the same if it was all gone. I just don't like being told what to do, basically like anyone.'

The band had previously been wildly accused of being Nazi sympathisers in the eyes of some who felt that the AC/DC logo had some Third Reich connection.

'That actually came from Germany, though. They're the ones that started it. You know what it was? It was the actual lightning flash [in the band's logo]. They thought it was an S ... sort of an SS thing. So they took it as that. I always thought any publicity is good publicity. We never used to deny or even comment on these things a lot because it's best just leaving them. The people that know the guys knew they're not into it and they're the ones that really matter; everyone else will speculate. It builds an interest, I guess!'

The success of the *Razors Edge* album and tour had re-opened the door to a massive global audience for AC/DC and with it came a slight softening of the band's stance on various ideas and proposals which previously would have sneeringly been turned down flat.

One sign that AC/DC was now slowly becoming less a 'heavy metal band' and more a mainstream commodity was that cartoonists from the legendary Marvel Comics, home of Spiderman, contributed to the *Ballbreaker* album's cover art.

Malcolm: 'They'd actually drawn some things. They were really interested in song titles. We gave them a few of our older titles and they'd come up with some good things, so when it came album-cover time we felt it could be a good idea if these guys can come up with a little sketch around each one of the titles — this could be fun. So we let them go for it.'

A logical extension of Marvel Comics doing the back and inside cover art for *Ballbreaker* was the creation of an actual AC/DC comic that was planned for release in November.

Malcolm: 'They're quite good people, Marvel. As kids we'd go to Comic World. I think some Australian cartoonist — I'm not sure who — kept bugging the guys at Marvel: "How come you're not doing [an] AC/DC [comic]?" We found this out when the guys from Marvel met up with us. They'd been fully informed on the band, the background of the band and everything through this particular guy. So because they'd done their homework and everything we just sat down and had a chat with them and the next thing they sent us a few ideas.'

The Australian cartoonist was Adelaide's Dave Devris, who had to create a storyline from the band's lyrics to make up one part of the comic. The other part was to be a respectful bow to Bon with a gig in hell — after taking the highway there, of course — that would officially and finally bring closure to his era with AC/DC. Unfortunately, the comic never saw the light of day.

Angus' sessions with master Afro-American music figure Taj Mahal took place around the same time. Something like five songs were recorded but remain unreleased.

Taj Mahal: 'That was smokin'. We did a couple of tunes, 44 Blues, and worked on this kind of like semi-rap thing. It was really very good, a lot of fun. If there's a human version of the Tasmanian Devil, boy, I'll tell ya! That guy [Angus] just can rip it up.'

After filming videos for Cover You In Oil and Hail Caesar in November, rehearsals for the *Ballbreaker* tour took place in a London warehouse. There the band worked through 37 songs but only 23 made it to the touring stage. Big Gun was among those that were tried out but didn't make the final cut.

Staging and production rehearsals then took place in early January 1996 in St Petersburg, Florida, at the Thunderdome. From there it was straight into the first leg of the *Ballbreaker* US and Canadian tour from 12 January, with 12 of Angus' school uniforms in tow, just in case. With 49 dates in all with Australia's The Poor, featuring drummer James Young — another relative — opening the shows, the run included two dates in Mexico City, their first, in February.

But tragically, just as the band were starting to hit their stride, in late January four shows were postponed in California to allow Brian to fly home to Newcastle to attend his father's funeral.

Aerosmith's Joe Perry caught the tour in Miami and later his band paid tribute to AC/DC on their *Nine Lives* album.

Joe Perry: 'We did our AC/DC tribute with the song Nine Lives. We've always loved AC/DC from the first time that we saw them. One of my favourite things to do is play AC/DC songs at soundcheck. So it's always in the back of my mind — we've got to write a couple of songs that are as much fun to play as those. So, after we saw them play down in Miami, the next day when we were writing the record we were thinking about Whole Lotta Rosie and stuff, and that's when we wrote Nine Lives.'

Later, at an open-air show in St Louis in the stifling heat and humidity, Brian collapsed and it was left to Angus, who had rarely if ever spoken on stage, to give the crowd of 20,000 the bad news.

Angus: 'We made it through to the end of the show but he had fallen over just before the end, so we couldn't really go and do encores. So I had to tell them; I had to go out and explain to the audience to keep calm.

'When you go out there in front of 20,000 people, you can be a little bit nervous because they all look at you like one big, big animal. I did feel a little bit like the Christians with the lions.'

During the US dates, the band separated from manager Stewart Young, and from that point on would manage themselves, with their long-time business manager, Alvin Handwerker, at Prager & Fenton handling additional duties.

On 5 July, a blistering private concert on a small stage area was filmed in London for 'VH1's Uncut' in AC/DC's first-ever television performance with Brian and their first live TV exposure since appearing on 'Midnight Special' in the US in 1978.

The cracking 12-tune event — they originally intended to do just four — included several songs never previously performed with Brian, including Go Down (which they'd also never played with Bon), Riff Raff, Gone Shootin' and Down Payment Blues.

A few days later the band were playing before adoring Spanish audiences, some of AC/DC's most fevered followers.

Angus: 'When we're in Spain, there was a lot of kids that got emotional about when we're coming. It's really strange because you see these really big guys and they've got tears in their eyes because you're there playing and they actually got to meet you.'

In recognition of this fanatical support, the entire 10 July show in Madrid was filmed.

The final show of the 48-date European tour was the biggest outdoor performance of the year in France. Held in Bordeaux on the night of Bastille Day in front of 30,000 people, they were supported by Wildhearts, Sepultura and Silmarils.

Given the pace of the tour, Brian was more concerned about his heart than his voice. And he was more worried still about Angus and the damage he did to himself each night on stage.

'By the end of the European leg, it was getting plain daft,' he told Angus Fontaine in Sydney's *Daily Telegraph* on 7 November 1996. 'He was running around stage with bruises all over him, blood pouring out his back, blood all over his elbows and knees.'

They got to catch their breath for a performance of You Shook Me All Night Long at Bryant Park in New York for the movie *Howard Stern: Private Parts*, which was based on the radio shock jock and huge AC/DC fan's autobiography. After numerous takes of lip-syncing You Shook Me, the band played an impromptu live version of The Jack.

They warned Stern that the combination of AC/DC and movies was cursed, based on their experiences with Stephen King's *Maximum Overdrive* and then *Last Action Hero* with Arnold Schwarzenegger, both of which had died awful deaths at the box office.

The *Private Parts* soundtrack would be released in the US on 25 February 1997, just a day after the European release, while the movie would be unveiled in the US in March and include AC/DC performing You Shook Me All Night Long.

The connection with Stern was, at least, good publicity for the second leg of the US and Canadian tour that kicked off on 1 August. It was followed from 11 to 22 October with a South American tour, which saw the band play in Brazil, and, for the first time, Argentina and Chile.

As the show in Buenos Aires at the River Plate Stadium drew a crowd of 120,000 people, the band must have wondered why they waited so long.

Australia and New Zealand were next on the touring schedule, from 2 November. As of late September, 160,000 tickets had been sold for the 13 shows they originally planned to do. By the time they arrived, two more shows were added due to demand.

It was the final leg of the world tour and the end couldn't come soon enough for the band. The schedule over the past year or thereabouts had been extended almost daily to meet demand to the point where at one stage they had clocked up 13 gigs in just 14 days. Australia was no different.

Recalling the Stones' legendary 1972 American tour, Sydney radio station 2MMM gave traffic and weather reports for the shows.

One fan in Melbourne, who couldn't get through by phone to a radio station, decided to go there in person to get his request in for an AC/DC song. That it was 4 a.m. wasn't an issue for him. Also in Melbourne, a group of academics reportedly pushed for a statue of Angus to be erected in the city, in response to proposals for a monument to Michael Jackson.

In Brisbane, William Young (Jnr), one of Angus and Malcolm's older brothers, came to the show. When AC/DC were in town, the family were always out in force.

During this hectic touring schedule, AC/DC still found time to make some history with their first-ever performance in the outback city of Darwin, after 21,500 fans put pen to paper on a petition to get the band to include it in their crowded itinerary.

There was a certain grace and poetry about the beer-consumption capital of the planet hosting AC/DC. Bon would have loved it.

Malcolm had even dreamt of meeting up with Bon in the outback of Australia.

'Occasionally I've had a few dreams about Bon that I've met him in a place up the back end, up the north in Western Australia ... he'd never died — he just decided that things went really funny for him and he just decided to get out and disappear. A few little dreams like this. We still think that Bon's around, basically, and he is around because of the music, and that's what's so good.'

During their Australian tour, Malcolm shattered the dream of former New South Wales premier Neville Wran when they were both bidding for a home in Balmain in inner-city Sydney. Wran, so goes the story, didn't take kindly to competing against some tiny longhair, only to have said longhair outbid him and get the house.

No Bull — Live Plaza De Toros De Las Ventas, the performance that had been filmed in Madrid in July, was released worldwide on video during the Australian tour. It was a blistering show in a bullring, a very different setting to the *Live at Donington* package.

'The sound is very raw,' Malcolm told Phil Lageat in *Hard Rock* in February 1997. 'This is No Bullshit, No Bull!'

As the year drew to a close, during a mass, Cardinal Joseph Ratzinger, now the Pope, branded rock music an 'instrument of the devil' and made specific mention of The Beatles, the Eagles, Queen, the Rolling Stones and AC/DC. Vatican officials later cited Black Sabbath, Alice Cooper and AC/DC as the worst offenders, and church leaders also claimed that the band's initials 'referred not to alternating current or even bisexuality, but to the satanic phrase "Antichrist, Death to Christ"'.

2001

Ever get the feeling you're being watched?
Angus, Madison Square Garden, New York.

chapter 26
STIFF UPPER LIP

You can take the schoolboy out of Glasgow but you can't take the streets of Glasgow out of the schoolboy.

The show in Phoenix, Arizona, was ticking over like clockwork. That was until midway through the breakdown of Bad Boy Boogie when someone threw a drink at Angus. Typically, he didn't take this lying down. He walked over, pointed out the guy and beckoned him over. Then came another drink and that was it.

Angus took off his guitar, handed it to a roadie and lowered himself under the guard rail to get closer to the guy. When he was within reach, Angus firmly tweaked the guy's nose and dished out some verbal venom before the offender was led out by security. Reunited with his guitar, Angus bowed and the show, as always, went on.

While a low tolerance for bullshit had long been an AC/DC hallmark, some of their other attitudes had continued to undergo change and their defences were slightly lowered. They seemed more tolerant and more open to suggestion.

It showed in little things like the article in Sydney's *Daily Telegraph* on 26 August 1997 about a series of stamps that were to be issued commemorating Australian rock and roll. One was to feature an image of Angus with his school bag with the words 'long way to the top'.

A greater example of the shifts that were taking place came with the *Bonfire* boxed set, a rewind exercise that returned the spotlight to Bon Scott, with rare and unreleased recordings and legendary live performances.

The band had never favoured 'greatest hits' type packages. More importantly: AC/DC virtually had two careers — one with Bon and then another with Brian; one governed by fate, the other by determination. Respectfully mixing the two, at one time, had seemed like a near impossible task. But now it seemed time and age had healed those wounds and bridged that divide.

In an open tribute to Bon, material with his imprint that had never seen the light of day, such as Dirty Eyes, the song which evolved into the classic Whole Lotta Rosie, was gathered together. In addition, the band's legendary 1977 Atlantic Studios radio broadcast, which had long been a ridiculously expensive bootleg fetching anything up to $300, was included, as was, at the suggestion of Arnaud Durieux, co-author of this book, one of the scorching Paris concerts from late 1979 that was recorded for the movie *Let There Be Rock*. Durieux had unearthed the original tapes and although the 24-track masters had been destroyed a few years back, a master of the final mix had survived.

In a tip of the cap to Brian, AC/DC's landmark transition album, *Back In Black*, was also included, which effectively killed off the band's long-expressed desire not to resell to fans what they all already had. And tens of millions already owned *Back In Black*.

The project stemmed from an idea of Bon's in the late '70s when it seemed every member of every successful rock band, such as Kiss, was doing a solo album.

While Bon initially had nothing but contempt for the idea, he eventually came around.

Angus: 'He told Malcolm once, "If ever I make it big . . . and they want me to do a solo album, I'll call it *Bonfire*!" His words were, "When I'm a fucking big shot!"

'I think [the hardest part was] tracking everything down, things that we could remember and the places that we'd done shows with Bon throughout the world and then getting hold of some of the tapes, because, believe it or not, a lot of them went astray or the quality of them was poor. They might have had a copy of a copy of a copy. We've had things like that in the past. I remember years ago we tried to track down some footage in Australia and I think there'd been a fire somewhere and they couldn't find it.

'I think the track that impressed me the most was She's Got Balls from the Lifesaver in Sydney. It was the first night Cliff had joined the band — it was his first time on stage with us, really. It really shocked me when I first heard it. I thought at first — it being Cliff's first night — it might be a bit shaky but it certainly cooks! And Bon, of course, shone.'

Compiling the material for *Bonfire* became an act of affirmation and a source of great pride for the band two decades on. Simply put, AC/DC's core values and sound hadn't shifted in the slightest; they worshipped at the feet of Chuck Berry, the most important part of any song was its swing and rhythm, and they were proud standard bearers for rock and roll at its most fundamental.

'The basic characteristics were the same,' Angus told Winston Cummings in *Hit Parader* in May 1998. '[But] we grew to better understand our music.'

On 17 November, *Bonfire* was released in Europe and Australia, and the following day in the US. The UK release came a little later on 6 December. The album's US release coincided with sales of 16 million copies of *Back In Black* in America, which made it the country's second-biggest-selling hard rock album of all time.

All the while, progress was slowly being made on a new album, and, by February 1998, the writing process, which had begun in the summer of 1997 in London, was completed.

The songs had been written in Australia, in Angus' home in Holland where he had lived for some time, and also in London, with Malcolm on guitar and Angus on drums.

But there were a few sidebar moments before recording began.

In March 1998, Brian and Cliff jammed at a benefit at the Opera House in Sarasota, Florida.

Then, the following month, Florida outfit Neurotica released their album *Seed*, which had not only been produced by Brian but featured him on back-up vocals. The previous year, Brian had appeared on Jackyl's album *Cut The Crap* on a song called Locked And Loaded, which he sang and co-wrote.

In August, work got serious on the new AC/DC album in London, a schedule which was pleasantly interrupted one night when Angus and Brian made a rare offstage public appearance to collect the band's Lifetime Achievement Award from *Kerrang!* magazine. It was another sign of more relaxed times.

Work on the new material continued for many months, during which time Malcolm's old friend Herm Kovac received a call.

'[Malcolm] rang me up asking if I could get him a deal on a drum kit. The Scottish thing coming out in him. Guy's a multimillionaire and rings me up [to ask] could I get him a deal on a Ludwig kit! I think I'd instilled into him through Simon Kirke [Free and Bad Company drummer, much admired by Malcolm] that Ludwig drums are great, Malcolm being a guy that when he does a home demo doesn't want to know about drum machines — he just wants to play a drum kit himself.'

Recording plans were tragically thrown into chaos on 17 May 1999 with the death of producer Bruce Fairbairn at the age of 49. Malcolm and Angus had great respect for Fairbairn for his work ethic, the great ease with which he made it possible to get things done, and his strong sense of family. Both of them flew to Vancouver to attend his funeral.

But the show, as always, had to go on and in July they entered Bryan Adams' Warehouse Studios in Vancouver, Canada, an environment with a similar feel to the original Albert Studios in King Street, Sydney, which had been demolished during the '80s.

George Young was coaxed out of an unofficial semi-retirement to act as producer, although he no longer worked with Harry Vanda. Mike Fraser, who had proven himself on *Ballbreaker*, took on the role of co-producer.

Having George back at the console was one of life's simple, reassuring pleasures as far as the band was concerned. As Brian once joked, if his dick broke in half, George would be able to find him another that was a perfect fit. Maybe even bigger.

And the teaming up of George with Malcolm made for a powerful creative combination.

Angus: 'I've been a little bit lucky for myself, probably from the beginning, because I've always had Malcolm. I could dream up some idea some time and he'd tell me if it was stupid or something. Other times he'd go, "That's not bad," and he would make it happen. He's probably more practical than me. I'm a bit of a dreamer so I'm lucky in that sense. He has more get up and go.

'George will plug into me and Malcolm and keeps us at bay sometimes, too, when we want to kick the shit out of each other! So he's a bit of a mix of me and Malcolm. It's a funny thing. If we come up with ideas and stuff, I'll look at Malcolm and every time it amazes me. I'll sit and hear what he's got — an idea off a tape or something — and it's always different. It's way ahead and in front of anyone I've ever met. It's unique. I like tapping my foot. For me, if you give me just a straight out rock and roll tune I'm happy, whether it's a TNT or a Whole Lotta Rosie or something like this, or a Highway To Hell where it's just [taps his foot three times] straight — that's what I love best. But Malcolm always looks, he'll try and be one step ahead with the approach to things. And he'll tell you, "Look, Ang, you've done that before," or "We've done that."

'George knows his rhythm,' Angus told Patrick Donovan in *The Age* on 6 February 2001. 'That's all you've got to have in this band, and a lot of producers don't have that. They've got the ears and timing, but no rhythm. It's mathematics to them; they don't understand the swing.'

As for Brian, being in the studio with Malcolm and Angus was one thing; being in the same room as Malcolm, Angus and George was another.

'It's like a shit sandwich, isn't it, Brian?' Malcolm laughed on the Allan Handleman radio show on WRFX on 25 March 2001. 'And you're trapped in the middle!'

'We get along great and we've got the bullet holes to prove it!' Angus chimed in later when the subject turned to the relationship of the three brothers.

The new album was intended to be a back-to-basics exercise where less sounded like much more with minimal technology.

Angus: 'We've got just two guitars and your bass and drums, and really the only colour they all use is me for a bit of the guitar work. You try to keep everything minimalist, I suppose, if you're thinking in an art way — you keep it basic. The good rock and roll bands are always the bare bones stuff.

'I always think the best rock out there is stuff that has got that blues element in it. They're sort of bombarding us these days with image, and that seems to be more and more the case. I think they're all sort of losing track.'

Overall, the basic concept was yet again to continue to refine what AC/DC started 25 years earlier.

'Something, somewhere near what the guys in the '50s were doing,' Malcolm told Tim Henderson in *BW + BK* magazine in June 2000. 'We want to keep the flag flyin'. I think we're the only guys, with the exception of the Rolling Stones.'

As usual, songs were nailed within a few takes. Malcolm played the solo on Can't Stand Still, while Angus did the backing vocals on Hold Me Back.

During the sessions, The Clash's Joe Strummer called in, as did the studio's owner, Bryan Adams, who walked into what must have been the clean-living vegetarian's worst nightmare — a studio thick with cigarette smoke and the sounds and smell of Brian happily cooking dead animal.

A member of The Beastie Boys called Malcolm to ask permission to use the riff from Back In Black as a sample for the re-release of The Beastie Boys' 1984 song Rock Hard on a new compilation album. He turned them down flat. Sampling was against everything AC/DC stood for and believed in.

Angus: 'As Malcolm once said [in a similar instance], "Well, if you're so fucking talented, why didn't you write it? Where's your hit? You've taken these guys' hit!" They probably spent a lot of time and effort and sweat to get it. Hell, they come up with something original and make a hit and that's their hard work. It's like some guy spending a couple of years on a book. You don't want to pick it up and see that Paragraph C's plagiarised, or if I made a movie, I wouldn't like to see chunks of it used to sell another movie.

'[People] want to take your song, take what they think's the hook, keep the hook and they'll write their name on it like it's a work of science. Malcolm even said to them [The Beastie Boys], "You're quite free to do that; there's nothing can stop you from doing that … but hell, fella, we know it as Back In Black and all those people out there who bought that album *Back In Black* know it as Back In Black. You might want to call it whatever you call it, but it's Back In Black."'

A total of 18 songs were recorded for what would be the *Stiff Upper Lip* album and were mixed by Mike Fraser in Vancouver during October and November.

On 25 and 28 February 2000 respectively, the album was released in Europe and Australia, and on 29 February in the US and Canada.

The concept behind the album's title, *Stiff Upper Lip*, came to Angus when he was stuck in traffic one day. It occurred to him that lips were a vital part of rock and roll culture, from Elvis to Mick Jagger, and carried a certain defiance. There was also maybe a sense of the traditional meaning of 'stiff upper lip' — keeping the flag flying and pressing on.

Angus: 'There was a bit of that and also with us there's always a bit of humour, too. Even from when we started, I used to always say, "I've got bigger lips than Jagger and I've got bigger lips than Presley when I stick them out." Actually, if you look on the *Highway To Hell* album, there's my lip stuck up there like this [curls his lip].

I remember when I was a kid I saw an early black-and-white movie of Brigitte Bardot and she had those pouting lips and you go, "Well, yeah! I like what she's serving!"'

Just as *The Razors Edge* and *Ballbreaker* had done, the album quickly charted exceptionally well around the world, reaching the Top 5 in most countries. The statue of Angus on the cover was like a rock and roll Trojan horse. He looked harmless enough until he was plugged into the power mains.

Angus had long been the focus on the covers of the band's albums from *Powerage* onwards but it was a role that had never sat comfortably with his offstage shyness.

Angus: 'I'm always weird about it. I think Malcolm said, "We'll put you [on the cover]." I said, "They always put me down for something somewhere on the cover." He said, "But people know you; they know you as part of AC/DC; they can focus. Even if somebody doesn't know your name, they know it's the kid in the shorts or the guy in the shorts." See, I always crawl to be up the back, hiding. Even in the beginning, it was the same, too. Malcolm and George used to always say, "You've got to get up the front. We all know you can play guitar but the people have got to know!" And I used to say, "But [the front] is where they're throwing missiles, too!"'

Can't Stop Rock N' Roll from the album harked back to earlier days and was a virtual re-statement of the sentiment of Rock And Roll Ain't Noise Pollution.

Angus: Some people try to plug into the fashion of the day. They're looking at now or what's around them locally and they forget. Music becomes fast food in that sense. It's so freely available but when it's freely available there's also the abuse of it. I can understand it when the media's always going, "We've got to have something new. I'm writing a newspaper column every day on music. I've got to have something new." I can always understand that side of it. But it kind of freaks you in a little way when … you've got the guy [Pete Townshend] that wrote [The Who's] My Generation turning around and coming out with things like, "Ah, rock and roll music's dead," and things like this. And you go, "You haven't been to my household!"'

The *Stiff Upper Lip* album was released just a little over 20 years since Bon passed away but it wasn't deliberately intended to mark that moment. For Angus, Bon's memory was to be privately celebrated every day rather than being the centre of any sort of ritual each February.

Angus: 'I've never done anything. I don't sort of sit and celebrate. See, the time Bon passed away I was also just married. So you've got a period you remember and there's also my anniversary. And, if you forget that, there could be another death! [laughs] I'd be seeing Bon quicker than what I thought!'

Memories of Bon could be triggered in the most unlikely situations.

'Me and Malcolm heard a blues guy on the car radio. Malcolm went, "Fuck!" There was just an element [of Bon] there. It might be the whisky voice or the bourbon or whatever but there was just that element. Then I remember hunting through records once and I was listening to an old blues [track], just an acoustic, and it had been made in 1928 and I heard it and went, "Fucking hell! Is that his voice?" As soon as I heard it, my hair was up.'

Just as startling was Angus, Malcolm and Brian performing an acoustic version of You Shook Me All Night Long live on the 'Out To Lunch' show on K-ROCK in New York.

Times certainly had changed and even the media suddenly seemed to be universally supportive, even those more high-brow publications who previously had rolled their eyes at the mention of the band's name.

Audiences were now studded with celebrities in AC/DC T-shirts. Some even boasted AC/DC tattoos.

In March, the band shot a video for the title track of the new album in New York, while two additional videos were done in LA two months later. This time Elektra did not choose to hire their long-time favourite director David Mallet. Malcolm was not amused.

That same month, the band played live on MTV's 'AC/DC@MTV' and a week later they did it again — this time for 'Saturday Night Live' where they were dwarfed more than usual by the other guests, wrestlers The Rock and Triple H. Their appearances on both were the sort of situations they had long avoided like the plague but, with their tour still months away, such events were a good early opportunity to ram the new album down a few million throats.

Just as surprising in terms of uncharacteristic appearances by the band was the Warner Music Juno Awards after-party in Toronto, which Angus, Malcolm and Phil not only attended but joined The Royal Crowns on stage to play Stiff Upper Lip.

The most tangible marker of the inroads AC/DC had made into mainstream culture came on 22 March when Calle De AC/DC — AC/DC Street — was officially unveiled in Leganes, Madrid, Spain, a tribute to the band's immense popularity there.

Almost as surprising was the fact that Malcolm and Angus were present for the ceremony, along with some 1000 fans, and later gave a media conference.

Angus: 'They keep saying that a lot of fans keep knocking off the street signs, so they've replaced it six times I've heard so far.

'I think it's better [that the street was named after] us. It's either that or some local civil servant that everyone's going, "Who?" So, why not, you know? The actual area is like a music area. They've got a bit of culture and music and stuff and it's in a working-class area of Spain.'

The obvious change in headspace within the band reached a climax in June.

Since day one of their career, AC/DC had been the very loud musical accompaniment to the photos in magazines like *Penthouse* and *Playboy*. Few would have thought the band would ever feature in such publications in anything other than a written piece. German *Playboy* magazine fixed that.

The interview with Angus was one thing, but the amazing eight-page spread of him modelling the latest men's fashions, surrounded by lizards and other exotic creatures, was on another level altogether. And there wasn't a schoolboy uniform in the viewfinder in any of the shots.

It was, in a sense, AC/DC's proud political incorrectness on high beam.

Angus: 'In the end these [PC] things become fucking law. That's the scary side of it. No record has ever fucking shot somebody in the heart, but there's plenty of dead bodies from ideology.

'My father used to hammer that into us when we were growing up. He used to always say, "Fuck 'em, son." He'd get annoyed if I'd go to school and some teacher was on a soapbox about an issue or a government thing. He used to say, "I'm sending you to a fucking state school and I don't want you to come out like a member of some fucking Reich!"

'I always found it strange that they would try to drag a political thing [into music] when, fucking hell, as everyone knows you've had samples of all the left and the right and the fucking centre, and as far as the general public is concerned, left and right is "which side of the plane am I sitting on?"

'For some reason I could tell a country was more left wing by how rough the fucking toilet paper was! I used to say, well, I don't think this fucking culture's going to go far. Every band I ever knew that went to fucking Moscow, the first item on the list was [toilet paper]. That was the hot item because you weren't going to get fucking toilet paper. That was proof number one. I thought, well, they can say what the fuck they like about capitalism, but they sure know what soft tissue is!'

Tour rehearsals took place in July in Grand Rapids, Michigan at the River City Studios and then moved to the DeltaPlex for full production preparations. Touch Too Much, Can't Stand Still and You Can't Stop Rock And Roll were rehearsed, but didn't make the cut.

On 1 August, the 33-date first leg of the US and Canadian tour began, supported by Slash's Snakepit, the new outfit for the former Guns N' Roses guitarist.

Apart from the band, the focus of attention on stage was a huge statue of Angus in the image of the *Stiff Upper Lip* cover. While it must have taken Angus a while to get used to sharing the stage with a demonic-looking model of himself several storeys high, at one show Malcolm got a close-up when it almost fell on him.

Angus: 'A bit of it had wobbled about one night because it's in sections, you know? And I think one of them was loose and sort of plonked and he [Malcolm] had just moved. He didn't really notice, he said, but he felt something go *swoosh* near the back of his leg.'

AC/DC's audience was now crossing several generations. Parents who might have seen the band on the *Back In Black* tour were now coming to the shows with their kids. Few had ever seen Bon perform, and for most, AC/DC's frontman had always been Brian.

For the singer, the show was still great fun but bloody hard work for a few hours each night. He also had a hell of a lot of words to a hell of a lot of songs to remember every night, and grudgingly decided he needed a teleprompter to nudge him along when necessary.

'My brain isn't big enough to learn all the songs,' Brian told Roger Lotring in *Metal Edge* in June 2003. 'What is it, 17 albums out there?'

That tally was well short of the recorded output of someone like John Lee Hooker, but being inducted into the Hollywood Rock Walk with The Hook, and other heroes like BB King, Eric Clapton and Jimi Hendrix, was reason to smile.

Again, they actually attended the ceremony and had their hands pressed into the cement at the Guitar Center on Hollywood Boulevard.

Meanwhile, rumours had been circulating for several months that AC/DC would be part of either the opening or closing ceremony at the Olympic Games, which were being held in Sydney in September 2000. But nothing eventuated and just as well.

AC/DC might have been a national treasure and crossed over to a broad audience, but the band would have been a bit overpowering for many in a situation such as that. Besides, miming was not something they wanted to be involved in, and the whole thing had very little to do with rock and roll, anyway.

'We failed the drug test!' Malcolm laughingly told Cameron Adams in the *Herald Sun* in Melbourne on 8 March 2001.

In any case, they had to prepare to take the *Stiff Upper Lip* juggernaut to Europe on 14 October. The tour went smoothly, apart from a gig in Madrid when Malcolm decided they should play an unrehearsed Sin City and poor Brian stumbled through the song, barely able to remember half the lyrics.

The *Stiff Upper Lip* tour hit Australia for 15 dates from 19 January, supported by The Living End. Shows had to be added to meet demand with six nights at the Sydney Entertainment Centre, while they performed in Hobart, Tasmania for the first time in 24 years.

Angus: 'A guy came along and he had a cap from that [previous] time, that he got off one of the crew. It was a genuine cap.'

Tasmania brought back all sorts of memories, such as seeing a dramatically smaller Rosie for the last time in February 1976 and Phil Rudd partying with a bikie gang during the Giant Dose tour.

When they arrived in Adelaide, Phil felt like the full weight of Rosie's original figure was concentrated on his lower abdomen. He keeled over at soundcheck and the show was postponed: he was later diagnosed with a kidney infection.

In Queensland, a radio station ran a competition in which, to win tickets to see the band at the Brisbane Entertainment Centre, all entrants had to do was provide photographic evidence of their dirtiest deeds.

One fan was filmed eating worms, another drinking vomit. Not to be outdone, another took himself into a pub and rolled around in the urinal.

Piss-Trough Man won the competition and took his other mates to the show, meeting the band backstage afterwards. He asked Angus to sign his arm, not too wild a request, but when he rolled up his sleeve, the guitarist was stunned to see several of his signatures from previous encounters tattooed in place.

Japan — a country AC/DC had never really cracked — was the next stop on the tour, but one Japanese fan couldn't wait. Tomoaki Baba was going to eight shows on the Australian tour and, as part of his pilgrimage, he and his wife turned up at Albert's in Sydney and asked if anyone wanted to see his tattoo. On his back, stretching from neck to waist, was an etching of Angus from the cover of *Highway To Hell*.

He returned a few days later with something else to show off. But this time he dropped his pants, and tattooed across his bum in large letters was AC/DC — just as Bon had once dreamt of doing.

The Japanese tour, the band's first since 1982, began on 19 February immediately after the Australian visit. They hadn't been in a hurry to return to Japan after their previous trip when there'd been technical problems using their full stage production and at some shows the Hell's Bell wasn't even unpacked.

By this point, *Back In Black* had clocked up sales of over 19 million in the US alone, making it one of the 10 best sellers ever in that market. The sales figures of the band's entire US catalogue to date tipped the scales at 63 million, which made AC/DC the ninth-biggest-selling act of all time in the States, and the fifth-best-selling band behind The Beatles, Led Zeppelin, Pink Floyd and the Eagles. It was the perfect way to stride back into the second leg of the US and Canadian tour which kicked off on 18 March.

In April, the band returned to Salt Lake City for the first time since the tragedy 10 years earlier. Behind the volume, lights and excitement, the horrific memories of their last visit weren't far from anyone's mind.

Towards the end of the 34-date tour, some shows were postponed due to Brian suffering from throat problems. That wasn't the only maintenance issue.

Angus: 'I think the shoes are the ones that take the toll. They get the worst of it. The shoes seem to run out of tread so quick these days. One night I got on and I was slipping a lot from the sweat on the stage and I asked one of the guys, "Can you sort of throw a bit of Coca-Cola and make it a bit sticky up there?" And because they've got a see-through part of the stage, he said, "I was looking up at your feet and you've got to get some shoes! The tread's gone off them!"'

Guitars also quickly got ruined by the sweat.

'They get kind of like surfboards, they get waterlogged. So nearly every week they're stripping them down and having to replace a lot of the parts because they rust so quick.'

Like the *Razors Edge* and *Ballbreaker* tours before it, satisfying demand to see the band was a task in itself, hence the massive 15-date tour of open-air European stadiums between June and July. It was the biggest exercise AC/DC had ever undertaken and spanned 15 cities with various support acts such as Megadeth, The Offspring, Buddy Guy, The Black Crowes and Die Toten Hosen.

The fact that it was a return visit meant rethinking some of what was to be played.

Angus: 'We'd done Europe in the winter months and we didn't know we were coming back in summer. We thought we wanted to do it a little bit different so we figured that probably the best thing is to play a few songs that a lot of the audience hadn't heard us do live, well, for a long time. The last time we ever played Up To My Neck In You would have been during one of the first times in America with Bon, I think, in San Francisco in an old club. So some of them we hadn't even attempted [since then]. We must have felt bold!'

The response was such that in some cities a second encore — unprecedented in the band's modern history — was demanded after their traditional closer of For Those About To Rock.

The reaction in Paris, which earlier in their career had been anything but welcoming, was amazing and not just from the 80,000 people in the audience which made it the city's biggest-ever show. A fleet of police on motorbikes escorted the band, who were staying in the same hotel as American president Bill Clinton.

The Paris performance was filmed and for the first time in the band's history the bluesy Ride On was included in the show, at the very end of the set. It had been quickly roughed up in the dressing room. John Lee Hooker had passed away the day before, an event hardly lost on blues nuts like Malcolm and Angus, although Ride On was not a tribute to the blues elder as such.

It was an indication that Bon might be gone, but more than 20 years on, he was anything but forgotten. The moment was also for Brian, who'd long felt that the song was too much of Bon's own to touch himself. But now it felt right.

Brian was moved and thrilled all at once. 'This is a Bon Scott song,' he announced, dressed, as were the rest of the band, in the uniform of the French soccer team who'd won their first World Cup in the same stadium three years earlier. It was like Brian's final rite of passage, even though he'd earned his stripes long, long ago.

It was fitting that, at the same time, Kirriemuir in Scotland had opened the Gateway to the Glens Museum in June to honour its cultural heritage. Local boy Bon and AC/DC were, of course, featured.

Meanwhile the reaction to the German leg of the tour was as enthusiastic as it had been in Paris. The show at the Olympia Stadium in Munich before 80,000 people had been the first date to sell out and the decision was made to film it.

The conditions on the day weren't ideal. Some people who couldn't get in to the show positioned themselves on a hill outside. Unfortunately, that was where a huge fireworks display was set up, so the police had to be brought in.

The decision to return for a second encore was both an extra act of thanks to the fans and an attempt to calm some hot heads.

Angus: 'I think during that day it was also going to prevent a little bit of trouble too, because you've got the police out there sort of doing their thing shoving people around [and] you figure, well, you don't want it to get nasty.'

Such was the success of the German leg of the tour that the band received an award from the promoter for ticket sales exceeding half a million for just seven shows.

The resulting DVD and home video, *Stiff Upper Lip Live*, was released in Japan and Europe in November, and in Australia and the US the following month.

The success of the tour must have had the marketing departments of numerous major corporations salivating at the sponsorship possibilities. But as far as Angus was concerned, any such deal would have taken him and the band right back to square one.

'I think over the years we've had a number of different people come and want to sponsor you for various stuff. But you get to a point where you go, well, I'm a chain smoker if anything but I still wouldn't sit there and say, I'm going to be sponsored by a cigarette company or something [he said before dragging heavily on a cigarette].

'Because I think then there's another one [company] you're working for. In the beginning you really were saying, well, this was the reason why I got into rock and roll in the first place. You always said, well, who knows? In the end I won't have a boss!'

2001

Where it all began: Brian and Angus, Hammersmith Apollo, London.

chapter 27

NO PARTICULAR PLACE TO GO

*M*ick Jagger, Keith Richards, Ron Wood and Charlie Watts looked puzzled at the Rolling Stones' Australian press conference in Sydney in February 2003. The problem was that the journalist's question had spewed forth as one garbled word: 'Andyouarefansofacdc?'

The reporter's second attempt was much clearer.

Mick Jagger: 'Keith likes them.'

Keith Richards: 'Oh yeah! Yeah! I love Accadacca, Angus and Malcolm, a great team, man. Great. Really.'

It was a prophetic, if brief discussion. Fast forward 30 hours to Sydney's Enmore Theatre where the Stones' intimate performance was the hottest ticket the city had seen in many, many years. An hour into their show, the tiny frame of Malcolm Young could be seen at the back of the stage in the semi-darkness. He was having a ball miming along to Start Me Up and punching the air around him in a manner that probably had as much to do with nerves as it did with sheer gleeful disbelief at the situation he was in.

After Start Me Up, Jagger, without much ceremony, introduced Malcolm and an until-then-unseen Angus, who quickly moved to the lip of the stage and took a customary bow.

With Angus in jeans — rather than his usual school uniform — and the shortest haircut he'd shown in public for almost 30 years, taking the stage alongside the not-immediately-recognisable Malcolm, it took a minute or two for the true significance of the moment to register. Then all hell broke loose as Keith, Ron, Angus and Malcolm formed a four-way guitar front line for a version of Rock Me Baby.

Malcolm stuck with Wood and rhythm guitar at the back of the stage, despite what seemed to be Jagger's urgings to step up and out. Angus needed no encouragement and moved about the stage as if it was his, with Wood even following his duckwalk at one point. The sight of Angus facing off with a grinning Richards was utterly priceless. Then they were gone.

Back in August 2001, with the *Stiff Upper Lip* tour over, Brian had taken the opportunity to step out on his own himself. Firstly, he joined Ringo Starr on stage in Florida at St Peterburg's USF Sun Dome. Then in September and October, he rejoined his old mates in Geordie II for a short tour of the clubs in northern England that had been their stomping ground in the '70s. Brian even proudly led them on stage at Newcastle's Opera House. To capture the moment, the band recorded two traditional North East songs — Geordie's Lost His Liggy and Biker Hill — in Newcastle for a compilation album.

Brian was still smiling fit to burst in March 2002 when he and Cliff Williams, who had recently composed the music for a movie called *Chalk*, joined Billy Joel on stage in the Ice Palace in Tampa, Florida, for a rendition of Highway To Hell.

But the AC/DC frontman had bigger and more dramatic plans than being a guest at the gigs of others. In April, he announced that he was working on a musical based on Helen of Troy with Robert De Warren.

The $1.2 million production, which had quietly been in the works for six years, had music and lyrics written by Brian with British actor Brendan Healy.

All this was pleasantly interrupted on 7 November 2002, when it was announced that AC/DC would be inducted into the Rock and Roll Hall of Fame along with The Clash, The Police, Elvis Costello and the Righteous Brothers.

The occasion was more high profile and prestigious than Cliff Williams' plans at the time. He was about to embark on four club dates in late November and early December in Bosnia-Herzegovina with Croatian band The Frozen Camel Project. Cliff also played on their album.

In December, it was announced that after a 27-year association, AC/DC were leaving the Warner Music group to sign a new deal with Epic/Sony Music worth a reported $50 million for the band's back catalogue and new recordings. The fact that Epic's president was their former co-manager Steve Barnett certainly helped.

In the New Year, Malcolm and Angus were back in Australia, a visit which coincided with the Rolling Stones' tour. With AC/DC's former production manager Jake Berry now with the Stones, it was arranged for the pair to join their heroes on stage in Sydney.

While they had never met the Stones before, Angus was well aware Keith Richards was a keen AC/DC admirer.

Angus: 'I know [Keith] Richards is a big fan. Somebody said some guy was interviewing him and Jagger and the guy said, "I hear you're a fan of AC/DC." And he went, "Yes I am," and Jagger said, "Yeah and he's got it on all fucking night!"'

When the Stones played at the Enmore, Malcolm and Angus were hardly going to pass up the chance to pay their respects.

'They're playing in our backyard,' Malcolm told Rollingstones.com in February 2003. 'We're 10 minutes away … but it's great to meet them after all the years. We were more concerned they'd beat the fuck out of us!'

On 10 March, the Rock and Roll Hall of Fame induction ceremony was held in the ballroom of the Waldorf-Astoria, one of the world's plushest hotels, in New York City. While being inducted by heroes such as Chuck Berry or Keith Richards — who is said to have nominated AC/DC on several previous occasions — would have been perfect, the fact that Aerosmith's Steve Tyler did the honours still suited Malcolm fine.

Again, the rhythm guitarist had a long memory. AC/DC had toured extensively with Aerosmith in 1978 and made their first appearance at Bill Graham's massive Day On The Green festival in San Francisco with the Boston outfit in July of that year. When Foreigner had objected to having AC/DC anywhere near them on the bill, Tyler, who jammed with the band at the Hall of Fame on You Shook Me All Night Long, stood up to be counted and issued an ultimatum: if AC/DC don't play, then neither do Aerosmith.

AC/DC, who were never at ease in such self-congratulatory circumstances as the Hall of Fame, would have preferred to accept the award by some sort of satellite hook-up or have it delivered by mail or courier, rather than in a ballroom before tables filled with the world's music industry elite.

They weren't ungrateful, but in a sense they were being signed up to a club that — thanks all the same — they had specifically chosen not to join for the previous 30 years. If they'd never even been nominated, that would have been fine.

Angus: 'I think it's a kind of misnomer in a way when they say "rock and roll" and then you see somebody like James Taylor sitting there [he bursts into the giggles]. You know what I mean? It becomes a little bit abusive.'

But at least Bon was represented by his nephews Paul and Daniel Scott, who were introduced by Brian in a warm gesture from the man who had proudly replaced their uncle.

The Clash, without the late Joe Strummer, were part of the ceremony and they too were not used to such adoration from the industry. But while AC/DC were at least familiar with The Clash, the punk veterans' bassist Paul Simonon knew next to nothing about AC/DC.

'To be honest, I'm not familiar with their music at all. Mind you, maybe if I heard a track on the radio ...'

Malcolm had no problem with The Clash but took great, yawning exception to the length of the speech given by The Edge from U2 to mark the passing of Strummer.

'We were at the side [of the stage], waiting, and getting madder and madder,' Malcolm told Geoff Barton in 2005's *Metal Hammer and Classic Rock Present AC/DC* magazine. 'When they said to go, we fuckin' took off. It was an anger-fuelled performance. We ripped the place apart. They were dancing up in the balconies in their tuxes. It was quite a moment for us.'

The day after the Hall of Fame ceremony, AC/DC played a free low-key show at New York's Roseland Ballroom attended by 3000 contest winners, with Billy Joel and Steve Tyler side of stage.

The connection made with the Stones in Sydney was played out again in June, but on a far larger scale, when they were asked by their heroes to be special guests for three enormous outdoor shows in Germany for a reported $4 million fee.

The circle that began at Chequers in Sydney 30 years earlier with a fledgling band and a set that included a handful of Stones songs was completed. As had been the case at Sydney's Enmore Theatre, Malcolm and Angus joined the Stones for a version of Rock Me Baby at each date.

'Their tightness has always impressed me,' Keith Richards said in the *Four Flicks* DVD in 2003. 'Doing these gigs together, we've all enjoyed each other, and I kinda like being taller than another guitar player as well!'

AC/DC also did two club dates in Munich and Berlin. The 1700-seat Munich show was filmed by Epic/Sony and it was so hot that Malcolm was sweating almost as much as Angus. In a highly unusual move, 10 minutes after AC/DC had left the stage, and with many people leaving the venue thinking the show had finished, the house lights went out again and the band came on and played Whole Lotta Rosie.

In July, rehearsals took place at Cherry Beach Sound in Toronto, Canada, where their joint venture with the Stones continued on 30 July as part of a huge outdoor benefit concert at an old military base to help the city get back on its feet after the SARS virus had ravaged its economy.

In addition to the Rolling Stones and AC/DC, the event included The Guess Who, who Malcolm had seen in Sydney in the early '70s, Rush, and The Flaming Lips. A mammoth 490,000 attended the show and, again, Malcolm and Angus jammed with the Stones on Rock Me Baby.

Despite the obvious mutual respect between the two camps, AC/DC hadn't lost their competitive streak.

'The greatest thing I've ever done with this band was smoke the Rolling Stones into the weeds in Toronto in front of 485,000 people,' Phil Rudd told Don Zulaica in *Drum* in June 2005. 'The Stones gave us an hour — that's a dangerous thing to do. You don't give us an hour before you go on, mate ... The whole band just nailed it. We got into the van offstage and went, "Yeah, fucking follow that!"'

In June 2004, Warner Home Video released *Toronto Rocks*, a DVD compilation of the event, which included two AC/DC tracks (Back In Black and Thunderstruck) and their jam with the Stones.

More history was made, or perhaps just revisited, on 21 October 2003 when the band returned for their first show at London's Hammersmith Apollo — formerly the Hammersmith Odeon — in 21 years. The gig sold out in four minutes through internet sales, but almost had to be cancelled as Brian was ill and had to have his lungs pumped out shortly before.

Primal Scream's Bobby Gillespie was among the lucky few who secured tickets.

'It was as exciting as seeing The Clash or Thin Lizzy when I was a kid. You know when you first go to rock gigs when you're a kid and it's all new and it's exciting and every second's amazing? It was that kind of experience, that exciting. It was like a movie or something. It was so perfect it was unreal. That's my girlfriend's favourite band since she was a teenager. She goes, "This is a great date!"'

In November 2003, Epic/Sony Music issued *Live At Donington* — the performance from 1991 — for the first time on DVD, with a remixed and remastered soundtrack. It would eventually sell over one million units worldwide, and attain Platinum status in the US six times over.

By early 2005, Brian was working with Florida band Big Machine, co-writing all of their material with friend and guitarist Doug Kaye. Some of those songs were previously recorded by The Naked Schoolgirls in 1995. Big Machine made their live debut on 24 March at Khrome in South Florida and Brian joined them on stage.

The singer hadn't written lyrics for AC/DC since 1988's *Blow Up Your Video*. All songs since had been strictly Young-Young credits.

Phil Carson (Atlantic Records): 'Brian is a brilliant frontman and a brilliant writer and it's unfortunate that he's been excluded from the writing of AC/DC over the last few years. I've heard rock songs that Brian's written — including one that Jesse James Dupree of Jackyl put out — they're great rock songs. His songs are starting to get to other people — there's a song he wrote called Deadly Sin that I know [Mötley Crüe's] Vince Neil wants to record. But there's a slew of songs that he wrote that would be smash hits for AC/DC.'

The release of the *Family Jewels* DVD set included classic footage of Bon and Brian. It would go on to be the biggest-selling music DVD ever in Germany where it spent 11 weeks at the top of the charts. It did similar business in no fewer than nine countries and became one of the most successful products in AC/DC's history, which was ironic for a band that had always despised videos.

In September, Brian jammed with Velvet Revolver on Led Zeppelin's Rock And Roll at Orlando's Hard Rock Live, and in November a very nervous Angus introduced Ozzy Osbourne at the UK Music Hall of Fame in London's Alexandra Palace. Phil Rudd produced the debut album for New Zealand band Jaggedy Ann in February 2006.

Brian and Cliff continued to keep their hands in with Classic Rock Cares, a charity project aimed at giving less fortunate children a musical grounding in their education. The venture included, among others, Joe Lynn Turner, formerly of Deep Purple, and Mark Farner of Grand Funk Railroad fame, and they not only did some recording but played five shows of AC/DC classics and an original song called Chain Gang On The Road in the US in July 2007.

October saw the release of AC/DC's live career retrospective, the three DVD set, *Plug Me In*. Such was the hunger for the band, advance orders eclipsed all previous records and not surprisingly it debuted at the number one spot on DVD charts all over the world.

All the while, Angus and Malcolm worked on new songs well away from the limelight and, from 2002, were in and out of the studio doing demos.

Cliff Williams: 'I think they're [Malcolm and Angus] in the studio — Mal's little studio in London — pretty much five days a week and do whatever they do and then take a break and then do it again; it's just the lifestyle that they've created. If one of the guys gets ready to do a project, like an album, we get a phone call. That's how it's worked for 30 years, and it works just fine like that.'

Early in 2008, when Malcolm and Angus were finally ready, that call came. A second Classic Rock Cares tour of the US that had been scheduled for February was cancelled.

On 1 March, the band entered Vancouver's Warehouse Studios where the *Stiff Upper Lip* album had been forged to record their 20th effort and first new album in almost nine years. While Mutt Lange, who had worked on *Highway To Hell* and *Back In Black*, was among those seriously considered to produce the album, the task went to Brendan O'Brien (Bruce Springsteen, Pearl Jam, Stone Temple Pilots).

The recording sessions spanned March and April.

With the new album completed, on 22 April three of the tracks recorded in 2007 by Brian and Cliff with the Classic Rock Cares project — Chain Gang On The Road, Who Phoned The Law and Chase That Tail — were featured on the soundtrack of the movie *Totally Baked*. Brian was also credited as executive producer for the comedy.

On 15 August, things started to really get serious, as AC/DC made their first public appearance in five years in front of three hundred specially invited fans in London for the filming of the video for the new album's first single, Rock N Roll Train, which was directed by long-time associate David Mallet. They ran through several takes of the song, much to the delight of the crowd, who were later treated to an impromptu autograph signing session by their heroes.

On 28 August, the rest of the world had the chance to hear Rock N Roll Train — which was originally called Runaway Train — when it debuted on radio and online.

A director's cut of *No Bull* followed on 9 September with footage of two bonus tracks not performed at the original show in Madrid: the cracking and rarely played Down Payment Blues (from the Ocean Center, Daytona, Florida in January 1996) and Cover You In Oil (from Scandinavium, Gothenburg, Sweden in April 1996). The teasing continued in October when AC/DC's classic Let There Be Rock was featured as the lead track in the hugely popular video game Rock Band 2.

While AC/DC are one of the last remaining artists who proudly refuse to distribute their music through iTunes — they hate the MP3 format and will not allow single track downloads — they still enjoy enormous sales figures in a decaying CD market and were second only to The Beatles in catalogue sales for the years 2005 to 2008, proving that their bold business decision has so far paid off.

Then on 20 October 2008 it finally came; the hugely anticipated *Black Ice* album was released worldwide by Columbia Records. With 15 tracks it's the longest of the band's recordings and was released with three different cover variations, including a 'deluxe' edition with a 30-page booklet.

In the US, the album is exclusively available through Walmart and Sam's Club stores and by mail order through the band's new official website.

An 18-month world tour — AC/DC's longest-ever road trip — kicked off in the US late in October. The response at the ticket office was extraordinary.

For those who missed out, the next best thing was AC/DC's very own Rock Band video game, AC/DC Live: Rock Band Track Pack, which was released in November. It provided virtual on-stage jam access to the complete *Live at Donington* DVD and all from the comfort of any hot and sweaty bedroom.

The release of *Black Ice* marks the triumphant return of one of the world's great rock bands, and it's been a truly amazing journey. Who would ever have thought that two Scottish brothers fired up by the sounds of the Stones and The Who in their bedrooms in suburban Sydney would eventually be admired by those same heroes and share stages with them? That their cartoon-like antics on 'Countdown' would develop into massive stage productions with blow-up dolls, a bell, cannons and a towering statue of Angus? That an incredibly slightly built guitar player in a schoolboy uniform could, for 30 years, hold audiences across the globe spellbound without the novelty of his get-up ever wearing thin? That despite Malcolm and Angus' deep love of the simple feel of blues, jazz and '50s rock and roll, they'd be pigeonholed by some as a heavy metal band and targeted by American political forces for their alleged 'satanic' links? And that despite caring little, if anything at all, for any music that's been produced since the late '60s or, at a stretch, the very early '70s, they remain the yardstick for almost all modern bands?

They are, and have always been, a study in focus and determination, with a painstaking attention to detail where others can't see any fine print.

'This is this,' Robert De Niro said in *The Deer Hunter*. AC/DC similarly are AC/DC.

And as Brian asked in the *Los Angeles Times* on 12 April 2001, 'Who's going to take the place of this band when it's gone?'

The answer is no-one. No-one at all.

DISCOGRAPHY

Albums

HIGH VOLTAGE

(Australia — Albert Productions) February 1975
Baby, Please Don't Go ◆ *She's Got Balls* ◆ *Little Lover* ◆ *Stick Around* ◆ *Soul Stripper* ◆ *You Ain't Got A Hold On Me* ◆ *Love Song* ◆ *Show Business*
PRODUCED BY HARRY VANDA & GEORGE YOUNG

T.N.T.

(Australia — Albert Productions) December 1975
It's A Long Way To The Top (If You Wanna Rock 'n' Roll) ◆ *The Rock 'n' Roll Singer* ◆ *The Jack* ◆ *Live Wire* ◆ *T.N.T.* ◆ *The Rocker* ◆ *Can I Sit Next To You, Girl* ◆ *High Voltage* ◆ *School Days*
PRODUCED BY HARRY VANDA & GEORGE YOUNG

HIGH VOLTAGE

(UK & Europe — Atlantic ◆ USA — Atco) April 1976
It's A Long Way To The Top (If You Wanna Rock 'n' Roll) ◆ *Rock 'n' Roll Singer* ◆ *The Jack* ◆ *Live Wire* ◆ *T.N.T.* ◆ *Can I Sit Next To You, Girl* ◆ *Little Lover* ◆ *She's Got Balls* ◆ *High Voltage*
PRODUCED BY HARRY VANDA & GEORGE YOUNG

DIRTY DEEDS DONE DIRT CHEAP

(Australia — Albert Productions) September 1976
Dirty Deeds Done Dirt Cheap ◆ *Ain't No Fun (Waiting 'Round To Be A Millionaire)* ◆ *There's Gonna Be Some Rockin'* ◆ *Problem Child* ◆ *Squealer* ◆ *Big Balls* ◆ *R.I.P. (Rock In Peace)* ◆ *Ride On* ◆ *Jailbreak*
PRODUCED BY HARRY VANDA & GEORGE YOUNG

DIRTY DEEDS DONE DIRT CHEAP

(UK & Europe — Atlantic) November 1976

Dirty Deeds Done Dirt Cheap ◆ *Love At First Feel* ◆ *Big Balls* ◆ *Rocker* ◆
Problem Child ◆ *There's Gonna Be Some Rockin'* ◆ *Ain't No Fun (Waiting
'Round To Be A Millionaire)* ◆ *Ride On* ◆ *Squealer*

PRODUCED BY HARRY VANDA & GEORGE YOUNG

LET THERE BE ROCK

(Australia — Albert's ◆ UK & Europe — Atlantic, LP only) March 1977

Go Down ◆ *Dog Eat Dog* ◆ *Let There Be Rock* ◆ *Bad Boy Boogie* ◆
Overdose ◆ *Crabsody In Blue* ◆ *Hell Ain't A Bad Place To Be* ◆ *Whole Lotta
Rosie*

PRODUCED BY HARRY VANDA & GEORGE YOUNG

LET THERE BE ROCK

(USA — Atco) June 1977

Go Down ◆ *Dog Eat Dog* ◆ *Let There Be Rock* ◆ *Bad Boy Boogie* ◆ *Problem
Child* ◆ *Overdose* ◆ *Hell Ain't A Bad Place To Be* ◆ *Whole Lotta Rosie*

PRODUCED BY HARRY VANDA & GEORGE YOUNG

POWERAGE

(USA — Atlantic ◆ Australia — Albert Productions) May 1978

Rock 'n' Roll Damnation ◆ *Down Payment Blues* ◆ *Gimme A Bullet* ◆ *Riff
Raff* ◆ *Sin City* ◆ *What's Next To The Moon* ◆ *Gone Shootin'* ◆ *Up To My
Neck In You* ◆ *Kicked In The Teeth*

PRODUCED BY HARRY VANDA & GEORGE YOUNG

POWERAGE

(UK & Europe — Atlantic, LP only) May 1978

Rock 'n' Roll Damnation ◆ *Gimme A Bullet* ◆ *Down Payment Blues* ◆ *Gone
Shootin'* ◆ *Riff Raff* ◆ *Sin City* ◆ *Up To My Neck In You* ◆ *What's Next To
The Moon* ◆ *Cold Hearted Man* ◆ *Kicked In The Teeth*

PRODUCED BY HARRY VANDA & GEORGE YOUNG

IF YOU WANT BLOOD

(Atlantic) October 1978

Riff Raff ◆ *Hell Ain't A Bad Place To Be* ◆ *Bad Boy Boogie* ◆ *The Jack* ◆
Problem Child ◆ *Whole Lotta Rosie* ◆ *Rock 'n' Roll Damnation* ◆ *High
Voltage* ◆ *Let There Be Rock* ◆ *Rocker*

PRODUCED BY HARRY VANDA & GEORGE YOUNG

HIGHWAY TO HELL

(Atlantic) July 1979

Highway To Hell ◆ *Girl's Got Rhythm* ◆ *Walk All Over You* ◆ *Touch Too Much* ◆ *Beating Around The Bush* ◆ *Shot Down In Flames* ◆ *Get It Hot* ◆ *If You Want Blood (You've Got It)* ◆ *Love Hungry Man* ◆ *Night Prowler*

PRODUCED BY ROBERT JOHN 'MUTT' LANGE

BACK IN BLACK

(Atlantic) July 1980

Hells Bells ◆ *Shoot To Thrill* ◆ *What Do You Do For Money Honey* ◆ *Given The Dog A Bone* ◆ *Let Me Put My Love Into You* ◆ *Back In Black* ◆ *You Shook Me All Night Long* ◆ *Have A Drink On Me* ◆ *Shake A Leg* ◆ *Rock And Roll Ain't Noise Pollution*

PRODUCED BY ROBERT JOHN 'MUTT' LANGE

FOR THOSE ABOUT TO ROCK

(Atlantic) November 1981

For Those About To Rock (We Salute You) ◆ *Put The Finger On You* ◆ *Let's Get It Up* ◆ *Inject The Venom* ◆ *Snowballed* ◆ *Evil Walks* ◆ *C.O.D.* ◆ *Breaking The Rules* ◆ *Night Of The Long Knives* ◆ *Spellbound*

PRODUCED BY ROBERT JOHN 'MUTT' LANGE

FLICK OF THE SWITCH

(Atlantic) August 1983

Rising Power ◆ *This House Is On Fire* ◆ *Flick Of The Switch* ◆ *Nervous Shakedown* ◆ *Landslide* ◆ *Guns For Hire* ◆ *Deep In The Hole* ◆ *Bedlam In Belgium* ◆ *Badlands* ◆ *Brian Shake*

PRODUCED BY AC/DC

'74 JAILBREAK

(Atlantic) October 1984

Jailbreak ◆ *You Ain't Got A Hold On Me* ◆ *Show Business* ◆ *Soul Stripper* ◆ *Baby, Please Don't Go*

PRODUCED BY HARRY VANDA & GEORGE YOUNG

FLY ON THE WALL

(Atlantic) June 1985

Fly On The Wall ◆ *Shake Your Foundations* ◆ *First Blood* ◆ *Danger* ◆ *Sink The Pink* ◆ *Playing With Girls* ◆ *Stand Up* ◆ *Hell Or High Water* ◆ *Back In Business* ◆ *Send For The Man*

PRODUCED BY ANGUS YOUNG & MALCOLM YOUNG

WHO MADE WHO

(Atlantic) May 1986

Who Made Who ✦ *You Shook Me All Night Long* ✦ *D.T.* ✦ *Sink The Pink* ✦ *Ride On* ✦ *Hells Bells* ✦ *Shake Your Foundations* ✦ *Chase The Ace* ✦ *For Those About To Rock (We Salute You)*

PRODUCED BY HARRY VANDA & GEORGE YOUNG, ROBERT JOHN 'MUTT' LANGE, ANGUS YOUNG & MALCOLM YOUNG

BLOW UP YOUR VIDEO

(Atlantic) January 1988

Heatseeker ✦ *That's The Way I Wanna Rock 'n' Roll* ✦ *Meanstreak* ✦ *Go Zone* ✦ *Kissin' Dynamite* ✦ *Nick Of Time* ✦ *Some Sin For Nuthin* ✦ *Ruff Stuff* ✦ *Two's Up* ✦ *This Means War*

PRODUCED BY HARRY VANDA & GEORGE YOUNG

THE RAZORS EDGE

(Atco) September 1990

Thunderstruck ✦ *Fire Your Guns* ✦ *Moneytalks* ✦ *The Razors Edge* ✦ *Mistress For Christmas* ✦ *Rock Your Heart Out* ✦ *Are You Ready* ✦ *Got You By The Balls* ✦ *Shot Of Love* ✦ *Let's Make It* ✦ *Goodbye And Good Riddance To Bad Luck* ✦ *If You Dare*

PRODUCED BY BRUCE FAIRBAIRN

LIVE

(Atco) October 1992

Thunderstruck ✦ *Shoot To Thrill* ✦ *Back In Black* ✦ *Who Made Who* ✦ *Heatseeker* ✦ *The Jack* ✦ *Moneytalks* ✦ *Hells Bells* ✦ *Dirty Deeds Done Dirt Cheap* ✦ *Whole Lotta Rosie* ✦ *You Shook Me All Night Long* ✦ *Highway To Hell* ✦ *T.N.T.* ✦ *For Those About To Rock (We Salute You)*

PRODUCED BY BRUCE FAIRBAIRN

LIVE — COLLECTOR'S EDITION

(Atco) October 1992

Thunderstruck ✦ *Shoot To Thrill* ✦ *Back In Black* ✦ *Sin City* ✦ *Who Made Who* ✦ *Heatseeker* ✦ *Fire Your Guns* ✦ *Jailbreak* ✦ *The Jack* ✦ *The Razors Edge* ✦ *Dirty Deeds Done Dirt Cheap* ✦ *Moneytalks* ✦ *Hells Bells* ✦ *Are You Ready* ✦ *That's The Way I Wanna Rock 'n' Roll* ✦ *High Voltage* ✦ *You Shook Me All Night Long* ✦ *Whole Lotta Rosie* ✦ *Let There Be Rock* ✦ *Bonny* ✦ *Highway To Hell* ✦ *T.N.T.* ✦ *For Those About To Rock (We Salute You)*

PRODUCED BY BRUCE FAIRBAIRN

BALLBREAKER

(EastWest) September 1995

Hard As A Rock ◆ *Cover You In Oil* ◆ *The Furor* ◆ *Boogie Man* ◆ *The Honey Roll* ◆ *Burnin' Alive* ◆ *Hail Caesar* ◆ *Love Bomb* ◆ *Caught With Your Pants Down* ◆ *Whiskey On The Rocks* ◆ *Ballbreaker*

PRODUCED BY RICK RUBIN, CO-PRODUCED BY MIKE FRASER

BONFIRE

(EastWest) November 1997

CD box set including:

Live From The Atlantic Studios: *Live Wire* ◆ *Problem Child* ◆ *High Voltage* ◆ *Hell Ain't A Bad Place To Be* ◆ *Dog Eat Dog* ◆ *The Jack* ◆ *Whole Lotta Rosie* ◆ *Rocker*

Let There Be Rock The Movie — Live In Paris: *Live Wire* ◆ *Shot Down In Flames* ◆ *Hell Ain't A Bad Place To Be* ◆ *Sin City* ◆ *Walk All Over You* ◆ *Bad Boy Boogie* ◆ *The Jack* ◆ *Highway To Hell* ◆ *Girl's Got Rhythm* ◆ *High Voltage* ◆ *Whole Lotta Rosie* ◆ *Rocker* ◆ *T.N.T.* ◆ *Let There Be Rock*

Volts: *Dirty Eyes* ◆ *Touch Too Much* ◆ *If You Want Blood (You've Got It)* ◆ *Back Seat Confidential* ◆ *Get It Hot* ◆ *Sin City* ◆ *She's Got Balls* ◆ *School Days* ◆ *It's A Long Way To The Top (If You Wanna Rock 'n' Roll)* ◆ *Ride On*

Back In Black: For song titles, see above

STIFF UPPER LIP

(EastWest ◆ Elektra) February 2000

Stiff Upper Lip ◆ *Meltdown* ◆ *House Of Jazz* ◆ *Hold Me Back* ◆ *Safe In New York City* ◆ *Can't Stand Still* ◆ *Can't Stop Rock 'n' Roll* ◆ *Satellite Blues* ◆ *Damned* ◆ *Come And Get It* ◆ *All Screwed Up* ◆ *Give It Up*

PRODUCED BY GEORGE YOUNG

BLACK ICE

(Columbia) October 2008

PRODUCED BY BRENDAN O'BRIEN

Notes:

All post-1979 Atlantic releases were issued in Australia by Albert Productions. All US albums were remastered by Epic/Sony Music in 2003 and issued worldwide.

Compilations of Interest:

ALBERT ARCHIVES
(Australia — Albert's) March 1980
Contains *Rockin' In The Parlour*
PRODUCED BY HARRY VANDA & GEORGE YOUNG

BOOGIE BALLS & BLUES
(Australia — Raven) October 1988
Contains *Dirty Deeds Done Dirt Cheap live in Sydney, January 1977*

LAST ACTION HERO — MUSIC FROM THE ORIGINAL MOTION PICTURE
(Columbia) June 1993
Contains *Big Gun*
PRODUCED BY RICK RUBIN

PRIVATE PARTS
(Warner Bros) February 1997
Contains live version of *You Shook Me All Night Long*

Singles of Interest

Only listed here are singles containing tracks unavailable on albums, marked *.

7" *Can I Sit Next To You, Girl** ◆ *Rockin' In The Parlour**
(Australia — Albert's) July 1974

7" *Jailbreak* ◆ *Fling Thing**
(Australia — Albert's ◆ UK — Atlantic) June 1976

7" *Dog Eat Dog* ◆ *Carry Me Home**
(Australia — Albert's) March 1977

7" *Whole Lotta Rosie* ◆ *Dog Eat Dog (Live)**
(Australia — Albert's) 1978

12" *Touch Too Much* ◆ *Live Wire (Live)** — *Shot Down In Flames (Live)**
(Europe — Atlantic) March 1980

12" *Let's Get It Up* ◆ *Back In Black (Live)** — *T.N.T. (Live)**
(Europe — Atlantic) January 1982

12" *For Those About To Rock* ♦ *Let There Be Rock (Live)**
(Europe — Atlantic) April 1982

12" *Nervous Shakedown — Sin City (Live)** ♦ *This House Is On Fire (Live)**
*— Rock 'n' Roll Ain't Noise Pollution (Live)**
(Europe — Atlantic) July 1984

12" *Shake Your Foundations* ♦ *Jailbreak (Live)*
(Europe — Atlantic) January 1986

12" *Who Made Who (Extended)** ♦ *Guns For Hire (Live)**
(Europe — Atlantic) May 1986

12" *You Shook Me All Night Long* ♦ *She's Got Balls — You Shook Me All
Night Long (Live)**
(Atlantic) August 1986

CD-Single *Heatseeker — Go Zone — Snake Eye**
(Europe — Atlantic) January 1988

CD-Single *Moneytalks — Mistress For Christmas — Borrowed Time**
(Europe — Atco) November 1990

CD-Single *Moneytalks — Mistress For Christmas — Down On The
Borderline**
(Australia — Albert's) November 1990

CD-Single *Highway To Hell (Live) — Hells Bells (Live)** *— The Jack (Live)**
(Europe — Atco) October 1992

CD-Single *Highway To Hell (Live) — Hell Ain't A Bad Place To Be (Live)** *—
High Voltage (Live)**
(Europe — Atco) October 1992

CD-Single *Dirty Deeds Done Dirt Cheap (Live) — Shoot To Thrill (Live) —
Dirty Deeds Done Dirt Cheap (Live)**
(Europe — Atco) February 1993

CD-Single *'5 Titres Inedits En Concert' Whole Lotta Rosie — Shoot To
Thrill** — Back In Black — Hell Ain't A Bad Place To Be** — Highway To
Hell (All live)*
(Warner Music — France) February 1993

CD-Single *Big Gun — For Those About To Rock (Live)** — Shoot To Thrill
(Live)**
(Europe — Atco) June 1993

CD-Single *Hail Caesar — Whiskey On The Rocks — Whole Lotta Rosie (Live)**
(Europe — EastWest) December 1995

CD-Single *Hard As A Rock* — Dog Eat Dog* — Hail Caesar* (All live)*
(Europe — EastWest promo) November 1996

CD-Single *Stiff Upper Lip — Hard As A Rock (Live)* — Ballbreaker (Live)**
(Europe — EastWest) March 2000

CD-Single *Satellite Blues — Whole Lotta Rosie (Live)* — Let There Be Rock (Live)**
(Europe — EastWest) October 2000

CD-Single *Safe In New York City — Cyberspace* — Back In Black (Live)**
(Europe — EastWest) June 2000

Videos

All available on DVD except where noted. Titles released in Australia by Albert Productions.

LET THERE BE ROCK
(Warner Home Video, VHS) July 1985
Movie filmed in Paris, December 1979

FLY ON THE WALL
(Atlantic, VHS) September 1985
Clips from *Fly On The Wall* album

WHO MADE WHO
(Atlantic, VHS) November 1986
Clips from 1980–1986

AC/DC
(Australia — Albert Productions, VHS) December 1987
Clips from 1975–1979

CLIPPED
(Atco, VHS) June 1990
Clips from 1988–1990

FOR THOSE ABOUT TO ROCK — MONSTERS IN MOSCOW

(Warner Home Video) October 1992
Includes four AC/DC tracks live in Moscow, September 1991

LIVE AT DONINGTON

(Atco, VHS) October 1992
Concert from Castle Donington, August 1991

NO BULL

(Warner Music Vision) November 1996
Concert from Madrid, July 1996

STIFF UPPER LIP LIVE

(Elektra) November 2001
Concert from Munich, July 2001

LIVE AT DONINGTON

(Remixed) November 2003
Concert from Castle Donington, August 1991, remastered and remixed

LIVE '77

(Japan — VAP Video) January 2003
Concert from London, October 1977

FAMILY JEWELS

(Epic) March 2003
40 tracks, promo clips, TV appearances and live tracks, 1975–1991

PLUG ME IN

(Columbia Video) October 2007
Two-DVD set, live tracks from 1975 to 2003, five hours of footage
Deluxe edition with bonus DVD, additional two hours of footage

NO BULL — THE DIRECTORS CUT

(Columbia Video) September 2008
Re-edited and remixed concert from Madrid, July 1996

ACKNOWLEDGMENTS

The information in this book, which was five long years in the making, has been sourced from a sea of interviews given by, and articles written about, AC/DC over the past 30 years.

Magazines that were our 'rocks', if you will, were: *Juke (The Age)*, *RAM*, *Go-Set*, *Kerrang!*, *Guitar World*, *Mojo*, *Classic Rock*, *NME*, *Sounds*, *Melody Maker*, *Record Mirror*, *Rock Hard* and *Hard Rock*.

We also wish to acknowledge our respectful plundering of the following sources:

2JJ, 2JJJ, 2MMM, 2SM, 2UE, 5KA, 92 City FM, 98 Rock, A2, ABC (Australia including 'GTK' and 'Countdown'), ABC (America), AC/DC No Nonsense website, AC/DC Resource Center website, *Adelaide News*, Albert Productions, *Album Network*, AlexisKorner.net, 'The Allan Handelman Show', American Forces Radio, Antenne 2, *Arizona Republic*, Atco Records, *Atlanta Gazette*, Atlantic Records, *AXS*, *BAM*, *Bass Player*, Bayern 3, BBC NorthEast, BBC Radio 1, BBC Sheffield, *Beat*, *Beat Instrumental*, *Best*, BFBS, *Billboard*, *Boston Globe*, *Boston Herald*, BR3, *Bravo*, Brisbane *Courier Mail*, *Daily Sun*, *Buffalo News*, *Burrn*, *BW&BK*, *Calgary Sun*, Canal+, Canoe.ca, Capital Radio, *Cashbox*, Channel Seven, Channel Nine, *Chicago Sun Times*, *Chicago Tribune*, *Cincinnati City Beat*, *Circus*, *Columbus Dispatch*, 'Continuous History Of R&R', *Cornerstone*, *Creem*, *Daily Mirror*, *Daily Planet*, *Daily Telegraph*, DC 101, debbiekruger.com, *Denver Rocky Mountain News*, *Desert News*, *Detroit Free Press*, *Disc*, *Drum Media*, *East Coast Rockers*, EastWest Records, *Edmonton Journal*, Elektra Records, *Enfer*, *Esky*, Europe 1, *Evening Chronicle*, *Everybody's*, *Express*, *Eye*, *Faces Rock*, FHM, *Florida Times-Union*, *Foundations*, FR3, Fun Radio, GalleryOfSound.com, *GAS*, *Geelong News*, Gibson.com, *GIG*, *Goldmine*, *Grand Rapid Press*, *Guitar*, *Guitar Club*, *Guitar For The Practicing Musician*, *Guitar Heroes*, *Guitar One*, *Guitar Parts*, *Guitar Player*, *Guitar School*, *Guitar Shop*, *Guitare & Claviers*, *Hard Force*,

Hard N Heavy, Hartford Courant, Heavy Metal Creem, Heavy Rock, Hit Parader, Hitkrant, HM, Hobart Mercury, Hollywood Press, Hot Metal, Hot Press, 'In The Studio', International Musician, Island Ear, It, It's Here, It's Only Rock & Roll, Jamm, Joepie, Juice, KISW, KNAC online, K-Rock, KSJO, Le Monde, Let It Rock, London Daily Express, Long Beach Press Telegram, Look-In, Los Angeles Times, M6, MCM, Mean, Media America, Melbourne Herald, Melbourne Observer, Melbourne Sun, Metal Attack, Metal CD, Metal Edge, Metal Forces, Metal Hammer, Metal Mania, 'Metalshop', Miami Herald, Milesago.com, Minneapolis City Pages, Minneapolis Star Tribune, Modern Drummer, Montreal Gazette, MTV, Much More Music, Much Music, Music Box, Music Express, Music Life, MusicMAX, Music Star, Music Week, Music Week Australia, MusicCentral.com, Musician, Musicians Only, Musik Joker, Muziek Express, National Rock Star, NDR, New York Times, Newcastle Chronicle, Newcastle Evening Chronicle, News & Observer, News Journal, 'Nights With Alice Cooper', 'Off The Record', On The Street, OOR, Orange County Register, ORB, Orlando Sentinel, Penetration, People, Perth Daily News, Philadelphia Inquirer, Piccadilly Radio, Pix People, Playboy, Player, Pollstar, Pop, Pop Corn, Pop Rocky, Popswop, Popular 1, Poster, Prairie Sun, PRO7, Punk, Pure Concrete, Q, Q104, Q104.3, Radio & Records, Radio Clyde, Radio Forth, Radio Hallam, Radio Stockholm, Radio Trent, Radio Victory, Ralph, RAW, Record Collector, Record Review, Remedy.com, 'Retrorock', Riff Raff, RIP, RMF FM, Rock & Folk, Rock En Stock, Rock Gossip, Rock Power, Rock Radio Network, Rockcentral, Rockline, Rolling Stone, Rolling Stone Australia, Rollingstones.com, 'Royalty Of Rock', RTL and Francis Zégut, RTL2, SabbathLive.com, Salt Lake Tribune, Salut, Sarasota Herald Tribune, Scene, Scream, SDR 3, Seattle Post Intelligencer, Seattle Times, SF1, Sky Channel, SonicNet.com, Sono, Sony Music, Sony Music TV, Sound Blast, Spin, Spunky, Star News Pasadena, St Louis Dispatch, St Petersburg Times, St Paul Pioneer Press, STGT3, Sudfunk, Sun Herald, Sun Sentinel, Super Polly, SVTV1, Switch, Sydney Morning Herald, Sydney Sun, Sydney Sunday Mirror, Tampa Tribune, Tamworth Herald, Tele24, Tele5, Ten,

Tennessean, TF1, *The Age*, *The Aquarian*, *The Chronicle*, *The Herald Sun*, *The Journal*, 'The Source', *The State*, *Times Picayune*, *Toledo Blade*, *Toronto Globe & Mail*, *Toronto Sun*, *Total Guitar*, *Triad*, *Trouser Press*, *TV Week* (Australia), TV4, TV6, TVE1, Tyne Tess, 'Up Close', *Vancouver Province*, *Vancouver Sun*, Van Halen.com, *Veronica*, VH1, VH1 Classic, Viva, VIVA2, VPRO, WABX, Warner Brothers, *Washington Post*, WBCN, WEA, WEBN, *Weekend Australian* supplement, *Wellington Evening Post*, *West Australian*, *Westword*, *Who Put The Bomp*, WIN, *Winnipeg Sun*, *Wisconsin State Journal*, WITN, WMMR, WRFX, *Young Guitar*, ZDF and ZTV.

We *think* that's everything. Hopefully our work goes some way towards doing justice to the efforts of all those involved.

Several books also helped us along the way. In particular, Clinton Walker's ground-breaking effort *Bon Scott: Highway to Hell* was crucial in mapping Bon's final days and remains the benchmark on the great man's life and times generally. Mark Putterford's *Shock to the System* was also of assistance.

The chapter on The Easybeats would have been virtually inconceivable without Glenn A. Baker's staggeringly exhaustive liner notes to *The Easybeats' Absolute Anthology 1965–1969*, which, at least in vinyl form, constitute a sizable book in their own right.

In addition to these sources, the authors conducted many of their own interviews.

It wasn't always an easy road. The entire memories of some witnesses suddenly, and somewhat unnervingly, evaporated overnight. In other instances, recall of well-documented events became inexplicably vague, while others were reluctant to respond in any way at all to the most innocent queries.

Thankfully, there were many who were far more accommodating — often above and beyond the call — and we wish to place on record our warm thanks to the following individuals who happily submitted to an inquisition:

Colin Abrahams, Angry Anderson, John Andreoni, Ray Arnott, Barry Bergman, Buzz Bidstrup, Big Al, John Bisset, John Brewster, David Brown, Jen Jewel Brown, Coral Browning, Michael Browning,

Colin Burgess, Bernie Cannon, Phil Carson, Brian Carr, Helen Carter, Russell Coleman, Perry Cooper, Stuart Coupe, Roger Crosthwaite, Bob Daisley, Leeno Dee, Bob Defrin, Eric Dionysius, Paul Drane, Mal Eastick, Phil Eastick, Phil Emmanuel, Dave Evans, Allan Fryer, Chris Gilbey, Ed Golab, Roger Grierson, Peter Head, Warner Hodges, Kim Humphreys, Noel Jefferson, Ian Jeffery, Herm Kovac, Eddie Kramer, David Krebs, Geordie Leach, Lobby Loyde, Richard Lush, Greg Macainsh, Barrie Masters, Paul Matters, Bob McGlynn, Wyn Milson, Steve Morcom, Philip Morris, Rick Neilsen, Mark Opitz, Fess Parker, Guy Picciotto, Tony Platt, Paul Power, Jason Ringenberg, John Rooney, Neil Smith, Mark Sneddon, Colin Stead, John Swan, Deniz Tek, Doug Thaler, Billy Thorpe, Jon Toogood, Chris Turner, Larry Van Kriedt, Peter Wells, Wizard, Simon Wright, Yogi and Rob Younger.

Thanks also to those who preferred that their contribution remain anonymous.

We would like to shine a particularly bright light on Sam Horsburgh, Fifa Riccobono, Herm Kovac, Ian Jeffery, Christie Eliezer, Anthony O'Grady and Glenn A. Baker for all their help.

Thanks also to Joel McIver, Clinton Walker, Mark Brennan at Captain Oi Records, Bob Stevenson and Tom Oliver for the Scottish geography lesson, Alan Paul, Ian MacKaye, Henry Rollins, Jenny Lens, Steve Lorkin, Maggie Montalbano, Vince Lovegrove, Jonas Herbsman, Rod Yates, and Craig Regan and I-94 Bar.

2SM, Simon Kain and ABC Australia also kindly opened their archives for us and we express our gratitude.

To our publisher at HarperCollins, Alison Urquhart, who believed unswervingly in this book from day one, and our editor, Patrick Mangan, who did a superb job and whose razor-sharp skills and wit lifted the project to another level entirely, we are delighted to have been involved with you both.

Murray: Thanks first and foremost to my long-suffering family — Tracey, Kylie and Keira — and my utterly wonderful parents, Milton and Lillian. Words cannot express. No-one could ask for better friends, counsel and/or sounding boards than Mark and Ruth Corbett, Tim Pittman, Robert Grieve and Mississippi Peter Smith.

Special thanks to Christie Eliezer, who not only falls into the esteemed category above but has the added honour of being my mentor and general godfather figure.

Thanks also to Peta Levett for her enthusiasm and encouragement to finally get this project out of the garage, and Sarah Levett and Atosha McCaw for all their support.

Arnaud: Personal thanks for the support, lost weekends and endless nights during this project, to Sydney; for enduring the decibels all these years, to my parents, Bernadette, Alain, Bertrand, Christophe and Sophie; for being here, Angus and Ascar — the best.

Thanks to the ever-enthusiastic AC/DC 'fan-gang' — Carl Allen, Brian Carr, Cyril Desagneaux, Stephan Deshaie, Mark Franklin, Goulash, Anders Hedman, Dan Johnson, Loic Kermagoret, Philippe Lageat, Alex McCall, Neil McDonald, Thierry Nourry, Pekko Paivarinta, Sam Prevot, Michel Remy, Glenn Robertson, Thomas Shade and Alan Shailes.

And last, but of course by no means least, to AC/DC, we both salute!

Arnaud Durieux runs the highly respected and authoritative AC/DC website www.ac-dc.net. Comment and feedback on this book at info@ac-dc.net are welcome.

PHOTO CREDITS

Dick Barnatt/Redferns (page 4, bottom)
JonathanPostal.com (page 5, top left and bottom)
© Jenny Lens Punk Archive (page 5, top right)
Tony Fasulo, Sydney (page 6, top left)
Alan Perry www.concertphotos.uk.com (page 6, top right)
Michel Chaurand (page 7, middle; page 8)
Copyright 1979 Michael N. Marks (page 7, bottom)

PHOTO SECTION THREE

George Chin (page 1, bottom left)
Worth Chollar (page 1, bottom right; page 2, top left; page 4)
Michel Ludovicy (page 2, top right)
© 2005 Ron Pownall/Boston (page 3, top)
Charlyn Zlotnik/Redferns (page 5, top left)
Alex Mitram/Intervision (page 5, top right)
© 2006 Tom Farrington (page 5, middle right)
Alan Perry www.concertphotos.uk.com (page 5, bottom)
Janet Macoska Photography (page 6; page 7, top right)
Arnaud Durieux (page 7, top left, middle and bottom left; page 8)

PHOTO SECTION FOUR

Bob King (page 1; page 2, top and bottom; page 3, top)
Bob King/Redferns (page 3, bottom)
George Chin (page 4, top left and right)
Mick Hutson/Redferns (page 4, bottom)
Philippe Lageat (page 5, top left and right)
Martin Philbey/Redferns (page 5, bottom)
RodolpheBaras.com (page 6, top left)
Stefan M. Prager/Redferns (page 6, top right)
Arnaud Durieux (page 6, bottom left)
Kevin Mazur/WireImage (page 7, top)
William Martin (page 7, middle)
www.GaelleGhesquiere.com (page 7, bottom)
Paul Frati/Intervision (page 8)

Memorabilia items courtesy of Arnaud Durieux, Dan Johnson and
Mark Franklin.

INDEX